Small Business Marketing Made (Stupidly) Easy

Vol.1 – Vol.8 of the Punk Rock Marketing Collection

By Michael Clarke
Publisher, Punk Rock Marketing

Printed in the United States of America

First Printing, 2019

ISBN: 978-1-970119-18-3

Punk Rock Marketing
6912 Ohio Ave.
La Mesa, CA 91942
(310) 751-0343

PunkRockMarketing.com

To Jewyl,

for the love, for the support and for letting me give cubicle life a wave goodbye

Table of Contents

About the Author

Michael Clarke is a former cubicle monkey and founder of Punk Rock Marketing Magazine, a publication devoted to helping small-business owners kick ass, make money and thoroughly rule the world.

He spends his days cursing Mark Zuckerberg and figuring out marketing shortcuts that help him — and small-business owners everywhere — avoid getting a "real" job.

How to Use This Book

Reading this book will NOT make you a "digital media expert" or a "social marketing guru."

You will NOT become a "thought leader" or grace the cover of WIRED.

You may not EVEN know enough to chair a "web 2.0" panel at the 2016 Eastern Delaware New Social Media Branding Conference-Palooza.

That's because: I don't even LIKE social media very much.

- ☑ Facebook is a self-involved navel-gazing waste of time where 300 of my closest "friends" share every personal DETAIL about themselves.
- ☑ Twitter is a shallow, superficial metaphor for a world with ever-lowering attention spans and an OBSESSION with celebrities whose last name is Kardashian.
- ☑ YouTube is a weigh station for shut-ins and show-biz wannabes whose PRIMARY goal in life is to get "10K views on their YouTube video" and anonymously ridicule each other in fresh forms of comment torture.

And yet…

…social media is ALSO the quickest, cheapest and most-effective way for small business folks to dominate their competition, turn casual customers into die-hard fans and survive the ups and downs of a world economy in turmoil.

Knowing the difference between the two is what this book is all about.

"Stand in the Place Where You Were"

While this book may not teach you much about "engagement" or "authenticity"...

It will walk you step-by-step through the LEAST you need to know to make this whole "social media thing," and marketing in general, work for you. (And by work, I mean make you a metric crapload of money.)

You'll discover:

- ☑ A simple system for using Twitter to not only get your business massive exposure, but also sell more of your product and services — without spending a single cent in advertising. **(Part One — "Twitter Marketing in 2019 Made (Stupidly) Easy")**
- ☑ A step-by-step process for creating brain-dead easy-to-make videos that help you conquer the ever-elusive Google rankings — in a matter of a few weeks. **(Part Two — "Video Marketing in 2019 Made (Stupidly) Easy")**
- ☑ Strategies for turning strangers into fans and fans into customers — without breaking the budget on pointless, non-performing Facebook campaigns that do nothing but annoy people in the Facebook newsfeed. **(Part Three - "Facebook Marketing in 2019 Made (Stupidly) Easy")**
- ☑ Insider secrets for turning pins into profits, using one of the hottest — if misunderstood — social networks around. **(Part Four - "Pinterest Marketing in 2019 Made (Stupidly) Easy")**
- ☑ Your very own roadmap for navigating those strange Instagram waters and learn how to get past the selfies and pictures of vacations and find a consistent source of leads. **(Part Five - "Instagram Marketing in 2019 Made (Stupidly) Easy")**
- ☑ A no-brainer, paint-by-numbers system for using LinkedIn to attract lucrative clients and establish yourself as an industry resources, no matter what you sell. **(Part Six - "LinkedIn Marketing in 2019 Made (Stupidly) Easy")**
- ☑ A detailed — but easy-to-follow — blueprint for turning lukewarm email subscribers into fanatical, repeat customers. **(Part Seven - "Email Marketing in 2019 Made (Stupidly) Easy")**
- ☑ Finally, you'll discover the most recent, updated strategies for

cracking the Google search rankings code and delivering steady (and free!) traffic to your most precious marketing resource, your website. **(Part Eight - "Search Engine Optimization in 2019 Made (Stupidly) Easy")**

More importantly, you'll learn what NOT to do. (Because there's a helluva LOT not to do.)

And #1 on the list is to NOT try every strategy in the book. (I had to because, you know, I'm obsessive. But I wouldn't wish that misery on anybody.)

Instead, look through the book, and decide on 3-5 things you'll try RIGHT NOW to boost your small business.

And then do them.

"Now, for the Bad News..."

Spoiler alert: I do not cover EVERY single social network on the face of the Earth in this collection. I've only included strategies I've actually used AND made money from. (Not just ninja hacks for how I got a few hundred retweets or upped my Klout score.)

If you're looking for extensive deep-dive looks at platforms such as Google+, Snapchat, Tumblr, Reddit — or whatever shiny, new Internet venture some fresh-faced, Birkenstock-infused, Harvard dropout hipster just came up with — then let me suggest you check out the MANY social media guides on good, old Amazon. (There are a number of tomes. Some of them are even slightly non-sucky.)

But if you want to know what works — to find out what strategies will get you where you want to go without all that extraneous bull crap — then give the strategies in this book a try.

I can't guarantee you'll get a Ph.D. in Social Media Studies, or that you'll acquire more Twitter followers than Lady Gaga...

But I do guarantee you'll learn a system for using Facebook, YouTube, Twitter, Pinterest, Instagram — and even Email! — that can help you promote your brand, market your products and make a hell of a lot of money.

As Francine Jay said: "The goal is not to get more done, but to have less to do."

It's my goal that this book helps you do FAR LESS…and achieve WAY MORE than you ever thought possible.

Good luck! (And don't let all that social media bull crap stand in your way.)

Michael Clarke
PunkRockMarketing.com
Michael@punkrockmarketing.com

TWITTER
MARKETING
in 2019
MADE
(STUPIDLY) EASY
Vol.1
of the Small Business
Marketing
COLLECTION
Michael Clarke

Twitter Marketing in 2019 Made (Stupidly) Easy

Vol.1 of the Small Business Marketing Made (Stupidly) Easy Collection

PROLOGUE:
What Am I Gonna Do With 140 Characters, Anyway?

~~140~~ 280 characters. That's what ya get.

That's the character-limit Twitter imposes on its micro-messaging platform.

And even ~~140~~ 280 characters is at the uppermost limit of what people can handle these days. (Tweets 120 characters or longer are seen as "verbose" and get read and engaged with far less than their less "wordy" counterparts.)

Doesn't give us much to work with, does it? (And it doesn't speak well of our "sad, illiterate world" - as my old English lit professor used to call it.)

And yet if we're gonna live in this ADD-inflicted, attention-span challenged, "everyone is a smartphone zombie" apocalypse, then Twitter might be the ultimate weapon in finding new zombies... err...customers who'll buy our products and services.

Because no content platform dispenses information as quickly, efficiently, and effortlessly as Twitter. With a simple scroll on a smartphone, a user can get updates from hundreds, if not thousands, of different sources on the "Twitter roller coaster."

And though Twitter doesn't offer the lasting impact (or at least not at the outset) that platforms such as Facebook or Pinterest do, the fact that human life in the 21st century is only gonna get more hectic, more overwhelming, more disjointed...

...plays into Twitter's greatest strength.

Its ability to let people organize the world in a small, digestible way.

And if you're somehow able to become a trusted resource in a person's smartphone organization of the world - and in this book

I will show you how to do that - then not only can you turn that one follower into a possible customer...

...but with a simple click of the "retweet" button you'll find your message shared (and vetted) to hundreds, if not thousands of possible leads. (Who might also share your message with hundreds, if not thousands, of folks.)

Because that's what them zombies do. They multiply.

So, as we plunge into the deep end of the Twitter pool try not to get too bogged down in the weird jargon - Twitter has got a lot of that - or the slightly deranged rants - Twitter has got plenty of those...

...just remember Twitter is like a haiku, that ancient form of Japanese Zen poetry.

It's short. It's rigidly structured. But if you're able to play within the "rules" of the art form then you can create something powerful. (In just minutes.)

And getting serious marketing benefit - in just a minute - is something any small-business non-zombie can appreciate.

So, if you're ready to begin your quest in this post-apocalyptic marketing wasteland, let's learn the LEAST you need to know about the Twitter social platform.

Chapter 1:

A Beginner's Guide to a Very Strange Tool

"We shape our tools, and therefore our tools shape us."

-Marshall McLuhan

Don't read this chapter.

Seriously.

If you're already using Twitter regularly and looking for some ninja marketing techniques to move the needle on your business, you can skip this chapter.

(You're busy. Ya got things to do. Like watch all those "Law and Order" reruns.)

But if you're a Twitter newbie -- who doesn't know his tweets from his Twitterati -- then I want to assuage your fears by letting you know: My 79-year-old aunt is on Twitter.

And if she can work this micro-messaging service to devious and nefarious advantage - and this is a woman who hasn't programmed the correct "time" on her DVD player in 12 years - so can you.

The REAL learning curve on Twitter is deciphering what all that ridiculously-named terminology means.

So, here's the briefest of brief overviews to help you get a B.A. in Twitter Studies and prepare you for the rest of our journey:

1. The Tweet

This is the building block of Twitter. These are short messages (280 characters max; used to be 140) a Twitter user sends out via their news feed.

Unless somebody "retweets" your tweet, or finds your tweet in a Twitter search, the only people who "see" your Tweets are your followers. This is why getting followers is crucial.

Tweets can be of almost anything: links to your website, or a video, or a blog post, or simply whatever status update you'd like to share with your Twitter followers. ("Just had lunch with Lady Gaga. #NotImpressed")

You can either send a tweet from your Twitter profile page — type in the status bar and hit "update" — or you can send a tweet from one of the many third-party Twitter dashboard tools available.

We'll go over these in a later chapter.

2. The Retweet

This is the "I scratch your back, please, oh please, will you scratch my back…" part of Twitter. This is where a Twitter user "shares" someone else's tweet with their own followers. (Hoping the favor will be returned at some point.)

"RT @JohnnyDepp Think I'll dress up as Jack Sparrow Scissorhands today!"

You can retweet anybody's tweet — your neighbor, Vladimir Putin, that strange man who talks to himself on the subway — meaning you don't have to follow them and they do not have to follow you to share their tweet with your followers.

The "how" of a retweet is pretty simple: You click the "retweet" button either on your Twitter page or on a third-party tool when viewing the tweet.

When you hit "retweet," it opens the tweet into a new field, with the symbol "RT" preceding your tweet. (This is how you can recognize a retweet from a regular tweet in your Twitter feed.)

The COOL part about retweets is that the person you retweeted is sent a copy of your tweet. (Helpful if you're trying to connect with a real Twitter heavyweight, such as Katy Perry or your moody teenage daughter.)

And you also get to throw in your own editorializing before the original message if space permits. (Editorializing and attitude are major pluses on Twitter.)

If you think that clunky "RT" looks too artificial, you can also use the more subtle "Via" to let people know where you got your Twitter content.

3. The Reply Message

This is where you send a message to someone on Twitter, by simply adding their Twitter handle (user name) with the @ symbol in front of it (Example: "Hey @Madonna, what's with the weird British accent?")

But this reply is not private as all your followers will be sent a copy of your correspondence with the "Material Girl." So, don't give away any national secrets here.

The supercool part of this action is that if the person replies — say @KimKardashian responds to your question about "What exactly is your talent, again?" — then all six million of Kim's followers will see the reply. (And you might pick up 1.7 million new Twitter followers/enemies in the process.)

4. The Direct Message

This is like the "Early Bird Special" of Twitter. This is where you send somebody a PRIVATE message on Twitter. (The trick is, both of you have to be following each other to see the message.)

Sure, it's an option and it's something you CAN use with your more intimate Twitter friends, but most people don't use the DIRECT MESSAGE function.

Ever.

And…I don't really know how to say this politely…but sending a DIRECT MESSAGE is a slightly uncool, old-fashioned — eat dinner at 4:00 p.m. — way of doing things.

Reply messages and retweets are the much better way to go.

One thing people often do is set up an automated system where each "new" follower gets an instant DIRECT MESSAGE thanking them for the follow and asking them to check out whatever crap they're promoting.

Don't do this. Nobody reads this crap. (And they come off as very spammy.)

5. The Hashtag

This might be the most misunderstood — though effective — part of the Twitter ecosystem. This is where Twitter users add the # (pound) sign in their tweets followed by a specific phrase. (Example: #Kony2012; #DarkKnight, #RealHousewivesOfDelaware, etc.)

Just remember to have no spaces in your hashtag. (Writing #Dark Knight, is the same as writing #Dark.)

Because there are so many tweets every nanosecond, hashtags are a quick, easy way for your tweets to be found.

Generally, it's best to jump onto an existing hashtag, if you're hoping to reach a large number of people. (But the key is to find the right #hashtag.)

#SelfPub and #SelfPublishing might appear the same to us fleshy humans, but in the Twitter world the first is still the hands-down winner in terms of number of tweets.

You CAN create your own hashtag, to promote an upcoming special event, or to build interest and momentum in a cause or movement you're behind.

We'll go over hashtag best practices later, just know they're important. (And that most people royally screw them up.)

6. Twitter Lists

Twitter lists are a simple, but effective, way to organize all the info in your Twitter feed.

You can organize your lists by industry, customers, competitors or teenage miscreants who hope to date your daughter…whatever.

7. Twitter Favorites

This often overlooked feature allows users to "favorite" specific tweets.

And while it feels all warm and fuzzy when somebody "favorites" your own tweet, the real benefit comes from your ability to "favorite" tweets that specifically talk about your business.

It's like having a portable list of testimonials you can use to show how your customers connect with your business. (There are even tools that let you publish this info on your site.)

The Journey Begins...

So, that's about it. The rest you'll pick up as you go. This isn't brain surgery, though it may feel like it, after reading the Twitter feed of somebody like Justin Bieber.

It's just a simple micro-messaging tool...that just so happened to have changed the world. And in the next chapter we'll dive into the basics of HOW to make money from Twitter.

CHAPTER Key Takeaways:

- **The "tweet" is the basic building block of Twitter.** This is the micro-message, maximum of 140 characters, that followers of your account see when you hit "publish."
- **The "retweet" is a way to share other people's tweets with your followers.** It is pre-populated with the designation "RT", but you can remove this and go for something more elegant, such as "Via."
- **The "reply" message is a way for you to "message" somebody on Twitter without them following you back.** Though, be careful, that "private" message will be shared with your followers.
- **The "DM" or "direct message" is a way to send a private message to somebody who is following you**. It's okay, but a bit old-fashioned. And whatever you do, don't set up automated DM's. (It's spammy.)
- **The "hashtag" is a way to categorize your tweets**. These can be very effective for boosting the discover-ability of your content. And allow you to embrace your inner ironic hipster. #HashtagsAreSo2014.)
- **"Twitter lists" are a way for you to create organized lists of Twitter accounts, independent of your main Twitter feed.** A fantastic way to filter your Twitter feed content and spare you the agony of sifting through all the junk that comes through.
- **"Twitter favorites" are a way to highlight particular tweets that catch your eye.** A great way to collect testimonials for your business.

Chapter 2:

How to Make Money With Twitter

"Anyone who lives within their means suffers from a lack of imagination."

-Oscar Wilde

Ah, yes. Money.

How DO we make money with all this ~~140~~ 240-character crap?

This is the MOST ASKED question I get from would-be Twitter marketers. (Aside from "Why isn't Jennifer Lawrence responding to my tweets?")

So, before we jump into the trenches of creating your Twitter account, and outlining your Twitter content strategy for total world domination…

I'd like to dig into how all those "retweets and "followers" and weird apps like TweetDeck and HootSuite and TwikiBoo…

…will help you do the one thing the founders of Twitter still haven't figured out how to do…

Make money.

So glad you asked: there are essentially THREE ways to make money with Twitter:

The Direct Approach to Making Money With Twitter

This is simple, and straightforward: You "tweet" out a link through your Twitter account which asks for some action by the person reading your tweet, which directly relates to income.

This could be:

- A link to a webinar you're running.
- A link to a sales page selling your latest widget.
- A link to a special event you're hosting.
- A link to a product or service you're an affiliate of.
- A link to a coupon or special offer.
- A link to a website squeeze page where you ask for an email opt-in. (Not sure what this is? We'll get to it later.)

Anything that asks people to go to some location and act (so you can either sell them something or market to them in the future) is a DIRECT APPROACH to Twitter marketing.

And trust me, these DIRECT approaches work. (We'll go over in a later chapter just how to use them for top effectiveness.)

But they're like eating gluten-free, vegan (no eggs harmed in the making of this dessert) brownies. A little goes a long way. (And they certainly don't work with everybody.)

The Indirect Approach to Making Money With Twitter

This is more subtle and doesn't have the ROI (Return on Investment) other forms of marketing do.

But, that doesn't mean it's not powerful. Because this is about:

- Answering questions people have about your area of expertise
- Responding to customer service concerns
- Offering to help people who are having trouble (even if it's dealing with your competitor)
- Sharing cool content (that you didn't create)
- Sharing cool content (that you created but lives on a platform like YouTube, Pinterest, Tumblr, Facebook)
- Providing news and important how-to info that improves people's lives

- Sharing personal (but not too personal) details about your daily life that reminds folks you are not a robot

I would contend, it's the last one that is key. I know all the "social media guides" tell you not to mix business with the personal.

But a quick TwitPic of your Jack Russell terrier chewing a pillow may do more for your marketing than all the coupons and free offers you can dream up.

And an honest tweet about something your company screwed up, and are working hard to rectify, can go a long way toward people seeing you as a trusted and humane company.

And not just somebody who's out for a quick buck. (Even if you ARE just out for a quick buck.)

The Sneaky, Ninja Approach to Making Money With Twitter

Though I use all three of the approaches I'm outlining here, this last one is probably my favorite. Because it isn't as blatantly promotional as the "direct approach" and it's a little more goal-driven than the "indirect approach"...

...and it just frickin' works so well.

And that is by sending Twitter followers to content that lives on my website - whether it be a video or a photo gallery or a how-to blog post - and then "retarget" all those visitors on platforms such as Facebook and Google.

Now it's beyond the scope of a book on Twitter marketing to go too deep on this but here's how ya do it:

- Throw some Facebook and Google retargeting code onto your website. If you don't know how to do this, hire your neighborhood 13-year-old genius to help you do it.
- Find a couple of your best (and super-helpful) pieces of website content. (Videos and short blog posts work great.)
- Share that content with your followers on Twitter.

- Set up retargeting campaigns to "follow" website visitors on Facebook and Google and display your offer to them whether they ever visit your site again.

The cool thing about this strategy is it's cost-effective.

For just $3-$5 a day you can triple the number of leads you get, by simply tweeting out content.

But it's also a great way to break through your would-be customers initial reluctance to marketed to.

You're leading with stuff that helps them solve a problem and then following up later in a place where they feel most safe…on Facebook and Google.

But all THREE approaches have their place in a successful Twitter marketing campaign. And in the next chapter we'll build the foundation for your Twitter marketing strategy of awesomeness… and Twitter profile that kicks serious marketing ass.

CHAPTER 2 KEY TAKEAWAYS:

- **There are three ways to market through Twitter**: DIRECT (sales pages, webinars, email opt-ins, affiliate offers, etc.), INDIRECT (brand building, expert status, pictures of your destructive canine, etc.) and SUPER NINJA (sharing our website content and then "retargeting" visitors)
- **The DIRECT method works well to achieve a specific goal.** But conversion rates tend not to be very high.
- **The INDIRECT works well to boost your brand and give your business some much-needed personality.** But the ROI can be fuzzy.
- **The SUPER NINJA approach is probably the most cost-effective way to increase leads and boost sales through Twitter.** Though it requires you have content on your website that actually helps people. (And doesn't just encourage people to buy your vacuum cleaner.)

Chapter 3:

4 Keys to a Kick-Ass Twitter Profile

"Not doing more than the average is what keeps the average down."

-William Lyon Phelps

We ain't gonna spend a ton of time on this.

Frankly, too many Twitter manuals go on and on about the need for a sleek, compelling background to your Twitter profile, before plunging into the deep waters of the Twitter-verse.

Yeah, that may have been important back in the Mesozoic era (you know, way back in 2010), but today few readers of your Twitter updates will see your tweets on the Twitter platform. Most likely they'll consume them via a Smartphone app or on some Twitter dashboard client like HootSuite or TweetDeck.

But there are FOUR KEYS you need to nail down when creating your profile before we start on your journey to Twitter awesomeness...

...and they will all go a long way toward ensuring your Twitter marketing success going forward. So, let's get started with:

Twitter Profile Key No. 1: Pick a Name That Doesn't Suck

When you create your Twitter account, and verify the email connected to that account, you will be asked to come up with your Twitter name, or handle.

You'll be tempted to use the name of your business or company. And most times this will be entirely appropriate. But there are a couple of reasons you may NOT want to do this:

- **If your company's name is super long** - If somebody retweets one of your tweets, your name will be included in that 140-character limit. So, if you go with a Twitter name of @PetesDenver-PoolSupplyInc, that'll gobble up precious Twitter real estate. Go with something shorter instead.
- **You want to use your given name** - If you are the "face" of your brand then this will probably be the way to go. Just add a period between your first and last name. ("michael.clarke" NOT "michaelclarke.")
- **You want to distinguish yourself in a crowded marketplace with some personality** - If I were in crowded, corporate field - such as real estate or accountancy or crime-fighting superheroes - then I'd go for something offbeat like @RealtorBob, @TheTaxKillers or @CrimeFighterJoe.
- **You want to create separate Twitter handles for different areas of your biz** - If you're a big enough fish in the Twitter pond create separate handles to handle separate duties. (Such as: @MatrixSupport, @ShoeBarnSales, @LindsayLohanParoleOfficer, etc.)

Twitter Profile Key No.2: Pick a Twitter Bio Picture That Doesn't Suck

Now, saying I'm not the most photogenic person is like saying Kanye West is not the most "humble" individual.

But I recognize the importance of a good Twitter profile avatar. (This is the small thumbnail photo that accompanies each of your tweets in a follower's Twitter feed.)

And in my experience, here's what you gotta know about Twitter avatar pictures:

- **The ideal size for your bio photo is 400x400.** This ensures your photo doesn't look Pixelated, or any important photo material is cut off unintentionally.

- **Close ups of faces are always better than far away shots.** Forget that pic of your entire staff in the break room. (Nobody will ever see it.) Instead go with a close-up shot of somebody's face.
- **Unless you are a HUGE brand, go with a person over a logo.** Now if you're McDonald's go with the "golden arches." But for most small businesses putting a human person in the photo will pay off more in the long run.
- **Get a professional photographer to take the shot if you can.** This isn't required, but a pro shutterbug will produce something more vivid and eye-catching than that random pic you've got floating around on your iPhone.
- **Go easy on the heavy-duty Instagram photo filters.** I know that's all the rage on Instagram, but those over-saturated bio pics can look strange in the Twitter feed.

TWITTER PROFILE KEY NO. 3: USE WHAT YOUR MAMA (AND THE TWITTER BIO) GAVE YA

Now we've got the username and pretty bio pictures taken over, it's time to focus on the most valuable real estate on your profile - the Twitter bio.

You'd think people wouldn't read this stuff…

But you'd wrong.

I'm continually shocked how many leads and squeeze page opt-ins I get from this tiny little bit of real estate. (People just want to know more about other people, I guess.)

The key, as with any aspect of social media, is to NOT be boring with your bio and to give people a reason to click over to your website or opt-in page.

Here are five tips to remember when creating bios:

1. **Use real words that real humans use.** NOT "We are an Austin-based accountancy firm who provides structured tax solutions for individuals and businesses alike." Instead: "We're

based in Austin. We like to save people money with taxes and stuff. Most of us majored in Math. (God knows why.)"

2. **Put a link in your bio EVEN if it's the same as your website link.** As a Twitter initiate, you're provided two opportunities to add links to your site, in your dedicated website link field and your Twitter bio. By far the MOST important link is the one in your bio. (This will be seen when people mention your tweet or add you to a Twitter list.) But point to two different web locations. (Just make sure the MOST IMPORTANT link is in your bio.)
3. **Use Friendly URLS.** A friendly URL is one that appears like humans created it, not some robot in an evil lair. (For example, you'd want to use http://JimsAutomotive.com/Deal…NOT… JimsAutomotive.com/site-Page4as90.aspf.) If you're not sure how to use "redirection" on your website to create a "friendly" URL, contact your local teenage computer hacker. (He/she can help you out.)
4. **You can CHANGE your bio whenever you want.** You don't have to be married to the bio you come up with when you create your profile. If you have a special deal, offer or product, be sure to change up your bio to reflect the new stuff going on.
5. **You can add #Hashtags here.** In a later chapter we'll go over hashtags and the proper use of these strange little inventions, but right now this is a good place to add them if there are some common hashtags that are used by your industry. (Such as #CruiseVacations or #DogTraining.) Nobody does this. So doing so will really make you stand out from the competition. (And help you get discovered.)
6. **Offers of FREE and discounted stuff do well in your bio, if done smartly.** You don't want to sound too sales-y in your bio, but something like "For your FREE copy of '10 Biggest Plumbing Mistakes Homeowners Make' eBook, head over to http://PlumbingPhoenix.com" would be appropriate.

7. **You CAN put almost anything in your Twitter bio.** Keywords, links to your Facebook page, your email address, your second grade report card. Whatever you want. Just experiment and see what works for you.

Twitter Profile Key No. 4: Get Your Twitter Profile Registered & Recognized

So, this last step is one many Twitter marketers neglect to do, or even know about. But due to Twitter's rather open-source platform, there are many Twitter directories that archive information about almost every single Twitter account.

And all ya gotta do is create an account, and you'll not only boost the exposure of your Twitter account but also get your website some much-needed Google backlink juice. (Never a bad thing.)

Note: For each of these Twitter directories, replace the "username" with your OWN Twitter username.

Here are the top Twitter directories I recommend you head over to and create an account with:

- Twitter Counter - Another good Twitter directory that lets users get a detailed look into their Twitter activity over time.
- Twitaholic - Another Twitter monitoring tool. Lets you know where you rank geographically. Not that useful, except as a directory backlink.
- Retweet Rank - Don't worry about where you rank with this tool. It's just another way to get people back to your website.

PUNK ROCK MARKETING
AMPLIFY YOUR MESSAGE

CHAPTER 3 Key Takeaways:

- **Choose a Twitter handle that sounds fun, but descriptive.** (Avoid complex, dull-sounding corporate names.) If you're gonna use your real name, be sure to separate your first and last name with a..."period."
- **With Twitter profile photos go with 400x400 square pics.** Also, try to use close-ups of human faces, over impersonal logos.
- **Fill out your bio with key information about your company that doesn't sound like a press release.** (Don't forget to put your most important link in your bio, even if it's the same as your website link.)
- **Change your bio to reflect your latest product or service you're offering.** Links to FREE downloads, reports, videos or offers do really well. Add relevant hashtags to help your profile get discovered.
- **Boost the visibility of your tweets by adding your Twitter account to Twitter directories.** Some even let you edit your specific bio and add your social links. (All good stuff!)

Chapter 4:

Yeah, But What the Hell Do I Tweet About?

"The secret of getting ahead is getting started."

-Mark Twain

Okay, so you've got a killer Twitter handle picked out and your bio is optimized for marketing/cool person awesomeness.

Meaning you've got some juicy links in your Twitter bio that point back to webpages that can make ya some money.

Must mean you're ready to get out there and grab those 2,500 Twitter followers who'll voraciously devour everything you tweet and send you thousands of dollars a month by buying your stuff!

Eh…not quite.

First, you've got to show a nice mix of Twitter activity on your profile before anybody will even consider following you. (And getting people to follow you is what this whole Twitter marketing thing is all about.)

I would shoot for AT LEAST 20-25 tweets before you even try to get followers en masse. This will make you look less like a spammer, and more like a human being.

Which I hope you are.

So what should those 15 tweets be?

Well, I think they should be as diverse as your regular Twitter activity going forward.

So, now's as good a time as any for me to introduce you to my:

Ultimate Punk Rock Marketing Brain-Dead Tweet Formula

These are the five areas of my Twitter portfolio I stick to religiously. It's a breakdown of how I organize my tweets and schedule them throughout the week, in a variety of markets.

It doesn't matter whether you tweet 20 times a day or just once after lunch, follow this formula and you'll be SURE you're hitting all the important touchstones.

The Formula works like this:

- **20% of your tweets should be helpful, How-to Stuff.** This includes links to interesting blog posts, articles, industry-specific advice, the secret to why people watch the Kardashians, etc.
- **20% of your tweets should be Inspirational.** This includes inspirational quotes, motivating pictures, stories of courage, anything that make us hate the human race a little less. (I know this seem irrelevant. It's not! This stuff will get shared the MOST.)
- **20% of your tweets should be FUN.** These are funny videos, silly jokes, amusing questions, your snarky little comments about whatever, etc. (Bonus points if it has to do with movies, TV shows, or anything entertainment-based.)
- **20% of your tweets should be Retweets of Big Influencers in Your Industry.** Now some of the inspirational and how-to stuff you share CAN be retweets. (And that's okay.) Just be sure to retweet folks you KNOW your customers are following. (If ya get a retweet you might just find a whole new audience waiting to check out your stuff.)
- **20% of your tweets should be Promotional.** This is stuff that directly boosts your bottom line. Such as: links to webinars, contests, opt-in offers, coupons, sales pages. Now I don't recommend this ALL be sales-y stuff. (Doesn't work that well.) Instead, sprinkle in plenty of links to your own video rants…err…how-to content.

The BIGGEST problem most small biz folks make with Twitter is their balance of promo tweets is way too high. Trust me, any over 20% and you'll piss people off.

So what do you do if you want to send more promo stuff to your followers?

Simple...you send out more tweets.

I try to shoot for at least FIVE tweets a day, makes it easier for me to break things up.

One tweet about how-to stuff, one tweet about fun stuff, etc. But you can do more than that. (Many people do.)

Just start out slow and build gradually until you get the feel. In a later chapter, I'll show you some cool automation tools that can make this a lot easier, but for now let me give you a few quicks resources that can help you put all these tweets together.

Tweet Area No. 1: Helpful, How-To Stuff

This could be almost anything:

- A video related to your industry that helps consumers with an issue they're having.
- An online article about some trend in your area of expertise (people just love trends; makes them feel smart).
- A blog post featuring a LIST of the top (whatever) that people absolutely need to know about (the only thing people love more than trends are numbered lists)

And where you find these pieces of kick-ass content will depend on your business, but here are go-to resources I never leave my Twitter home without:

Google Alerts: This is so simple, it's criminal. All you do is set up an alert based on a specific phrase, such as "pool care," and Google will email you the latest news articles, blog posts, and message-board ramblings around that subject. (Be careful, though. The alert will grab EVERYTHING. So, if you put in "pool" you'll get articles about chlorine levels and pool sharks.)

YouTube: There is a video about almost anything. (Don't believe me? Just search for "Japanese poodle fitness video" and you'll see what I mean.) So, do a keyword search for your subject and share all the good helpful stuff you find. Just be sure to pick a video that has a majority of "likes" or "thumbs up." You don't want to share crap. (And there's a metric ton of crap on YouTube.)

AllTop: If you're not familiar with AllTop, then let me introduce you to your new Twitter best friend. This site is basically a blog aggregator (fancy word for collector of good stuff) broken out by subject. Not that extraordinary you say? Yeah, but this site uses humans, not robot algorithms. So, you can bookmark the relevant page for your business and share the best human-endorsed stuff around.

The Big News Sites: I scour Yahoo, New York Times, and CNN every once in a while to see if something interesting is happening. Most of them will even email you the most popular stories. (Hint: If it's popular for them, it'll probably be popular for your followers.)

StumbleUpon: I love this site because it's just so frickin' random. You can find ALMOST anything on StumbleUpon. Photo blogs devoted to locations that look like James Bond villain hideouts. Interior designers imagining what TV show houses REALLY look like. An infographic showing you how to never pay a utility bill ever again. As long as you keep your interests relatively focused, you can find some amazing stuff here.

TWEET AREA NO. 2: INSPIRATIONAL

Inspirational quotes do little for me. But I am in the vast Twitter minority.

Of all the kinds of tweets I've sent out over the years — in markets as diverse as self-publishing, real estate and even golf — by far the most retweeted, most shared and most downright "viral" have been quotes.

I think this is because of all the kinds of content floating in the world of social media they are so easily consumed.

You may not have time to read a blog post while you're checking your phone in the bathroom — and don't kid yourself, everybody does this — but who doesn't have time to read a single quote.

And "sharing" a quote can make you look smart. And witty.

And whatever the hell other reason people love quotes.

So, what quotes do you share?

Well, I think this depends on your business.

If you're running a restaurant, you'd want quotes about the joy of eating, drinking and being thoroughly merry. If you're a golf instructor, you'll want to share nuggets about maximizing your potential and not going insane working on your short game.

I think no matter what your business, quotes that underscore some form of: "Life is Short; Appreciate What You Got; Be Your Best" are usually winners.

And where do you find these choice tidbits of wisdom?

Well, you could do a simple search for "quotes" on the good, old Google. But I prefer not to have to work that hard.

So, I simply outsource it.

Two sites I highly recommend are Upwork and Fiverr. These are sites that help you find virtual assistants who, for a small fee, will do things such as collect quotes for your tweets…or even handle all of your Twitter duties.

When I NEED quotes I create a posting and mention I'm looking for a Virtual Assistant to help me collect 200-400 quotes on a SPECIFIC TOPIC. (You gotta be specific!)

This can cost as little as $10-$15. (And it can make a huge difference to your business.)

Tweet Area No. 3: Fun Tweets

This is where a lot of business folks on Twitter really miss out. They forget that social media is SUPPOSED to be social. (Not a platform where you hawk your wares endlessly.)

But sharing funny pictures, silly videos, random and crazy blog posts can be some of the best Twitter content to move the needle on your business. (And some of the most "shared" stuff you put out there in the Twitter-verse.)

Here are my go-to spots for fun Twitter material:

PopUrls: If you're looking for a way to waste time, this site is it. PopUrls aggregates EVERYTHING on the Internet. (Scary, huh?) I find most of my funny, weird gems here.

BuzzFeed: This is like PopUrls, but with a racier edge. (Which CAN be a good thing.) Whether it's the top porn search terms by country or the best soul-dancing videos, the random collection of weirdness that is BuzzFeed has got it all.

The Onion: I'm an unabashed Onion fan. I love their satirical tone and their headlines are hysterical. (Perfect for this Twitter world we live in.) And some of them can be offensive. (Which can surprisingly well.)

Funny or Die: Not everything on Funny or Die, the brainchild of Will Ferrell, is awesome. But most of it is, especially their in-house content. And funny videos do well in the Twitter sphere.

Tweet Area No. 4: Retweets

This one is self-explanatory: You give a little retweet love to a REAL PLAYER in your space on Twitter. (I like to call this "strategic retweeting.") Here are a few tips to ensure your retweets reach maximum effectiveness:

- **Retweet Twitter users whose followers you'd love to get access to.** If they reply or mention you, you'll get an added boost of promotion, and ya might pick up some more followers.
- **Retweet Twitter users who have at least 1,000 followers.** No point in retweeting messages from a ghost town.
- **Retweet stuff that doesn't suck or hasn't been done to death.** Sharing the video of Susan Boyle singing "I Dreamed a Dream" might have been cool three years ago, but it's now second-hand news.

- **Try to put a brief comment before the retweet.** Example: "You. Must. See. This. RT @jimmy.myers:..."This helps you put your own personality on things and encourages people to follow you. (And not look like some noob jumping on the retweet bandwagon.)
- **Use Twitter lists to find content from just your Twitter heavy-hitters.** We'll go over automation tools in a later chapter, but by creating Twitter lists, and adding high-profile users, it'll make it much easier to find the gold amid all that Twitter crap.

Tweet Area No. 5: Promotional

This is all you! This is stuff that can make you some serious money.

What you promote here will depend on your business model. But here are a few best practices to ensure you get the most Twitter bang for your marketing buck:

- **Sales pages work better if they seem like content.** Saying "Check out the No.1 secret to dealing with hair loss" is better than "Get 50% off the hair loss solution that is sweeping the nation - and will help me pay my bills."
- **Discounts and offers work best for small purchases.** If you're selling something for under $15 or so, then pitch away.
- **Discounts and offers work even better for purchases that have a time constraint.** Limited-time offers and coupons with expirations work like magic. (And people will share them with their friends. Seriously.)
- **Ask for a retweet if space allows.** People generally do what they're told, if they're told by someone they like. (And hopefully the other 80% of your tweets have made you someone they like.)
- **Links to free content that is an upsell in disguise work like MAGIC.** I love to tweet links to webinars or instructional videos or helpful blog posts...that turn out to be thinly veiled sales pitches. They work well, and they don't make people feel you're a sleazy salesman. (Even if you are.) And you can do that remarketing trick I discussed in Chapter 2.

CHAPTER 4 Key Takeaways:

- **Divide your tweets equally into FIVE different areas**: 1) How-to 2) Quotes 3) Funny Stuff 4) Retweets 5) Promotional
- **Use YouTube, Google Alerts, AllTop and StumbleUpon** to find the best helpful stuff to tweet.
- **For quotes, either do a Google search** or hire an outsourcer at a site like Upwork or Guru to help you out.
- **For funny stuff**, The Onion, Funny or Die, PopUrls and BuzzFeed are fantastic resources.
- **Set up a list of high-profile Twitter users** and retweet their stuff to get access to their followers.
- **Discounts and coupons work really well** for your promo stuff. (As do free giveaways that opt people into a list.)

Chapter 5:

The Best (and Worst) Times to Tweet

"The early bird gets the worm, but the second mouse gets the cheese."

-Willie Nelson

This might be the most important chapter you read in this humble tome.

Because knowing WHEN to tweet is almost as important as knowing WHAT to tweet.

As somebody who has listened to all the webinars and read all the crappy blog posts, I know there is virtually NO CONSENSUS about the best time to tweet. (Some will tell you the weekends are best, some will tell you stay away from weekends, etc.)

So, I'll just give you what time periods have worked for me repeatedly. (And I've tested 'em all.)

If you find something in my recommendations that isn't right for you, then tweak where needed.

Note: In a later chapter, I'll show you how to automate all this Twitter activity months in advance.

But in my experience these five principles can help you maximize your ability to market on Twitter, without wasting tons of time sending out tweets that nobody sees. (Or wants to see.)

Twitter Time Principle No. 1: Go Local or Global

What time you tweet will depend on what you're selling. If you're a local business, then your time-zone considerations are relatively tight. (And will probably be during weekday business hours.)

But if you're peddling software solutions around the world, then be flexible with your tweet times.

If you're looking for a hard-fast rule about tweet times, generally anything that hits the east coast of the United States in its Twitter sweet spot (more info in the next principle) is a good rule of thumb.

This is because the vast majority of online eyeballs are in the U.S. eastern seaboard. (East Coasters all believe they live in the center of the world…" and you know what, they might be right.)

Twitter Time Principle No. 2: Working Hours Are Golden

Sorry you night owls, but I find evenings pretty much comatose for Twitter response rates.

Yes, there's less competition in the evenings, but so what? Sometimes there's less competition for a reason.

For me, the absolute best times to tweet are anytime between 9:00 a.m. - 3:00 p.m. EST. So, for me on the West Coast this means I sprinkle my tweet times like this:

- 6:00 a.m. PST
- 7:30 a.m. PST
- 9:00 a.m. PST
- 10:30 a.m. PST
- 12:00 p.m. PST

But this will all depend on what your business is and who you're trying to reach. The big thing is: Don't tweet BEFORE 7:00 a.m. or AFTER 5:00 p.m. (Unless of course you try it and it totally works!)

And before you worry that my recommendations will force you to overtweet…don't worry! Your tweet will get lost in someone's feed so quickly that an hour and a half is plenty of time between tweets.

But five tweets a day may seem daunting at first. So, if you're looking for a minimum amount when you're just staring out, I would do:

- 9:00 a.m. EST
- 12:00 p.m. EST
- 3:00 p.m. EST

This is a decent way to break in and will get you a ton of traction with your followers.

Twitter Time Principle No. 3: Fridays Really Suck (Especially in the Afternoon)

Whatever it is — maybe the fact our working brains make a mental siesta at the end of the week — Friday afternoons just plain suck for Twitter engagement.

I still schedule tweeting on Friday morning, just to keep the old machine cranking, but it's not where I put my primo content, or my heavy-duty promotional stuff. (If you gotta prioritize, skip Fridays.)

Twitter Time Principle No. 4: Mondays are Okay, But Not in the Morning

Ugh. Mondays.

Not only are they rough on your followers who are getting back into the flow of work, but they're also pretty light on Twitter engagement, at least in the morning.

Unless you're trying to tap into that Monday escapist mindset.

Say you're a travel site offering vacation deals. Then Monday would be a fantastic day to tweet about your Acapulco vacation packages. (Especially in cold climates.)

Or if you run a Mexican restaurant touting "Margarita Monday," then you could do a whole bunch of tweets related to curing the cubicle Monday blues.

This will depend on your business, but putting your feet in the information-overloaded shoes of your customer is always a good starting point when trying to come up with your Twitter scheduling strategy.

Twitter Time Principle No. 5: Weekends are Okay, But Mostly on Sundays

I don't know what it is about Saturdays. But I have zero luck getting any headway with my Saturday tweets.

I know you're different. I know you've got the secret sauce to reach people and change the world, but I find most folks are too busy living their lives to be on Twitter.

Now, if you're someone who does a ton of business on Saturdays, like a realtor or a bail bondsman, then you'll want to jump on the Saturday Twitter boat.

But for me, Sunday mornings and Sunday evenings are the best times to schedule your weekend tweets.

And the 5-7 p.m. range on Sunday nights is just golden.

Maybe after a long weekend with the family, the last thing we want to do is talk to humans. (And would rather be on our phone or computer.)

So, I usually schedule some kind of promotion heavily on Sunday nights. (Engagement goes through the roof, and so do my opt-ins and sales.)

Twitter Time Principle No. 6: What the Hell Do I Know?

Again, what I advise may not be right for your business.

The quickest way to find out how utterly full of crap I am would be to test…and test and test.

Try out different times of day. Give Saturday a go. (Even though I know it won't work.) Tweet 47 times a day. Or at 3:00 a.m.

See what excites your audience. (And if you find something different, shoot me an email. I'd love to know what worked for you.)

But once you find your own secret sauce, don't deviate from your plan.

Once the plan is simple, successful, and repeatable, then you've got something you can scale. (And things you can scale can make you some serious money.)

CHAPTER 5 KEY TAKEAWAYS:

- **Determine if you need a global or local presence on Twitter**. (If you are global, shoot for the east coast of America during the morning and early afternoon.)
- **Mornings and afternoons are awesome.** (For starters: try to tweet at 6:00 a.m., 9:00 a.m. and 12:00 p.m. of your desired time zone during the week.)
- **Skip Saturday.** But don't forget about Sunday evening, 5-7 pm. (Great engagement and even better profit potential.)
- **Find your own system** with constant tweaking and testing.

Chapter 6:

Art of the Perfect Tweet

"Have no fear of perfection — you'll never reach it."

-Salvador Dali

We've talked a lot about what you should tweet out to your followers (don't worry, I'll soon show you how to get followers) and when the best time to reach those people who will hinge on every word you say.

But you might ask: What's the best way to organize your tweet? Do you really need hashtags? And should you use all ~~140~~ 280 characters? (Interesting note: Since Twitter expanded the maximum character limit people STILL write tweets that are roughly 140 characters.)

So, let's dig into some of the best practices of how your tweets should be constructed:

Perfect Tweet Tip No. 1: Write Tweets That 120-130 Characters

I know you've got ~~140~~ 280 characters to work with. So why am I asking you to stop at 120?

Because you want to give people "room" to retweet you. If they give you some retweet love and you take up all ~~140~~ 280 characters, then they have to do some editing to get your retweet out there.

And as anybody in the business world will tell you, people are inherently lazy and if you ask them to do anything that takes more than a .001% effort they won't do it.

So keep those tweets short and enjoy the retweet awesomeness.

Perfect Tweet Tip No. 2: Write Tweets Shorter Than 100 Characters If You Can

This one shocked me. But according to Buddy Media, tweets less than 100 characters experience a 17% boost in engagement. (I'm not sure how they define "engagement," but I'm sure it's better than "non-engagement.")

So, if it's possible, keep your tweets nice and short. (It'll make your tweets stand out from the usual crap.)

Perfect Tweet Tip No. 3: Place Your Link About 25% of the Way Into the Tweet

According to social media savant Dan Zarrella over at HubSpot the highest engagement on Twitter comes from tweets with links approximately a quarter of the way into the tweet.

So…

"Apocalypse is near: http://bitly.463 Michael Bay to remake Mutant Ninja Turtles"

…is better than:

"Apocalypse is near. Michael Bay to remake Mutant Ninja Turtles: http://bitly.463"

I have no idea why. I don't care. It's worked for me, and it'll work for you.

Perfect Tweet Tip No. 4: Kill the Passive Voice and Use Active Verbs

Twitter is like poetry. Ya gotta be tight and economical with your words. So, this wouldn't be super awesome:

"We are presenting a webinar later this afternoon, where we will discuss the merits of Twitter marketing http://bit.ly/twitter"

But this would be a helluva lot better:

"Crush your competition with Twitter. Find out how in this kick-ass webinar TODAY: http://bit.ly/Twitter"

Did ya notice how all those active verbs gave some urgency to the copy. That's what they do! (Let them do most of the Twitter heavy lifting for you.)

Perfect Tweet Tip No. 5: Don't Forget About Hashtags

Have to be honest. For the longest time I never used hashtags. (Just didn't understand their appeal.)

Well, was I a total moron. People love 'em and they can help your tweets get discovered.

There are three basic ways to use hashtags:

1. **Group your tweets within an existing hashtag category,** such as #asklochte; #writerquotes; #thingsgirlsdo; #tweetevent. The best place to find this info is at Hashtags.org and leverage the work somebody else has already done to find the optimal hashtag. (Don't reinvent the wheel - just steal it!)
2. **Create your own hashtag to brand your event, company or special offer.** This is a powerful strategy, and one that can get people to do a lot of social promotion for ya. Just be sure to research your hashtag before using. (The dessert company Entenmann's got in trouble for using the hashtag #notguilty at the same time supporters of murder suspect Casey Anthony were also using #notguilty. Uh, awkward.)
3. **Use a hashtag ironically,** such as #NoMoreShaveTech or #WhatWouldMichaelBayDo. This one may not have an immediate marketing benefit, but it can make you seem funny, articulate and somewhat human. (Even if you aren't any of those things.)

Perfect Tweet Tip No. 6: Try to Use a Real Hyperlink (If Possible)

If you're using any kind of automated Twitter service, such as TweetDeck or HootSuite, they'll usually offer some form of link shortening service.

Don't do it. (If you can.)

Putting a "real" hyperlink — http:yoursite.com/coupon as opposed to http://bit.ly/78$#2 — will boost your click-thru rates and help put some moolah in your pocket.

One exception to this might be the Amazon affiliate program, which lets you create an Amazon shortened link that looks something like "http://amzn.to/1lqbBXY." Here, you are leveraging the power of a big brand like Amazon.)

But I haven't done enough testing with this to determine its effectiveness. Stay tuned on this one!

PERFECT TWEET TIP NO. 7: USE INTERESTING CHARACTERS TO LET YOUR TEXT STAND OUT

Anything that helps your tweets stand out is a good thing. And I mean anything.

I love the tilde… (~)

It's just so weird and can convey, well, whatever the hell I want it to convey.

Colons (:) are also good right before a hyperlink.

As are any variety of characters: ($, %, ^, *, &)

And even ALL CAPS can be effective. (Just don't go overboard.)

And if you are going to feature a blog, video, or picture then be sure to add the following before the tweet:

- [BLOG]
- [VIDEO]
- [PIC]

It will help boost click-thru rates. (And make your tweets stand out in an overcrowded twitter stream.)

PUNK ROCK MARKETING
AMPLIFY YOUR MESSAGE

CHAPTER 6 KEY TAKEAWAYS:

- **Keep your tweets between 120-130 characters** to allow easy retweet-ability. (Don't make people THINK to help you.)
- **Keep your tweets below 100 characters** for maximum engagement.
- **Put your link a quarter of the way** into your tweet.
- **Get to the point.** Use verbs. Skip adverbs.
- **Use hashtags** to promote your special event or brand. (Be sure to check nobody is using the tag.)
- **Use real links** (if you can.)
- **Use interesting characters** to make your tweets stand out.

Chapter 7:

How to Get a Million Followers in 24 Hours

"To handle yourself, use your head; to handle others, use your heart."

-Eleanor Roosevelt

Okay, so maybe a MILLION followers are optimistic. But 500K for sure. :)

Seriously, though, we have come to the most CRUCIAL yet MISUNDERSTOOD part of Twitter marketing.

And that is: How to get some frickin' followers who can eventually turn into customers who put money in your pocket.

I must warn you though; this section is not for the timid.

If you don't like to offend or step on toes, then the techniques outlined here may not be for you.

But if you want to get a ton of Twitter followers quickly (but not so fast as to raise any red flags with the Twitter gods), then these tips will be right up your Twitter marketing alley.

So, here are my THREE Totally Ninja Techniques for Getting a Crapload of Twitter Followers Fast:

Ninja Technique No. 1: Follow to Be Followed

I know what most of the gurus tell you.

Mass following people on Twitter is spammy. And it's unethical. And it makes you look like a huckster.

Yeah, but it works. (If you do it right.)

The key is to have a plan and work that plan. (Without all those crappy mass-follow automated solutions that seem to spring up every week.)

So, here's what I do with every new Twitter account I've created, and it has worked EVERY single time.

1. **Find your tribe.** Choose 15-20 "big-time" Twitter users (at least 2K followers) whose followers represent your ideal customer. (Could be a competitor, a local celebrity, your favorite chef, the President of Denmark, etc.)
2. **Schedule three "following" sessions a week.** My ideal following times are Tuesday 12 p.m., Thursday 12 p.m., and Sunday 5 p.m. But you can do it whenever you like. (Just avoid Saturdays and late evenings.)
3. **For each session, follow the most recently active followers of 3-5 users on your big-time user list.** This is easy to do. Just find the Twitter profile page of the big-time user, click on the followers link and follow away. (I usually try to shoot for about 50-100 folks here.)
4. **Try NOT to follow companies or people without profile pictures and written bios.** Unless you're on the B2B (business-to-business) train, you're not interested in other businesses. And people without pictures aren't frequent users. (And folks without bios are usually Russian hackers.)
5. **Give people you just followed TWO FULL DAYS to follow you back and then unfollow any folks who didn't follow you back.** About 40% of everybody I follow will follow me back. (Not always, but it's a good general rule.) It's vital you give people a full two days, otherwise you'll be seen as a spammer and Twitter can shut down your account faster than a Taylor Swift romance.
6. **Go slow.** Twitter has a limit of how many people you can follow. The maximum number of users you can follow is approximately 10% more than the number of people who follow you. (Example if you got 1,000 followers, then you can follow 1,100 peeps.) But

don't worry, stick with it and you'll build a decent following in no time.

7. **Rinse and repeat.**

Ninja Technique No. 2: Put Twitter Buttons Everywhere

The first technique, by far, is the one where I see the quickest gains.

But it's this second technique, in which you place a "follow me on Twitter icon" in specific areas of your Internet footprint, that I see the most lasting and permanent connections on Twitter.

That's because these are people who already have affinity with me and want to know what else I'm up to.

And people like that make for great Twitter marketing buddies.

The HOW is pretty simple: just head over to the Twitter Button Resource page (PunkRockMarketing.com/TweetButton) to grab some code and make your own icon.

It's the WHERE that so many people neglect. So here are my favorite (yet often overlooked) places to put a Twitter icon to boost my follower count:

- **Email.** Total no-brainer here, but I'm surprised how many people don't take advantage of the real estate at the bottom of their email newsletters or info blasts that encourage people to follow them on Twitter.
- **Your website.** Here's another lost opportunity for many marketers. Online marketing newbies sure know how to cram a bunch of crap on their website, except for the stuff that actually lets them continue to market to their customers. So throw a twitter icon on your site so the conversation, and the selling, never ends.
- **Blog posts and articles.** If you do any kind of written website content, it's crucial you have some kind of "follow what I'm doin' on Twitter" nearby. (Especially if you're guest posting.)

- **Video.** If you have any kind of video or YouTube presence (and you damn well should), then putting your Twitter info can be invaluable here. (And you will usually get some easy retweets along the way.)
- **Flyers/Print Marketing.** If you have any kind of direct marketing, be sure to include your Twitter handle. Give people a reason to follow, such as: "Follow us on Twitter to find out about our specials." Not: "Follow us on Twitter to boost my pathetically low self-esteem."
- **Your Front Counter.** If you're a brick-and-mortar business, you're absolutely brain dead if you don't have some kind of thing at the front counter encouraging people to follow you on Twitter. Again, you gotta give 'em an incentive. Free, cheap stuff is usually good.
- **Your body.** I have a client who puts his Twitter handle, along with an offer of a free coupon, on his company-issued sandwich shop t-shirt. Twitter followers went up 300%! (Mostly from people standing in line to buy sandwiches.)

Ninja Technique No. 3: Answer People's Questions

Don't think I'm breaking any news here when I say good business is about helping people solve problems.

But for some businesses this can be difficult. It's hard to find people BEFORE they come looking for you. (Such as a personal injury lawyer or a Justin Bieber life coach.)

But Twitter is perfect for jumping right into the confused and muddled vortex your prospective customers find themselves in and deliver kick-ass solutions.

And all without chasing a single ambulance.

So how do you find people who need your help?

Here are a few super-secret ninja tricks I advise all my clients to use:

- Go to Twitter advanced search.
- Add your industry-specific keywords. In the "All of These Words" field put in your keyword (such as "sandwich" or "pool cleaner" or "dry cleaner") and a "?" (No quotes)
- Strip out the spammers. In the "None of These Words" field, put in the phrase "http" (no quotes). That will remove all the auto-posters (robots).
- Add question words. In the "Any of These Words" field put in "recommend," "how," "find" …or whatever words you think might fit your particular field. (No quotes)
- If you're a local business, specify your area. In the "Places" field put in your town or city.
- Hit Search.
- Look for questions you can answer. Be cool. Don't be sales-y. Just answer questions like a human being.

Trust me, do this for a little while and you'll be shocked how quickly you can grow a dedicated following. (That just so happens to give you money.)

Social media expert Gary Vaynerchuk built an entire wine-making empire, not to mention an insanely lucrative public-speaking career, by simply answering people's questions about vino.

You can do worse than follow his lead. (Just don't root for his beloved New York Jets. That simply doesn't have the ROI any good business person is looking for.)

PUNK ROCK MARKETING
AMPLIFY YOUR MESSAGE

CHAPTER 7 Key Takeaways:

- **Follow the followers of big-time users** in your industry to build up your Twitter following.
- **Be sure to give people you recently followed at least two days** to follow you back. Shoot for three following sessions a week.
- **Put your Follow Me on Twitter icons everywhere** (including email signatures, newsletters, store counters, your employees, etc.)
- **Answer questions** (with the Twitter question search above) to help people out and add people to your Twitter following.

Chapter 8:

Contests, TweetChats & Live Streams...Oh My!

"If you're not gonna go all the way, why go at all?"

-Joe Namath

So, at this point, you pretty much have a master's degree in Twitter Studies.

I think it's safe to say with the knowledge you've consumed so far, you know more than nearly 85% of all business peeps when it comes to Twitter marketing.

But now it's time to take your knowledge to the next level. It's time to get a full-on Ph.D. in Twitternomics. (Without all the crippling student loan debt.)

Because no matter how many followers, retweets or "engagement" you have, it really doesn't mean a damn thing until you can translate all that Twitter activity into paying customers.

And there may be no better form of social media marketing than Twitter for instantly converting browsers into buyers. Here are a couple of profit-generatin' techniques that work really well:

Super Ninja Twitter Technique No. 1: Twitter Contests

Want to build your Twitter following and customer base fast? Throw a Twitter contest.

People love to win free stuff. And the stuff doesn't even have to be that amazing. I'm constantly amazed at the FREE crap people scurry around trying to win on Twitter. (Imagine what would happen if you actually gave away something decent.)

Here's how to organize your very own Twitter contest of epic proportions:

1. **Come up with a prize that doesn't suck.** Could be an iPod. A dinner for two at your restaurant. A free one-hour consultation in your office. A date with Brad Pitt. Whatever.
2. **Create a special website landing page with details about the contest.** This could be on your blog, your website, your Facebook page, wherever. Just so long as it's a link. Have a picture of the prize that doesn't suck. (If you want a super easy tool for running a contest, give WishPond a try. They've got a FREE Trial that makes the whole process seamless.)
3. **Shorten that special website landing page URL.** This is where you take a clunky, long URL and shorten it using a site like Bit.ly or TinyUrl. (Example: http://bit.ly/89do) This is especially handy if you've got a bunch of extra analytics code at the end of your URL.
4. **On your contest detail web page, let people know how they can win the special something you're giving way.** You want them to follow you on Twitter and tweet out a phrase of your choosing to enter. (Example: "Just entered to win a FREE iPod. Follow @punkmarketing and retweet http://bit.ly/8&*2 #Freepunkstuff.) The unique hashtag is key. This will let you track entrants into the contest. Don't forget to come up with an original #hashtag nobody else is using. (Sorry but #freestuff is already taken.)
5. **Promote the contest everywhere.** On Twitter, Facebook, YouTube, forearm tattoo, etc.
6. **Allow the contest to run for about 4-7 days.** This will depend on your audience, but I generally like to keep my contests within that timeframe. (Anything longer feels more drawn-out than a "Downton Abbey" episode.)
7. **Pick a winner.** Use the hashtag search in Twitter search or Bing Social search to find a list of all the people who retweeted your tweet.

8. **Announce the winner…everywhere.** Again on Twitter, Facebook, YouTube, etc.
9. **Wait 6 months and do it again.**

SUPER NINJA TWITTER TECHNIQUE NO. 2: TWITTER Q&A

The one problem with Twitter contests is you get a lot of freebie-seekers. (And slightly deranged people should be on meds.)

Which is okay. To a point. But ideally you'd like people who'll give you hard currency for your efforts.

And that's why I like Twitter Q&A's.

The leads I've gotten from Twitter Chats are much higher than from Twitter contests. (Even if overall numbers are lower.)

And by riffing on your area of expertise, you not only can put a face to your business, but you become the go-to person — in your follower's mind — for your given industry.

Trust me: it's like holding your very own 30-minute infomercial, without all the bad lighting and ultra-expensive ad buys.

So, here's how you run a Twitter Q&A:

1. **Pick a hashtag.** This is important. You'll be using this to not only promote the event but also keep track of who's attending. Make it unique and make it somewhat not sucky. (#AskJim or #AskCompanyName would be good ways to go.)
2. **Schedule a time for the chat.** I think the sweet spot is anywhere from 30-45 minutes, though I've seen people go as long as 90 minutes. (Not something my ADD can handle, but if you can do it, knock yourself out.)
3. **Promote the event with the hashtag.** This is key. You gotta get the word out about your event. So, make sure everything you've got — your website, blog, Facebook page, Twitter account, back of your car — has the hashtag and the topic you plan to talk about.
4. **Tweet about it constantly.** This is a no-brainer, but still, many small-biz types miss out on this. You gotta let people know what you're doing. (Don't forget the #hashtag.)

5. **Write a press release.** If you think your chat isn't important enough to do a press release, then you should see the crap people write press releases about. Believe me, if you're answering questions in your knowledge wheelhouse, it's worth a press release. (And you can really get the word out. Not to mention help your Google rankings.)
6. **Do the Chat.** Here's how it works. When the event starts, send out a tweet letting people know to ask questions using the designated hashtag, then retweet their question, so people see it. And then you answer with another tweet. Su-per simple.
7. **Wrap up the chat with a call to action.** Thank everybody for attending and let them know if they've got more questions, or they want to get a copy of whatever free thing you're peddling, then they can reach you at your website. (Be ready to have some way to collect their info. Because they are now hot leads.)

Here's the thing, no matter what business you're in, you have some level of expertise that civilians/possible customers might find interesting.

Ninja Technique No. 3: Twitter Live Video (Via Periscope)

I know what you're saying. Streaming video? On Twitter? I'd rather watch all 12 "Transformers" movies. (In Bulgarian.)

That's what I thought. Until I did it. And now, I'm only sad I didn't do it earlier.

Whether you're recording a live event or talking from the comfort of your double-wide trailer, live video on Twitter can do some amazing things for your marketing.

And since Twitter purchased Periscope, for an insane amount of money, it now offers the super-simple Twitter Live Video feature.

It is built into the Twitter app — available for either Android or Apple devices — but once you've got installed, you:

- Log in to your Twitter app on your device
- Set up your phone/tablet for recording (Best if you use external microphone and tripod)
- Tap the compose icon (Looks like a pen and quill)
- Tap the live video icon (Looks like..well…a pizza with one slice missing)
- Swipe down and tap "End broadcast" when you're done

And if the thought of broadcasting live video strikes you with mortal fear — it might — you can tap the microphone icon and choose audio-only. (Not sure how interesting that would be, but worth a go.)

I've had clients as diverse as surf-school instructors, caterers and even dentists do these from a variety of locations.

And again something about video makes people "trust" you. (Even when you shouldn't be trusted.)

PUNK ROCK MARKETING
AMPLIFY YOUR MESSAGE

CHAPTER 8 Key Takeaways:

- **Throw a Twitter contest** by asking entrants to retweet a designated message. Be sure to use a special #hashtag to track results.
- **Plan a Twitter Q&A** where you can answer questions from folks. Don't forget to send out a press release to promote the event.
- **Do a high-tech Q&A** with Twitter Live Video. Use the Twitter app, along with a tripod and external mic, to get some high-quality live Twitter video out there.

Chapter 9:

The Strange (and Sometimes) Profitable) World of Twitter Ads

"Many a small thing has been made large by the power of advertising."

-Mark Twain

I had no intention of writing this chapter on Twitter advertising.

For three reasons:

- The Twitter advertising platform is so frickin' NEW any proclamations I make will be rendered obsolete in about a week
- Though Twitter ads offer great targeting, they can royally suck with click-thru-rates (Twitter users don't like to click on... well...nearly anything)
- If you think CTRs are low with Twitter, just take a gander at conversion rates when trying to "sell" (Good frickin' luck!)

And yet you see before you a chapter on Twitter advertising: what gives?

Well, though Twitter is not the social media ad juggernaut Facebook is — no one is — there are still a ton of great opportunities to be found with Twitter ads.

Especially if you're not overly "selling."

That's because:

- Hardly anybody uses the Twitter ad platform

- If they do use it, they probably suck at it
- If retargeting or lead-capture is your goal — instead of an instant sale — Twitter ads can really pay off.

As my brother-in-law likes to say, "Right bait for the right fish." So, if your customers/fish spend a significant amount of time, Twitter ads can be an effective (and quick) way to boost your bottom-line.

TWITTER AD STRATEGY #1: PICK A GOAL (THAT DOESN'T SUCK)

There are five different conversions you can focus your Twitter ad campaigns around:

- New followers
- Website clicks or conversions
- Promoted video views (I like this one a lot)
- In-stream video views (pre-roll)
- Tweet engagements
- Awareness (Whatever that means)
- App installs/re-engagements

I'm not an app/tech guy so I won't "pretend" to advise you on what to do with app installs. (For the longest time I thought "Pokemon Go" was a card game.)

And I don't advise marketers spend a lot of time growing their follower count. (Followers just ain't worth spending much on.)

But my three favorite Twitter ad conversions, in order, are:

1. **Website clicks/conversions** (Great for promoting content on your website)
2. **Promoted video views**
3. **Tweet engagements** (Good for boosting the overall popularity of your Twitter account)

I like to have a healthy mix of all three with my Twitter ad campaigns. My ratio looks something like this:

- 50% of my ad budget goes toward "website clicks"
- 25% of my ad budget goes toward "promoted video views"
- 25% of my ad budget goes toward "engagements"

But this will depend entirely on your business model. If you don't produce a lot of original content, or you've got high-ticket items in your funnel that pay off big, then conversions and Twitter cards are the way to go. But if you've got a content-rich website or you interact with people on Twitter a lot, then "engagements" and "website clicks" will do well for you.

If you've got your website and funnel dialed in. Speaking of…

Twitter Ad Strategy #2: Get Ready for All That Twitter Ad Traffic

Before you spend a penny on Twitter ads you want to make sure your website, landing pages (and/or sales pages) are "ready" for those millions of new visitors you're gonna get. (Okay, maybe not millions, but you get the idea.)

And by "ready," we mean you gotta:

- Install retargeting code on all relevant pages (This lets you track folks, even if they leave your website without opting in)
- Place "relevant" sidebar and/or footer offers in your content (Don't pitch stuff a Twitter user would never buy)
- Create a Twitter-only landing page to capture opt-ins (Not only keeps analytics organized, but lets you tailor your copy to a Twitter audience)

It's beyond this humble tome to go too deep into the "retargeting" rabbit hole. But here's the Cliffs Notes version of how it works:

1. **Sign up for a Google Adwords and Facebook ad account.** (You probably already have one of each.)

2. **Grab the retargeting code for both and install on every page of your website.** (If this freaks you out, get a coder at Fiverr do it for you.)
3. **Tell Google and Facebook** which web page represents a successful conversion goal — such as a "Email Opt-In Thank You Page" or "Thank You for Buying" page — for your funnel.
4. **Create ads for visitors who visit your website** — but DON'T reach your conversion page — and encourage them to join your funnel of awesomeness.

This is how I make most of my money with Twitter ads: I send 'em to a content page on my website, and then whether they opt-in or not I continue to market to them.

Sneaky, but effective.

But even if you don't have a ton of content, you'll be promoting with Twitter ads, you want to make sure you have the chance to "sell" to website visitors again and again and again.

Twitter Ad Strategy Ad No. 3: Pull the Trigger

Because Twitter ads are relatively new — and so few people are having real success with them — I can't tell you definitively the ONE way to create Twitter ads.

But let me share with you the step-by-step methods I use for my Twitter ads. (And if you find a system that works better drop me a line and tell me what an idiot I am.)

Promoted Tweets (and Website Clicks)

Purpose: Great for promoting a contest, live event, or sending people to a web page. (Offers and coupons work great!)

Anything where you want people to leave the confines of Twitter and take a specific action.

How I Do It

1. **Campaign** - Sign in to Twitter, click on Twitter ads, and name your campaign.

2. **Targeting** - Target either through keywords or similar followers to specific Twitter accounts whose followers represent your ideal customer. I prefer the latter, but test to see which works best for you. (Don't target your own followers!)
3. **Device** - Start with desktop ad placement, then slowly build out to mobile. (And I mean "slowly.")
4. **Tweets** - Manually select 2-4 tweets (or create 'em on-the-spot.) Make the copy clear, informal and personal. Conversational and fun is best. (Example: "Good organic pizza just got easier. Learn how to save 25% off your next Denverlicious pizza pie: link.com" Be sure to use your own analytics link — Twitter analytics suck!)
5. **Budget** - Set a total budget of $100, and a daily max budget of $10. (Don't worry, you can always pause the campaign if you need to)
6. **Location** - Start with the U.S. and then spread out from there. (Unless your customer base lives outside the good, old USA.)
7. **Pacing** - Pace the campaign evenly throughout the day. (Though if your offer is time-sensitive, then choose accelerated.)
8. **Cost** - Choose a cost-per-click that is 25% of the lowest suggested bid. This ain't Google Adwords where you gotta out-bid everybody else. Keep that bid low — and keep lowering it — until you find a dead spot. (That's your golden range.)

Twitter Promoted Video Views

Purpose: Great boosting the engagement of a video.

How I Do It

1. **Add the Twitter remarketing pixel to your website, if you haven't already.** Have a designer on Fiverr do if for you if this seems complicated.
2. **Create the perfect video.** I don't mean perfect in terms of quality, but perfect in terms that it's short, interesting and contains a CTA — usually in the text of the ad. This CTA will encourage

people to go SOMEWHERE and do SOMETHING after they watch the video. Otherwise it's a waste of money.

3. **Create ad and upload video** - Few people know you can upload your video direct to Twitter without creating a "sponsored tweet." This is why I like this ad. Cuts out any obstacles to a viewer watching the video.
4. **Use the same settings as the Promoted Tweet** - Device: Desktop; Total budget: $100; Daily max budget: $10; Location: U.S. at first, then spread out; Pace: evenly through the day; Cost per click: 25% of lowest suggested bid.
5. **Target your tribe** - Because you get charged for each video view — or Cost-Per-View (CPV) — I like to target people already "following" me on Twitter and folks who've landed on my website. (Leads to better conversions.)

TWITTER AD STRATEGY AD NO. 4: FIND THE WINNERS (DITCH THE LOSERS)

Once you've got a Twitter campaign or two running, it's just finding the ones that work and killing the campaigns that don't.

But how do you know if a campaign is a winner?

Well, this will depend on your business. But any Twitter ad that produces a lead at a cost-per-lead that works for your business model is a winner.

If you're selling $450k yachts, your cost-per-lead will be radically different than if you're selling a $7 eBook.

But here are a couple general guidelines to keep in mind:

- **When targeting @usernames, break your campaigns up in groups of five.** This will help you hone in on Twitter accounts that actually provide the biggest source of your leads.
- **If you're not getting a good response, try running ads between 6pm - 9pm.** (Might just be your audience ain't on Twitter during the day.)

- **Use existing customer demographic information in your Twitter ads.** (If your audience is 65% women interested in the "Food Network" use that intel to further refine your targeting.)
- **When you've got your Twitter ads rocking-and-rolling, try buying a couple of "paid tweets"** — in which you pay folks to spread your message for you. Tools for this include: SponsoredTweets.com, PaidperTweet.com, and BuySellAds.com.
- **Always trust YOUR data, over anybody else's.** Including mine, or Twitter's.

Twitter ads are NOT an overnight strategy. (Not even sure it's an over-fortnight strategy.) But if you've got a compelling offer — or irresistible coupon — the Twitter-verse would be brain-dead to not jump on, then dedicate some time and energy to Twitter advertising.

It may not pay off immediately, and it will take some work, but once you've got it honed in, it can be a surprisingly profitable way to make money, and outpace the competition. (Especially if that competition thinks "Pokémon Go" is a card game.)

CHAPTER 9 Key Takeaways:

- **Effective Twitter ads start with good goals that don't suck.** The author prefers "website clicks," "video views," and "sponsored tweets." (Skip "followers" — it just ain't worth it.)
- **Make sure your funnel is ready for that Twitter ad traffic before running your first campaign.** This includes setting up relevant offers and ensuring you've got all that retargeting goodness ready for prime time.
- **Set up your initial Twitter ad campaigns following the recommendations above.** (Don't forget to keep your cost-per-click low, and your copy simple and conversational.)
- **Always look to improve your winning ads and ditch the crappy campaigns.** Try running ads in the evening, purchasing a couple of paid tweets, creating different kinds of Twitter video ads, and using your existing customer demographic information to make sound Twitter ad decisions.

Chapter 10:

Setting It All on AutoPilot

"The first problem for us all, is not to learn, but to unlearn."

-Gloria Steinem

The beauty, and I mean the absolute beauty, of Twitter is that like those cheesy rotisserie grill infomercials…

You can "set it and forget it."

It's possible, if you've got enough content and quotes and funny videos and promotional links stored up, that you can schedule your Twitter activity months, if not years, in advance.

This is because (unlike other social platforms like Facebook, Pinterest and Instagram) Twitter has what techie types call an "open API."

Which is a nerd-alert way of saying Twitter lets developer-types grab their data and create toys that make your Twitter life easier.

Now, not all third-party Twitter tools are created equal. (In fact, some tool's names are as dumb as the tools themselves.)

There are a few I can't live without. While most of them have a free version, their premium versions can often make your life much easier.

But when you're first starting out, just grab the FREE tools and give 'em a test drive.

Twitter AutoPilot Tool No. 1: HootSuite

I believe the official term for HootSuite is that it's a dashboard client for Twitter.

It's just a kick-ass way to use Twitter and is pretty much my absolute number one tool I use day in and day out.

Why?

Well, HootSuite lets you feed multiple Twitter streams into one single dashboard.

Meaning, if you've got multiple Twitter accounts, you can handle all the scheduling, commenting, retweeting, replying, and cavorting in one place.

But, wait! That's not all! (Cue the music.)

These streams can be virtually anything: LinkedIn profiles and company pages, Twitter searches, Twitter lists, Facebook pages, Instagram profiles, YouTube channels, Pinterest profiles…

So, you can handle all your social media goodness in one place.

The FREE version lets you sync up to five twitter accounts, which is perfect for most businesses. The PRO version lets you handle up to 50 different accounts.

You also get a fair amount of analytics, so you can track what works and what doesn't.

Alternatives include: TweetDeck, SocialOomph and a bunch of other crappy tools I can't stand. For my vote, HootSuite is still the best.

Twitter AutoPilot Tool No. 2: Friend or Follow

The manual labor of having to "unfollow" masses of people in my quest to build up a Twitter follower base can be cumbersome.

But with Friend or Follow it's a breeze.

All you do is:

- Sign up
- Import your Twitter account
- Let the tool show you who is not following you back
- And then "unfollow" everybody who does not deem you worthy of their attention

Now, the process isn't as automatic as it once was. (Afraid you'll have to THANK Twitter for that. They changed their API.)

But it is still fairly easy. (And so easy a virtual assistant or disgruntled teenager can do it.)

Twitter AutoPilot Tool No. 3: SnapBird

I told you these names were ridiculous.

But as silly as SnapBird sounds, it's actually a pretty cool tool. Because SnapBird lets you find people based on keywords.

And way more powerful than the generic Twitter search.

Now like all these tools, there is a FREE and PAID version. (For unlimited search requests you gotta pay.)

But here are a couple of great ways to use SnapBird:

- Search for users who have engaged with you
- Comb through old tweets of yours you can't find
- Find the EXACT kind of lead you're looking for (Not just a generic group of might-be-leads)

Twitter AutoPilot Tool No. 4: Other Cool/Crazy Tools

There are some other neat tools I like, but don't use day in and day out.

Clicktotweet is a simple way to promote your stuff by letting people click a button which automatically updates their Tweet status with a pre-populated tweet promoting your Twitter goodness.

Twtqpon.com is probably the best of the bunch, as it allows you to create an online coupon code that your readers can redeem. It's a very cool way to spread the word (and the profits.)

And I'm sure by the time I finish typing this sentence, 1200 more Twitter tools will come out that can help you market to the masses.

Just try a couple out and see if they can help you. Chances are there's a fourteen-year-old RIGHT NOW inventing something in his basement that will help you make money in the future.

PUNK ROCK MARKETING
AMPLIFY YOUR MESSAGE

CHAPTER 10 Key Takeaways:

- **Try out tools like HootSuite or SocialOomph to manage ALL of your social media activity.** (And schedule your tweets weeks in advance — so you don't lose your frickin' mind.)
- **Rely on the ever-reliable Friend or Follow to help you build up your Twitter rapidly.** (By helping you get rid of the Twitter unfollower deadweight.
- **Use SnapBird to find users** who match your ideal customer interests and locations.
- **Explore crazy tools like ClicktoTweet and Twtqpon** to find that tool that'll make your Twitter marketing life much easier.

EPILOGUE:
This Wasn't Supposed to Happen

Twitter, like most technological innovations, was a total accident. (And was never intended to be anything but a side project for the guys working on it.)

It started off as a simple micro-messaging service that helped colleagues keep in contact during the workday. (The reason for the 140-character limit was based on SMS cell phone limits and had little to do with the relative merits of a super-short tweet length.)

And yet, Ev Williams and Biz Stone, the founders of Twitter, certainly couldn't have predicted they would create a technology platform that would change the way we write, read, communicate and live.

But they did.

And today, Twitter is used just as much by bored suburban teenagers who want to be vampires as it is by student protesters in the Arab world dreaming of a new life.

And that's the mind-boggling part of Twitter.

Messages can spread in a matter of seconds to thousands of people you'll never meet.

And unlike platforms such as Facebook or LinkedIn, Twitter isn't about getting membership into an exclusive club or building your "network of friends."

It's about breaking down the doors of the club and finding out if your message resonates with the world.

Now, it's possible you won't be sending out tweets that bring down a fascist regime.

But…

Every once in a while you will send out something that spreads like wildfire. (I sent out a bittersweet tweet about my mom's chemotherapy struggles that got 1,300 retweets and some of the most moving and heart-felt emails ever.)

So, as you plan your Twitter marketing calendar, just remember beyond the tech and the jargon and the ninja-hack strategies…

…in business we like to buy stuff from people we like and trust.

And people who remind us, in a simple way, how important it is to stay upbeat, strong and committed to what we want don't come off as marketers.

They appear as people, just like us.

Here's hoping the tips in this book help you not only become the trustworthy and likable Twitter ninja I know you can be…

…but bring a little "us-ness" to the world.

Vol.2
of the Small Business
Marketing
COLLECTION
VIDEO
MARKETING
in 2019
MADE
(STUPIDLY) EASY
Michael Clarke

Video Marketing in 2019 Made (Stupidly) Easy

Vol.2 of the Small Business Marketing Made (Stupidly) Easy Collection

PROLOGUE: Why You're a Total F#*$& Moron If You Don't Do Video

I remember the first time I heard the phrase, "THIS is the YEAR you MUST do Video…"

That was 2009. (Pretty sure I made a note in my Blackberry at the time.)

Since then, it seems, every nanosecond some rambling pundit, myself included, comes out with their prediction about how THIS is the year video will dominate everything…

…and how any small business owner who doesn't RIGHT NOW, THIS VERY MINUTE drop everything they're doing and pick up a video camera and create 45 YouTube videos…

…will fall into bankruptcy, lose their livelihood and wander the streets in a disoriented post-marketing stupor.

The truth is: RIGHT NOW represents an absolute, goldmine opportunity for marketers to do video.

Because creating, promoting and distributing your videos has NEVER been easier.

The best part: YOUR customers don't know that.

Most people are impressed by the fact it took you all of THREE MINUTES to talk to an electronic device with a blinking light…

…then spent the extra SEVEN MINUTES to cut out the boring parts where you forgot to turn the camera off…

…and then dedicated a monumental THIRTY SECONDS it took to upload the video and give it a title that isn't totally pointless.

So, before we jump into the nuts-and-bolts of video marketing (and there are quite a few nuts-and-bolts to contend with), here are a few major-league kick-ass reasons video marketing is not only an effective and rather inexpensive way to market to new customers...

...but a totally revolutionary way to do business.

KICK-ASS REASON NO. 1: VIDEO MARKETING IS CHEAP

But what about all that gear? And expensive editing software and all the time to memorize aspect ratios and HD video export formats?

Relax. Breathe.

Yes, there MIGHT be an initial investment in some gear. (If ya got a smartphone, that expense can be greatly minimized.)

But when it comes to managing your marketing costs — namely trying to get a ton of leads without taking out a second mortgage — video is the MOST EFFECTIVE and CHEAPEST FORM of marketing there is.

Just TRY to get on the first page of Google with a keyword-infused article on your website, or even worse, some clumsy Google PPC campaign.

And while your competition waits six months for the Googlebots to index their blog post or pays $7.50/click in an ultra-spendy Adwords campaign, you and I can rip off a quick video and get my video on the first page in a matter of a week. At nearly 10% of the cost. (About as kick-ass as it gets.)

KICK-ASS REASON NO. 2: VIDEO MARKETING IS FAST

And while your competitors spend two hours on that 400-word opus that Google may or may not rank them for...you and I can create ten videos and have an entire video editorial calendar wrapped up for the next two-and-a-half months.

And I say this as a guy who loves writing. (I'm one of those hopeless English Majors who actually read, and liked, "Moby Dick.")

But writing moves at GLACIAL speed compared to video. And, let's be honest, when was the last time you READ an entire 400-word "anything" online. (That's what I thought.)

KICK-ASS REASON NO. 3: VIDEO GETS SHARED A LOT

Know what gets shared the most on Facebook? Pictures of friends AND videos, the social engine that drives the Internet.

So, if you're looking to boost business at your burger joint, instead of pouring thousands of dollars into offline print marketing or PPC campaigns that have crappy ROIs…

…just make a funny behind-the-scenes video of your kitchen crew, and you'll get a much bigger bang for your marketing buck.

KICK-ASS REASON NO. 4: VIDEO PUTS A (HUMAN) FACE TO YOUR BUSINESS

All that snappy sales copy and reams of direct-mail pieces won't make people feel nearly as connected and interested in you, and your business, as video.

I could tell you it's because 90% of our judgments are based on what we can see. (Though that might be a part.)

I think the real reason is that video, by the medium's nature, just "feels" more intimate and personal. (Especially for the viewer.)

I can't tell you how many emails I've gotten from people who saw one of my vids and felt like they just "knew" me. (Stalker-ish? Yes. Good for business? Absolutely!)

And if you approach your video marketing with a sense of humor, and a willingness to look foolish, there's nothing that can stop you.

KICK-ASS REASON NO. 5: VIDEO MARKETING CAN HELP YOU OWN YOUR MARKET

I've done it countless times, where I've entered a market with long-time old-school established search-engine competition…

...and BLOWN them away in a matter of a few weeks with three or four strategic videos.

That's because videos give you instant credibility. And help differentiate you as a seriously big fish in a super-sized pond.

Because if most businesses dip their toe into video marketing, they suck at it. And most people are lazy and don't want to read anything more than a paragraph.

But give 'em a couple two-minute videos and they'll be putty in your hands. And, luckily, you can sell a whole lot of crap to putty.

Chapter 1:

Which Kind of Video Should You Do?

"If you don't make mistakes, you aren't really trying."

-Coleman Hawkins

So, what'dya need in a perfect piece of video marketing?

Well, not much marketing, for one. (But we'll get to that.)

First, let's break down some different forms of video marketing and see which may or may not be a good fit for your business needs.

Video Form No. 1: Talking-Head Expert Stuff

Just like it sounds.

This is somebody on your team, or maybe you, talking straight to a camera or smartphone mounted on a tripod, offering helpful tips on a topic.

It's simple, powerful and staggeringly effective for building rapport with viewers.

Mostly, because so many videos of this kind are truly abysmal. (Just head over to the freakshow that is YouTube to verify this painful fact.)

As with any video: audio quality is huge. Nobody will tolerate you talking 40 feet away from the camera into an external boom mic.

It can also be scary, especially for people who aren't Uber-comfortable on camera; in which case a script or series of bullet points is highly recommended.

Pros: Personable. Quick. Easy to produce. Great at building an emotional connection to you or your brand.

Cons: May require Valium for those frightened of being on camera.

VIDEO FORM NO. 2: SCREEN-CAPTURE TUTORIAL

This is where you record what's on your computer screen, whether it be a PowerPoint presentation or a software demo, with software such as Camtasia or Screenflow.

I know. Sounds mind-numbingly boring, but it's great for:

- Product Demos
- Sales Videos
- Technical Training
- Big Ideas That Require Text

And you know that whole "rule" about corporate PowerPoint presentations? Where you're not supposed to repeat the words on the slide?

Yeah, that doesn't apply here.

In a video, people actually like to read along as you go through the points of your presentation.

The downside is you don't get that intimate connection you do with "talking head" videos, but you know what? For some folks that's okay.

If you're camera-shy, this can be a great way to break into the video marketing field. (Without taking that paper bag off your head.)

Pros: Don't even need a camera! Easy to fix glitches and mistakes. Super cheap and easy to make.

Cons: Can be boring, if not focused. Need images to make video stand out.

VIDEO FORM NO. 3: BEHIND THE SCENES

This is self-explanatory; a video that shows viewers a behind-the-scenes look at your business.

Now, this may require you to tap into your inner Spielberg. But if you can, it can be worth it.

Ya just wanna go around your business and shoot some footage. Talk to your employees, give folks a look at what's it like behind the counter. Show people that your business is filled with…well… people.

Even if you're a solo-preneur, people still want to see what your desk looks like, what books are on your bookshelf, what kind of Star Wars bobbleheads you have in the window, etc. (I'm a "Boba Fett" guy, but maybe that's just me.)

We'll cover filming later, but here's the absolute KEY to a good behind-the-scenes vid: get good audio.

Too many of these behind-the-scenes videos have such bad audio, it makes them unwatchable. And don't talk about how amazing your company is. Talk about something interesting.

Got a policy where employees can bring their dogs to work? Film it!

Have somebody on your team who can break dance? Film it!

Is there an annual chili contest in the second-floor building of your company? Film it!

This is a great way to spotlight your team and get some cool marketing exposure in the process.

Pros: Really good (sneaky) way of marketing your brand. Fun. Boosts team morale.

Cons: Requires some editing time. Bit of technical know-how. (But not much.)

Video Form No. 4: Customer Testimonials

This is actually the most overlooked form of video marketing, but one of the most powerful.

Got a group of regular customers who love your stuff? Film them! Just have them do a brief 30-second talk about why they love your stuff.

(**Tip:** Be sure they start their response with "The reason I love (name)..." or else it will be hard to edit their response in context.)

Sell things virtually?

No problem. You can record people on Skype talking about your company, or even better...

Have them leave a voice mail message and put that into a video with a simple slideshow. (God knows why, but people just instantly believe things that are recorded on the phone.)

Now, you want to tread carefully here. Don't make it too over-the-top. (No need to have scores of customers gush about how your company is the most amazing thing that ever existed.)

But if you've got some good social proof going on, throw in some video footage of your products or services. It can do more for your video marketing efforts than all the talking-head videos in the world.

Pros: Very effective at increasing leads. Easy to film. Virtually no work on your part.

Cons: Can get very annoying quickly, if not done well. Sometimes hard to get customers to talk on-camera.

Video Form No. 5: Video Q&A

Have no idea what to do a video on?

Well, just ask people what their biggest questions/frustrations are...and then go ahead and answer them.

I had a client of mine who ran a pizza joint, and all he did was set up his iPhone and answer questions submitted to him via email. Think his tips on helping folks create the perfect crust hurt sales?

Absolutely not!

And in a later chapter I'll show you how to track the effectiveness of your video marketing to make sure you're not wasting your time with these types of videos.

Video Form No. 6: Anything But…

Notice what kind of video marketing I did NOT mention?

That's right. YOU talking about how amazing/wonderful/awesome your company is.

Nobody cares. (Really.)

You can talk about virtually anything on camera, just don't go on and on about the amazing features and benefits of your latest doo-hickey.

Unless it's a sales page video, and even then...

Not only will the "one ring to rule them all" in video distribution, YouTube, probably ban your video, but it won't help you reach any of your marketing goals.

PUNK ROCK MARKETING — AMPLIFY YOUR MESSAGE

CHAPTER 2 Key Takeaways:

- Talking-head videos are great for how-to tips and building personality into your brand.
- Screen-capture videos are fantastic for technical training and product demos.
- Behind-the-scenes vids are perfect for showing a funnier/lighter side of your biz. (Even if you don't have a lighter side.)
- Testimonials from your customers are great if done subtly.
- Video Q&As are a good way to help people out and allow you to be seen as a ready-made expert.
- Overt marketing videos are boring and lame; and nobody wants to watch them.

Chapter 2:

Anatomy of the Perfect Video

"To express yourself needs a reason, but expressing yourself is a reason."

-Ai Weiwei

Okay, so you got some ideas for what kind of video you might want to do. But what do you actually put in the video?

How do you structure your video? What do you say? What do you NOT say?

And how do you make sure the video actually does something for your business, you know, besides pad your ego?

Worry not! Here's my patented (I wish) FIVE Step Video Marketing Checklist to ensure your videos stay on track and get you the results you want:

Step No. 1: The Brief Intro

When I say brief? I mean...brief. Get in, get out.

And tell people WHY the hell they should be watching.

This is probably the simplest step in this process, but the one most people neglect. (Watch any DIY how-to videos on YouTube and this will become abundantly clear.)

This is what I say in my intro, to establish WHY people should watch, and I hardly ever deviate from this formula:

"Hi there, it's Michael from Punk Rock Marketing. And in this short video, I will cover the No.1 reason Facebook is a spawn of Satan on bringing down Western Civilization with its desire to plant electrodes in our brain...and what you can do about it."

Okay, so let's break it down a bit further:

- **"Hi, it's Michael…"**
- Put your name and your company in there fast. You have no idea where people will watch your video, so get your branding out there right away.
- **"In this short video…"**
- Tell 'em it will be short. This is key. Lets them know they won't be sitting in their chair for a hundred years as you show them how to change a spark plug.
- **"I'm going to cover…"**
- Tell them what they will get from watching the video. What solution will your video provide? What insight will it cover? What PROBLEM will it solve?

Step No. 2: The State of Things

This is where you take a slight step back. And tell people WHY it's important they know this thing you're going to tell them.

They may already intuitively know this, but this brief section will help nail it home, and give them confidence in your ability to help them.

Again, keep this brief.

I might do something like this:

"Facebook has built its empire on user data. But how do they get that data? With tiny electrodes they plant in our brain when we're sleeping next to our smartphone. That's how!

"Here's how you can keep the electrodes from invading your body…"

Notice how it moves seamlessly into the next step which is…

Step No. 3: The Meat and Potatoes

This is where you instruct. Or with more whimsical fare, such as the behind-the-scenes video and testimonials, fire off into the fun part.

Whatever form you're dabbling with, this is where you give up the goods. Where you deliver on the promise you set forth in the brief intro.

Here are a few tips to ensure your Meat and Potatoes don't go completely off the rails:

- **Don't ramble.** Just stick to the points.
- **Lists are great.** If you can tell us the three steps, five techniques, four tactics to solve the problem…. people will love you for it.
- **Keep the number of steps reasonable.** Don't do 19 ways to lower your car insurance bills. Do seven. Or one.
- **Cover one idea in your video.** You're not trying to cure cancer. You're trying to solve one problem. (Even if that solution has three or four parts to it.)
- **Remember people don't know as much as you do.** If there's a lot of technical jargon or complex ideas, try to keep things simple.
- **Tell stories.** People love personal anecdotes. (As long as they relate to the point. If not, cut 'em.)
- **Don't be boring.**

Step No. 4: The Action Steps

This is where you lay out the simple step-by-step blueprint you outlined in Step No.3 into easily digestible chunks of info anybody can understand.

In my Facebook example:

"First, you cover your head in tin foil. Step two, you bury your iPhone thirty feet below ground…."

If you're doing a talking-head video, and have editing savvy, then you could throw up a quick text image of the steps at the end of the video.

But the key thing is: give people something they can act on right now. (Even though most of them won't.)

Step No. 5: The Call to Action

Okay, you've been a supercool awesome person. You've given them some info and helped improve their lives. (Sorta.)

Now, it's time for them to pay it forward. And, trust me, they will.

Obligation is hard-wired in our brain, so if somebody does us a solid we feel (strongly) the need to pay it back.

So, here's what you do…in the call to action I usually ask people to do two things:

1. Share or comment on my video
2. Grab a free offer/coupon I'm offering

Here's an example:

"If you've enjoyed my anarchist ramblings about the cabal that is Facebook be sure to Facebook like, tweet, or comment in the field below.

"And if you'd like a FREE copy of my new eBook, "7 Ways Facebook is Trying to Eat Your Soul From the Inside Out," head on over to punkrockmarketing.com to get instant access."

The cool thing about this verbiage is that even if they don't take advantage of your offer, they can still help you out by making your video more popular.

But if they take advantage of the offer, after having watched you talk for 2.5 minutes, they are very much a qualified lead.

CHAPTER 2 KEY TAKEAWAYS:

- Start your video with a brief intro that tells people what they can expect to find out by watching.
- Follow that up with a short description of why your video is important.
- Get into the meat of your video. Don't ramble!
- Give viewers action steps they can use. Instantly!
- End your video with a call to action that asks people to social share and head over to your website to pre-qualify themselves.

Chapter 3:

Getting Geared Up on the Ultra-Cheap

"You can fool all the people all the time... if the advertising is right and the budget is big enough."

-Joseph E. Levine

Video equipment is like computers or guitars.

You can get as complicated and expensive, or as simple and bare-bones as you like. (Much of it will depend on your own personality.)

I'm weird. I LIKE to edit video. (Maybe it's the OCD control-freak in me.)

So, a good copy of video-editing software is a must for me, but knowing which F-stop setting or white balance control to alter on a camera literally puts me in a coma.

So, with camera choice I want something that looks great out of the box...not something I have to fuss with for hours.

That said, here are my recommendations for the gear you'll need (and may want someday) as you delve into the fabulous world of video marketing.

Remember there are only THREE MUSTS for video: good audio, something to record on, and something to say.

Everything else is just decoration.

Note: I've created a PDF downloadable Video Marketing Gear Checklist you can use as reference. Be sure to grab your totally FREE copy here:" PunkRockMarketing.com/VideoGear"

Video Gear Must-Have No. 1: The Microphone

What??? What about the camera?

I'm telling you, audio is your most important piece of gear.

The quality difference between the cheapest HD camcorder and the most expensive digital SLR is NOTHING compared to the quality difference between internal (built-in) microphones and external sound-capturing devices.

Believe me, the money you spend here will be well worth your while.

Ultra Cheap Option-Lavalier Microphone ($25-$100)

This is a simple tie-clip microphone that attaches to your lapel and plugs in directly into the camera.

Tip: Run the lapel wire under your shirt to avoid making the video look super ghetto.

I used to find these at Radio Shack for about $25. (But then Radio Shack decided to institute "losing money" as a business practice.)

There are a ton of great options on Amazon, including the Sony ECM series. (If you're going to do a bunch of talking-head vids, go for a condenser lav mic. It's worth it.)

Amazon Lav Mics:

PunkRockMarketing.com/LavMic

Elite Option-Wireless Lavalier Microphone ($500-$700)

Okay, I don't expect you to get one of these right out of the gate. But if you make some extra moolah from your video marketing efforts, then adding a wireless lavalier microphone to your video toolbox will be well worth it.

The sound is quite good, considering you're on a wireless channel, and it gives you a ton of flexibility in terms of movement and location. (You can even record live presentations you give.)

Tip: Don't go for the ultra-cheap wireless units. They ain't worth it.

Amazon Wireless Lav Mics:

PunkRockMarketing.com/WirelessMic

EXTRA ITEM - IPHONE LAV MIC ADAPTER ($25)

If you plan on shooting exclusively with your smartphone or tablet computer, then you'll need an iPhone adapterhttp://punkrock-marketing.com/iphoneadapter to plug in your lav mic.

Bonus: You can actually get a splitter to let you conduct interviews and get great audio from both you and your subject.

Amazon iPhone Mic Adapter:

PunkRockMarketing.com/iPhoneAdapter

VIDEO GEAR MUST-HAVE NO. 2: THE CAMERA

Okay. We're here. We're finally gonna get you a camera. (But wait! You might already have one lurking in your shirt pocket.)

Here's a breakdown of some options you have on the camera recording side:

Ultra-Cheap Option - Your Smartphone (Free-$500)

My uncle ran a videography business in the late 80s. His equipment cost him $30,000. Today he could do everything for under $50.

That's because the smartphone you hold in your hand, and will hold for years to come, can produce some amazing QUALITY video.

Now, if you don't have a smartphone, don't run out and go buy one for the video capabilities. It ain't THAT good.

But if you have an Android phone or an iPhone, you've got all you need to produce amazing video. (As long as you know what you're doing; we'll go over that in more detail later.)

Semi-Cheap Option- Rugged Adventure Cameras $95-$200

If you plan on doing a lot of action video — maybe, you run a ski lodge and want to film on the slopes, or you're a surf instructor who wants to shoot some action footage in the water — then there are plenty of rather cheap camera options, such as the GoPro and the Sony ActionCam, that will produce amazing video quality in a variety of rough settings.

The cool thing about these cameras is they're tough and can shoot video (almost) anywhere. Trouble is their sound quality often sucks. (Though they are improving with each new version.)

Mix up your action shots with some microphone assisted talking segments to get some very usable quality stuff. (No matter where you find yourself.)

Amazon Adventure Cameras:

PunkRockMarketing.com/AdventureCam

Somewhat Elite Option - Prosumer Camera ($400-$800)

The more you spend, the more features you can get with your video camera. Like better lenses, more controls, more stabilization, better ergonomics.

You wouldn't think ergonomics would make a difference. Wait till you have to hold a camera for ten minutes without shaking, you'll see what a difference it makes.

Unfortunately to get the best features around you need to spend upwards of $2500. (At least.)

Unless you go with a "prosumer" camera. These are camcorders that are in the middle region between smartphones and high-end DSLR camera. (And they'll usually set you back, at the high end, just under $1000.)

If you spend money on a "prosumer" model, I recommend you go with a Sony or Canon camera.

There are tons of nice camcorders out there, but these two manufacturers have the best lenses...which are probably the most expensive, and most important, part of a camera.

Amazon Resources: (Sony)

PunkRockMarketing.com/SonyCam

(Canon) PunkRockMarketing.com/CanonCam

UPDATE As I update this section of the book for 2019, I've had a tough time finding a wide selection for this type of camcorder. Canon still makes some good models in this category, but Sony seems to have de-emphasized offering here much.

It's as if they think this smartphone thing is gonna stick around. Word to the wise, buying a Prosumer camcorder now may sound good, but it could be difficult to get parts and service later.

Elite Option - DSLR Camera ($1500-Who Knows?)

This is where I must feign a bit of ignorance - I am not huge camera gear head. (If I were, I'd probably own a $4000 DSLR high-end camera that would make my footage look more amazing than an indie Hollywood film.)

But if you have the budget - and the patience - to work with a high-end camera (lots and lots of accessories are needed) then a high-end DSLR camera will give you the best footage on the planet. (And make your business look so much more profitable and professional than it is.)

Amazon DSLR Cameras:

PunkRockMarketing.com/DSLR

Video Gear Must-Have No. 3: Tripod

Unless you want your videos to induce vertigo, you're going to need a tripod. Here are a few options:

Smartphone Tripods - ($5-$50)

These can range from the arm tripods, ones in which you wrap them around nearly any surface, or traditional stand-on-the-floor models. (Popular brands include Gorilla and Joby, but whatever floats your boat should work.)

Amazon Smartphone Leg Tripod:

PunkRockMarketing.com/PhoneLegTripod

Amazon Smartphone Arm Tripod:

PunkRockMarketing.com/GorillaPod

Camcorder Tripod - ($19-$50)

This will depend mostly on your filming needs. If you're just going to shoot inside, go with one of the cheap, light tripods. (Nothing more than $25.)

If you're going to shoot outside a lot, particularly in windy conditions, you might need something a little more durable, but heavy. (You might even need a few sandbags to hold down the camera. Believe me, wind can be a cruel obstacle to filming.)

Either way, I find tripods generally have the shelf life of a reality show. (About eight months.)

Amazon Camcorder Tripods:

PunkRockMarketing.com/Tripod

Video Gear Must-Have No.4: Lighting

Now, the lighting you'll need will depend on where you will do most of your filming. If you shoot a lot outside, just use the sun. (It's the best lighting source there is.)

But if you shoot indoors, you're going to need something more than that horrible office neon lighting that makes everybody look like a zombie. So, here are a couple of options:

Super Cheap Option - Home Depot Clip-On Lights ($40)

If you plan to shoot stuff close, like sitting at your desk, or you're just not worried about executing high-quality footage, then a couple of clip-on lights from Home Depot will serve you just fine.

These stark lights can lead to extra shadows, but if you play with the positioning a bit, you can find a nice lighting set up on the ultra-cheap.

Somewhat Cheap Option - Simple Lighting Kit ($100)

I like the lighting kits from FancierStudio. But no matter which brand you use you'll want at least 2 lights - placed behind the camera - that point toward the subject at 45-degree angles.

Now I'm no lighting expert, far from it, but the key is to go for balance. (No intense shadows on the face.) Even crappy lighting can be fixed by boosting the saturation in a video editing program. As long the lighting balanced. But if it's all over the place, then it can be an absolute pain to fix.

Amazon Fancier Studio Lighting Kits:

PunkRockMarketing.com/StudioLighting

Somewhat Cheap Green Screen Option - Green Screen Lighting Kit ($150)

If you plan to do green screen videos - where you'll "key out" the background in your videos and insert a background of your choosing - then buy yourself a lighting kit + green screen combo.

You may need additional lights, but these can be exceptionally versatile. (And can turn even the most cramped office setting into a full-on video studio.)

Amazon Green Screen + Lighting Kit Combo:

PunkRockMarketing.com/GreenScreenKit

CHAPTER 3 Key Takeaways:

- Audio is super important. Invest in a lavalier microphone of some kind to improve your video quality.
- Your smartphone is a fantastic HD camera. (As long as you've got external audio.)
- Tripods are flimsy but required. (You may even need a sandbag or two.)
- Buy cheap desk lamps for a quick infusion of light into your video settings.
- Don't forget to grab your "No B.S. Video Marketing Gear Checklist!"

Chapter 4:

Your Super-Quick 5-Minute

"If you can't explain it to a six-year-old, you don't understand it yourself."

-Albert Einstein

Ya don't have to be Fellini to make great video marketing content. But there are a few, simple rules to making any type of filmed media…

And knowing these rules can make you look way more talented and professional than you are.

So, here's my super-brief Five-Minute Film School Tutorial that you can use to ensure your videos are watchable, compelling and they communicate your message in the best way possible.

Five-Minute Film-School Tip No. 1: Keep the Camera Still

I know there's a zoom button on your camera. That doesn't mean you have to use it.

The problem with the zoom function on most camcorders, and especially smartphones, is that they make the lens more sensitive to things like light, contrast…and your constant frickin' moving.

And, believe me, you're moving even if you're just holding the camera still.

So, put your video device on a tripod whenever you can. And if you need to go "handheld," use a nearby wall or chair to brace yourself.

And if you must "move in" to shoot something close, physically move the camera in. (Not the zoom.) It will look much better in the long run.

Five-Minute Film-School Tip No. 2: Keep the Light Behind You

Most photographers know this trick well, but if you're new to any kind of camera operation, it's a good rule to keep the sun, or major light source, behind you as you film.

The reason is instantly clear to anybody who has filmed on a sunny day. (It makes the subject's face dark and under-exposed.)

Also, if you're filming outside, it's good to know that early morning and late afternoon are the best times to film. (That's because you can control where the sun is.)

Noontime is the absolute worst. (Mid-day sun makes everybody look like zombies. And nobody likes to look like a zombie.)

As for that indoor lighting kit you've got, put your two most powerful light behind the camera at 45-degree angles.

(Here's a quick diagram [PunkRockMarketing.com/LightingDiagram] you can use for reference.)

And then if you've got another, softer light put that behind the subject to light their back. This will ensure you have decent, balanced lighting.

Five-Minute Film-School Tip No. 3: Keep the Central Subject Out of the Middle

This one surprises some people. I mean, aren't you supposed to put the camera subject in the middle of the frame?

No. It looks sorta weird…and way too geometric.

Instead, put the subject off to the side, with an interesting background filling in the rest of the shot. This will make the video look dynamic and interesting. (Even if the person talking isn't.)

Film-School Tip No. 4: Don't Leave Too Much Headroom

Headroom is that space between a person's head and the top of the frame. It's okay to have a bit, you don't want to cut someone's head off at the forehead.

But you don't want to have too much room at the top. There's an old photography trick, called the Rule of Thirds, which works great here.

Divide the frame into three equidistant horizontal lines (like the flag of Germany) and just make sure the person's head is somewhere near the top half of the frame.

Film-School Tip No. 5: On-Camera Etiquette

For being on-camera, here are a few guidelines to maximize your appearance and overall effectiveness:

- Don't wear sunglasses. People want to see your eyes.
- Wear mid-range colors. (Blues, greens, blacks.) No stripes and no white. (Takes attention away from the eyes.)
- No hats. (Distracts from the face.)
- Don't read from a script. Your eyes will look shifty, and unless you are Tom Brokaw it will be tough to pull off.
- Take a breath, exhale…and then perform. (Don't start without taking a breath…otherwise you'll do a gulp of air in the middle of your performance.)
- Pick one side of the camera to look at and stick with it. (Don't bounce…it will make you look shifty.)

Film-School Tip No. 6: Focus on Helping (Not Your Performance)

If you try to "perform" on camera, if you think you must somehow embrace your inner news anchor to do well on video, you will be sadly mistaken. The camera has an amazing ability to capture who you are. (Even if you don't want it to.)

And if your entire mindset is all about:

"Look at me! I'm on camera. I'm an expert! Buy my stuff! While supplies last!"

It won't work. (Or not as well as it could.) But if you step into frame and say…

"There's a problem many people have. Here's how I figured out how to solve it. Hope it works for you. Talk to you soon…"

You. Will. Crush. It.

Because so much of the crap videos out there are people yelling at the camera, hoping those "thousands" of viewers will take action NOW!

But if you, or your team, get on camera, and just help solve people's problems, there's no way the competition can stop you.

PUNK ROCK MARKETING
AMPLIFY YOUR MESSAGE

CHAPTER 2 KEY TAKEAWAYS:

- Keep the camera still. Seriously.
- Always keep the sun to your back. (Morning and afternoon are good times to shoot.)
- Put the subject off to the side to mix things up.
- Keep the subject's head in the top third of the frame.
- Don't wear sunglasses, white shirts or hats. Stick to mid-range colors like blue or green.
- Focus on solving people's problems to get past on-camera nervousness.

Chapter 5:

Crashing the YouTube Party

"Hobbies of any kind are boring, except for people who have the same hobby."

-Dave Barry

When it comes to looking for a place to house your video marketing efforts, there really is YouTube…and everybody else.

YouTube isn't just simply the largest video-sharing site in the world. It is the second-largest search engine in the world.

Read that again. The second-largest SEARCH ENGINE.

That means, for Internet traffic, there's Google, then YouTube, then Amazon, then Facebook…

…and then way, way, way down the list are other video-sharing sites such as Vimeo and Viddler and Voohoo (or whatever t they're called.)

This doesn't mean things won't ever change, or that you shouldn't place your videos on other sites. (In a later chapter, I'll show you a super-easy quick way to do so.)

It's just that, when I outline my video-marketing strategy for a project, I spend 99.7% of my time worrying about YouTube. (And then, in between episodes of "Law and Order," I think about other sites.)

YouTube has the eyeballs. (And by last count, nearly 1 billion unique visitors a month.) So that's where your videos need to go.

So, here is my SIX STEP process to uploading your video to YouTube that will increase your exposure and help you add a bunch of new leads into your marketing funnel of doom:

STEP NO.1: GET A BUDDY

Before you upload a single megabyte of video to the YouTube universe, I'd like you to strongly consider adding a powerful mentor/ally/kick-ass video Jedi to your marketing toolbox.

And that is the FREE (though there are paid options) tool: Tube Buddy.

Now before you freak out and say, "I need another marketing tool in my life like I need a six-inch hole in my head," let me give a couple kick-ass reasons this YouTube analysis tool is so awesome.

With a quick install of this Chrome extension — did I mention it's FREE? — you can head over to a popular video in your subject of expertise, or whatever your video is about, and with a click of a button you can:

- Find the best keywords (high traffic; low competition) for your video title
- Find the best tags (high traffic; low competition)
- Nail down the perfect TIME to publish your videos (based on user behavior)
- Collect a list of tags that you can save and manage for future projects
- Track your video ideas (so you don't forget them)

Seriously this tool has not only hours at a time, but exponentially improved my lead-generation efforts on YouTube.

My only complaint is that I could have used this tool about six years ago. (Or maybe I just need a time machine.)

And, yes, you could figure all this stuff out manually. But why put yourself through that?

Try this app out. Your world domination depends on it.

STEP NO.2: WRITE A VIDEO TITLE FOR ROBOTS AND HUMANS

Writing the perfect video title is equal-parts art and science. You want a title that contains the RIGHT keywords to get discovered, but you also want to encourage people to consume that video.

And boring, keyword-stuffed titles just won't cut it.

So, what do you do?

I like to incorporate one major keyword in my titles and emphasize how simple and approachable my video is.

I don't want people scared off thinking: "Oh God, that video looks like it's gonna be work." I want them to think: "That video looks short and easily digestible."

That's why I like to use descriptors like:

- "How to"
- "101"
- "Dos and Don'ts"
- "Tips"
- "Tricks"
- "Secrets"
- "Made Easy/Simple"

Let's say I run a blog that caters to would-be romance novelists. (Not sure what I would say to them, but let's go with it.)

And I've done my research in Tube Buddy — my video marketing Obi-Wan Kenobi — and I've found the phrase "Romance Novel Writing" is a good one to use in my title. (It has a score of 87/100 meaning high traffic, low competition.)

Well, I could title my video something like:

- How to Master Romance Novel Writing
- Romance Novel Writing 101
- Romance Novel Writing Dos and Don'ts
- Romance Novel Writing Tips the Competition Doesn't Want You to Know
- Romance Novel Writing Tricks the Pros Use
- Romance Novel Writing Secrets the Bestselling Authors Know
- Romance Novel Writing Made Easy/Simple/Understandable

You get the picture.

Now in earlier editions of this book, I USED to recommend people put TWO keywords in a title.

Such as:

"Romance Novel Writing Tips 101 | Romance Novel Writing Secrets"

But I have since moved away from that strategy. Not because it doesn't work from a keyword standpoint. It does.

But that over-optimized approach can turn people off. Make the video look overwhelming.

And as any copywriter will tell you, the most powerful weapon you have when writing sales copy is white space.

You want there to be space in your title and description.

As the old saying goes: "The confused mind says 'No.'" And having too much crap in your titles can sometimes lead to more "no's" than you envisioned.

STEP NO.3: RENAME YOUR VIDEO FILE ACCORDING TO YOUR KEYWORD

This one's a trick few people know about. But the name of your video file directly relates to its ranking and relevancy in YouTube. (And its ranking in good old Google.)

And what do you name it?

The keyword you want to rank for.

So, using the example above, you'd name your file "Romance_Novel_Writing_101" NOT "Video_1."

Now this is something you change on your computer before you upload it to YouTube. But it's super easy. Just click on the folder until the folder name is highlighted, type in the keyword…and you're done. (Simple, but it can really help.)

Step No. 4:Make Sure Your YouTube Channel Is Niche-Focused

If you haven't already created a YouTube account, then this won't be a problem. You'll be starting off with a clean slate and have plenty of room to keep your YouTube channel focused.

But if you've got a channel, and it's got videos of your kids playing soccer, you singing karaoke and that awesome slideshow of your trip to Yosemite...

...then I highly recommend you create a new, separate YouTube channel (you'll need a separate Gmail account as well) that just focuses on your video marketing.

I know it seems like a pain, but it's also part of Google's ranking of the relevancy of videos.

And if all your videos are about "lawn care," then it will assume your channel is about "lawn care." If your video library is a hodgepodge, then you won't get that same benefit of the doubt.

And if you're not sure what to name your YouTube channel, just pick one of the keywords off the research you just did in Tube Buddy. (Instead of Joe's Pizza Joint...you could do Best Denver Pizza and take advantage of the extra Google juice.)

Step No. 5: Write a Killer Description for Your Video

So, here's where most people screw up. They either have crappy descriptions or no description at all.

Which is sad because the description of your YouTube video is primo real estate. (And super important to how your video will rank in the good old search engines.)

So, your description needs to have five parts and it must be in this order:

1. **A hyperlink to your website.** This must be first and must include the http://.... etc... Example: http://punkrockmarketing.com

2. **Reiterate the FREE/awesome offer you made in the video.** "Head over to punkrockmarketing.com for your FREE copy of my Facebook Brain Protector eBook."
3. **Describe your video.** You are given 1,000 characters here. Use as much of that as you can. And be sure to include that handy-dandy keyword you found earlier a few times in there. If you're not sure what to write about, simply talk about WHY you feel the topic of the video is so important. And then give brief summaries of the steps/topics you cover in the video. (Don't worry, it won't hurt engagement. It will help…a lot!)
4. **Give out your digits.** If ya got a Facebook page, Twitter account, Pinterest doo-dad…whatever…put it here. (Remember to include the http:// part.)
5. **Repeat the FREE offer + your hyperlink.** Example: "Don't forget to head over to http://punkrockmarketing.com for your FREE copy of my Facebook brain protector eBook."

Step No. 5: Beg, Borrow and Steal Your Tags From Your Competitors

This is where Tube Buddy really comes in handy. All you do is:

- Click on the #1-ranked YouTube video for the phrase you want to rank for. (Here, "Romance novel writing.")
- Fire up Tube Buddy and let it analyze the video and find the tags the video creator used to define this video.
- Repeat for the next 2-3 top-ranked videos for that same term.
- Copy all relevant keywords — some might be too obscure to be helpful — and type them into YouTube as your tags.
- Rejoice because you have reverse-engineered your competitor's YouTube success.

Now you don't have to use TubeBuddy to find these tags. You CAN do it manually, by finding a top-ranked video, right-clicking and choosing "View Page Source," and manually finding the keyword embedded in a sea of gibberish-looking code.

And if you're a masochist and enjoy looking at lines of code, then knock yourself out.

But if you want a shortcut to the front of the line, then let Tube Buddy do the tag heavy-lifting for you.

Step No. 6: Upload Your Video

Here's the easy part.

You just click on "upload" at the top of the YouTube navigation and upload your video file, enter your title, description and tags… and you have a published video on YouTube.

But how is anybody gonna FIND your video? Well, that topic of YouTube world domination is what we'll cover in the next chapter.

PUNK ROCK MARKETING
AMPLIFY YOUR MESSAGE

CHAPTER 5 Key Takeaways:

- Choose a video title that gets a decent amount of traffic and is not competitive. (I use the FREE tool Tube Buddy to figure this out.)
- Re-title the file name of your video using your desired keyword.
- Keep your YouTube channel focused only on video marketing — no personal vids.
- Include a "http://" hyperlink in the beginning of your description.
- Use all 1000 characters of the description if you can.
- "Borrow" tags from other high-performing videos using the Tube Buddy in your corner.

Chapter 6:

How to Promote the Hell Out of Your Video

"I am always doing that which I cannot do, in order that I may learn how to do it."

-Pablo Picasso

If you've gone to the trouble of making a series of videos, then you damn well want to get them in front of the largest number of eyeballs possible.

But most people throw up a video or two on YouTube and simply "wait" for the masses to come banging down their door to give them money.

Sorry, don't work that way.

YouTube requires hustle and some promotional savvy to work. But the cool thing is, once you've got a system (which I'll share with you here) and work that system consistently, it becomes easy to outpace the competition in no time.

There are basically two different ways to promote your videos:

1. Stuff you can do INSIDE YouTube.
2. Stuff you can do OUTSIDE YouTube.

Let's start with the OUTSIDE stuff. It's super easy and doesn't require much brain power. Here are my THREE YouTube Outside Marketing Strategies I use again and again:

Outside YouTube Promo Strategy No. 1: Promote the Video Everywhere!

Once you upload your video and it's done "cooking" in the YouTube kitchen, you will get a unique URL. (Example: http://youtube.com/watch=S1uDnIP9L)

With that web address in tow, you can now promote that video on social networks like Facebook, LinkedIn, Twitter, Pinterest, Tumblr, your email newsletter, etc.

The key thing is to ASK people to "like" it or "share" it when they watch the video.

Lots of social activity around your video, especially when it's first uploaded, is a big sign to Google that this video is "important" and should be given a prominent place in the search engines. (Both in Google and YouTube.)

Outside YouTube Promo Strategy No. 2: Build Some Links to Your Video

Okay, this technique is a bit on the shady side. (And by shady, I mean if you tried doing this with your own website, Google would send your site to search-engine Siberia.)

But it frickin' works. What you're going to do is build backlinks to the video page.

In the crazy, strange world of SEO (Search Engine Optimization), most people spend time and money trying to get their own websites ranked super quick. (Which doesn't work very often.)

But for a big "authority" site, like YouTube, it can work exceedingly well.

So, here's what you do:

- Head over to Fiverr.com (This is a site where people offer services for five dollars.)
- Search for "SEO" services. (I like to buy ONE "link pyramid," ONE "social bookmarking" gig, and ONE ". Edu Backlink" gig

- Buy THREE "gigs." Choose people with high ratings.
- Have the gig master build backlinks to your video around your primary keyword. (And wait for the traffic to flow in.)

This won't provide an immediate, overnight boost. But it will help tremendously. (Because hardly anybody else does this.)

OUTSIDE YOUTUBE PROMO STRATEGY NO. 3: STOP THE PRESSES

If you have a little extra money to spend (about $25) and you've optimized your video to this point, then it's worth your while to send out a press release touting your video.

Huh?

A press release? About a YouTube video?

Before you freak out and tell me that your video isn't newsworthy, and nobody would read a press release about it…

First off, you should see some crap people send press releases on. (It's hysterical.)

Secondly, we are not sending it out in the hope that NBC News is going to ask us to join the broadcast.

We are doing it for the Google backlink love. And Google REALLY respects press releases. (God knows why, most of them are awful.)

For $25 you can head over to a site like WebWire and shoot out a press release about your video.

Couple of keys:

- **Write a decent headline by focusing on the problem you're solving.** Example: "Chicago Pizza King Reveals the Secret to Homemade Crust."
- **Write it in third person.** As if you were having an interview with yourself.
- **Make sure you include links back to the video**, along with the keywords we researched earlier.

Do these three things and you will be light-years ahead of the rest of the schmucks who put their crap on YouTube.

And if you REALLY hate writing, head over to Fiverr and have somebody else write the press release for ya. (Win-win!)

"Forget it, Jake. It's Chinatown."

Okay, now let's jump into the strange morass of insanity and awesomeness that is promotion inside the YouTube universe.

The three main goals of your videos on planet YouTube are:

- Likes
- Shares
- Subscribers

The higher these numbers, the more the Google/YouTube empire will see your video as an authority and you will blow your (feeble) competition out of the water.

So, how do we get more of all that YouTube community goodness? Here are my FOUR favorite strategies for getting more people into your YouTube army:

Inside YouTube Promo Strategy No. 1: Create YouTube Cards

YouTube cards are a way to create linkable text overlays onto your video. (But they're far better than those old, annoying YouTube annotations that looked as fresh and modern as a dot-matrix printer.)

You can use them to:

- Encourage people to subscribe to your YouTube channel.
- Provide links to your other videos.
- Link over to other YouTube users' videos who offer more resources.
- Have people donate to your cause or kick-starter campaign.
- Most importantly: Provide links over to your WEBSITE!

YouTube cards are super easy to create. All you do is:

- Find the video you want to add cards to and select "edit video."
- In tab at the top, select "cards."
- Select "add card" and choose the type of card you want. (I prefer "link cards" - but you can choose whichever one you want.)
- Click on "create"
- "Enable" cards - if you haven't done so yet. (You'll have to accept terms and conditions. Don't worry - they won't make you give up your first-born. Yet.)
- Enter the URL where you wanna send people.
- Upload an image. (Be mindful the image will be cropped to a sqaure.)
- Edit your title and call to action in the card. (Keep it simple. Don't get complicated. Tell 'em what they'll get by clicking.)
- Set a time for when you want the card to appear. (I'd say get one in within the first 30 seconds - and then space 'em out from there.) Don't put in more than three cards per video.
- Click on "create card" and you're done!

INSIDE YOUTUBE PROMO STRATEGY NO. 2: CREATE KEYWORD-FRIENDLY PLAYLISTS

Here's another technique a lot of YouTube creators miss out on. (And it's so frickin' easy.)

All you do is create a playlist around a specific keyword that includes your videos and a mix of other people's videos.

The key thing here is to include other people's stuff, not just your own. However, avoid adding your competitor's videos, unless you would like to help their business out.

To create your own YouTube playlist just:

- Click on "add to" underneath the video you want to add the playlist

- Choose a keyword-friendly playlist name
- Add some other videos that you didn't create

Bonus points: If you're feeling super-ninja you could head over to Fiverr and purchase some SEO gigs that point backlinks to the playlist URL. (But only if you're feeling super-ninja. If you're feeling just slightly ninja, then I would avoid.)

Inside YouTube Promo Strategy No. 3: Respond to Comments Within 24 Hours

I must admit, I'm not as good about this as I should be. But one of the biggest factors in determining the "authority" of your YouTube channel is your engagement with people who leave comments.

Especially within a day of the comment being left.

So, try to check in every couple of days to respond to comments. (You should get an email each time a comment is left.)

But...PLEASE...do not engage with negative commenters. (It's not worth it. Trust me.)

Inside YouTube Promo Strategy No.4: Build Your Subscriber Base Fast!

The best thing about subscribers is they comment. (Sometimes too much.)

And even more importantly, subscribers get an email from YouTube every time you upload a new video. This ensures all your future videos will have plenty of social buzz around them.

So, what's the catch?

Well, doing this is a manual process. (In the next chapter, I'll show you a tool that can help automate it.)

One of the most effective ways that I've found that boosted the views of my YouTube videos, literally overnight, is to "send messages" to my target audience inviting them to:

Check out my new video and/or subscribe to my channel.

Say I run an e-commerce site that specializes in Minor League Baseball apparel. (An interesting market.)

Well, instead of spending tons of money on Google PPC traffic, I could create a video on the Top 5 Coolest Baseball Caps in Minor League Baseball.

And then I could find out who the fans of those teams are, by searching for videos relating to those teams. (And sending messages to people who've commented on those videos.)

It's quite an easy process, you just:

- Search for videos related to your subject.
- Locate people who've commented recently — within the last two months.
- Click on their name to bring up their profile page.
- Click on the "send message" button. (Located in the drop-down arrow on the right side, under their name.)
- Send them a message like: "Hey. I noticed you're a fan of the Sacramento Bear Cats. I just made a video of the Top 5 Baseball caps in Minor League baseball and they made the cut. Thought you'd want to check it out. Thanks!"

Now, I know that sounds quite manual. (It is.)

I'll show you a tool in the next chapter that can handle it super easily, but in the interim maybe you could get an intern or some aimless teenager (maybe one who shares your last name) to do it for you.

No joke, this one technique will put your face in front hundreds of new people each day, and if you follow it up with the rest of the techniques in this chapter, you'll be dominating the YouTube universe in no time.

CHAPTER 6 Key Takeaways:

- Promote your YouTube video by sharing your unique URL on your various social media properties.
- Buy a few SEO gigs over at Fiverr.com to build some keyword-focused backlinks to your video.
- Write and distribute a press release about your video. (Nobody does this.)
- Create YouTube cards for your videos that have clear calls-to-action AND links to your external site.
- Build keyword-friendly YouTube playlists for extra exposure.
- Try to respond to all comments to your video within a day or two. (Skip the negative ones.)
- Send messages to commenters of similar videos inviting them to subscribe to your channel.

Chapter 7:

Super Advanced Ninja YouTube Tactics

"Great thoughts speak to the thoughtful mind, but great actions speak to all mankind."

-Emily P. Bissell

Before we jump into the deep part of the video marketing tool, let me just say…

…if you follow the tips I've outlined so far, and there's not a ton of competition out there for you in the YouTube stratosphere, then everything we've gone over to this point should be enough.

If you're a local business, chances are the restaurant or business down the street will not be employing the same strategies. And you're likely to crush them on the video side in a matter of weeks.

But if you're in a more-competitive market, say something in the weight-loss or financial-services markets, then you're going to find there are a lot more animals at the trough.

So, below are my THREE Super-Advanced YouTube Marketing Tactics you can use to destroy the competition and reign supreme as the YouTube King of your market:

Warning: These tactics are a bit technical and dorky. Consult your local teenage hacker if the methods detailed aren't clear.

Ninja Promo Tactic No.1: Tube Buddy

I know. I went over this tactic in Chapter 5.

But Tube Buddy is so powerful, and FREE, I'm going to reiterate again.

If you want to know:

- What video topics to cover
- What to title your video
- Which tags to use
- When is the best time

Then Tube Buddy is like the YouTube Obi-Wan Kenobi you deserve. (Hopefully Tube Buddy won't ever cut off a guys' arm in a bar. But you never know.)

Seriously, I use this tool every day and I can't recommend it enough.

Ninja Promo Tactic No. 2: Feed the RSS Monster

I'll be honest, I don't really understand how RSS works.

I mean I know what it is. RSS stands for (Really Simple Syndication) and refers to a technology that helps organize and distribute content around the Internet. (RSS Feed readers such as Feedly use them.)

And I also know it is dying as a mode of consuming media. (You can thank Facebook for that.)

But I don't care about any of that. All I care about is how feeds build super-quick bridges to my content. (Namely, my YouTube videos.)

And it works as a quick-and-dirty promotional tool to create little freeways around the Internet that lead straight to my videos.

Now because each of your YouTube videos are static web locations, not a constantly changing feed, you'll have to do a bit of manual work to make this strategy happen. (But it's really, easy.)

Here's what you do:

1. Grab the URL of your YouTube video.
2. Head over to Feedity. (This site allows you to create a feed from a web URL.)

3. Submit your video URL and create a feed.
4. Copy the feed URL Feedity gives you.
5. Head over to Ping-O-Matic and Pingler. (These are pinging sites that let the world know your RSS feed exists.)
6. Enter your new feed URL in the fields provided, along with your keyword, and ping the feed. (You only must do this once. Not continually.)

NINJA PROMO TACTIC NO. 3: PAY-PER-CLICK ADVERTISING (ESPECIALLY FACEBOOK)

Now I'm not suggesting you spend hundreds of dollars a day on PPC ads trying to drive traffic to your YouTube video. (Unless you really, really want to.)

But if you have experience in the PPC waters, such as Google, then on a strict, modest budget you can actually see a nice ROI for sending traffic to your videos.

As long as you know your numbers and know what a YouTube viewer is worth to ya.

That said: my favorite technique for promoting videos is to actually "upload" that same video to Facebook - don't just share the YouTube link on your Facebook page, but upload the video - and then promote that video with a couple dollars a day on your Facebook page.

Why do this?

Well, two reasons, it's easy to get .01 and .02 cent views on videos uploaded to Facebook. (In almost any niche.)

And if ya get at least 1000 views in a single day (which should be easy to do with a ten dollar spend) everybody who watches your video that day will be added to a "custom audience."

This will let you serve all those folks with retargeting ads for your other stuff.

Now it's a bit beyond this volume to cover Facebook entirely, but let me just say, taking each of your YouTube videos and uploading them to Facebook - and boosting them with a $20-$30 boost over a couple days can dramatically improve your results.

Not to mention help increase the engagement of your Facebook page.

Ninja Promo Tactic No. 4: Your Very Own YouTube Virtual Assistant

Back in the last chapter I talked about how sending private messages to viewers who are in your ideal target audience was the BEST, FASTEST way to build up your subscriber base…

…and get tons and tons of new people in your good old marketing funnel FAST!

My only lament was that, due to YouTube's rather strict messaging policies, it was a bit time-consuming to manually send out these messages.

Well, there is a tool that can automate it for you.

It's called Tube AssistPro (PunkRockMarketing.com/TubeAssist). And in a nutshell, here's what it does:

1. **You find a video with a bunch of commenters or a channel with a bunch of subscribers** who you'd like to message. (Your ideal customers.)
2. **You create a message template** of what you'd like to say to these commenters. (Example: "Hey There! Check out my new vid on Facebook Satanism!")
3. **Tube Assist Pro scrapes the video** to find the user profile info for all those commenters.
4. **Tube Assist SLOWLY sends out those messages**, over the course of a few days. (Thereby following YouTube's terms of service - and putting your message in front of hundreds, if not thousands of users over the course of a week.)

I've gotten amazing results from it. (And reached a bunch of people I never would have without it.)

And without question, Tube Assist Pro is my absolute secret weapon that helped me GROW an email list of nearly 10K in a matter of three months with just three videos.

Pretty awesome sauce.

I haven't asked you to buy any fancy tools up to this point, and you don't have to have Tube Assist Pro to have YouTube success, but I unreservedly recommend the tool. (The guys are great, the support is awesome, and the forum is friendly and helpful.)

PUNK ROCK MARKETING
AMPLIFY YOUR MESSAGE

CHAPTER 7 KEY TAKEAWAYS:

- To figure out what to title your videos — and which tags to use — consider adding Tube Buddy to your video marketing toolbox.
- Create an RSS Feed of your video and promote by pinging, for added promotional boost
- Use PPC campaigns - with strict budgets - to extend the reach of your videos. Focus specifically on Facebook. (There's real gold in 'dem hills.)
- The author highly, highly recommends Tube Assist for building your subscriber base up, and exponentially increasing your overall video views.

EPILOGUE:
Conquering the World One Video at a Time

In a previous life I wanted to work in radio. (I guess something about working 60 hours a week and living just above the poverty line appealed to me.)

For a brief time I got to work as an intern for a local sports talk radio station. (You know, the kind where two mentally-imbalanced individuals argue about whether the designated hitter is responsible for the downfall of Western civilization.)

I remember late one night I was messing around in the studio, working on my "reel." (This is a demo that a would-be on-air talent sends around in the hopes of getting a job.)

I was doing my melodramatic intro — "Hey all you sports fans out there! It's Crazy Mike! And I want to hear from YOU!"— when the grizzled, old station director walked by.

He popped his head in and gave me one of the best lessons I've ever learned.

He said, as radio professionals we "experience" the audience as a large group of people. But an audience does not "experience" radio as a member of an audience.

They experience radio as a one-to-one conversation. (One in which they happen to not have access to a microphone.)

And when you say something like "Hey sports fans!" it destroys the intimate connection an audience has with you. And people don't quite feel as emotional about the things you're talking about, nor are they likely to stick around, while you break away to air some car dealership commercials.

And you end up reaching nobody at all.

This YouTube stuff is addicting.

You'll create a series of videos and in a month you'll have 2,000 views, 100 comments and tons of new leads and you'll think I need to scale this.

I need to make more videos, and get more subscribers, and get more likes, and hire more video people, and buy some latest YouTube Hack automation tool that can do it all in five minutes or less.

Just remember, video works best when the person on camera is having a conversation with one person.

Trying to solve one person's problems. (Maybe even their own.)

People will email you and write to you to say they felt like you were talking just to "them."

Which you were.

If you can stick with that philosophy and not worry about what you look like on camera, or what aspect ratio your video should be, and do at least a couple videos a month…then there is absolutely nobody who can stop you from reaching all your video marketing go als.

Vol.3
of the Small Busines
Marketing
COLLECTION
FACEBOOK
MARKETING
in 2019
MADE
(STUPIDLY) EASY
Michael Clarke

Facebook Marketing in 2019 Made (Stupidly) Easy

Vol.3 of the "Small Business Marketing Made (Stupidly) Easy" Collection

PROLOGUE: Yeah, But How Do You Make Money With Facebook?

Just so you know, this isn't one of those books that will tell you how to "connect" or be "authentic" on Facebook.

Truth is, I hate Facebook.

I hate "engaging" with annoying friends from high school who share every single photo of their zip-lining vacation in Costa Rica. (Especially when I'm sitting at a desk. Working.) I hate "connecting" with my cousin's weekly political rant on what's wrong with Washington politics.

Can't stand "being authentic" on a media platform that barrages me with "Bubble Safari" requests and "Mafia Wars" clues and "You Should Like This Crappy Page Because Your Friends Liked This Crappy Page" suggestions.

Facebook is annoying, shallow, pretentious, invasive…

And that's why it pains me to say this: for reaching the largest, most targeted customer base ANYWHERE — at the cheapest, lowest ad cost — nothing works like Facebook.

"Always Be Selling"

If you're reading this book, chances are you fall into one of two categories:

1. **You've tried Facebook in the past**, had lousy results, wasted a bunch of time and money and don't know what the fuss is all about. *But other people seem to do well with Facebook marketing and you want to know their secret.*

2. **You've avoided Facebook like the plague**. You think it's a technological fad that creates a lot of marketplace noise but doesn't lead to sustainable profits. *But other people seem to do well with Facebook and you want to know their secret.*

Either way, you've come to the right place.

There's no better evangelist than the converted, and I have swung from hating (nearly) everything about a company who turned "friend" into a verb and designed their entire color scheme around the fact their CEO is color blind…

…to understanding that Facebook is poised to become THE tool that people use to do nearly everything.

Not just A tool.

THE tool.

Facebook is going after every part of your experience. (How you search on the Internet, buy products, read books, watch movies, find restaurants, check out those photos of that girl you had a crush on in high school, etc.)

And if they accomplish just 10% of what they want to, they'll be an overbearing, intrusive, obnoxious presence in our lives for decades to come.

And one that we as marketers can use for our own benefit.

The Magic Formula

So, the big dilemma about Facebook marketing comes down to this...how do all of those "likes" and "friends" and "pages" and "posts" lead to actual customers?

The process is simple. It goes a little something like this:

1. Create content that doesn't suck (and doesn't put people into a coma)
2. Build a Facebook Page that doesn't suck
3. Attract people to like and follow your pages and posts

4. Send these fans (and non-fans) to content that lives on your site
5. Retarget these folks with Facebook ads
6. Rinse and Repeat…and count your money

That's what I'm going to show you in this book. Step by step.

I've replicated this system in a bunch of different markets, with a bunch of different customer segments. And the only time I haven't had success is when I've deviated from this formula. (Or skipped a step because I was lazy.)

So, if you don't mind, we're gonna leave the talk about "connecting" and "being authentic" for the other guys (and girls).

We're just going to talk about what works. And kick some serious Facebook marketing ass in the process.

You ready?

Chapter 1:

5 Ways to Find Rocket Fuel for Your Fan Page

"All things are ready, if our mind be so."

-William Shakespeare

Before we jump into the nitty-gritty of creating your Facebook fan page — and there is quite a bit of nit and grit — it's good to create a reserve of that most valuable Facebook marketing resource… content.

I know what you're gonna say: "Content? But I want to create a zombie army of Facebook fans who do my bidding and buy my crap."

Sounds like you've been drinking the Facebook Kool-Aid from 2010. (Ya know, the good, old days when you could post something on Facebook and actual humans would see it.)

The trouble is, these days, getting people (and that includes your own fans) to see the content you put out on Facebook is just slightly harder than finding a Transformers movie that doesn't suck.

Gone are the days when we could just post a silly "fill in the blank" question and get 35 comments — "The person I'd least like to see President is_____."

We must be more strategic. Thoughtful. Super-ninja.

The good news is most marketers on Facebook, and that includes your competition, are still doing things the old way. (Wave to them as you zoom past them in the sales charts.)

But it all starts with creating CONTENT that doesn't suck. (That we can then use to boost engagement on our page — and attract leads into our funnel.)

So, here are the Five Pillars of Non-Sucky Content Every Business on Facebook Should Have:

Non-Sucky Piece of Facebook Content #1: A Killer Blog Post (With a # in the Title)

I know. Blog post? What 19th-century rock did I crawl out from under?

Don't I know we live in a post-selfie world where everybody Snapchats and Vines their way through life.

Here's the thing: SOME people prefer to learn about a topic through words. (Not just Instagram posts.)

And studies have shown if somebody READS more than 75% of your blog post, they are 10x more likely to become a lead, and 5x more likely to be a customer.

Now, a blog post doesn't have to be a 5,000-word essay about tax annuities. (Though it can be.)

A killer blog post can be things like a:

- How-to article walking the reader through an important topic
- Interview with a notable person in your industry
- Collection of YouTube videos around a specific theme (Even videos you didn't create)
- Excerpts from blog columns/posts (you didn't write) around a specific theme (Be sure to ask permission)
- List of recommended resources
- Case study showing results you or your clients have gotten
- "Best Of…" post (this can be on almost anything)
- Mission Statement/Declaration (In which you say "you're mad as hell…" about something in your industry and "you will not take it anymore")

Whatever you think will cause your target audience to sit up — take notice — and click on your post as they scroll through their Facebook newsfeed on their smart phone is the way to go.

And if you're able to weave a "#" in your blog post, all the better. There's just something about "#s" that calms the brain and reassures people that a task is manageable. For instance, which would you rather read: "How to Survive a Tax Audit" or "5 Secrets to Surviving Tax Audit."

Neither is pleasant, but I'll bet you'd rather read the "5 Secrets" one. (And if you do happen to know how to survive a tax audit, I'm all ears.)

Non-Sucky Piece of Facebook Content #2: A Killer Video (That Explains Something in a Fun, Interactive Way)

Now, once ya got your blog post created, it's time to appeal to the 91% other people out there...with a killer video that explains a confusing/important topic in a fun, interactive way.

Don't worry, this video doesn't have to be super long. (These days, anything over three minutes feels longer than a "Lord of the Rings" movie.)

But you want your video to cover ONE single topic exhaustively. (Don't tease at a solution, give people what they need to know.)

And try to put yourself (or someone on your team) in the video. (Either by talking straight at the camera or using a white board to explain something.)

If you have a brick-and-mortar store, you could also do something where you walk people through your shop. (The "Dollar Shave Club" guys do this brilliantly.)

Just resist the urge to do a screen capture video where you ramble over a Power Point presentation. (These. Are. Boring.)

And when you figure out the topic you're gonna cover, here's how I recommend you structure your video:

1. **Start by asking people to click on the video as you point downwards**. (" Click to hear the video! Click to hear the video!") I know this is weird, but this will encourage folks to click on your video as they scroll past on their phones.)

2. **Introduce yourself and yer topic.** (" Hi, this is Michael Clarke, author of Facebook Marketing Made (Stupidly) Easy and in this video I'm gonna talk about the microchip that Mark Zuckerberg is trying to implant in your brain.")
3. **Go through the step-by-step instruction and content of your video**. This is the part people are there for.
4. **Give 'em action steps for what to do next.** ("First, you remove the microchip...")
5. **Congratulate them for already acting even if they haven't.** ("And presto! You are now microchip-free.")
6. **Thank them for watching and ask them to "like" the video.** ("Thanks for your time and if you'd be so kind to 'like' this video I promise to be your best friend.")
7. **Give them your offer!** ("And if you'd like a free copy of my 'Removing the Chip' eBook just head over...")

And that's it!

Please, don't over-think this. This isn't rocket surgery, as my Dad would say. Just a killer piece of video content - that you can use to awesome (and totally nefarious) means with your Facebook marketing.

Non-Sucky Piece of Facebook Content #3: 5 Touchy-Feely Images of Inspirational Quotes

You probably already know what these are: those motivational quotes you find ALL OVER social media where somebody slaps some inspirational words over a colored background. (Or a view of a sunset. God, how they love sunsets.)

And I find these as inspiring as a late-night infomercial. But I am in the vast minority. (These are like Facebook catnip, people love 'em.)

So, here's how you make 'em:

- Type into Google "Quotes about (insert adjective related to your business)" and collect FIVE quotes (along with the speaker.) If in doubt just do something about adversity or perseverance. Everybody wants to overcome that.

- Head over to Canva. Totally FREE photo-editing tool. Perfect for creating quotes.
- Choose "Facebook Post" size as your template.
- Choose a neutral, colored background that catches your eye. Nothing too dark or too light.
- Add text boxes, and type in the quote and the person who uttered it.

Export…and you're good to go!

Non-Sucky Piece of Facebook Content #4: 5 Links to Funny Articles/Videos

I know you THINK what your fans really want is to read those erudite 10,000-word essays you found on the "New Republic" Twitter feed.

But the truth is most people are stressed-out and tired and just want something funny, dumb and silly while they're in the bathroom at work.

And if you're able to churn out at least one of these a week, your fans will realize your page isn't just there to sell crap and "educate." Your page is fun! (Even if it really isn't.)

Some of my favorite go-to places to find stuff like this is:

- PopUrls - Pretty much a "best of" containing the coolest - and weirdest - the Internet has to offer.
- BuzzFeed - Most of their stuff is outright click bait, but sometimes you'll find a funny piece of content or two you can share with your tribe.
- The Onion - I frickin' love "The Onion." ("Mom Thinks You'd Enjoy Restaurant She Can't Remember the Name Of.") Their stuff is always good for a chuckle or seven. (And perfect for sharing in your Facebook feed.)

- AllTop - This site is like the NY public library of the Internet. (Where everything is categorized and rated by actual humans.) Perfect for a targeted little piece of content here and there. (Best of all, you can set up RSS feeds so you'll be notified when new content, fitting your area of expertise, pops up.)

Non-Sucky Piece of Facebook Content #5: 5 Super-Simple (No-Brainer) Questions Your Tribe Can Answer

There was a time, way back in the Mesozoic era (or what we call 2010) when every Facebook page out there would fill their news feeds with this social media sludge. ("Reeses or Snickers?")

And though they aren't quite as effective as they used to be, they still have a place. (Especially for boosting the popularity of your page.)

The key is to use questions that have "some" connection to your brand. ("My favorite horror movie is___?" is a great fit for my screenwriter audience, not so much for my golf tribe.)

So, here are a couple of my favorite go-to's when trying to find brain-dead questions so simple even a Kardashian can answer them:

- "My favorite (insert) is ___?"
- What's your biggest frustration/gripe about ___?
- What's one word that describes ___?
- Write a caption to a photo.
- Trivia questions.
- "(This) or (that)?"
- "If you were trapped on a desert island and could choose only one (insert)...what would it be?"

I know these are pandering. But for what you're asking this content to do — get Facebook users past their overpowering laziness and type words on a screen — they are devastatingly effective.

And as with all these forms of content rocket fuel, they're perfect for attracting new fans and distracting your existing ones from the fact that you're eventually gonna sell them something.

Which is what we'll cover in the next chapter.

PUNK ROCK MARKETING
AMPLIFY YOUR MESSAGE

CHAPTER 1 Key Takeaways:

- **Having one killer blog post can go a long way towards not only connecting with your existing fans but attracting new fans.** (Note: Blog posts don't have to mean boring, 5000-word essays. They can be things like "best of" columns, curated video, case studies, and resource lists.)
- **One killer video is not only an awesome way to reach people who would otherwise never read your blog post**, but it can also be the vehicle for some of the cheapest (and most effective) advertising on the Internet. (More on that later.)
- **Images with touchy-feely, motivational quotes STILL do well as Facebook page content.** Despite the author's best efforts to remove them from the Facebook-verse.
- **Funny videos/articles are perfect for entertaining your stressed-out, totally bored tribe.** (And they get your fans to look forward to your future Facebook posts.)
- **No-brainer questions aren't quite as effective as they used to be**, but they're still perfect for boosting the "engagement" of your page. (Which Facebook uses in their witchcraft algorithms, so they're kinda important.)

Chapter 2:

6 Keys to a Profitable Facebook Sales Machine

"There is no one giant step that does it. It's a lot of little steps."

-Peter A. Cohen

I know you're champing at the bit to get your Facebook page of unstoppable profit awesomeness up and running…and we're gonna get to it. Promise!

But I'd like to encourage you to begin at the end and work backwards. (Like all those "self-help" books tell you to.)

Don't worry, I'm not gonna ask you to do any mantras. We're just gonna set up the foundational goodies you'll need to turn those likes and fans into cold, hard cash.

Because "engagement" and "branding" sound great, but it doesn't keep the lights on. (Unless your landlord is a lot more flexible than mine.)

So, here are 6 Keys to Setting Up the Ultimate Facebook Sales Machine:

Facebook Sales Machine Element #1: Facebook Retargeting Code on ALL Your WebPages

Facebook retargeting code? What's that? (Does it involve Wookies and the Millennium Falcon?)

No.

Retargeting code is simply a batch of nonsensical gibberish that lets you "remarket" to folks weeks, if not months, after they've visited a page on your website.

This is how, after you look at a product page on a website, ads for that very product seem to "follow" you all around the Internet.

Aside from the obvious "Big Brother" connotations, remarketing is a super-powerful strategy. (And one that can cut your lead acquisition cost by 50%.)

But, for now, all you gotta do is:

- **Generate your Facebook pixel.** (Head over to PunkRockMarketing.com/FacebookPixel for a walk-through of how to do this.)
- **Have your web designer - or local neighborhood 12-year-old hacker - install it on every page of your website.** (Especially those email capture and thank you pages hosted on other platforms.)
- **Count your money** like Scrooge McDuck.

Okay, we're not quite at the "Scrooge McDuck" phase…yet. (But we will be when we get to Chapter 7.)

Just know you have now taken a first step in a much larger world. (You didn't think I was gonna let that "Star Wars" thing go, did you?)

Facebook Sales Machine Element #2: A Freebie Thing-a-majiggy That Doesn't Suck

No matter what yer business model is, the best way to attract leads (who hopefully become lifelong customers) is to offer prospects some kind of freebie or special offer in exchange for an email address.

Unfortunately, many of the freebies/special offers that businesses offer are:

- Vague
- Overwhelming

- Cliché (Been done to death)
- Underwhelming (Doesn't promise big results)
- Boring
- **Solve one problem (or satisfy one desire.)** Don't offer an eBook that covers every aspect of a topic, or a coupon that offers 10% off anything on the menu. Have the eBook solve ONE problem ("My #1 Secret to Buying a Used Car") or have the coupon offer a discount on one item ("Get 25% Off All Lobster Dishes on Thursdays After a Full Moon.") The confused mind says no, so don't let 'em get confused.
- **Video ain't as awesome as it used to b**e. There was a time when people offering "video tutorials" was a big deal. (Mostly because nobody had any idea how they did it.) But these days it just ain't that impressive and watching a video "sounds" like work. PDF's and audio formats not only sound like high value, but they're easy to consume too.
- **If offering information, make it sound secretive.** Cheat sheets. Insider guides. Toolkits. Resource Lists. Anything that sounds like you're saving people a crap load of time — and offering them something other people don't know about — is a good thing.
- **If offering a coupon, choose the discount that "sounds" higher.** "Save 50% off" sounds a heckuva lot better than "Save $.43." Do some testing to see which works best with your audience.
- **Free trials work great for software and monthly programs**. Not just because most people forget to cancel. But because it lowers the bar of resistance and shows you have confidence in your product.
- **Scarcity is a powerful Mofo**. If you can instill some kind of limited-time period — especially for a discount — that can work staggeringly well. (Later we'll go over how to use Facebook contests.)

- **Don't spend HOURS working on your freebie and/or coupon**. You'll probably have to change it in a year anyway…so don't spend YEARS crafting the perfect freebie. Just get it done and get it

Facebook Sales Machine Element #3: A Short Video "Selling" Your Freebie

Huh? A video "selling" the freebie? What is this craziness I'm having you do now?

Relax. This video is only gonna be about 90 seconds long. But it might be the most important (and profitable) part of your Facebook sales machine.

Because eventually we're gonna "show" this video to warm prospects and it should literally help your lead costs nose-dive.

Now, in Chapter 8 I go over my entire step-by-step outline for how to create this pre-sell video. (So, no need to create it right this minute.)

But for the time being, think about how you might answer the following questions:

1. Who's the best person for our business to put on camera to talk about our business? (Skip photogenic, go for passionate.)
2. What pain point does my product/service solve?
3. What are the main obstacles standing in the way of our customers solving this problem? (What beliefs or habits get in their way of success.)
4. Can the person on video talk about their OWN experience or connection to the product/service? (Beyond..."Hey, I'm getting paid to talk about this!")

This video can be as short as 60 seconds or as long as 2 minutes. (Or even LONGER if the offer warrants it — things like a webinar sign-up may need more information.)

And don't worry about making it perfect. Just make it honest. And human. (Even if the aliens are controlling your brain.)

Facebook Sales Machine Element #4: A Landing Page That Doesn't Suck

This is probably the SECOND most important element of your Facebook sales machine, and that is having a landing page that doesn't suck.

And by "doesn't suck," I simply mean: a webpage that converts. (Industry standard is about 25% — though the tips I'm about to share should probably boost that well above 40%.)

So, how do we achieve this? Well, after testing this a ton (and making every landing page mistake in the book) I've found good landing pages have the following elements:

- **A picture of the FREE thing yer giving away** (Such as a book cover or coupon graphic — you can get this done on Fiverr)
- **A headline that makes it clear WHO this freebie is for** — ("Attention golf instructors"; "To All Denver Oral Surgeons!")
- **An emotional, action-packed description of what the free thing is** and what subscribers will get if they opt-in) — ("Download my FREE report "7 Ways to Offer a Free Report" and You'll learn my secret strategies for boosting your profits 1300%!)
- **A button they can click** to enter their info

And that's about it!

Unfortunately achieving this through a simple WordPress template - or HTML coding - can be difficult and expensive. (Especially if you hire designer.)

I recommend the following tools:

- LeadPages (The tool I use)
- Instapage

Both are good tools for letting you use pre-built, mobile-responsive templates to create landing pages that look super killer.

I prefer LeadPages because they give you conversion stats about your pages right there in the dash. (No need to keep checking Google Analytics.) But InstaPage is good too.

And the COOL thing is you can use this same tool to create a killer "Thank You" page where you can sell your stuff RIGHT AWAY.

Facebook Sales Machine Element #5: A Way to Collect and Send Emails

So, I'm not gonna spend a ton of time on this, because chances are you've already got some email collection (and email sending) tool in your arsenal.

But in case you don't.... I highly, highly recommend you get one. (They're vital for establishing long-term relationships with your customers and creating offers that can cut through the social media noise and get noticed.)

There are a lot of players in this space. I use ConvertKit, mostly because it gives you most of the features of a $1000/month platform, at a fraction of the cost.

But you could just as easily use a service like iContact or MailChimp. They're all good, they're all cheap. And they're all essential.

Whichever way you go, choose something. (You'll regret it if you don't.)

Facebook Sales Machine Element #6: Obnoxious (But Effective) Opt-In Crap on Your Website

The last piece of the Facebook Sales Machine puzzle is to have lead-capture mechanisms in place for when people visit your website.

Now some of these are simple to execute, and other require more technical know-how. (If you're not sure how to do any of this just find a talented, unemployed hacker on Fiverr to do it.

Here are methods I recommend:

- **Right sidebar lead-capture widget** — This is a simple vertical widget placed on every page of your blog or website. (Or wherever you think is appropriate.) You don't even have to design it, just use your email service to create the code and then place it on your site.
- **Blog post footer widget** — Here's one most folks forget about. And that is have a horizontal widget at the end of each of your blog posts or articles touting your latest freebie. (Best of all, once you create this you can put it anywhere you want — including in the middle of long articles.)
- **Obnoxious Exit Pop (Optional)** — Okay, so this one is on the spammy side. But this is where you install an exit-pop plugin on your site that forces people to "confirm" they want to leave your website and give them one last chance to opt in. Spammy? Yes. Effective? Absolutely! Something that will piss people off and lower your opt-in rates? Not even close.

CHAPTER 2 Key Takeaways:

- **Having Facebook retargeting code installed on your website will save you a lot of wasted energy** — and put money directly in your pocket.
- **Successful Facebook marketing requires a freebie (or offer) that doesn't suck.** Keep it specific, easy to consume, and quick to produce. (Don't spend years on it.)
- **Creating a short video that "sells" your freebie is one of the smartest (and most effective) things you can do for your Facebook marketing.** Don't forget to a) encourage people to click b) establish your authority c) get right to their pain point d) offer a solution and e) tell 'em to click in the post.
- **Ya gotta have a landing page that doesn't suck to make this whole thing work.** And that means having a picture of your freebie, a headline that tells folks who the freebie is for, body text that tells people what they'll get, and a button they can click.
- **This whole Facebook Sales Machine needs a way to collect email addresses** and send out pre-generated emails. I use ConvertKit, but you can use any tool you like.
- **Don't forget to add lead-capture opportunities into your website design.** Right sidebar widgets and blog post footer widgets are must-haves. (And if you can stomach the possible "spammy nature" of them, exit-pop plugins are devastatingly effective.)

Chapter 3:

The Ultimate Facebook Fan-Page Makeover

"When all the details fit in perfectly, something is probably wrong with the story."

-Charles Baxter

I wish I could tell you looks don't matter. I wish I could tell you lots of things.

But how your Facebook Fan Page looks — how cool, fun and relevant to your audience your page appears to be — makes a huge difference in the success of your Facebook marketing.

So, before we get likes and fans and (more importantly) customers, we will need to pimp out our Facebook fan page to make it sleek, modern and one kick-ass lead-generatin' machine.

Note: If you've been living under a zombie-proof bunker for the last six years — and don't have a Facebook page yet — head over to Facebook.com/Pages and "Create a page".)

So, here's my Five-Step Facebook Makeover checklist to help your Fan page look like you spent thousands of dollars on getting it designed, for just the price of a latte:

Facebook Page Makeover Step No. 1: Choose a Facebook Page Name (and Username) That Doesn't Suck

Page Name Vs. Username. This one always confuses. (And no wonder, they sound exactly the same. Thanks, Facebook!)

Here's the deal: Your "Page Name" is the name that shows up right next to your profile thumbnail on your Fan Page.

Below the Page Name is the number of likes and number of people talking about your page.

It is also the name that will show up when you run ads to either boost your number of likes or promoting content.

So, it's very important.

Your Facebook Username, on the other hand, is what is in the actual URL of your page: http://Facebook.com/MyUsername.

So, here's what I recommend for USERNAMES:

- **Choose something you're comfortable having on your business card.** I find with most of my clients, the Fan Page ranks well ahead of my actual website in the search-engine results. So, it's good to go with something you like the sound of.
- **Try to avoid hyphens or underscores if you can.** Not always possible, but it makes it a lot easier for your page to get found if the "page name" doesn't have these.
- **Beg, borrow, and steal your way to 25 likes for your Page.** Until you got your 25 likes, you'll have to stick with an abysmal username like Facebook.com/profile.php?id=52984566. So, once you choose a username, get those 25 likes as soon as you can.
- **Choosing a Facebook username is like having children.** Once you have 'em, you have 'em for life. So, choose wisely.
- **If somebody grabbed your username, and it does happen, choose something else related to your business**. Facebook doesn't check to see if usernames match the pages. They don't care. They are Facebook. So, if somebody grabbed "PlumbingPatrol" and that was the actual name of my business, then I might go local, such as "SanDiegoPlumbers" or "PlumbersSanDiego" or even do something more broad such as "BestPlumberSanDiego" or "FindAPlumber."

Okay, that's USERNAMES. Now let's turn to your PAGE NAME:

- **Get a keyword in there if you can.** You can get some serious SEO Google juice from your Fan Page. So, try to get a keyword in there subtly. Not: *Joe's Pizza - Best Denver Pizza, Best Denver Italian, Best Calzone Denver"* but *"Joe's Pizza - Best Denver Pizza"* would be fine.
- **Don't force a keyword in there if it doesn't sound right**. There's nothing worse than a Fan Page that sounds like a keyword factory. (Always ask...would my customers be into this?)
- **If branding isn't important, then go with something "fun" and "personal."** If getting your business name in there isn't crucial, then go with something like "I Love French Press Coffee" or "BBQ Grill Gurus" or "Bull Riding News." Remember Facebook is all about fun, social activity. (Not just a place to sell your crap.)
- **You can create as many Facebook Pages as you want.** If your business caters to different audiences, you may want to create separate Fan pages for these segments and take advantage of the SEO boost some keyword-laced page names can offer. (I worked with a law firm who created a separate Facebook page for each of their divisions, such as "bankruptcy"; "DUI" and "personal injury.")
- **You can only change your page name if you've got fewer than 200 likes.** So, choose carefully and get this whole Page Name nailed down before you get too popular. Trust me, by following the tips in this book, you'll get to 200 likes in no time, so neglect this tip at your own peril.

Facebook Page Makeover Step No. 2: Put Keywords (Almost) Everywhere

So, we've talked about some SEO benefits that a few well-placed keywords in your username and Fan Page name can do for you.

But here's where the real SEO magic happens. Lucky for us, it's an area where most marketers fail to take advantage of — the "informational" fields that are all over your Facebook Fan Page.

This includes your:

- "About" section
- "Description"
- "Short description"
- "Products" field

To update these fields on your Fan page, simply click "edit page" and then select the "basic information" tab.

Now, you don't want to go overboard. You don't want to say:

"Drain Patrol is a Modesto plumber you can trust. When it comes to choosing a Modesto plumber, Drain Patrol should be your first call. We have many Modesto plumbers at your service."

Sounds like somebody drank a bottle of Nyquil before writing that.

But you want to sprinkle in keywords your customers might use to "find" you.

"We specialize in ***data recovery,****" "Jimmy Cobra voted #1* ***LA Tattoo artist,****" "Looking for* ***Pittsburgh Steeler Jerseys****? Steeler Town has got 'em all."*

If I was trying to include "Denver tax preparer" in my "about" section, I might do something like:

"John Smith is a dedicated Denver tax preparer whose sole mission is to help people reach their financial goals, build for their economic future and defraud the IRS."

Quick Tip: Don't forget to include your website in the very first part of your "About" Section. This is the most visible area for you to include a link on your Facebook Fan Page. And can lead to lots of additional traffic back to your own website.

FACEBOOK PAGE MAKEOVER STEP NO. 3: CREATE A TIMELINE COVER PHOTO THAT DOESN'T SUCK

I don't encourage small-biz types to spend a ton of time on the creative for their social media profiles. But Facebook is different.

So much of the real estate on your Facebook fan page is devoted to photos. (Facebook knows most people are lazy and hate to read.)

And there's one photo you need to focus on. That's the Timeline cover photo — the image at the very top of your fan page that stretches horizontally over the entire width of your page.

And it's important.

It's like your very own 24-hour billboard. (Without the spendy rental costs.)

- **Use a photo-heavy design that incorporates the vibe of your company.** And by vibe, I don't mean your boring conference room. What is the mission of your company; what feelings do you hope to convey to your customers; what's the core benefit of your products or services? Put that in your photo.
- **Unless you have an inner graphic designer in you, hire an outside designer to make this photo awesome and not sucky.** Upwork and Fiverr are great places to find talent for super cheap.
- **Add text and calls-to-action — but sparingly.** Couple years ago, Facebook removed the restriction about having no more than 20% text in your Timeline cover pics. (Thank God.) But don't go overboard. Just have your text focused on one action you want folks to take.
- **Make sure the photo is right-aligned and NOT left-aligned.** This just means you want all the action of the photo happen on the RIGHT side. (And not on the left side where it'll get gobbled up by your thumbnail photo.)
- **Pick warm colors (red, brown, orange).** Anything that contrasts with the LA Dodgers color scheme Facebook forces upon the world.
- **Unless your brand is instantly recognizable, include a tag line that tells us what your company does.** So, your company is named Marketing Mojo, but what the hell does that mean? If it's not clear from your company name, add a bit of tag line, something like: "Training, Support, Solutions" or "Your Social Media Sherpa."

- **If relevant, add in testimonials (along with head shots) of your customers.** Social proof is HUGE. And having that baked in to your timeline photo can do absolute wonders.
- **Create a new cover photo for any upcoming promotions, events or product launches.** Got an upcoming webinar? Or a new mini-course you're teaching? Or maybe a live conference event you're organizing? Create a new cover photo to act as a billboard for your shiny new thing you're promoting.

Fan-Page Makeover Step No. 4: Create a Profile Photo That Doesn't Suck

The profile photo is the small thumbnail in the Timeline Cover Photo, on the lower left-hand side. While it doesn't have the sheer "Look at Me, and All of This Cool Stuff I Can Sell You" potential that the Timeline cover photo does…

…it does have a valuable function.

It quickly separates you from the rest of the pack in your fans' newsfeeds. (And most of the time your fans will see this 90% more than they do your timeline cover photo.)

So here are some best practices when it comes to creating a killer profile pic:

- **Start with a quality photo.** Sounds like a no-brainer. But I'm still shocked by how many people use a less-than-stellar pic for their profile spot. (Make sure to upload a square image.)
- **Go with a shot of a person if you can.** Unless you're a huge company, I always recommend going with a head shot over a brand logo. (You are trying to sneak into the news feed, and logos scream "I'm a business who wants you to buy stuff so don't worry about reading me.")
- **When in doubt, go with images over words.** This profile pic will eventually be sized down to 160x160px, so if you can't see your great verbiage at that size, you should probably remove it from the picture altogether.

- **Don't keep changing your profile pic.** The timeline cover photo can/should be changed frequently. But once you hone in on a good profile pic, stick with it.

Fan-Page Makeover Step No. 5: Add Your Company's Greatest Hits to Your Facebook Timeline

Everyone loves a good success story. And that includes your Facebook fans.

For some unknown reason, people like to scroll through fan pages to find out about the history of a company. (Sounds boring but trust me, people do this.)

And not only that, but these milestones can be a great way to send traffic back to your own website.

So, it behooves you to take a few minutes to brainstorm 8 or 10 key milestones for your company.

These could include:

- The day your company opened its doors.
- The day your company reached a certain profit threshold.
- The day your company served a famous (ish) person, or a specific-numbered customer.
- Products or services you launched.
- Key partnerships you entered into or huge contracts you were a part of.
- Employees who joined the team.
- Awards your company won.
- Special events your business was a part of.
- Key events in your local community. (Charity stuff works well here.)

So, what do you do when you've got your list of "milestones?" Well, here's what I do:

- **Find a LARGE photo that corresponds to the milestone.** 1200x628 px is the ideal size for these milestone pics, so BIGGER is always BETTER.
- **Add your milestone to your Fan Page Timeline.** To do this, just click on "Offer/Event" in the status update bar of your page, and then select milestone. (Include a keyword, if you can, in the event or story fields.)
- **Add a CTA (call-to-action) in the "Story" field.** (Example: "Here's a picture from my first seminar. (When I had more hair.) To check out our brand-new marketing seminars, head over to http://coolwebsite.com/seminars.")

CHAPTER 3 Key Takeaways:

- **One of the most important makeovers you can do for your Page is to come up with a username and page name that doesn't suck.** You want to aim for a blend of branding, SEO and something that appeals to humans.
- **Facebook pages offer a myriad of SEO keyword opportunities.** This includes some under-utilized areas like "descriptions", "about me" sections, "products", and "company overviews."
- **Create a kick-ass (left-aligned) Timeline cover photo that captures the vibe of your company.** And highlights any important calls-to-action or upcoming events you've got going.
- **Facebook profile photos should be of actual human beings, if possible, and high quality.** (No shaky cell phone pics.)
- **Create a "greatest hits" of your business on your Facebook Timeline.** (It's not self-serving, it's interesting to your customers.) Be sure to incorporate corresponding photos and stories. (And stuff involving employees and humans is always more interesting than product shots.)
- **Facebook apps are a great way to replicate whatever you've got on your website** — such as a menu, video, shopping cart, opt-in form — on your Fan Page. Just try off-loading the app creation to somebody who likes that tech crap.

Chapter 4:

Getting Your First 1000 Fans (in 60 Seconds or Less)

"Only one man in a thousand is a leader of men — the other 999 follow women."

-Groucho Marx

Okay, maybe it'll take longer than 60 seconds. (Might take as long as 90 seconds.)

But all those inspirational quotes and pictures of kittens and bunnies on your Facebook Page Timeline won't do you much good if there are no eyeballs to see 'em.

Like a junior high school dance where students are too scared to be the first one on the dance floor, sometimes you've got to scrape and claw your way to your first 1000 fans — so the rest of the universe thinks your page is worth "liking" and "interacting" with.

So, here are my seven favorite (mostly free) techniques to boost your fan base overnight and make your brand look way more popular than it is:

Super-Quick Fan Strategy No. 1: Leave a "Follow Us On Facebook" Suggestion Everywhere

And when I say everywhere, I mean everywhere. This could include areas such as:

- Email signature
- Forum or message board profile
- Your other social network profiles (such as Twitter, YouTube, Pinterest.)

- At the end of every blog post your write (whether on your site or on somebody else's site)
- In the description of every YouTube video you upload
- Your brick-and mortar store's front counter
- Employee t-shirts
- Any direct mail or offline promo materials
- Media Buys, such as TV, radio, print, or online

And how do you get people to follow you?

- "Follow Us on Facebook for Special Offers"
- "Like Us on Facebook for Members-Only Content"
- "Like us on Facebook for Members-Only Coupons"

Ya gotta give people an incentive, other than it would really help your teetering self-esteem. If you do, you'll see your fan count — and overall self-worth — rise in no time.

Super-Quick Fan Strategy No. 2: Put Facebook Icons on Your Blog or Website

This one SHOULD be a no-brainer, right? I mean, it's your website. (So why wouldn't you have "Like Us on Facebook" stuff there.) But many marketers still neglect to do this. (And if they do it, it's usually not done well.)

I think it's because Facebook makes the entire "liking" experience so damn confusing. People can "like" your blog post, but not necessarily "like" your Page.

They can "like" a comment, but not "like" the blog post itself. (Only Mark Zuckerberg could make me "hate" the word "like" so very much.)

Here's what you got to know…there are two prominent areas on your website or blog that you want to have Facebook icon placement:

Placement #1 - A Facebook "Like" box on the sidebar of your website.

These are those cool-looking square boxes visitors that not only show how many fans you have — and how many of those fans are their own friend — but gives visitors a chance to "like" your page without leaving your website.

This is, by far the most effective way to get new fans from visitors who frequent your website. (It's like you're getting two leads for the price of one.)

To install this like box, just head over to the Facebook Like Box Developer Page. (PunkRockMarketing.com/likebox) (They've got some, surprisingly, straightforward documentation there to help.)

You basically just:

- Create the like box plugin on the Facebook developer page.
- Insert the code into the sidebar of your website. If you're using WordPress there are plugins that specifically do this. Otherwise you can find a developer-for-hire on Fiverr.com to help.

Placement #2 - Add Facebook Comments to Your Blog Posts and/or Web Articles

Want immediate and instant feedback to the stuff you publish on your website? (I know. Scary, right?)

Don't worry, the possible downside to hearing brutal feedback from your visitors is outweighed by the awesomeness of having comments on your website, show up in your visitors' — and their friends' — newsfeed. (Talk about viral.)

Just another in a long line of reasons to ensure your website content has killer titles that catch the attention of people who have no idea who you are.

To add comments to your site, just check out the Facebook Developers Comments page for instructions on how to do it. (http://punkrockmarketing.com/commentsbox)

SUPER-QUICK FAN STRATEGY NO. 3: BEG YOUR FRIENDS TO LIKE YOUR PAGE

This one may sound pathetic. (And it is.) But it works.

Considering the average Facebook user has an average of 240 friends, asking your existing (personal) Facebook network to "like" your page can be the quickest way to boost that fan total, especially for a brand-new page.

What I usually do is make an appeal that's both whimsical and self-deprecating:

"Hey guys!

"I created this awesome, amazing new Facebook Page that will completely revolutionize the entire world, and quite possibly save civilization. Unfortunately, we've only got three fans so far. (One of them is my mother.)

"Will you help us out by clicking 'like' and becoming a fan? A grateful nation thanks you."

Feel free to leave out the "mother" part. Otherwise, the rest works well.

SUPER-QUICK FAN STRATEGY NO. 4: ASK YOUR SOCIAL MEDIA FANS/FOLLOWERS TO "LIKE" YOUR PAGE

This is a super-easy, but often under-utilized, method for getting fans (many of whom already know you.)

And that is by asking your tribes on other social media platforms to "like your page" — or better yet respond to one of your Facebook page posts.

This includes platforms such as Twitter, Instagram, Pinterest, Tumblr…almost any you can think of. (In my experience, Twitter and Instagram are perfect for this. I wouldn't recommend Google+ however…don't want to piss off the Google gods.)

As we mentioned before, this works best if you "tease" the request to "like" your page — such as "Follow us on Facebook to get a 10% off coupon" — or link to exciting content you've placed on your Facebook page. (I love to use surveys and quizzes in this way.)

Super-Quick Fan Strategy No.5: Put a "Follow Us" Link on Your Thank You Pages

Once somebody has bought something from you, or has opted into your email list, they are what you might refer to as a "hot lead."

So why not add them to your Facebook tribe at the same time? (And possibly keep selling to them in different ways repeatedly.)

To add some "Follow Us" code, just head over to the Facebook Developer Follow Button page (PunkRockMarketing.com/followbutton), and put in your website info and drop the code into your website.

Super-Quick Fan Strategy No. 6: Run a Contest

We're gonna go over contests in a lot more detail in Chapter 10. Just know when it comes to getting fans — FAST! — nothing beats a good, old Facebook contest.

The trouble with Facebook contests is they tend to lead to freebie-seekers — and not folks who necessarily translate to actual customers. (These are people who like to win "free crap.")

But when it comes to boosting your fan counts, Facebook contest absolutely rock.

Contests are a bit involved, technically, so head on over to Chapter 10 for more of a deep-dive on the topic.

Super-Quick Fan Strategy No. 7: Run a "Like Page" Ad

Okay, so maybe this is more of an advanced strategy. (Mostly because it requires hard-earned moolah.)

And if you're able to get 1,000 fans using the methods above, I encourage you to do so. (Even if it means forcing all your nieces and nephews to act as unpaid social media assistants.)

But if you're STILL not able to get much traction with your Page in the "fans" department, then it might be time to invest in a "Like ad" campaign.

Here's what you should know about "Page Like" ads in the Facebook ecosystem:

- **Facebook "like ads" do one thing, invite people to "like" your page**. Don't expect them to link out to your sales page or deliver you an email subscriber.
- **They are stupidly expensive.** Especially considering what they give you. ("Like ads can run anywhere from $1-$2/like.)
- **They boost the performance of other types of Facebook ad**s. We're gonna cover ads in far more depth in later chapters, but just know that having an ongoing "like ad" can really help the performance of your more targeted types of ads. (Not fair, but 'tis the way it is.)
- **You can see results by spending as little as $1/da**y. You don't need to spend a ton on these. Even $1/day for just a couple of days will help the popularity of your page.

So, how do you set these types of ads up? Su-per simple!

1. Head over to your Fan page. Click on the link that says "Promote your page"
2. Select your page. (If you have more than one page.)
3. Put in a headline. I like to sell the benefits of the page for headlines. (Whether it be special offers or insider tips.)
4. Choose a placement. Start off with mobile and right column placements. (Desktops get way too expensive for "like ads.")
5. Choose fans of pages that are like yours. (Go for an audience at least 2-3 million in size.)
6. Set up your daily budget. I like to do about $1-$2 a day.
7. And let the "like ad" do its thing.

Again these "like ad" campaigns aren't gonna put instant money in your pocket. (Sorry this isn't Forex trading or multi-level marketing.)

But it is part of an overall strategy of boosting the popularity — and more importantly the "perceived" popularity — of your page. Which will come in handy, in the next chapter.

CHAPTER 2 KEY TAKEAWAYS:

- **Place a "Follow Me on Facebook" link in any online — and offline — place you can think of.** That includes email signatures, online profiles, business cards, print ads, and in-store merch. (Just make sure to give 'em a reason to follow you — such as free stuff!)
- **Put Facebook icons on your website and/or blog to boost your fan count.** This includes a sidebar "like box" and a "comments box" to your blog posts. Don't worry about the "feedback," it'll be worth it.
- **Beg your friends to like your Fan Page.** Plead shamelessly, if required.
- **Reach out to your fans and followers on other social media profiles and ask them to "like" your page.** (Better yet ask them for their feedback on hot-button topics.)
- **Use your Fan Page to like and comment** on other Pages. (But in a non-spammy, human way.)
- **Create a "Follow Us" link on your thank you pages.** (Nearly 50% of all people who opt-in to your email list will "like" your page, if you give them a reason.)
- **Run a simple Facebook "like" contest to increase your fan count…FAST!** (Just don't expect a ton of these new fans to turn into instant customers.)
- **Use "Click Like" ads to boost your fan base.** Even as little as a $1/day for a couple of days could do the trick. Super helpful when running more conversion-focused ads.

Chapter 5:

The How, What, When and Where of Facebook Posting

"Our chief want is someone who will inspire us to be what we know we could be."

-Ralph Waldo Emerson

Here's where we dig into the trenches of Facebook Marketing. Where we answer such eternal questions as…

- What the hell am I going to post on my Facebook Page?
- When is the best TIME to post?
- How do we attract the largest audience possible with our posts? (I.e.: Get fans to share stuff for us because we're too lazy to do it ourselves.)
- How do I make sure I don't waste my time with all this posting crap?

And all the tips I'm going to share in this chapter have been tested and refined the hard way. (Meaning I tried a bunch of other crap that didn't work, until I accidentally hit up on stuff that did work.)

Here's what I want you to know upfront: just because you post something doesn't mean ANYBODY is gonna see it.

Sorry, but it's true.

Since Facebook's recent Machiavellian updates…err…algorithmic changes, LESS of our stuff gets seen by OUR fans, unless we spend money "boosting" our posts.

Which means it's all about QUALITY posts, less often, over a QUANTITY of posts in the hopes that "something" catches the attention of fans.

So, now we got the bad news out of the way, let's jump right into the dos and don'ts of Facebook posting with my Facebook Publishing FAQ:

FACEBOOK POSTING FAQ #1: HOW OFTEN SHOULD YOU POST?

If this were five years ago, I'd have said you should post to your Fan Page EVERY day. (Maybe even 2x a day.) And if your business creates a ton of timely content, such as an online magazine, then this frequency count will still work for you.

But these days I'd say 2-3x a week is optimal — and way less time-consuming than the old "gotta post 3x a day" mandate all the gurus recommend.

You can post way more than that. But try your best to get at least 2-3 good status updates a week. (And if NOBODY is responding to any of your posts, then just hit a "boost post" to any of your updates and that'll help get your stuff noticed.)

FACEBOOK POSTING FAQ #2: WHAT TIMES OF THE WEEK SHOULD YOU POST?

This might be the most contentious topic in the seedy, underground world of social media guru-ness. I wish I could tell you there was absolute agreement on this subject. (But getting people to agree on a brand of coffee, let alone ideal Facebook posting times, is nearly impossible.)

But let me share with you what I've learned, having done this in a few businesses (and worked with clients to find their ideal posting time):

- Best days to post are Thursday and Friday (and to a lesser extent, Saturday)
- Worst days to post are Monday & Tuesday (more hectic the work schedule, the less Facebook-ing there is)
- 3-7pm EST is ideal for weekday posting
- 9am-12pm EST is ideal for weekend posting

Now the usual disclaimers about "this will depend greatly on your individual business" …blah, blah, blah…apply here.

But if it were me, I would focus my prime Facebook marketing energies on the period between Thursday - Saturday.

And let the rest of the business schmucks waste breath trying to fill their Facebook page with content every day.

FACEBOOK POSTING FAQ #3: WHAT KIND OF STUFF SHOULD YOU POST?

In Chapter 1, I went over some ways to generate content for your Facebook page posts. (Such as blog posts, videos, motivational quotes.) And you can do your own testing to find a weekly content quota that works for you.

But let me give you a rough weekly breakdown of the kinds of stuff I like to share on my Facebook page — and on which days I like to feature them:

- Thursday - Blog post (created in-house)
- Friday - Motivational Quote
- Saturday - Hot-Button (Fill-in-the-Blank) Question

- Thursday - Video me (created in-house)
- Friday - Funny video
- Saturday - Hot-Button (Fill-in-the-Blank) Question

- Thursday - Infographic or blog post (created in-house)
- Friday - Motivational Quote
- Saturday - Hot-Button (Fill-in-the-Blank) Question

- Thursday - Video pitching something or promoting something for sale

- Friday - Motivational Quote
- Saturday - Hot-Button (Fill-in-the-Blank) Question

Couple things you might have gathered from this weekly breakdown:

- **The only thing I share on Friday is "motivational" quote**s. That's because human brains have Kardashian-level potential on Fridays. (So, all ya wanna do is give 'em something to silly to look at.)
- **Thursdays are where I focus my in-house content and special offers.** This is where I find my most captive — and lucrative — Facebook fan audience.
- **Saturdays are great for engagement with posts that don't require a lot of time**. I don't recommend you ask your fans to read your 12K-word blog post on a Saturday, but having people answer a survey or check out some other fun, visual piece of content is wholly acceptable.
- **I only "promote or sell" something once a month.** That's because my stuff is on the higher-ticket range. You may want to promote lower-ticket items (more often).
- **I promote with a video.** In Chapter 8, I'm gonna walk you through exactly how to use video to create devastatingly effective ads. But for now, just know if yer selling "anything" that requires more than a $20 investment, it's helpful to have a video that "pre-sells" the product or service. (Doesn't have to be long, just something that educates them about why they need the product or service RIGHT this frickin' moment.)

Facebook Posting FAQ #4: How Do I Actually Post Something on Facebook?

So, once you've got your posting schedule nailed down — and have a rough idea of the kinds of things you'll be sharing on your Facebook page — it's time to get that stuff published for public consumption.

Here's my eight keys to the perfect Facebook post:

1. **Try your best to "schedule" and "publish" your posts through the Facebook platform**. I know there are plenty of third-party tools, such as HootSuite and Post Planner, that let you handle all your Facebook publishing. But evidence suggests Facebook "penalizes" content published through these tools.
2. **Always attach a photo to your post** — unless it's a video. And if yer promoting content that lives outside Facebook, try to use the same photo found on that landing page.
3. **Ideal Facebook photo size for your posts is 1200x630 pixels**. This will be probably change by the time I finish typing this sentence but aim for this size for now.
4. **Keep your Facebook posts less than 80 characters if possible**. Turns out posts under 80 characters get 23% more interaction. Which might be easier to explain when you realize 75% of all Facebook posts are longer than 80 characters. (You'll stand out!)
5. **Use brackets to categorize your pos**t. For example, you could do something like: [blog] or [video] or [question of the week] or [quote]. This not only provides a shorthand for Facebook users to understand what yer pitching, but the special characters also stand out in a sea of content.
6. **Pick your posts when asking people "What do you think?"** There was a time when I suggested folks asked "What do you think? Let us know in the comments below" in every single post. But that's passé these days. (And takes up valuable real estate.) So, be judicious about asking for feedback. (Don't worry they'll give it.)
7. **If you're promoting a good cause, ask people to "like" and "share" your post.** Back in the olden days of 2011, you could ask folks to "like" every single thing you put out there. (But now it's seen as obnoxious.) Unless you're promoting something on the charitable end of things. Then knock yourself out.

8. **Super-sneaky trick:** once you publish your post click on the "date stamp" and this will bring up a URL of your individual post. With this URL you can promote your individual page posts in places like Twitter, Pinterest, Instagram, LinkedIn…or wherever else you can think of!

CHAPTER 5 Key Takeaways:

- **Ya don't need to post every day.** In fact, 2-3x a week seems like a good weekly posting mix for Facebook.
- **Best days to post are Thursday and Friday.** (With 3-7pm EST being the Facebook post sweet spot.)
- **You can post whatever you want…but I like to share quotes** (especially on Fridays), blog posts, videos, and the occasional promotion. (No more than 1x a month.)
- **Posting your content on Facebook is dead easy.** Try to keep your post text under 80 characters, use bracket descriptors, and aim for a photo size of 1200x630.

Chapter 6:

Creating a Facebook Ad Strategy That Doesn't Suck (and Actually Makes You Money)

"It's not the impression you make,
it's the impression you leave."

-Marilyn Schwartz

Ah, yes…Facebook ads. The scourge and bane of most every small-business owner who's dipped their toes into the pool of Facebook marketing.

Trust me: I know how FRUSTRATING running Facebook ad campaigns can be.

And if you've tried Facebook ads in the past, with inconsistent results, just know, it's not your FAULT. (The system is pretty much set up for you to fail.)

That's because:

- Facebook likes to change the "look" and "feel" of its ad platform every 12 seconds
- Facebook "might" have the most user-unfriendly ad dashboard ever created (and I've used the Bing ad platform!)
- Facebook is notoriously picky about which ads they will — or won't — allow
- …most important of all, Facebook users HATE clicking on ANYTHING that has the appearance of marketing

And if Facebook didn't hold the key to the most targeted, focused leads our business could ever find…

…then I'd say you can tell those Silicon Valley Millennials to take their $1.32/like ads and shove it up their newsfeed.

But, alas, Facebook ads DO represent an under-utilized and super-ninja way to find a swath of new leads and long-term customers.

And once you figure out how to get some successful Facebook ad campaigns running on auto-pilot — and over the next few chapters I'm going to show you how to do just that — not only will you be making a crap load more money…

…but you'll also chuckle to yourself as the competition complains about how "hard" Facebook ads are to run. ("Let them eat cake… and their crappy Facebook ads.")

So, if you're READY to begin your quest for world domination, let's jump right in with my 4 Keys to Profitable Facebook Ads:

PROFITABLE FACEBOOK ADS KEY #1: KEEP YOUR EYE ON THE BIG PICTURE

Having spent enough money on Facebook ads to buy my first car, a 1983 Honda Civic, SEVEN times over…

…I can tell you the NUMBER ONE reason most Facebook ads fail is not targeting or bid strategy or bad copywriting (though all of that can certainly derail even the best ad)…

…it's unrealistic expectations.

We create Facebook ads like we do any other piece of paid media. We design ads that tout our latest offering and serve it in front of eyeballs we think SHOULD be interested…and wait for the cash register to start cha-ching.

And when it doesn't, we consider ourselves, or the entire Facebook ad platform, a total failure.

But that's because we're expecting a tiny little ad — which most people will see while scrolling on their smart phone on the toilet — to do all this sales heavy-lifting for us.

When what we need to do is understand the Facebook ad long game. And that "long game" is:

- **Step #1: Introduce Yourself to "Cold" Prospects (With a Content Ad)** — In which you share your best content — your most passionate, kick-ass stuff — with your ideal target audience. (And sneakily add that website visitor to your "retargeting" contact list.)
- **Step #2: Offer Your Freebie to "Warm" Prospects (With a Pre-Sell Video Ad)** — In which you create a video that tells people, who've ALREADY consumed your stuff, what your freebie is about (and why they desperately need it.)
- **Step #3: Offer Your Freebie Again (Nicely) to "Warm" Prospects Who Haven't Opted In yet (With Facebook Retargeting Ads)** — In which we create super-sneaky retargeting ads that "follow" our would-be leads throughout the Facebook universe.

Now each of these ad steps are super important — and require some precision to make work — so we're gonna break 'em up into the next three chapters. But for now, just digest this: no SINGLE Facebook ad lives in isolation. (They all work together to create a wonderful symphony of marketing awesomeness.)

Because approaching Facebook ads lets you:

- Get past a Facebook user's usual resistance to clicking on ads
- Disguise sales pitches as actual content (Totally ninja)
- Squeeze MORE profit out of every single drop of website traffic (the part I really love)

So, no matter what Facebook ad "hangover" you may have — give this method a try. You'll be surprised how profitable — and less stressful — this strategy can be.

Facebook Ad Key #2: Sync Your Account With Facebook Business Manager

Before you freak out I'm asking you to sign up for ANOTHER weird social media contraption, just know Facebook business manager is:

- A great tool for keeping all your Facebook page and ad activity in one centralized hub (away from your personal stuff)
- The perfect way to manage numerous Facebook pages (and multiple admins) without wires getting crossed
- Likely to be the only way in the future for you to access more advanced Facebook marketing features (such as Power Editor and Ads Manager)

To sign up all you gotta do is head over to business.facebook.com and sign in with your current account and follow the steps to migrate your account over to a business account.

And though you could certainly avoid this step — if you prefer to keep your existence as Zuckerberg-free as possible — I heartily recommend you make the big leap over to Business Facebook Manager. (If only so you won't have to create ads with that annoying "Dodger blue" color scheme staring back at you.)

Facebook Ad Key #3: Get That All-Important Targeting Code Set Up

We went over this in Chapter 2, but this is a good time to double-check you've got that all-important Facebook retargeting code set up on every page on your website. (That includes landing pages and thank you pages that live on other platforms, such as LeadPages.)

Trust me: you want to do this as soon as possible. (Otherwise you're leaving money on the Facebook advertising table.) And if you're unsure HOW to do this, find a degenerate developer on Fiverr or Upwork do it for you.

Bonus Tip: While you're at it, pasting code all over your virtual kingdom, you might as well get your Google Analytics and Google Retargeting code in there as well. (It's better to have too much data, rather than not enough.)

Facebook Ad Key #4: Have Your Marketing Funnel as Bullet-Proof as Possible

Marketing funnels evolve over time. (So, you don't have to make sure it's perfect before jumping into the world of Facebook ads.)

But right before you set up your first campaign take one last tour through your funnel. (Or better yet have a total stranger do it.)

You want to make sure the messaging (and the user experience) is exactly how you want it in areas such as:

- Your freebie giveaway
- Your landing page
- Your email follow-up sequence (if you have one)
- Your sales pages
- Your upsell pages (and downsell pages) — if you got 'em
- The look and feel of your Facebook page
- Your website (especially those "About Us" and "Contact Us" pages, which I find interminably boring, but users actually do check it out)

Does the copy and imagery on all these different touch points deliver on your CORE MESSAGE? (Do you have a core message?)

Do these different tentacles of your marketing octopus do a great job of: Presenting a compelling offer AND Converting on that offer.

If not, rewrite it. Or re-design it. Or cut it out of the funnel.

But if you feel you've got your funnel dialed in, then you ready for one of the coolest, most ninja ways to use Facebook — promote your kick-ass marketing (disguised as content.)

CHAPTER 6 Key Takeaways:

- **The #1 key to Facebook advertising success is to remember it's a long-term gain with THREE key components** — 1) Introducing yourself with content ads 2) which you follow up with pre-sell videos that tout your freebie 3) then follow up with retargeting ads that (gently) nudge people to sign up for your email list.
- **Facebook Business Manager isn't just an obnoxious term for Silicon Valley world domination.** It's a convenient tool to manage all your Facebook marketing activities — and gives you access to the shiny toys Facebook provides marketers, such as Power Editor.
- **Set up that Facebook retargeting code before running your ads.** The Author really encourages you not to be dumb like he did and wait six months before doing this.
- **Do a test-run through your entire marketing funnel before running your ads.** The Author also strongly encourages this as he wishes he had a time machine and had done this before spending thousands of dollars on Facebook ads.

Chapter 7:

How to Use Content Ads to Boost Your Brand (and Bottom Line)

"Nobody reads ads. They read what interests them. Sometimes they happen to be ads."

-Howard Luck Gossage

I know you're gonna have resistance to running these kinds of ads. And trust me, I get it. I HATE running any kind of ad, especially on shallow social media platforms, that don't IMMEDIATELY put money in my pocket.

But here's the thing about Facebook: Nobody, not even your most die-hard, stalkerish fans open their Facebook app on their smartphone so they can learn how to get 50% off your Google Adwords course or discover how they can take advantage of your limited-time dental marketing coaching plan.

They go to Facebook to comment on pictures of their friends' kids — or watch videos of pugs dressed up like "Yoda." They DON'T want to make decisions or spend money or do anything.

There's a reason Facebook is called the "modern smoke break." People use it to "turn off" their brain — not discover how you can help them consolidate their student loan.

But if you're somehow able to cut through the noise and offer them a shortcut or ninja-hack strategy or crazy funny video that speaks to the situation they're in at that moment — and I'll show you how to do just that — you will move into a different part of their brain.

The part of their brain they reserve for cool, funny people they "like" and "trust."

And there's no quicker route to that part of their cerebral cortex than a good, old piece of kick-ass content. (Supported by a content ad or two to make sure it gets seen by the eyeballs of your future customers.)

FACEBOOK CONTENT AD STEP #1: HAVE YOUR KILLER PIECE OF CONTENT READY TO GO

We went over this in Chapter 2 in some detail — check back there if you need a refresher course — but the key here is to have a signature piece of content that shares your message and genuinely helps improve the lives of people who check it out.

What kind of content should you share? Well, that'll depend on your audience. If you're trying to reach lawyers, that 60-second Instagram selfie video you shot standing in front of your bathroom mirror probably isn't a good fit.

And if you're looking to connect with "World of Warcraft" fans, then a 2000-word article on LinkedIn will do nuthin' for ya.

But, really, it comes down to this question:

What piece of content (and more importantly what form of content) can I create that will get people to stop scrolling through their smart phone and check out my stuff?

In my experience "list-type" blog posts — such as "5 Things Every CEO Can Learn From Ozzy Osbourne" — or benefit-rich videos work well. ("My #1 Secret to Creating a Viral Video (Without a Camera or Anything to Say.")

Though may need to test which works better for your audience, text-driven content or visual-driven content.

For my niche businesses catering to writers — they prefer the written word above video. But for my business catering to realtors, they'd rather have an icepick to the brain then read anything over 500 words.

Just know you want to make this your BEST stuff. Your super dazzling piece of amazing-ness that causes rioting in the streets — and brings a revolution to your industry. (Or at least to the minds of your potential customers.)

Facebook Content Ad Step #2: Know the Facebook Ad Lingo

So, there's a Facebook elephant in the room I'm having to deal with before we can move forward. And that's the confusion surrounding two similarly named types of Facebook content ads: boosted posts and page posts.

I know this is confusing because it took me months to get these straight. (I'm certain Mark Zuckerberg did this intentionally to make me feel dumb.)

But here's what you need to know:

- A "**boosted post**" is where you create a usual, run-of-the-mill status update on your Facebook page where you include a link to your piece of content — but as a bonus you choose the "boost post" option. For just a few dollars you can get your post seen by many your fans and followers. (Simplest type of content ad to run.)
- A **"page post"** is where you create an ad in your Facebook ads manager — not directly in your Facebook page platform — and create a special Facebook post that allows you more text and better targeting options. (More complex, but you can get your ad in front of targeted eyeballs.)

How do you KNOW which type of content ad to run? I'm so glad you asked…

Facebook Content Ad Step #3: Make a Content Ad Plan

Here's what I like to do for each of my pieces of KILLER CONTENT:

- **Phase #1: Share that content on my Facebook Page as a status update** — and then "boost" that content to my existing fans. I'll usually spend $10-$15 over the course of a couple days to do this. Just helps prime the pump — not to mention get some much-needed engagement going on my page.
- **Phase #2: After the "boost post" campaign is done, I'll create a "page post" campaign** in my Ads Manager. I generally like to start with a small daily bid for this type of ad — about $5 or so — and give it three days. (If it ain't getting at least a 3-5% click rate — or view rate, for video — then I'll tweak the ad. Or try another piece of content.)

And that's the plan. Su-per simple. And once ya got that, it's time to put together the creative assets for your content ad…

Facebook Content Ad Step #4: Create a Compelling Picture (For Text-Based Content)

If yer gonna share a video, don't worry about this step. (Your video will dynamically generate a thumbnail for ya when you create a Facebook content ad from it.) But if you're sharing any kind of written content, you'll want a compelling image to grab people's attention.

And though I am the world's worst graphic designer — and the world's second-worst photographer — here are a couple guidelines I've picked up when procuring that all-important Facebook content ad picture:

- **Ideal size for your picture is 1200x628**. Though this could change by the time I finish this sentence. Until then, opt for a picture in this ratio.
- **Faces looking directly at the camera**, or strong abstract visuals always work well. Your job is not to be subtle, it is to be seen.
- **Black and white pictures stand out well**. Especially in a sea of other Facebook posts. Try it out, you might be surprised.

- **Use colors that contrast nicely with the BLUE Facebook color scheme**. Oranges, reds, and yellows work well. Blues and purples, not so much.
- **Insert a text overlay at the TOP that bears the "title" of your piece of content.** Ya can't assume people are gonna read the copy of your post. Let the image do the talking — and that talking should include "Here's the awesome cool thing this content is about. (And put it at the top, or middle, so it doesn't get cut off at the bottom.)
- **Make sure text doesn't take up more than 20% of the overall image.** This is an iron-clad Facebook rule, if you violate it they will reject your ad.
- **Create 2-3 different images for each piece of content**. I know this is a pain and a little bit of extra work, but you'll be surprised how different images can lead to very different results.

And once ya got your photo set up, it's time for…

Facebook Content Ad Key #5: Write That Killer Ad Copy

Because there are essentially two kinds of content ads — the initial "boost post" ad and the "page post" ad — there are two bits of ad copy ya gotta create. (But don't worry I've got templates for both that you can follow.)

Here's how I like to organize my "boost posts"….

Bracket Descriptor + Juicy Benefit-Laden Headline (Along with a reminder how this benefit is way easier to achieve than people think)

Examples would be:

[blog] 5 reasons why carrier pigeon messages will become the new social network (and how to master it in 5.3 seconds)

[video] My 3 best webinar marketing strategies — and none of them take longer than five minutes

Remember these are all about: Killer results WITHOUT pain, time, or effort. (Skip the fancy copywriting books and focus on that.)

For the "Page Post" copy, we get more text to work with. There are three areas we need to focus on: The Text, Headline and News Feed Link Description.

Here's how I break them down:

- **Text** - this is the big block of text at the top. (ABOVE the headline…I know. Weird, right?) And this is where I like to include a) who I'm talking to b) what benefit my piece of content will offer 'em and c) who I am and why they should listen.

  Example: "Hey Screenwriter! Curious what legendary filmmaker Buster Keaton can teach you about writing for the screen? Find out in this new column from your screenwriting Sherpa, Michael Rogan, of ScriptBully Magazine."

- **Headline** - Again, the headline is BELOW the description. (Boggles the mind.) But this is simple. Just use a bracket descriptor and a title headline for the piece of content. (Not unlike what you used in the "boost post" copy.

  Example: "[blog] 5 Hacks Every Screenwriter Should STEAL From Buster Keaton"

- **News Feed Link Description** - This is the piece of text at the very bottom. And this is an area most marketers screw up — because they think this is ABOUT "selling" the content. Instead they should see this as an area of "previewing" the content. Just jump right in and give 'em a quick slice of what you're gonna do. (Add a "No.1" if you can. Makes it sound more official.)

  Example: "Screenwriting Hack #1: The More Serious Your Characters Are, the Funnier They'll Be..."

And when you've got your status update copy nailed down, for both the "boosted post" and the "Page post" you'll be ready for the final step…

Facebook Content Ad Key #6: Upload That Sucker

This is the easiest part of the whole system. Don't believe me? Just watch:

- **Step #1 - Share your content as a status update and simply click "boost post."** Depending on the # of fans you have, plan on spending $10-$20 over the course of a few days. (You don't need total saturation, just some likes and comments.)

  Note: Don't target "friends of fans" unless you feel they are part of your ideal demographic. (For instance, if you were running a local business.)
- **Step #2 - Create a "Page Post" ad,** when your "boost post" promotion has run its course. Give it at least 3 days before ditching the Page post.

Now the actual process for creating these types of ads seems to change weekly — so I recommend you check out the documentation that Facebook creates for these types of ads. You can access that by heading over to PunkRockMarketing.com/PagePost.

But a few things to keep in mind:

- **Choose "Video Views" or "Clicks to website" as your campaign objective.** Don't worry about conversions.
- **You want to create what's called a "dark post."** This just means you'll create an ad that won't be published to your page. (Ya don't need it. You already covered that with your "boosted post.")
- **Try "Desktop" and "Desktop Right Column" as ad placements first.** And then add "Mobile" or "Instagram" if you're getting good performance from the ad.
- **For "suggested bid" choose an amount .10 over the minimum range suggested.** You can always lower it later...ya just want to give your ad a chance out of the gate.
- **You want to target "Fans" of your competitor's pages** — or fans of pages that are in a similar industry as yours. (For example, if I

was a golf shop then I'd target fans of golf magazines, golf blogs, golf manufacturers…in addition to other local golf shops.)

- **Specify you want your ad to show only in the U.S., Canada, U.K. and Australia.** Unless, of course, your business caters to non-English-speaking countries.
- **Feel free to use a "tracking link" in the ad under website URL.** (Google Analytics is perfect for this.)
- **Start with a small daily ad spend limit — about $5 or so**. And then work your way up from there. (You want to see results before you invest more.)
- **Have a target audience of at least 500K- 1 million folks before you run your ad.** Any less than that and you might not be reaching anybody.
- **If you're sharing a video, upload that video straight to the Facebook ads manager**. Don't just share a YouTube video. (You'll get better results if you upload the video straight to your Fan Page.)
- **Don't get too hung up on instant conversions.** You want clicks and video views. (Don't forget if you've got your retargeting set up properly, then you're collecting them as a lead already.)

CHAPTER 7 KEY TAKEAWAYS:

- **The biggest key to Facebook content ad success is…well… killer content**. The type of content you present will depend on your market. (But list-type blog posts and "my #1 strategy" videos work well.)
- **There are two kinds of Facebook ads — they have annoyingly similar names.** They are "boosted posts" — which are simply status updates that are "boosted" and "page posts" which are Facebook ads that promote content to very targeted audiences.
- **The ideal Facebook content plan** "usually" includes 2-3 days of "boosting" a post, and then 3-5 more days of a targeted "page post."
- **If you're going to promote a text-based piece of content, then you'll need a killer picture to promote that content.** Key features of this killer photo include standout colors (no blues or purples), final photo size of 1200x628, and a text overlay that contains the title of your piece of content.
- **Write your ad copy BEFORE you head over to the Facebook ads manager.** Sell benefits of the content — as well as a brief reminder why they should listen to you. (Bonus ninja tip: Use the News Feed Link Description field in your page post to "preview" your content. Nobody else does this.)
- **Uploading your ad (finally) is relatively easy.** (Even if the process changes every week.) Don't forget to: choose "video views" or "website click" as your goal, find fans of competitor (or industry) pages, gather an audience at least 500K-1 Million in size, and start your bidding off low (about $5/day) and raise slowly up from there.

Chapter 8:

How to Get Super-Cheap Leads With Facebook Video Ads

"The absolute aim should be to make money out of satisfying customers."

-John Egan

Finally! We're going to, at long last, get to the MEAT of this whole Facebook ad strategy...and that is get some actual frickin' leads into our marketing funnel.

Now, you can go straight to this ad type — and skip the whole content ad step — if you really, really want to.

But I don't recommend it.

Having gone through this dog-and-pony show quite a few times I can confidently assert if you introduce yourself using content ads FIRST, before you go for the Facebook marketing kill, you will be rewarded with:

- Lower ad costs
- Higher click thru rates
- Higher conversion rates
- Lower refund rates
- More long-term customers

And the reason is simple: by introducing yourself first (and offering value first) you'll lower folks' resistance to your message. (And put them in a state where they're ready for your Jedi marketing tricks.)

Okay, enough of the pedantic lecture. Let me walk you through my 5-step Facebook Pre-Sell Video Ad Process:

PRE-SELL VIDEO AD STEP #1: FIGURE OUT WHAT YER GONNA SAY

I know you're champing at the bit to get in front of that camera and riff away about your wonderful, dynamic, earth-changing video.

But here's what you gotta remember:

- People get bored and distracted easily (So if you don't grab their attention, you're toast)
- People don't want to say "yes" to you (Which is why you've got to make it imperative they act)
- People are always wondering WHO the hell is this guy or girl talking to me?

Now we went over this pre-sell video structure in some detail So, before you begin riffing away, I recommend you follow this simple, but effective Pre-Sell Video Ad Formula that I follow:

1. **The "Click Start"** — Start off your video by looking directly at the camera and saying, "Click to hear the video" TWICE as you point downward (near your chest). There's a reason for this, it encourages people to click on your video in their feed while on their Smartphone. This alone will boost click rates nearly 40%.
2. **Introduce yourself** — You wanna keep this brief, but it's important you tell them who you are (and why you're talking.) "Hey this is Larry Rothschild from MicroChip Remover and in this video and I want to tell you about HOW to remove that microchip from your brain the Facebook thought police implanted there..." — Note: If you have different customer segments, create different versions of this video so there's a better message to market match.
3. **Tell them the WHY** — Give them context for WHY it's so damn important they grab your freebie, stress urgency and pain

if they don't do it — "All of us know free will is important…but did you know Mark Zuckerberg is controlling your every thought and movement from an underground bunker in Menlo Park…"

4. **Acknowledge their obstacles** — "The trouble is, it's hard to find the time or motivation to deal with the microchip. Or even know how to get started."
5. **Introduce your freebie** — "I think I may have found the perfect solution and it's all revealed in my FREE REPORT 'How to Remove the Facebook MicroChip from your brain…."
6. **Brief story about your journey** — "I first realized I had my own Facebook micro-chip problem when I wandered through Silicon Valley, naked, asking for "my buddy Mark Z. And I said to myself: 'There has to be a better way!'"
7. **Tell 'em how to get their freebie** — "And to learn my micro-chip removal system…all you gotta do is click in this post."
8. **Wish them well** — "Hope to see ya on the other side, but in case I don't I wish you much good luck in your pursuit of being the best and micro-chip free person you can be."

Pre-Sell Video Ad Step #2: Film and Edit the Damn Thing

I know the thought of turning that camera on might induce enough anxiety to require a Lexapro prescription, but just know your video doesn't have to be PERFECT.

It doesn't even have to be in the kingdom of perfect. (In fact, in some markets, the more polished and professional your video looks, the worse it converts.)

But here are FOUR must-haves your pre-sell video needs to be successful:

1. **Good Sound** — This is a deal-breaker. You MUST have good sound. If somebody can't hear your video, if it's recorded with an external Mic that makes you sound like you're speaking from a Sears washer/dryer, nobody will ever watch your video.

So, whether you film on a $2800 DSLR or your smart phone make sure you've got decent audio. (And this usually means having some kind of external microphone plugged in to your camera.)

2. **Video Performer Who Gives a Crap** — This might be you. (And probably is.) But resist the temptation many small biz types fall prey to do to put the most "photogenic" or "attractive" person on camera. "He/She who cares most, wins…" and whoever that is in your business, makes sure they're the ones doing the communicating.
3. **A Mix of Fast and Slow** — This is an advanced public speaker tip, but one of the best ways to really engage listeners is to vary the tempo of your message. So, when you get to the part of your video that's important…slow it down. Give it more emphasis. But you when you want to do drum up excitement, speed up. (Simple, but effective.)
4. **Photos to "Cut Against"** — Sorry, 'bout the video jargon, but it's good to have a couple of still images (that relate to your topic) that you can "cut to" while you keep talking. We want to do this because a) It hides our mistakes (even though you and I both know you're not going to make any) and b) It breaks up the monotony of people looking at your mug. (Break up a static image every 15-20 seconds.)

And though this isn't a book about video editing — Thank God! — I do want to say video editing is like changing the oil in your car. If you enjoy doing it, knock yourself out. But if it fills you with mortal dread, just have somebody else do it.

PRE-SELL VIDEO AD STEP #3: UPLOAD THAT SUCKER

Here's the fun part! Where we get to upload this piece of marketing art you've created.

Now, as I've detailed earlier, Facebook likes to "change" their ad process quite a bit. But here are guidelines to keep in mind when you create your video pre-sell ad:

- **Target people who checked out your content — such as a blog post or a video — but did NOT reach your "Thank You" page.** You do this by creating a "custom audience" that includes anybody who visited any of your website pages...but did NOT visit your "Thank You" page. By targeting people who've already encountered your brand you'll be paying next to nothing for leads.
- **You can either use the Power Editor or Business Manager to create your Video Ads.** There is talk of doing away with one if not both. But, at this moment, Power Editor gives you more options — but is harder to figure out. Ads Manager is easier to use — but has less options. (I'd recommend creating your first couple ads with Ads Manager and then easing yourself into the deep end of the Power Editor pool.)
- **Choose "Video Views" as your ad campaign objective at first.** And when you've got a bunch of data to work with, and you're getting leads, ease up to a "Conversion" objective.
- **When it comes to ad copy for a video ad, there are two components ya gotta nail:** a) The verb-filled copy to sell the benefits of the video. "Discover my #1 secret"; "Uncover the #1 Thing Google Doesn't Want you to Know..." and b) A LINK to your freebie "Get It Here==> www.microchip.com" (Note: You don't really have to "introduce yourself" the copy. The video does that.)
- **Choose "Learn More" as your "Video CTA."** You have a choice of "video CTA" text options, such as "Download." Just remember people love to learn — and hate "downloading" things.
- **Keep your bidding low — as low as $1-$2/day**. Because you're targeting folks who've already checked your content your # of video views will be low — but your cost of lead acquisition will be super low. (When you see gains, slowly move that bid amount up.)

PRE-SELL VIDEO AD STEP #4: SLOWLY BROADEN YOUR VIDEO AD'S REACH

Here's where things get really ninja.

Once you've got a video pre-sell ad that's working for you — that's bringing in leads at an acquisition cost you're comfortable with — it's time to broaden that video out to the bigger Facebook world.

Not just folks who've already checked out your content in the past.

I highly recommend you wait to roll this type of video ad until you're sure you've got a winner on your hands. (And by winner, I mean something that's making money.)

But once you've got a video that's resonating with your ideal customer demographic, feel free to SKIP the whole content ad process and see how your video does with a much-larger Facebook target audience.

The process for publishing these ads is nearly the same as we just outlined in Step #3, with just a couple of tweaks:

- **Start with "Video Views" as the objective**. After a week, change it to "conversion." (Using your "Thank You" page as the destination.)
- **Start with a daily bid that's higher than the earlier video ads, somewhere in the $10-$15 range.** (At least for the first day.) The reason for this is, if you're able to get 1000 video views in that first day — and with video view costs hovering around .01-.02 per it's totally doable — Facebook will create a "custom audience" based on people who watched your view. (This means you can present these folks offers at a future date, even if they watch your video and NEVER opt-in to your email list.)
- **Experiment with segmenting your target audience further and further** until you can't improve your ad's performance anymore. This is the real secret sauce to your Facebook ads. To keep refining your target audience, slowly and steadily, until it's so awesome you're practically printing money from Facebook ads.

And what we've gone over so far will not only get you a Ph.D. in Facebook Ad Studies but will also help you crush (in a nice way) the competition…and literally get 200-300% more profit from your existing ad spend.

But it's in the next chapter where we're gonna go over my favorite absolute sneaky, clandestine — and super-powerful — form of online marketing going these days.

And it's a strategy that can not only help you sell a crap load of your stuff to new customers — at bargain-basement ad prices — but help you encourage those pesky non-buying past customers of yours reach for their wallets, again and again.

PUNK ROCK MARKETING
AMPLIFY YOUR MESSAGE

CHAPTER 8 Key Takeaways:

- **Before you film your pre-sell video, take time to map out what you will say.** Follow the system I outlined earlier, paying attention to the story you're telling, and the pain points you're hitting. (Don't sell…tell!)
- **When it comes to "performing" your video, just remember good audio is always more important than good video.** (And put the person MOST passionate about the subject — not the most photogenic — on camera.)
- **And as for editing: if you enjoy it, do it.** If you don't, have somebody else do it.
- **Setting up your video ad is easy.** (You can use either the Power Editor or Ads Manager.) You just want to target folks who've already visited your website. (And ya need little in terms of daily ad budget, couple dollars a day will do.)
- **When you've got a pre-sell video ad that's working** — people are clicking on it and you are getting new leads — expand that video ad to target your ideal customer demographic.

Chapter 9:

Facebook Retargeting Ads… The Final (Profitable) Frontier

"I find it useful to remember that everybody lives by selling something."

-Robert Louis Stevenson

This is where things get Exciting. Almost "too" exciting.

In fact, you probably shouldn't read this chapter. There's just way too much awesome ninja marketing info here.

And, for your brain's sake, you might want to close this chapter and move on to something more palatable. (Like that "alien invasion" sci-fi novel you've got in your Kindle queue.)

But…if you're looking for a way to wring every ounce of profit out of your prospects, leads, and customers then I want to introduce you to the fabulous, wonderful world of Facebook Retargeting Ads!

A Brief Primer on Retargeting

Just in case you're not up on your oddly named marketing terms — most likely because you were busy trying to run an actual business — retargeting is a process in which:

- A website visitor lands on one of your webpages
- That web page places an invisible piece of "tracking code" on that visitor's page (Through the use of harmless "cookies")
- You "follow" that user throughout the Internet — both on Facebook or Google or wherever — by offering "targeted" ads related to the webpages they've already visited

This is how Home Depot "seems" to be reading your mind as they show you Black and Decker power drill ads as you surf the Internet. (Do people still "surf" the Internet? Does that expression make me sound old? Probably yes on both counts.)

The Cool Ninja S*#&@ You Can Do With Retargeting

Okay, now you know how it works. Here's where the mind-blowing part comes in. Because with retargeting you can do things like:

- Remarket to landing page visitors who don't opt-in
- Remarket to new email subscribers who don't buy your initial offer
- Remarket to new customers who don't take your upsell (or downsell)
- Offer existing customers different products (such as upgrades, further training, automated services)
- Re-engage existing customers who've stopped opening your emails
- Ask existing customers/subscribers to provide a testimonial, fill out a survey, leave an online review, "like" your Facebook page… do almost anything you want them to

Retargeting (or remarketing) ain't about selling stuff. It's about cutting through the distraction and clutter of modern life — and start up a one-on-one conversation with a member of your tribe.

Might be the most powerful weapon us marketers have been given since the sales letter.

But how do we get started with this powerful (though somewhat technical) marketing strategy? Well, here are SIX key methods I'd use in your Facebook retargeting efforts:

(Note: This isn't a book about retargeting, but the strategies I outline could be used with Google retargeting, or any other retargeting platform, with relative ease.)

Cool Ninja Facebook Retargeting Method #1: Share Your Content With Email/Blog Subscribers (Easy)

This is probably the simplest retargeting method there is, and yet many marketers who produce content on a somewhat regular basis neglect to do this. And that is for just a couple bucks promote every piece of NEW content (or OLD content) to folks who haven't seen it.

Why would you want to do this?

- It boosts the SEO of your content (The more eyeballs and social shares you get, the better your content will rank)
- Gives value to your subscribers/customers (Nice deposit in the future goodwill bank)
- Gives folks who haven't opted in yet, but have read your content, a chance to "finally" join your funnel
- Most important: Helps you segment your subscriber/customer base (If I share a blog post on "Facebook marketing" and 40% of my subscribers check it out, then I can create an even more targeted future Facebook offer for just those 40%)

Now for this type of retargeting ad, I wouldn't go to the trouble of creating a video. (Think that's just overkill.) All you gotta do is:

- Create a Facebook custom audience based on your existing email subscriber list or customer list (You can do this by just uploading an Excel sheet of your contacts)
- Create a Facebook content ad (we went over these in Chapter 7)
- Target that ad to both your subscriber/customer custom audience, and target anybody who visited your website and did NOT opt-in
- Set the daily bidding for that campaign at $1-$2/day
- Sit back and watch all that delicious, new traffic to your content (and the new leads this traffic will provide)

Cool Ninja Facebook Retargeting Method #2: Get Warm (ish) Prospects to Opt-In to Your Email List (Finally!)

This one's self-explanatory. All you do is:

- Create a Facebook custom audience compiled of ANYBODY who visited ANY page on your website — or watched one of your videos on Facebook — but did NOT land on your "Thank You" page
- Create a Facebook retargeting ad that gives them another chance to opt-in
- Set the bidding at $1/day

The real magic comes from how flexible this type of retargeting ad can be. You can:

- Share a piece of content that answers any "objections" you think they might have
- Point them to a page where you've got testimonials and social proof of people who've consumed your freebie
- Show 'em the "same" pre-sell video you created before — or send 'em straight to the same email capture page

What you do will depend entirely on WHY people aren't opting in. (Might have nothing to do with the landing page and everything to do with the audience that's consuming it.)

But in my experience answering objections — especially about how "easy" and "simple" a solution is — and testimonials is the best way to use this form of retargeting.

Cool Ninja Facebook Retargeting Method #3: Remarket to Shopping Cart Abandoners

Everybody knows this form of retargeting. This is the "Big Brother is following you all around the Internet showing you that same DAMN Hewlett Packard printer from Costco" feeling.

The reason you see so many of these types of ads is they work. (Devastatingly well.) The trick is to make SURE you balance proper follow-up with respecting people's privacy.

Here are some recommendations when creating these types of retargeting ads:

- **Limit time length these ads can be shown to 30 days**. Don't bother marketing to folks who went to your page eight months ago.
- **Cap the frequency of these ads to 15-20 times a month, per person.** Any more than that and you risk a good, old restraining order.
- **Make sure ad touts the exact product or service the would-be customer was looking for.** Don't offer them everything in your suite of products. Just show them what they were interested in.
- **Videos and/or articles that offer testimonials — and answer objections — work grea**t. Especially the testimonial part, I've seen those collect as much as 50% of lost shopping cart revenue.
- **Be nice and self-deprecating.** Don't be a spammy, creepy jerk with these ads. ("I noticed you DIDN'T buy our thing!") Just present the offer in a slightly different way, with more information.
- **If people aren't buying, re-think your product's pitch**. Might be your product isn't resonating with people. (For whatever reason.) Use this type of retargeting ad as the cheapest focus group of all time.

Cool Ninja Facebook Retargeting Method #4: Offer an Upsell (or New Product) to Your Existing Customers

This might be my favorite form of retargeting ad…and that is to offer upsells (or new products) to people who've already bought from me in the past.

And the reasoning is simple: the conversion rates on these types of ads are stupidly high. (And is probably the most profitable ROI you'll get from any kind of retargeting ad you run.)

That doesn't mean these types of ads are simple. (You can easily bug the ever-living crap out of your existing customers with too many of these.)

But if done properly, it can be some of the most impactive advertising you can do for your entire business.

Here's what to keep in mind about these upsell/new product retargeting ads:

- **Segment your customer base (first!) and then create your retargeting ad**. Not all your customers are gonna be interested in every damn thing you must sell. Do your best to segment them out, either through filtered email lists or Facebook custom audience based on user behavior, so your ad is relevant and timely for your customers.
- **The best upsells are always related to your existing product** — and make things faster/easier/more customized for your consumer. This is a strategy that took me forever to figure out. (Unfortunately.) But you want the upsell to seem like a "no-brainer" proposition. Just ask folks if they'd like help getting your product or service set up. Or if they want personal attention from you or your team. (A good portion of your customer base will want this. So why not let them pay for it?)
- **Videos seem to work best with these types of ads**. In which you provide more information, and hammer home the benefits they'll be getting if they take advantage of the offer.
- **Try to add an urgent time limit if you can.** This isn't always possible but if you stress the offer is gonna expire in 7 days — and you really hope they take advantage of the opportunity before it goes away — you'll get a much higher conversion rate.
- **Just like with other retargeting ads, keep the frequency to about 15-20 times per month**. (And don't hammer your customers with the same ad for more than 30 days.)

- **This same process can work for freebie opt-ins,** where you're trying to your customers to pre-qualify themselves for a new email list. In that case a text ad that links directly to a landing page will work just fine.

COOL NINJA FACEBOOK RETARGETING METHOD #5: REDUCE REFUNDS (WITH A SHOUT-OUT TO CURRENT CUSTOMERS)

This is a strategy I hit upon by accident. (Found it while helping a client who had a profitable coaching package but couldn't get his refund rate down.)

So, we created a simple Facebook retargeting ad — targeted at NEW coaching clients — that just said: "Thanks so much for checking out the coaching package. If ya got any questions, don't hesitate to ask."

And guess what...his refund rate dropped by 50%. (Considering his packages cost $1000/month, $1/day wasn't too bad an investment in ads.)

These do not have to be elaborate. Or time-consuming to create.

But if you've got an issue with refunds — especially for higher-ticket stuff — then I encourage giving these a try.

Here's what worked for my client:

- **Start with "Thank You."** Just having a banner ad that said "Thank You for Joining the Program" cut my client's refunds by half. (And the ad didn't offer anything else...just a message of thanks.)
- **Tell 'em you want them to succeed — and you KNOW they'll succeed.** Studies have shown the biggest reason people refund stuff isn't because they don't like the product...it's that they don't feel it'll work for THEM. (Or that they'll ever figure out how to use it.) So, just allay these fears and give 'em a nice encouraging nod forward.
- **The more expensive your product/service, the more complicated these should be**. In fact, for my client selling the coaching

packages, we created a series of follow-up weekly videos that would check-in and see how people are doing. (You do this by segmenting customers into email lists that designate what week they're in a program — and then creating Facebook custom audiences based on those lists.)

- **These kinds of ads work even with folks who REFUNDED your product.** Instead of getting bitter and angry, just create a simple ad thanking folks for giving the product a try and ask them if they'd fill out a survey about their experience. (You will learn more about your marketing funnel this way then 10K in consultancy fees.)

Cool Ninja Facebook Retargeting Method #6: Reach out to Warm Customers...Who've Grown Oh-So-Cold

We've gone over different ways you can use retarget to would-be and existing customers on Facebook. But this LAST one might be the most lucrative because you're simply re-energizing an asset you already have...but can't seem to figure out what the hell to do with.

How do you get your once red-hot customer base — that has suddenly grown colder than a hockey rink? Well, here's how I do it:

- **Decide on HOW you want to reach out your "once-awesome" customer base.** Do you want to offer them a special coupon or discount? Offer them a freebie? (Insider guides and free consulting works well.) Or maybe just ask them to fill out a survey so you can figure out how better to serve them.
- **Segment your existing email list**, or customer database, into a manageable asset based on a determining factor of your choosing. I generally like to target folks who haven't opened one of my emails in 3 months or so. But you may have a different set of factors you'd like to target. (Such as folks who haven't upgraded their software or downloaded your latest app.) Whatever it is, you gotta segment them in some way that Facebook can understand.

- **Create your ad and upload your customer data to create a Facebook custom audience.** I generally like to run these types of ads for a limited amount of time — usually for a week or so — every couple months. That way you don't over-saturate these folks.

And don't get too overwhelmed by all the options I've outlined here. (These are just possible retargeting directions you can go in. You don't have to employ each single one.)

But the cool thing about these retargeting campaigns is you can extend that chance to make the sale weeks, if not months, beyond initial contact. (Which can put unexpected windfalls of money into your pocket.)

And speaking of putting money in your pocket, in the next chapter we're gonna cover some of the more advanced ninja Facebook marketing tools and tricks you can use to not only exponentially grow your bottom line — but automate much of this Facebook marketing "stuff."

CHAPTER 9 Key Takeaways:

- **Retargeting is the process where you "follow" visitors to your website** — through tracking code — so you can market to them on Facebook, or most any other place on the Internet.
- **One of the simplest, though hardly used, forms of retargeting is to promote content you must existing customers and email subscribers.** (Not only does it help the SEO ranking of your content, but it also helps segment your audience for future marketing.)
- **One of the most common, and effective, forms of retargeting ads is to give folks who didn't opt-in to your email list ANOTHER chance to opt-in.** (Adding testimonials or answering objections are great ways to use this form of ad.)
- **The most used — and "Big Brother-y" — form of remarketing is to follow shopping cart abandoners and give them one more chance to buy their stuff.** Keep the frequency to these types of ads to 15-20x per month, or else you risk pissing them off.
- **My favorite type of remarketing ad is the "upsell" or "new offer" to existing customers.** They've already bought from you — some very recently — and they are primed to buy more good stuff from you in the future.
- **Reducing refund rates is a cinch with remarketing.** Just create some "Thank for buying! Got any questions!" type ads to make sure your customers are feeling satisfied and confident in their abilities to use your product or service.
- **Perhaps the most ninja form of remarketing is to reach out to customers who haven't responded to any of your marketing messages lately.** You could offer them discounts, freebies — or simply ask them how you can help them. (If they don't take the bait…feel free to remove 'em from your tribe.)

Chapter 10:

Contests, Offers and Facebook Live...Oh My!

"If you don't set goals, you can't regret not reaching them."

-Yogi Berra

This might be the most profitable part of this book.

Because this is where we leverage all the hard work we've done up to this point and create some rather cheap and easy customer funnel activities that directly affect our bottom line.

But you gotta do the prep work.

You must build your Fan Page and post regular, frequent content that gets people to answer insipid questions and offer their opinions on a variety of subjects...

...and you've got to get some ad campaigns going that bring in new fans, leads and paying customers. (And maybe even a couple of ads that reclaim older customers from your marketing salvage yard.

Because when you've got all that going, you'll have so much engagement and social activity around your Facebook page, you'll be in a perfect place to run out the three super-ninja Facebook weapons of marketing awesomeness:

- Contests
- Offers
- Facebook Live Events

Now, you could certainly try these out before you run your first ad, but I highly recommend you master running a couple successful (if cheap) ad campaigns — and have a Facebook page with at least 2,000 fans — before rolling these out.

These are powerful strategies that work best when you've got the infrastructure in place to make it happen.

So, let's dig right in and get started with the first pillar of my Trinity of Facebook Promotion Awesomeness, which is:

Facebook Promotion Awesomeness Pillar No. 1: Contests and Sweepstakes

I'm still amazed how popular Facebook contests are. (I don't get particularly jazzed about entering a photo contest to win a free smoothie, but I am not most people.)

Mostly, contests and sweepstakes can be an excellent way to not only build your fan base and spread the word about your product or service — but also add some nice profits to your P&L sheet.

But it helps to know the difference between a contest and a sweepstakes, and what you have to do with each of them, to comply with Facebook's terms of service.

So, here's the scoop on Sweepstakes:

- **What They Are?** Chance-based promotions or random drawings usually hosted on a Facebook tab or on a 3rd-party solution. (More on that later.)
- **Do They Work?** Oh yeah. Especially if the prize is cool.
- **How to Set Up?** Easy to set up. Especially with a third-party sweepstakes app from a company such as WishPond, just fill in the fields and publish on a Facebook custom app. (WishPond has a 15-day free trial. Plenty of time to give your contest a try.)
- **What info do you collect?** Entrants often fill out a single form, usually involving the submission of their name and email (and often location and a phone number for future text marketing).
- **Who to target?** The barrier to entry for a sweepstakes should be quite low, which leads to a bigger pool of entrants. (Be aware, some people will enter more than once. Just the way it is.)

- **What Should the Prize Be?** Anything that is relevant to your fanbase. And cool!

Best Practices:

- Keep the entry form simple and to the point.
- Have good pictures of the prize on your landing page.
- Choose a sweepstakes app that has mobile capabilities. (Sweepstakes spread super quickly through mobile devices.)
- Keep the sweepstakes to about 5-7 days in length. (Longer than that and people will forget.)

Contests require a little more effort on the part of your fans, which can be good or bad.

Here's the skinny on Facebook Contests:

- **What They Are?** Contests are promotions where entrants must perform a specific action (such as upload a photo, write a caption, shoot a video, make a comment, dash off a quick essay.) to win a specified prize.
- **Do They Work?** Exceptionally well. When people go to the trouble of creating "something" for a contest, they often share it with all of their friends. (This stuff can spread REALLY fast.)
- **How to Set Up?** Just like a Facebook sweepstakes, you'll want to set up through a third-party app, such as WishPond. Let them handle the technical and legal crap that goes with setting up a contest.
- **What Should I Ask People to Do to Enter?** Well, there are tons of different ways to go here. You could ask people to: like your page, comment on a post, leave a photo caption, write a fill-in-the-blank, answer a Q&A…even crowdsource something. (Such as your new creative design or product idea.)
- **What Info Do You Collect?** Same as the sweepstakes. Name and email, at a minimum, and then location and phone number if you have a plan to use it. (Don't ask for more than that.)

- **Who to Target?** Whomever you think will act and enter the contest. Will retirees in Phoenix upload their Instagram photos from their latest Friday night? Probably not. But goth teenagers might.
- **What Should the Prize Be?** Not only relevant, but something commensurate with the effort required for the contest. If you're asking people to write an essay, you need to offer them more than a Slurpee coupon.

Best Practices:

- Make sure to create ads around your contests. (I love video ads for these. Helps you get your message out there — and get new entrants.)
- Make the entry form SUPER CLEAR about what's needed to win. (Unclear contest guidelines can lead to huge headaches.)
- Like sweepstakes, make sure the app you use is mobile-friendly.
- All things being equal, go for photos over videos and captions over essays. (Make it easy, and more people will enter.)
- Create a separate email list for these entrants and create follow-up emails welcoming them to your tribe. Go easy on the soft sell. Wait till you've established a relationship.
- Keep the sweepstakes to about 5-7 days. (Longer than that and people will forget.)

FACEBOOK PROMOTION AWESOMENESS PILLAR NO. 2: OFFERS

I hate to break it to ya...but 57% of all Facebook users like a brand or company for the "discounts and offers" they receive.

That means your fans are selfish. They don't love your brand, they love a great deal.

Which is why Facebook offers are so frickin' awesome. Here's how they work: (And yes! They still work!)

1. **Create an offer.** You can either do this straight from your page or from your Ads Manager.
2. **Promote your offer.** You can use many of the ad types we mentioned in the previous chapters. (I especially like the Promoted Posts, Video Ads, and retargeting ads.)
3. **Sit back and collect your money** as people redeem your offer.

One quick downside to Facebook offers is that you must have 400 fans for your page before you can start using them. (Or at least as of the writing of this book.) Otherwise these things totally rock.

So, what's so great about Facebook offers?

Well…

- You can choose whether people redeem them online or print them out and redeem them in person. (Ideal for online and local businesses alike.)
- The offer is tied to the email address that the user has connected to Facebook with. (This means they'll get it and use it!) And it won't be some spam filter email address.
- You can set a time limit for the offer.
- You can set up a quantity limit for the offer.
- If you promote with a page post ad, you can do some seriously cool location targeting. (This is awesome for local businesses.)
- The offer can show up in the newsfeed for maximum visibility.
- Promoting your offer can be surprisingly cheap. (Especially with all them different ad options we mentioned earlier.)

What kinds of stuff can you promote with a Facebook offer? Obviously, coupons and discounts work well.

But so do webinars, online trainings, video courses…pretty much anything where there is something of high perceived value being offered at some kind of special price.

Here are a couple of tips when crafting your Facebook offer to get the most bang for your buck:

- **Get to the point in your copy.** You've only got 90 characters so no futzing around talking about the features. Get right to the deal and what people can expect to get from the deal. Example: "Click to receive 2-for-1 Pizza deal at New York Joe's."
- **Tell people to act.** "Click here," "Click now," "Download now," "Grab yours now..." Don't be shy. Tell 'em what to do.
- **Set up an initial budget of about $30-$40 to get started.** This will get you a ton of exposure if your targeting is halfway decent.
- **Always opt for dollars saved, over percentage off.** Which sounds better: "50% off all blazers at Macy's," or "Save $20 on a Macy's blazer today"? Specific always beats vague.

Facebook Promotion Awesomeness Pillar No. 3: Facebook Live!

So, why would we want to use Facebook Live? I mean, don't we want to just use YouTube for our video.

Well, first off, Facebook and YouTube are in a death struggle together to carve out video share. And that Facebook Live is…well… live means you could use it to stream video of your:

- Live events
- Product launches
- Behind-the-scenes looks at your business (Such a meet-the-team video)
- Weekly (or daily) how-to tip
- Webinars or seminars
- Coaching programs
- Q&As (I think these could be powerful)
- Breaking news

There's a reason Facebook is paying content partners like the New York Times to create content specifically for Facebook Live. (And those guys in Silicon Valley pay for anything they don't have to.)

They want to create unique, live content that is exclusive to their platform. (And I believe they will go to great lengths to promote it.)

So, if you're already doing a weekly blog — or monthly article/ column — I would encourage you to focus all that energy on frequent Facebook Live offering.

Not only will it help establish you as an authority to your existing tribe and future customers, but I suspect that Facebook will give you some same promotional push they give to media stalwarts like The New York Times.

Which, if nothing else, is an awesome trivia question you can share at parties: "Guess what me and The New York Times have in common?"

PUNK ROCK MARKETING
AMPLIFY YOUR MESSAGE

CHAPTER 2 Key Takeaways:

- **Set up a sweepstakes or contest using a 3rd-party app, such as WishPond, to give away a cool prize** relevant to your business, and don't forget to make it mobile compatible.
- **Good ideas for contests include** having folks like your page, make a comment on a post, answer a Q&A, leave a photo caption…or anything cool that you can think of.
- **Yes, offers still work!** Especially if you've got one that sounds irresistible. Just create an offer and promote it through Facebook ads. Have your copy get to the point and don't forget "dollars off" usually sounds better than "% off."
- **Facebook Live is awesome for broadcasting your live events, Q&As and weekly how-to content** — anything that lets you talk to the peeps in real-time. (Maybe even…like..sell something.)

EPILOGUE:
If You Don't Like the Weather…

You could spend months, if not years, trying to become a Facebook expert.

Don't.

It's just not worth it.

The (somewhat) Draconian rules and regulations that Facebook forces upon its ~~victims~~ advertisers can be changed at any moment. (Without any warning.)

And that Fan Page community you've spent years cultivating can suddenly disappear because Facebook changed its quantum affinity algorithm flux capacitor and you're left out in the Status Update cold.

And, though I have done my best to brain dump all the little ninja Facebook tricks and tactics I've learned the hard way (and at quite an expense)… minutes after I finish typing this epilogue, some of the things in here may already be obsolete.

Just remember that as many new little tools and tweaks and "you gotta have this one thing" service Facebook offers…

…the principles will never change.

Facebook is that kid's tree house in the backyard.

It's a place where people like to meet up with their friends, catch up on gossip…even get into a couple of arguments.

But it's their place. Their zone. Their home away from the parents.

And it's your job as a Facebook marketer to build that tree house.

To fill it with comic books and Barbie dolls and baseball cards and an EZ Bake Oven and let the kids just ramble on and have a great time and feel important and feel like this is the safest place in the world.

So, when you have a product or service you think they'd like, or would enjoy, or could possibly improve/change their lives…

They'll pounce on it. Because they trust the tree house. (And the person who built it.)

And though I'm straining metaphors here, I truly believe that (whether I like it or not) the only marketing that will survive in the competitive years ahead will be marketing that doesn't feel like marketing.

Selling that doesn't even remotely feel like selling.

Web properties that feel like tree houses.

Here's hoping this book provided a nail or two to help you build some tree houses for your business.

Pinterest MARKETING IN 2019 MADE (STUPIDLY) EASY

Vol.4
of the Small Business
Marketing
COLLECTION

Michael Clarke

Pinterest Marketing in 2019 Made (Stupidly) Easy

Vol.4 of the "Small Business Marketing Made (Stupidly) Easy" Collection

PROLOGUE:
How I Stopped Hating Pinterest (and Started Making Money)

I used to think Pinterest was the Lady Gaga of social networks. (Without the dress shaped like an egg.)

That even though Pinterest was hip and popular and visually engaging and was giving us a glimpse of what users would want to consume in the **future...**

It was also something that wasn't designed for ME. (I don't sell Prada purses or kitchen cabinet installations.)

But then the strangest thing in the world happened - I made MONEY with Pinterest.

Real money. (With little effort.)

That's because:

- Pinterest users GLADLY share advertorial images of products and services (with the price tag attached!)
- Pinterest delivers more referring website traffic than LinkedIn, YouTube and Tumblr COMBINED...
- Pinterest users BUY more often than users of other social networks. (And when they buy, they spend a hell of a lot more money than Facebookers and Twitterers combined.)

And though I was resistant at first - like being dragged to "Bath and Body Works" by my wife - I swallowed my pride, and my inherent distrust of yoga photos, and jumped into the swirling vortex of Pinterest.

And, I made EVERY mistake a Pinterest marketer can make. (Most of which I will help you try to avoid.)

But, gradually, I started to NOT suck so badly. And what I found was a-stounding. Pinterest didn't just boost my traffic. It:

- Increased my sales
- Boosted my email subscriber counts
- Reduced product return rates
- Cut down on customer support costs
- Put me in contact with affiliates and JV partners
- Created more leads (and more customers) than Facebook and Twitter

And that's when it occurred to me: Pinterest's appeal isn't just pretty photos accumulated in a virtual scrapbook.

Pinterest allows people to ORGANIZE their world.

To put their life experience into themed boards that shows their friends — and the rest of the Pinterest universe — who they REALLY are. (Or perhaps who they'd desperately like to be.)

Unlike a Facebook page, which can have a multitude of voices and rants and complaints (all without any context to one other)...

...or a Twitter feed, which is like drinking from a 140-character social media fire hose...

...or YouTube which is like visiting the cantina from Star Wars. (Who knows what you'll find in there?)

A *Pinterest board*, such as the popular Nordstrom "Shoe Lust" board with its 156K followers, is about as simple as it gets.

It's about pictures of pretty shoes. That's it.

It's not about users or profiles or friends or retweets or likes or RSS feeds or blog posts or anything that feels like homework...

...it's about a single place where people share pictures of a SPECIFIC thing, such as triathlon exercises, DIY bathroom ideas, Indian curry recipes...whatever.

And having something in our lives that simple, focused, fun, and ultra-visual (meaning we can consume it in a matter of a few seconds) provides real benefit to people living in a smartphone-infused world.

And if we as marketers can tell a simple STORY about our products and services, that connects to people on a primal, emotional level…

Then not only will we **sell more stuff,** but we'll be helping our customers connect to that magical, inspirational, kick-ass part of themselves.

And doing that can impact your business, and the world, in ways you can't imagine.

Still skeptical?

Think I'm full of Pinterest bull crap? That's okay.

I would have thought I was full of it too. (Nothing changes one's mind like adding commas to a bank balance.)

So…let's enroll in the department of Pinterest studies and go make you some moo-lah!

Chapter 1:

Pinterest Made Super Simple

"The best way to predict the future is to create it."

-Peter Drucker

Before we jump into the deep end of the Pinterest pool, I want to make sure we're all on the same page. (Nothing more confusing in this world than a social network and all its oddly named components.)

So, if you feel you got a good handle on what Pinterest is, but you just want to start crushing it from a marketing side, then jump over to Chapter 2.

But if you're relatively new to Pinterest, and don't know your pinboard from your repin, then up your Pinterest IQ with these answers to these Pinterest FAQs:

Pinterst FAQ No.1: How the Hell Do I Make Money With Pinterest?

How do we turn all these pins and repins and likes and pinboards into hard currency?

Most social networks FROWN on overt selling. (Just see how many times you link out to your sales pages on Facebook before you incur a "fan" revolt.)

But Pinterest is different. For one thing, the entire Pinterest ecosystem is based on people pinning pictures of:

- Stuff They Want
- Stuff That Represents Their Style
- Stuff That Inspires Them

Market your stuff in a way that touches on one, if not all of those, and you have something that doesn't "feel" like marketing.

Best of all, Pinterest users ARE buyers. They want to spend money on cool stuff.

And studies show they spend a ton more than any other social network user. (Nearly double what Facebook and Twitter users spend, combined.)

And if your cool stuff is aligned with their themed pinboards, and the boards of their friends, then you will find a new source of leads who not only share your content and follow your company…but they also **buy your stuff**.

The important thing is you GOTTA tell a story with your product or service. You know, besides, "We sell stuff so we can make money."

Come up with a compelling WHY for your company — "We're an organic diaper company who believes in a no-chemical childhood…" "We're a group of accountants who wear blue jeans and motorcycle jackets to work…" — and you're 75% of the way there with your Pinterest marketing.

Pinterest FAQ No. 2: Yeah, But What If I Don't Sell to Women?

There's no getting around this: 65% of all Pinterest users are women.

But maybe that's not a bad thing.

According to She-Conomy, women represent nearly two-thirds of all consumer spending. (That means whether your product or service is for men OR women, chances are women will end up buying it at some point.)

Now, if you're selling a product or service that absolutely no woman would ever want to look at (or even imagine thinking about it) — such as a seduction dating information product or a Hooter's video series — then think seriously before plunging forward with your Pinterest marketing strategy.

This doesn't mean, though, you can't sell products *designed for men*.

As any advertising expert will tell you: Old Spice's ingenious "The Man Your Man Could Smell Like" campaigns were NOT intended for men. They were designed for my wife. Guess what I'm using for deodorant now.

Pinterest FAQ No.3: What's a Pin?

A pin is simply an image or video that users add to their Pinterest profile. Somewhat like the Pinterest version of the "tweet" or the Facebook "status update."

That's it. Don't over-think it.

Pinterest FAQ No.4: How Do I Pin?

There are four different ways to pin something:

- Clicking the "Pin It" button on a website page.
- Clicking on your Pinterest bookmarklet in your browser.
- Adding the website URL in the "Add From a Website" field of your Pinterest dashboard.
- Upload an image or video directly to Pinterest.

All pins link back to their original source. (No matter how many times they are shared.)

Pinterest FAQ No.5: What Do I Put Into My Pin?

We're going to cover this in some detail in Chapter 5, but for now just know that when you "pin" something there are three things to consider:

- What specific image or video on a web page the pin will feature.
- What specific pinboard the pin is associated to.
- What's in the text description of the pin. Example: Caption, links, calls-to-action, etc.

Again, this is vital marketer real estate. In Chapter 5, we'll go over the whats and hows of the perfect pin to help you reach your marketing goals.

PINTEREST FAQ NO.6: OKAY, SO WHAT'S A PINBOARD?

Pinboards, or boards, are themed collections of pins. They're kind of like mini-Facebook pages, but without all the Mafia Wars invites.

The whole concept of the pinboard can be confusing the first time out. Just know:

- Each pin is associated to a specific pinboard
- You can create as many pinboards as you want
- Followers of yours can follow either your entire profile, which means they get updated on everything you do, or they can follow specific, individual boards.

PINTEREST FAQ NO.7: WHAT SHOULD I CREATE PINBOARDS ABOUT?

Almost anything you want!

As long as you don't go with what Pinterest gives you out of the box. As a Pinterset user, you are given a few default boards upon signing up. They are called "My Styles" and "Places and Spaces."

These need to be changed immediately. These are horrible names for anything, let alone a Pinterest board.

You can organize a board around almost anything:

- A theme
- An event
- A special promotion
- A product or service
- Your customers (or a segment of your customers)
- Testimonials

- Quotes
- A special private board that only invited users can contribute to
- ...anything!

And in Chapter 4, I go into a ton more detail on the best practices for creating boards.

Pinterest FAQ No.8: Is a Repin the Same Thing as a Pin

Repins are like retweets. **Sorta.**

Like retweets, a Pinterest user finds an interesting pin they think is cool. They then repin it to one of their "boards." The original pinner still retains credit for the pin, no matter how many times it is repinned.

Nearly 80% of all the activity on Pinterest is *repins*. They are an important part of your Pinterest strategy, but to separate yourself from the Pinterest pack you'll need to do more pinning than repinning.

Pinterest FAQ No.9: What's a Like? Is it Like a "Facebook Like"?

Yeah, kinda.

When you "like" a specific pin, it is added to your profile's collection of "likes." (I suppose for those folks who feel that the four seconds it takes to "repin" something is far more than they're willing to spend.)

"Likes" are not added to a user's particular pinboard, but are instead added to a user's "likes" page. (This is more of a social vote, than a traffic-getting strategy.)

To "like" a pin, simply hover over the pin and "click" on the HEART icon.

Pinterest FAQ No.10: How Do I Make Sure I Don't Waste My Time With Pinterest?

Well, you're reading this book, aren't ya? :)

Seriously, here's a minimum-effort strategy I'd like you to think about before crashing the Pinterest party.

Can you or somebody on your team commit to:

- Pinning 5-20 pins a day? Remember each of these take about three seconds. (That's almost a full minute's work.)
- Following 25-50 other Pinterest users per day?
- Creating 10-20 boards for different themes and topics relates to your business? (Just need these to get up and running.)
- Throwing an occasional contest to boost your fan base and increase your amount of leads?
- Adding pretty pictures to the web content you produce?

If you can do that, and it seriously shouldn't take you more than 10 minutes a day, you will be light years ahead of 92% of the businesses out there on Pinterest. (And you'll be making a hell of a lot more money than them too.)

Chapter 2:

4 Steps to a Kick-Ass Pinterest Profile

"If you have nothing to create at all, then perhaps you create yourself."

-C.G. Jung

Before we jump into the creation of your fabulous Pinterest boards and grow your Pinterest follower base (and make some serious money from our new Pinterest efforts) we need to create one seriously kick-ass Pinterest profile.

Because a Pinterest account isn't just where your pins and pinboards live, it's also a huge source of referral website traffic. (And that traffic is especially effective when sent to opt-in pages and sales pages.)

And don't forget your Pinterest profile provides a serious SEO boost to whatever external location it links to. (Way bigger than your Facebook or Twitter profiles ever will.)

So here are my FOUR Kick-Ass Steps to Creating an Awesome Pinterest Profile to get you primed for domination:

Kick-Ass Pinterest Profile Step No.1: Create a Business Account

Just like with the Facebook universe, there are two kinds of profiles for Pinterest: personal and business.

We want the business.

Not just for the obvious reason — that we are, in fact, doing business-y things. But there are basic, though important, reasons for having a business account:

- Promoting your wares on a personal account violates Pinterest's terms of service. (And could get your account banned.)
- You can designate your business name as the profile name for a business account. Sounds obvious, but this is not something you can do with a personal account, in which you have to have a regular (first name, surname) naming structure.
- As of the writing of this book, Pinterest will plans to add some new features for business accounts down the line. (My guess? Cool analytics and more creative profile display options. But then again…I thought Cyndi Lauper would be a way bigger success than Madonna. So what'dya I know?)

So how do you set up your business account? Here's how:

- **Go to the dedicated Pinterest business page**. You can find it at: http://business.pinterest.com.
- **Click "Join as a Business."**
- **Fill out the key info**. Make sure your company name hasn't already been taken by somebody else. (It happens.)
- **Add a keyword in the username if you can**. It's not required: but the username carries a HUGE SEO boost to your profile. (Meaning your Pinterest boards could eventually show up in Google rankings for important keywords.)
- **Verify your website.** Huh? Verify your website? What the heck does that mean? Well, funny you should ask, because…

Kick-Ass Pinterest Profile Step No.2: Verify Your Website

You'd think this would be easy. You'd be wrong.

Pinterest requires all business accounts be "verified" by having the user place code on their website or blog. (Check Out

Yeah! Code! Sounds fun, doesn't it?

You can do this two different ways:

1. By uploading an HTML file (generated by Pinterest) to your website's server
2. By adding a meta tag (generated by Pinterest) to your website's home page

If what I said sounds like I'm speaking Klingon, then I'd like to make recommendation: Head over to a site like Fiverr.com and pay the five bucks to have somebody do it for you. For somebody who knows what they're doing, it'll take five minutes. For us technically challenged schlubs…who knows?

If you know your way around FTP and the back-end of your blog, head over to http://punkrockmarketing.com/pinterestverify. There, I've got some detailed instructions on how to do it.

Again, if you're not sure, hire a professional. (Or that precocious 12-year-old cousin of yours who seems to know everything.)

Kick-Ass Pinterest Profile Step No.3: Create an "About Me" Section That Doesn't Suck

This is where a lot of Pinterest marketers totally screw up.

The "about me" section of your Pinterest profile is valuable real estate. And shouldn't be wasted on some rambling pointless dissertation of what kind of DIY bathroom project you're into or your favorite flavor of homemade incense.

In the "About Me" section you can:

- **Talk about the benefits of your company's products or services.** Remember: People care about benefits, not features.
- **Add in appropriate keywords.** If you're not sure which keywords are the best, head over to http://punkrockmarketing.com/keywordtoo l. I've got a step-by-step process on a FREE resource to help you out.
- **If you're a local business, USE geo-targeted keywords.** Not abbreviations; good, old spelled-out cities.

- **Put in your email.** Unless you don't want people to email you, which you might not.
- **Link to a landing page other than your home page.** Such as a place to collect email addresses. (You are collecting email addresses, aren't you?)

Kick-Ass Pinterest Profile Step No.4: One Killer Profile Image to Rule Them All

Ya wouldn't think this would make a difference. You'd be wrong.

Pinterest is all about pictures and nowhere is that more evident than with your Pinterest profile image.

Here's what you need to know about profile images:

1. **The image should be square.** Pinterest recommends an upload size of 600 pixels by 600 pixels to allow for the highest amount of resolution. (And if that's what they recommend, that's probably what we should do.)
2. **The image should focus on one subject.** The picture will be resized to 165 pixels by 165 pixels and group shots can look muddled at that size. (So can vague, indeterminate nature shots.)
3. **People shots are best if they're crisp.** No blurry, fuzzy iPhone shots you took in the dark holding a margarita…err…I mean a library book.
4. **The image should evoke a "feeling" that relates somehow to your company.** This can be loosely defined, but go for whatever positive feeling you'd like associated with your product and website. (Whether it's a rainbow, or your CEO. Or your CEO standing in front of a rainbow!)
5. **Avoid logos, unless they're awesome.** I don't like logos used as profile images. (Think they appear too artificial.) But if you got a killer one, then use it.
6. **The name of the image should contain your company name.** Not "IMG_1" or "Pinterest_Logo," but instead "ABC-Accounting" or "Joe's-Pool-Cleaning." This will give your Pinterest account some extra SEO juice.

CHAPTER 2 Key Takeaways:

- **Create a Pinterest business account.** (It'll make your life much easier.)
- **Verify your website.** If you're tech-y, you can upload an HTML file or meta tag to your website. If not, hire somebody to do it for you.
- **Fill up the "about me" section of your profile with goodies.** Add keywords, links and benefits of your business in this valuable part of your profile.
- **Find a great profile image** that is: 600 x 600 pixels, features one subject, shows people (or a great logo) and has your company name in the file name.

Chapter 3:

7 Tools Every Pinterest Marketer Must Have

"If all you have is a hammer in the toolbox, everything looks like a nail."

-Bernard Baruch

Okay, here's where we separate from the pack.

Here's where we stand out from the rest of the Pinterest hobbyists and flex some serious Pinterest marketing muscle.

Most of the tools I advocate below are 100% FREE. (And my favorite tool of all costs less than a couple of bucks a month.)

But no joke...adding these tools to your Pinterest marketing arsenal will make it SO MUCH EASIER to attract new leads and find those elusive, paying customers.

So, here are my SEVEN Must-Have Pinterest Tools to get you ready for maximum Pinterest marketing supremacy:

Must-Have Pinterest Tool No.1: A Camera That Doesn't Royally Suck

Nothing sells a product on Pinterest like a kick-ass photo. And chances are you already have a decent well-stocked camera sitting in your pocket.

That's right. Your smartphone!

Most smartphones made in the last couple of years pack plenty of camera-taking punch to suit your needs. (If you know how to use it right.)

Here are a few quicks tips when taking photos with your smartphone:

- **Turn the phone sideways.** This gives you more photo-editing area to work with later. Nothing screams "amateur" like a vertical smartphone photo.
- **Tap on the screen to indicate the subject of the picture before hitting "click."** This lets the phone do all kinds of auto-focus and stabilization stuff that'll make your photo sing.
- **Lean against a wall or some kind of flat surface.** This avoids needless movement which can affect crispness and photo clarity.

And what do ya do if you don't have a smartphone?

Well, for just a couple hundred dollars you could buy something from the very under-rated and high-performing Canon PowerShot series.

You could spend a lot more on a Digital SLR camera. But if that's the case, you don't need my camera-buying tips.

No matter what your camera of choice, here are a couple of general tips when shooting people or products:

- **Shoot outside if you can.** Natural light is always better than artificial light.
- **Late mornings** (8:30 a.m. - 10:00 a.m.) and **late afternoons** (4:00 p.m. - 6:00 p.m.) are "magic" times to shoot photos because the lighting is warm. Noontime is the worst, it makes people look like vampires.
- **"Don't look into the light!"** Always try to shoot with the sun to your back.
- **Keep the light even**. If shooting inside, try to keep the light source behind you consistent on all sides. (You can buy desk lamps and clip them behind you, if needed.)

Must-Have Pinterest Tool No. 2: Free (and Legal) Sources for Photos

Not all the images you share on Pinterest are gonna be ones that came from your camera. (Nobody wants to look at your product pics all day. Secondly, you gotta a frickin' business to run.)

That's why it's crucial to find sources for FREE (and legal) photos you can use under the Creative Commons license.

Note: Creative Commons has a wide variety of rights distinctions. It's worth learning about. Just head over to: http://en.wikipedia.org/wiki/Creative_Commons to get more information about it.

The LEGAL part of "Legal and Free" is important. You don't want to just grab pics from Google Images. It's wrong, and could get you thrown into a Bulgarian work camp.

Here are some of my favorite places to grab open-source photos: (Note: Be sure to check the copyright on all images before using)

- Flickr (http://flickr.com)
- Morgue File (http://morguefile.com)
- PixaBay (https://pixabay.com/)

And when you're on the look-out for photos remember:

- **You gotta GRAB people.** You want crisp, sharp photos...that stand out! Better to be shocking than boring.
- **Forget pretty, go with real.** Stock photos of supermodels doing "ordinary" things look staged and really DUMB.
- **Go with your gut.** Find photos that evoke a "feeling," don't just look for photos that make literal sense.

MUST-HAVE PINTEREST TOOL NO.3: PICMONKEY

The cool thing about photo-editing tools, such as the supremely awesome **PicMonkey**, is it makes you look like a much better photographer than you actually are. (As a very mediocre photographer myself, this is a great asset.)

Now, you don't HAVE to use PicMonkey. You could use FREE tools such as Gimp, or expensive tools like Photoshop.

But PicMonkey is my secret Pinterest marketing weapon because it's:

- Cheap — they have a FREE option and a very reasonable paid option.

- Easy to Use
- Powerful — lets you correct lighting issues and offers a TON of out-of-the-box effects perfect for making your photos POP.
- Made for non-techie folks (like me).
- Lets you add a company watermark to your images

But I think the BIGGEST benefit PicMonkey gives you is the ability to add a text overlay to your photos.

This is HUGE. With a text overlay you can:

- Add quotes to images. Wanna create a viral meme? Just put a quote over a pretty picture.
- Ask people to visit your website.
- Ask people to "pin" a photo.
- Suggest people sign up for your email list to get that FREE THING you're giving away.

And the crazy thing is: just asking people to "pin" your photo increases engagement by 80%.

I know. It shouldn't be that easy. Telling people you want them to do something…then having them do it.

But it can be! And PicMonkey is in, my never humble opinion, the best friend a Pinterest marketer can have.

MUST-HAVE PINTEREST TOOL NO.4: PICTURES (AND LOTS OF 'EM) ON YOUR WEBSITE

This one isn't so much a tool as it is a best practice.

If you aren't already adding a picture to every piece of content you publish on your site — whether it be a blog post, essay, FAQ, About page, deranged manifesto about the government, etc. — then you are missing out on a huge source of Pinterest traffic.

We've touched briefly on what KIND of photos to look for. (Crisp, interesting, no supermodels using laundry detergent.) But here's what you need to know before uploading actual photos to your site:

- **"Name" the photo with a keyword**. For instance, if the blog post is about "How to Make Decorative Candles," then a great picture name would be: "Decorative_Candles," not "Photo1."
- **Get in fast**. Try to get the photo in the first couple paragraphs of your blog post or webpage.
- **Caption this!** If you have room for a caption, be sure to include a keyword there.

Must-Have Pinterest Tool No.5: Pinterest Buttons...Everywhere!

Pinterest buttons let you leverage the existing website and blog traffic you are already getting to your site and encourages those visitors to pin your existing content. (Now you know WHY it's so important to make sure all your groovy content is adorned with killer images.)

Creating the button is simple; it's just a matter of generating code you throw onto your site.

To do this, head over to http://punkrockmarketing.com/pinterestbutton to generate the code. You'll find a couple of design and text options. Nothing super fancy here, but it'll get the job done.

There are two important types of buttons to focus on:

a. **The Pin It Button:** This lets folks pin a photo located on a specific web page to the pin board of their choosing.
b. **The "Follow" Button:** This lets people "follow" you on Pinterest.

So where do we put these buttons?

Here's how I use them:

"PIN IT" BUTTON

- In the body of a blog postThe sidebar of a website
- The header of a website
- The footer of every blog post
- Next to every video

"FOLLOW ON PINTEREST" BUTTON

- The "Thank You for Subscribing" page
- The checkout page
- The email signature
- The message board profile signatures
- The website footer

And if that sound super complicated - or something reserved for people with a Ph.D. in Internet engineering - then just hire your designer or local unemployed fifteen-year-old to help you out.

MUST-HAVE PINTEREST TOOL NO.6: GET A PINTEREST BOOKMARKLET

I know. I hate the term bookmarklet too. (Offends my English-Major sensibilities.) But they're huge Pinterest time-savers.

Basically a "bookmarklet" is an extension you install on your web browser of choice that lets you "pin" things to your Pinterest profile with the simple click of a button. (Told ya Pinterest takes way less time than other social networks.)

To set up the bookmarklet, just head over to http://about.pinterest.com/goodies/ and you can grab the bookmarklet thing-y. (You can even get the Pinterest smartphone app there.)

MUST-HAVE PINTEREST TOOL NO.7: PUT A BOARD WIDGET ON YOUR WEBSITE

Before you say: "What the hell is a board widget? And why should I care?..."

...a board widget is a piece of code you throw onto your website that shows your website visitors the latest pins from your Pinterest account.

Another good reason to separate personal from business with your Pinterest activities.

Now, in the early days of your Pinterest career, this widget will look a little skimpy. But before you know it, you'll have a robust Pinterest offering.

And what better way to show off your Pinterest efforts and "spice" up your website, visually, than adding a little board widget action?

To generate the code, just head over to that same location I mentioned earlier (http://punkrockmarketing.com/pinteresttbutton) to get your board widget created and your website looking somewhat less sucky.

PUNK ROCK MARKETING AMPLIFY YOUR MESSAGE

CHAPTER 3 Key Takeaways:

- **Make sure you have a halfway decent camera.** You don't need a full-on DSLR, your smartphone will most likely work.
- **Shoot outside, if possible.** And always keep the camera steady, with the light to your back.
- **Find free photos, legally.** Great places to find free (legal) photos are PixaBay, MorgueFile and Flickr. (Be sure to check on the rights of every photo you use.)
- **Get awesome photos with PicMonkey.** Be sure to add text overlays that encourage folks to "pin" your photos.
- **Go photo crazy.** Include a crisp, interesting photo with every piece of content you publish on your site.
- **Add Pinterest buttons — both "Pin It" buttons and "Follow Me" buttons — everywhere on your site.** That includes headers, footers, sidebars, thank you pages and in the body of all your content.
- **Grab the Pinterest bookmarklet** to save you a bunch of time.
- **Place a board widget on your site**, especially if your site needs sprucing up.

Chapter 4:

The Marvelous & Fantastic World of PinBoards

"Great works are performed not by strength but by perseverance."

-Samuel Johnson

This chapter will blow your mind.

Seriously, when you discover some of the cool, awesome things you can do with Pinboards you might just need hospitalization from your instant Pinterest awesomeness.

While it's true most casual users experience Pinterest through the pins they use to tag whatever catches their eye…it's really the BOARDS where we find our biggest marketing potential.

Because Pinboards are like little silos of super-focused, ultra-targeted awesomeness that let users check out our products, share our content and eventually buy our stuff.

Earlier I said, unlike its social-media cohort Facebook, a Pinterest user does not follow EVERY single thing you do on Pinterest.

That means users can just "follow" and check out the things they want.

Example: A user can "follow" a Nordstrom board dedicated to Prada shoes, without having to follow the "Coach handbag" board, which they may or may not have any interest in.

And it means you can meet your prospective customers in a huge variety of ways. (And sell them a huge variety of products and services.)

So, now you've got the 411 of how Pinterest boards work, let's show you how to plan, create and fill those boards with awesome money-making content.

And we'll do that with my THREE Step Blueprint to a Kick-Ass Pinterest Board:

Kick-Ass Blueprint Step No.1: Realize What's Possible

I used to think Pinterest boards were just a place to house all my product photos and affiliate crap.

Boy, was I wrong.

There is (virtually) no limit to the things you can do with Pinterest boards. There are a couple of obvious ones:

- Create a board for each different product or service you offer in your business.
- Create a board where customers can give you feedback on your products.
- Create a board where customers can find out about any big company news or future product launches.
- And that's all nice. But it doesn't EVEN scratch the surface. Because you can do things like create:
- A testimonial board for your products where followers and customers can leave comments.
- A board highlighting members of your company. (People LOVE these.)
- A board showing behind-the-scenes stuff about your company. Videos work great here.
- A board promoting and recapping a live event.
- A board that offers how-to advice on a specific topic. (Lowe's does a great job of this with their DIY boards.)
- A board that offers supplemental training. (This can work great for info-product creators and those in the educational space.)

- A board that spotlights some of your top clients or customers. (You can imagine some of the goodwill this might create.)
- A board specifically for affiliates.
- A board for virtually any special offer, coupon, contest, promotion, or product you've got in the works.

The possibilities are endless. If you've got rich media (photos, video, audio) that can be themed and organized…then putting them into a board is a no-brainer idea.

Kick-Ass Blueprint Step No.2: Come Up With a Board Plan

Now you've got some idea of what you COULD create, it's time to figure out what you SHOULD make.

Not all the boards I mentioned earlier will apply to your business. And that's okay.

What you want to do is be daring. Come up with interesting, creative ways you can show off your company and its offerings.

Here are a couple of questions to get you started:

- How many **products and services** does my business have?
- Do we have **happy customers/clients** we'd like to spotlight?
- Are there certain **areas of expertise** where we could be a resource to potential customers?
- What would be the best way to **break up these areas of expertise** into separate boards? (Again, Lowe's does this really well: breaking up the DIY boards by project.)
- Do we have upcoming **events** that would make for cool boards? (If so, make damn sure SOMEBODY takes a lot of photos and video.)
- Do we have any **future product launches** or new services that could use a board?
- What would be a cool, interesting way to **feature our team**? (Videos? Blog posts? Pictures of our employees' pets?)

Try to shoot for at least 10 or so boards that could house at least 25-50 pins apiece. This will be enough to get you started and help your Pinterest account look thriving and robust.

Kick-Ass Blueprint Step No.3: Create Your Boards (and Give 'Em Non-Sucky Names)

Okay, so now you got a plan! It's time to dig in and create your boards.

The HOW is pretty simple. You just:

- Click the Add+ button in the upper right-hand corner of your Pinterest home page.
- Select the "Create a Board" option.
- Enter the name, category, and (any) contributors to the board... then click "Create Board."

But there's a couple important things to keep in mind when creating your boards:

- **Try to get a keyword in if you can**. Your SEO ranking will thank you for it.
- **Put a twist at the end** to give your board name personality. Instead of "Marketing Tips," you could do: a) "Marketing Tips From Andy" or "Marketing Tips From the Lab" or the very simple "Marketing Tips That Don't Suck."
- **You CAN change the name of your board later.** BUT changing the name changes the URL. So if you have links to that board, it may break those links.
- **Don't stress the "category" choice** too much. Pinterest doesn't give you a lot of options. And most of the ones they give you are boring.
- **Add contributors**, if relevant. Pinterest boards can create some cool micro-communities. So if it's part of the board plan, specify here who can contribute to your board.

CHAPTER 4 KEY TAKEAWAYS:

- **There are TONS of different ways you can theme and organize your Pinterest boards.** My personal favorites include: 1) Highlighting customers 2) Collecting testimonials 3) Employee spotlights 4) How-to resources 5) Affiliate boards and 6) Future product launches.
- **Brainstorm different boards that might work for your business.** Anything that tells a "story" with pictures and video would work.
- **Be sure to include keywords in your board names.** And add "spice" at the end to stand out from the pack.

Chapter 5:

6 Keys to Creating the Perfect Pin

"Bite off more than you can chew, then chew it."

-Courage Wolf

Ah, yes. Pins.

The raw currency that makes the Pinterest economy go.

Pins aren't like Facebook status updates and tweets. For one thing they last forever. As opposed to tweets and Facebook updates, which seem to have the half-life of a nanosecond.

And pins aren't a "vote" for something a user likes. Such as a Facebook "like" or "retweet."

When somebody "pins" a photo, they decide which "board" that "pin" will live in. And that "pin" becomes a part of their board ecosystem, not just something to fill their newsfeed.

So, offering compelling and interesting content that people will "pin" and "repin" is our primary job as Pinterest marketing gurus.

And filling our boards with pin-worthy goodies is an important first step to attracting followers and building up our Pinterest street cred.

So, that's what we will do.

In this chapter I will show you my SIX Keys to the Perfect Pin. But first let's go over the mechanics. How do we actually "pin" and "repin" stuff the RIGHT way?

How Pinning Works

1. **You decide on something to pin.** Either through uploading a photo or video, using your bookmarklet browser extension, clicking on a web location's "pin it" button or pasting the URL directly into your Pinterest dashboard.
2. You choose **which of your boards** the pin will live in.
3. **Fill out the pin's description**...and you're done!

How Repinning Works

This is even simpler. You find a "pin" somebody else has already shared on Pinterest and:

1. Hover over the pin and click "Pin It"
2. Select which board you want to add the repin to
3. Click "Pin It"

As my 15-year-old emo cousin would say: "It ain't rocket surgery."

What You Should Fill Your Boards With

This is really the big question facing us as marketers. How much NEW, original pinning do we do?

And how much repinning (or using other people's content) should we do? Especially since repinning is a great way to grab new followers. (More on that in the next chapter.)

If it's a board focused on internal/company stuff — such as an "employee spotlight" board or a "client appreciation" board — then obviously the pins associated with that board will be limited in scope. And repinning will play less of a role.

Although, when appropriate, opening up the board to outside contributors can lead to some interesting content you hadn't thought of being shared on the board.

But if it's a board that is about a more general theme or area of expertise — such as a "DIY Bathroom Project" board — I like to keep the mix of pins somewhere in the neighborhood of:

- 50% repins
- 25% pins of other resources (Such as blog posts, YouTube videos, anything I didn't create)
- 25% featuring my own company's blog posts, images, videos, and photos.

Now you may NOT have enough visual content to fill up that 25%. And that's okay. Do what you can.

Just commit you and your team to creating more visual content — could be as simple as putting an inspirational quote on a pretty picture — from here on out.

All right, enough of the jibber-jabber…let's get to the 6 Keys to the Perfect Pin!

PERFECT PIN KEY NO.1: FIND COOL STUFF TO PIN

This will depend on the specific board you are pinning items to, but here's the stuff that's worked best for me:

- **Inspirational quotes** over pretty pictures. (This NEVER fails.)
- **Product stills.** Make sure they are crisp and non-sucky.
- **Photos and videos of my team** doing human, non sales-y things.
- **How-to videos.** Both that we created and curated from somewhere else.
- **Infographics.** If you want resources on how to create your own FREE infographic, check out http://punkrockmarketing.com/infographic.
- **Funny videos and pictures.** If you can get an animal in there, even better.
- **Checklists, insider guides, cheat sheets.** Anything that smells like a resource.

- **Repins of other Pinterest users** that fit in with the theme of your board.

And where do you find these assets?

Well here are some of my favorite go-to spots:

- **PopUrls:** This "best of" collection of the stuff that's viral and popular on the Internet is my browser home page. (You'll find a broad range of content here, from the profane to the scholarly erudite.) Poke around and you might just find the perfect stuff to add to your Pinterest stew.
- **AllTop:** This is a site that collects the best blog posts on the web about a topic. And it's done by humans! Check it out, there's virtually a page about everything here.
- **Photo of the Day:** There are tons of Photo of the Day sites. Pick one that fits your business and use it to fill up your Pinterest archive.
- **Google Alerts:** This tool allows you to set up alerts, based on keywords, that will have ALL of the latest blog posts, news stories, discussions, etc., about that topic delivered to your inbox.

I like to create a Google Doc where my team and I can throw in URLs for interesting visual stuff we come across during of our workday. (You'll be shocked how quickly your Pinterest reserves can fill up.)

The key thing is to mix it up. Don't pin everything you see from The New York Times and The Daily Beast. Keep it varied.

Perfect Pin Key No.2: Decide Best Time to Pin

This is not written in stone.

But according to Reachli, a Pinterest analytics company, the best times to post on Pinterest are between 2:00 p.m. - 4:00 p.m. EST and again from 8:00 p.m. - 1:00 a.m. EST.

And I have to agree.

Pinterest is definitely an afternoon after-work activity. So experiment with your posting times, but lat afternoon and evening definitely seem to work best. If you're a local business, start with evenings and work backwards to find your pinning sweet spot.

Perfect Pin Key No.3: Gather Great Imagery

Doesn't matter whether your pin should promote a new blog post or the fact you made squash soup for the first time, making sure you have good, eye-catching imagery is VITAL to your Pinterest success.

But what makes an image good? And eye-catching?

Well, I'm no photo creative expert, but here are a couple things that the data has shown:

- **Think "lifestyle" first** - No matter what you're hawking ask yourself: "Does this image sell an ideal lifestyle?" Pinterest is creative and aspirational; it should not feel like homework. So, make sure your imagery captures the mood you want.
- **Light over dark** - Dark images don't do well. Light images do well. 'Nuff said.
- **Sharpness is key** - Your photos should pop off the page. If they are blurry or unfocused, keep shooting until you have what you want.
- **Saturation over Desaturation** - Saturation is just a fancy term for color intensity. And while you don't want to go overboard, opting for bright colors over desaturated grays that look like a Russian penal colony is always better.
- **White background (especially for product shots)** - This is hard to appreciate until you see your Pinterest image next to the rest of the Pinterest universe. But it can make a big difference to helping your pin stand out.
- **Simple is best** - Don't clutter your image with TOO many things, unless you're pinning an infographic. One subject for one pin image.

- **Things over faces** - This goes against most conventional thinking. But on Pinterest it's best to choose images of things, or abstract items, and less on human faces. (Could be because shots with faces often look like stock photos.)
- **Earth tones over etheral tones** - I can't tell you WHY this is. But if your images have reds and oranges they will do exponentially better than images with blues and grays. (Not mine to question, only to do the bidding of the Color Gods.)

Perfect Pin Key No.4: Size Your Imagery

Just as important as what the image looks like is the sizing of the image.

Many people mistakenly believe there is only ONE top of image dimension you can use, the skyscraper "much taller than wider" type of image.

But this isn't true.

There are four types of images that work well on Pinterest:

- **The skyscraper** - This is the one you know and love. According to Pinterest the size that works best for this type of pin one that is 600 x 900 pixels or any photo in the 2:3 ratio.
- **The infographic** - Despite rumors to the contrary these still work. The key is to make sure your image is no bigger than 600 x 1260 pixels. (Otherwise Pinterest will crop your image and make it look strange.)
- **The Instagram portrait** - This plays well with Instagram. If you create an image in Instagram and want to repost on Pinterest — and why not? — then you'll automatically get a 600 x 750 pixels image you can use with great effect on Pinterest. Or you can custom-make an image in this portrait size.
- **The square** - People think square pins don't work. They do. You want to make sure you have an image that's 600 x 600 pixels, otherwise it'll look Pixelated.

Perfect Pin Key No.5: Write a Great Pin Description (and Tell People What You Want Them to Do)

It's in the description of your pin where the juicy marketing stuff happens.

There are SIX key elements to include in every pin description you write:

1. **A description of the what the hell people are looking at.** This should seem brain-dead obvious, but I'm shocked how many pins don't have a simple a caption telling us what we're looking at. (People are scrolling on their phone while they see your stuff. Don't make them think.)
2. **Keywords in body of text.** But not in an overdone, spammy sort of way. This will help people find your pins and boards in both the Pinterest search engine and external website search engines. (I generally try to shoot for one keyword, two max.)
3. **A call-to-action** that tells people to either find out more about your product or service, opt-in to your email list or buy your product or service outright.
4. **An external link** for people to follow, based on the call-to-action you give them. Don't put in a shortened URL, such as http://bitly/375. These tend to be seen as spam. Put the entire link, including "http," in the description.
5. **One hashtag related to your specific business**. Such as #punkrockmarketing #discounttire #OldSpiceContest
6. **(Optional) The price of the product featured in the pin description.** This is done by typing the $ or £ in your description and adding the amount. (Pinterest will automatically add the price in a text overlay on the photo. Cool, huh?)

So, it would look something like this:

My newest Doctor Who themed steampunk jewelry piece! Check out our entire collection at: http:steampunkstuff.com #steampunkjewelry

I know some Pinterest gurus recommend you add TONS of #hashtags to your Pinterest description. You know, to help your pins get easily located in the Pinterest archives.

I don't advise this.

Adding a hashtag in your description simply gives people an invitation to leave your pin and check out a bunch of other people's stuff. (Pinterest users have a short enough attention span. I need not help it along any with some needless hashtags.)

Perfect Pin Key No.6: Share your Pin on Facebook and Twitter

You have a Facebook Page and Twitter account? Right?

Well, Pinterest makes it super simple to have your pins automatically show up as updates and tweets in your other social media platforms.

All you do is:

- Look under Pinterest settings
- Click on "Social Networks"
- Choose which social network you'd like Pinterest to share your activity with.

And yet, I'd like you to tread carefully with this.

The Twitter integration is fine, I ain't too worried about that. Twitter moves so fast, and there's so much stuff out there, that it's hardly worth worrying about.

But, with Facebook, it's possible to overload your fans. Studies have shown posting more than twice a day on a Facebook page suppresses engagement.

So instead, I recommend you add a Pinterest tab to your Facebook page. That way if people want to check out your "pins" they can do so there, but they won't feel overloaded with content.

To install the Pinterest app on your Facebook page, download and install the FREE WooBox Pinterest app.

All you gotta do is:

- Head over to WooBox.com
- Click "Get Started for Free"
- Sync the app up with your Facebook Page (You must be signed up to do this)

...and you're done! Su-per easy. (And it makes your Facebook page look a lot more filled out.)

PUNK ROCK MARKETING
AMPLIFY YOUR MESSAGE

CHAPTER 5 KEY TAKEAWAYS:

- **Pinning success starts with finding great content to share.** (PopUrls, AllTop, Google Alerts and Photo-of-the-Day sites are perfect for this.)
- **Keep it visual.** Other good pieces of content to pin include: infographics, how-to stuff, product stills that don't suck, quote overlays on photos, and behind-the-scenes content.
- **Watch the clock.** The best time to pin SEEMS to be late afternoon, and after dinner. (Test to find the best time for you.)
- **Use the description wisely.** Include keywords, price points, and external links to your site in the description.
- **Promote your pins on Twitter and Facebook.** Set up the Twitter integration within the Pinterest dashboard, but create a Pinterest custom tab on your Facebook page to avoid fatiguing your Facebook fans.

Chapter 6:

7 Killer Strategies for Getting a Crapload of Pinterest Followers

"Why join the Navy if you can be a pirate?"

-Steve Jobs

All the pins and pinboards in the world won't do you much good if you don't have followers.

And that's what we will cover in this chapter: the subtle (and not-so-subtle) art of attracting Pinterest followers. (Who we can eventually turn into customers.)

In the next chapter I will show you how to make money from your Pinterest tribe. But for now, we gotta build the tribe before we can ask them to do things. (Like buy stuff from us!)

So, here are my SEVEN Top Tips for Finding a Collection of Rabid, Passionate (and Buying) Pinterest Followers:

Rabid Pinterest Tribe Tip No.1: Pin More Stuff

What? You mean I gotta pin...like...more stuff?

'Fraid so.

Pinterest rewards the dedicated, and slightly obsessed, with a ton of new followers. But those followers are like four-year-olds in a Chuck E. Cheese restaurant.

Very. Easily. Distracted.

That's why you got to keep the flow of pins, and pepperoni pizza, coming.

Research shows that the ideal pin sweet spot seems to be around 4-25 times a day.

Which sounds like a lot. (I know. Believe me.)

Until you realize it takes all of four seconds to pin something. (And if you've got the Pinterest bookmarklet added to your browser, less than that.)

The key thing is to come up with some kind of pinning routine that everybody on your team can follow.

This is the schedule I follow:

- **Noon** - Lunchtime: Three pins (1 promo pin, 2 cool stuff I found pins)
- **3:30 p.m.** - Afternoon break: Three repins
- **7:00 p.m.** - Evening pin session: Three pins (1 promo pin, 2 cool stuff I found pins)
- **10:00 p.m.** - Late-evening pin session: Three repins

Seriously, this takes me less than 10 minutes total. Each day.

And by following this system I get myself 12 pins a day. Have other people on your team pitch in and before you know it your Pinterest pin total will be through the roof.

Rabid Pinterest Tribe Tip No.2: Repin Folks

This works the same as it does with Twitter. (Even more so.)

The fact is: after you repin somebody, they are likely to follow you back. (Most people are still NEW to Pinterest and having some kind of social interaction with people is cool.)

To keep it simple, I dedicate specific blocks of my pinning time to repinning. As my aforementioned schedule revealed, I focus my afternoon and evening sessions to repinning. (Which is good, because at those times all my brain cells can really handle is repinning.)

This does a couple of cool things.

If somebody is on their lunch break, and gets a smartphone notification I repinned them, they're **likely** to follow me.

And for the after-dinner session, early evening is prime Pinterest time, so I've got a great chance of adding that user to my tribe while they're amid some serious Pinterest activity.

But experiment. Find out what works for you.

Just make sure you devote time to repinning. (Your bank account will thank you.)

Rabid Pinterest Tribe Tip No.3: Follow Your Ideal Customers

This tip requires detective work. (And manual labor.)

But you want to put yourself in the mind of your ideal customer by asking:

- What type of boards would my ideal customer follow?
- What keywords or phrases would they type into Pinterest?
- What are they looking for? (If your product or service fills a need or solves a problem, how would they find you?)

And then it's as simple as:

1. Type a keyword related to your ideal customer in the Pinterest search bar.
2. Choose the "Pinners" tab.
3. Start following "pinners" who share "pins" related to that keyword.
4. Follow approximately 50-100 people per "following" session.
5. Give 'em three days to follow you back. If they don't, unfollow them.
6. Rinse and repeat three times a week.

This is the same process I use to build my various Twitter tribes into the tens of thousands.

It's slow. It's monotonous. (And it totally works.)

Rabid Pinterest Tribe Tip No. 4: Follow the RIGHT Boards

This is exactly the same process as following "pinners." Only after you put your keyword in the Pinterest search bar, you choose "boards" instead of "pinners."

Give the creator of the board a couple of days to follow you back. If not, unfollow them. (Same as the pinner strategy: I like to do this three times a week, shooting for 20-30 new boards to follow each time.)

Rabid Pinterest Tribe Tip No.5: Comment on Popular Pins

This is a super easy technique that a lot of Pinterest marketers neglect. All you do is:

- Head over to http://pinterest.com/popular.
- Find a couple of cool images that genuinely move you.
- Make a comment that doesn't suck.

You don't want to just say: "Cool share," "Agree," or "That's great."

Take time. Look at the image.

Read the description and make a halfway decent, meaningful comment. People love recognition, especially when it's sincere and heartfelt.

If you're stumped, just show you're passionate for the subject. (Even if you aren't.)

Rabid Pinterest Tribe Tip No.6: Find Your Friends

This only works if you have actual, human friends. If you're a hermit living in a cave in eastern Mongolia, this won't help.

Once you've connected your other social networks to your Pinterest account — we went over this in **Chapter 5** — you can easily look for those same friends and fans on Pinterest.

All you gotta do is:

1. Click on the name of your business account in the upper right-hand corner
2. Select "Find Friends"
3. Follow those "friends"
4. Wait for your Pinterest follower numbers to skyrocket

Rabid Pinterest Tribe Tip No.7: Run a Contest

Pinterest and contests go together like Lennon and McCartney. Simon and Garfunkel. Lady Gaga and…whatever weird outfit she's wearing these days.

Pinterest users LOVE contests. And they are a fan-tastic way to build your follower base FAST.

Which is why we're devoting an entire chapter to Pinterest contests in Chapter 8. (They're that awesome!)

PUNK ROCK MARKETING
AMPLIFY YOUR MESSAGE

CHAPTER 6 Key Takeaways:

- **Pin to win.** The more you pin, the more followers you'll get.
- **Repin to find followers.** People love recognition, and if you repin them they are likely to follow you back.
- **Find your ideal customer.** Use keywords in the Pinterest search bar and search for "pinners" who are pinning about areas related to your business.
- **Follow related boards.** Use the same "search" feature to find Pinterest boards that might contain folks who would make great followers for your account.
- **Hang with the popular kids.** Head over to pinterest.com/popular and comment on popular pins that are zooming up the Pinterest charts.
- **Find your friends (if you have some).** Use your Pinterest dashboard to connect with your existing social circle to broaden your Pinterest fan base.

Chapter 7:

7 Super-Ninja Ways to Make Money With Pinterest

"Nothing makes a man so adventerous as an empty pocket."

-Victor Hugo

Okay, we've gone over some traditional ways to incorporate Pinterest into your marketing arsenal. Create boards, pin stuff, sell your wares, buy yourself a yacht…

But there are real out-of-the-box ways you can use Pinterest to kick-ass marketing effect.

And, trust me, your competition isn't doing any of these!

So, here are my SEVEN Super Ninja Ways to Use Pinterest That Nobody Knows About (But Now You Do):

Super-Ninja Pinterest Money-Making Tip No.1: Use Pinterest as Social Proof

Social proof is just a fancy phrase for using other people's positive opinions about a product or service to help future customers buy more of your stuff.

And it works really, really well.

If you've got an array of products for sale on your website, why not put a little button next to the products that are most popular on Pinterest?

That your organic eco-friendly baby diapers got 345 pins may not mean that much to you, but it means something to your customers.)

As consumers, we are always trying to compare and judge things in our brain. That's why Amazon reviews and Consumer Reports ratings are so important. So make that job easier for your customers by putting a product's Pinterest popularity front and center.

Note: This works even better with a brick-and-mortar store where shop owners can put ACTUAL Pinterest stickers on price tags.

Super-Ninja Pinterest Money-Making Tip No.2: Have Customers Vote

The only thing people love more than sharing their opinion, is sharing that opinion when it counts for something.

One Pinterest technique that works really well is to display two products on your store's showroom floor, or show pictures of two products on a dedicated website landing page, and have customers "vote" on their favorite, with the "winning" item being put on sale for some period.

Talk about consumer power.

Later on you can feature the winner in your store or on your website as a Pinterest bestseller. (You could even do a press release around the winner, with background on how you ran the contest. Journalists love behind-the-scenes stuff like that.)

And all of that interaction with your Pinterest account makes it much, much more likely that customers will eventually become Pinterest followers (And, hopefully, long-term customers.)

Super-Ninja Pinterest Money-Making Tip No.3: Create a Product Bundle Board

Folks love getting a deal. And there's nothing that feels quite like a killer deal than a product bundle.

If you've got a suite of products or services, then why not create a board that shows off these assets and offers a bundled price as well? (Say, if you were a flower company offering "wedding flower packages.")

All you do is set up a board with all your relevant products, and link each of the pins' descriptions to a landing page with a discounted bundle price.

And don't forget to promote this themed bundle on all your other social media platforms. A press release wouldn't hurt either.

Super-Ninja Pinterest Money-Making Tip No.4: Create a Client-Specific Board

Earlier we talked about creating a board that specifically recognizes a special client or board. But this tip takes that strategy much further.

What if you were a wedding planner? Would creating a client-specific board be a good idea?

Hell yeah!

Or what if you were a realtor? Would creating a client-specific board showing them photos of possible houses be a cool way to give them housing options?

I'd say so!

This may not be practical for everybody, especially those who sell low-ticket items.

But if you deal in any kind of sizeable margin items with your business, this would be a great way to offer your clients and customers a fantastic visual way to have their needs met.

And a reminder that you really care about them and don't see them as just customer automatons.

Super Ninja Pinterest Money-Making No.5: Run the Cheapest Focus Group Ever

Would knowing what your ideal customer wants, fears, and secretly desires be helpful to selling more stuff?

Uhh...yeah!

Well, skip the $500/hour consultant and run your very own focus group.

Check out the boards of your followers and find out:

- What their passions are
- What super expensive merchandise they dream about owning
- What they want to look like
- What they feel is lacking in their life
- What kind of life they dream of having

And then collect all that data into a spreadsheet. (Interns, and teenage children, are perfect for this task.)

Once you have your data, brainstorm new products and services that solve these problems and connect with your customers on a deep and personal level. (Where all the real selling takes place.)

Super Ninja Pinterest Money-Making Tip No.6: Do What You Do Best

My grandfather had an expression: "Feed the stallions and starve the ponies."

And while my Grandad may not have been a contributor to the SPCA, the truth is he was right: you gotta exploit what's working and minimize what's not.

Nowhere is that more true than in your inbound marketing. And there's no better way to find what's working — and what's not — on your website than to discover which content from your website people are pinning.

To find this out, all you have to do is add your website into the following path:

Http://pinterest.com/source/yourwebsiteurl.com/ (Just to be crystal clear: you replace "yourwebsiteurl" with your own website. Don't want you wandering off into some weird corner of the Internet.)

This will give you a visual look at what's catching people's eyes. (And what's just sitting there like a mouse fart.)

Bonus: you might even come up with a couple of cool product ideas based on the content people are responding to.

SUPER NINJA PINTEREST MONEY-MAKING TIP NO.7: SHOW OFF YOUR TEAM (AND YOUR EXPERTISE)

As any overpriced marketing guru will tell you, we buy from people we like.

Ever been to a bookstore and suddenly you come across that "Staff Picks" section? (You know the part of the store where over-qualified English majors share their literary faves?)

Suddenly you buy that depressing novel about Seattle oyster farmers in the 1890s because "Katie" the cashier said it "changed her life" and helped her appreciate the "moody, turbulence" of the Pacific Northwest.

Without you realizing it, they've put a human face to their brick-and-mortar business and made you feel "connected." (And sold you crap you didn't want.)

So what better way to up the "like" quotient of your team than create a dedicated Team Pin Board where your staff can share:

- Cool things that inspire them
- Recent company outings
- The latest visually creative stuff they're working on
- Possible creative choices that followers could vote on (People love to feel included)

And you can also use this Pinterest real estate to:

- Call out a team member's recent accomplishment
- Brainstorm ideas for future products
- Share company logos (old and new)

PUNK ROCK MARKETING
AMPLIFY YOUR MESSAGE

CHAPTER 7 Key Takeaways:

- **Use testimonials.** Create a dedicated board where your customers and fans can gush about your products and services.
- **Let them vote.** Pit two of your products against each other to see what the Pinterest community likes best. (Be sure the winner goes on discount after the contest.)
- **Create a bundle board.** Organize your products and services into bundles you can place on a board and offer at a discounted group price.
- **Recognize your special clients.** Create a dedicated board for your best customers. (They'll love you for it.)
- **Run a focus group.** Do product research by poking around your ideal customers' boards and pins.
- **Find out what's working.** Check out what people are pinning from your site to discover the effectiveness of your content and potential product ideas.
- **Show off, but in a nice way.** Create a board that touts your team's accomplishments, passions, tastes and whatever else you like.

Chapter 8:

Pinterest Contests Made Supremely Easy

"A business absolutely devoted to service will have only one worry about profits. They will be embarrassingly large."

-Henry Ford

Everyone loves to win FREE stuff. Everybody.

And throw in the rather low barrier-to-entry of a Pinterest contest — you ain't asking people to write an essay, all they gotta do is upload a picture or create a board — and you've got the perfect marketing engine to attract tons of followers, boost your brand awareness and turn those freebie-seekers into paying customers who buy your wares.

But there's a new Pinterest sheriff in town.

And the old "Pin It to Win It" model of Pinterest contests is being phased out. Pinterest thinks these type of contests are spammy. (They're right.)

So, before we dig into the nuts-and-bolts of your Pinterest contest campaign let's go over what you CAN'T do:

- Require people to "pin" your contest guidelines. (Big no-no)
- Run a contest where pinners vote with likes, pins or repins.
- Require people pin a single image, or a selection of images, to enter the contest.
- Set up a contest where each follow, pin, or repin represents a single entry.
- Suggest that Pinterest endorses your contest.

Well, that kinda puts a crimp in things, don't it?

Don't worry.

All it did was kick the Internet hucksters out. (And leave room for us ethical marketers.)

So, here are my SIX tips for running a Pinterest contest that doesn't suck (and will actually make money):

Pinterest Contest Tip No.1: Set Your Goals

I know. Setting social media goals is about as much fun as filing a tax return.

But without a clear set of goals for your Pinterest contest — that you and your team understand beforehand — you'll be unsure of:

- How long to run the contest
- What kind of prize to offer
- How much money in advertising to put behind it... (Yes, it's possible you may have to spend money to spread the word about your Pinterest contest. But it'll be worth it.)

Here are some of the more common Pinterest contest goals that marketers have used successfully:

- Increasing your number of Pinterest followers
- Finding more subscribers for your email list
- Promoting an upcoming product launch
- Getting publicity for your brand, product, service or cause
- Procuring feedback for...well...almost anything
- Boosting the amount of traffic to your website
- And...selling more stuff!

In my (not-so-humble) experience, the goals that I've had the most success with are getting more Pinterest followers, building up my email subscriber base and promoting a product launch.

I've had less success with getting "publicity" — whatever that means — and I find trying to simply sell more stuff hasn't worked out well for me.

But I don't move in the e-commerce space. If you sell physical products, you shouldn't have any problem.

And it's okay to have more than one goal with your Pinterest contest. But tread lightly...

Having more than two, maybe three, contest goals can water down your marketing efforts significantly. Don't worry, you can always run another contest next month to achieve different goals.

PINTEREST CONTEST TIP NO.2: GET CREATIVE WITH YOUR CONCEPT

This is where you get to flex your real marketing muscle. You just can't roll out the good-old "Pin It to Win It" contest model. It just means we need to be a little more creative, is all.

Here are a couple of contest concepts I've had REAL gains with:

- **Have users upload a photo or video of themselves** using your product, or doing something related to your business.
- **Create a board** where users can come up with the most creative/interesting/funny/heartfelt idea for a specific project or topic. (People love to feel like they're part of your behind-the-scenes brainstorming.)
- **Have users "vote" on two prospective products or projects.** Make sure the winning product or project is offered on discount. And a couple of lucky winners get the item for free.
- **Have users create their OWN board around a theme** of your choosing. Carnival Cruise Lines had great success with this when they asked users to create four boards related to four different dream destinations. (If only their maintenance crew was as innovative.)

- **Have users FIND missing pieces of a pinboard puzzle**, somewhere on your website. Audi crushed this when they showed close-up images of a car and had people search their website for pictures that would fill in the rest of the automobile.

Pinterest Contest Tip No.3: Decide on the Rules

This is really just a matter of working out how long the contest is going to be (I recommend a week, no longer), what people need to do to win the contest and whether you are running a "sweepstake" or a "merit-based contest."

In case you're a little rusty on your contest terminology, a **sweepstake** is where somebody enters a contest and a winner is chosen at random.

A **merit-based contest** is where somebody performs an action, such as uploading a video or creating a board, and then the contest organizer picks the winner.

Both are great. Both work really well.

If you're running a sweepstake, you want to be careful you don't run afoul of Pinterest terms of service. (You can get all their info at: http://business.pinterest.com/brand-guidelines/)

As for what you should have entrants do, you could have them:

- Create boards
- Opt-in to your email list
- Follow your account
- Follow a specific board
- Upload a photo or video

I usually do a combination of things. Have them FOLLOW me and enter their email address. (Or have them upload a photo or video.)

Just make sure you get some way to market to the entrants in the future. (Email is STILL my favorite way to go here.)

Pinterest Contest Tip No.4: Come Up With a Prize That Doesn't Suck

This will depend heavily on what type of business you have, and what kind of targeted lead you are trying to acquire.

Obviously if you're marketing to PR professionals than a one-hour coaching call might be something those folks would be into.

But if you're trying to reach a "non-marketing" population, then talking "marketing" for an hour may sound like government interrogation.

Just put yourself in your user's point of view. What would be cool to them?

- A one-year supply of Greek yogurt?
- A master bedroom set?
- A big-screen TV?
- A subscription to the Smithsonian Magazine?
- A candlelight dinner with Justin Bieber?

Whatever you do, keep the prize simple enough to understand that it can be explained in a single image.

A Victoria's Secret gift card is self-explanatory. (And in my wife's case… awesome.) A TCP/IP corporate network security firewall is not.

Pinterest Contest Tip No.5: Outsource the Anxiety

Right now, I'm going to share with you my secret weapon when it comes to Pinterest contests.

I handle none of it.

Really, most of the heavy lifting is done by an awesome, innovative company called Wishpond.

They are basically the go-to company for social media contests and sweepstakes. I love Wishpond because their tools offer:

- Eye-catching imagery you can use to promote your contest.
- Custom entry forms. (Works great for email opt-in forms.)
- Sweepstakes compliance. (So you don't have to deal with any of the boring legal stuff.)
- Templates that make you look like an awesome web designer. (Even if you aren't.)
- The ability to "schedule" your contests in advance. (I've run contests while sitting on a beach in Oahu.)
- Landing-page templates that are mobile-friendly. (This is huge!)
- The ability to set up follow-up emails and customize entrant's messages to their friends.
- Killer analytics to let you know what's working. (And what's not!)
- The ability to promote your contest on Twitter and Facebook really easily.

Sorry for the gushing **endorsement**. I like the services that WishPond offers. Makes things SO MUCH easier.

And if you're extremely cheap, like I am, you can always run a 7-day contest within your two-week FREE trial and get all the benefit, with none of the cost.

Pinterest Contest Tip No.6: Promote the Contest Everywhere

Bit of an easy decision, this one. But it's still true. Promote your contest on:

- Twitter
- Facebook
- Instagram
- Your Blog
- YouTube
- Press Release
- Email Newsletter

…anywhere you can think of! (Again, if the prize is good, and the contest is creative, you WILL get a great response.)

And you may suddenly have thousands of new leads, for the price of a Victoria's Secret gift card.

PUNK ROCK MARKETING AMPLIFY YOUR MESSAGE

CHAPTER 8 KEY TAKEAWAYS:

- **Come up with contest goals first.** Are you going after new followers, new email subscribers…or simply trying to get press attention? Decide on goals, then come up with your strategy.
- **Go beyond the usual.** Come up with a creative concept that asks people to do MORE than just create a board or pin an item from your website.
- **Lay down the law.** Come up with the rules of your contest. (And make sure, if it's a sweepstake, you follow Pinterest terms of service.)
- **Find a quality prize.** Bonus points if it fits in with the area of your company's expertise.
- **Let somebody else handle the contest.** Choose a tool like WishPond to handle all the tech-y stuff associated with your contest.
- **Promote!** Spread the word about your contest on your blog, Twitter feed, YouTube Channel, Facebook page…anywhere you can think of.

Chapter 9:

Standing on the Shoulders of (Pinterest) Giants

"The mind is not a vessel to be filled, but a fire to be kindled."

-Plutarch

WORDS can only do so much.

I've tried to share some of the tips and tricks I've learned (the hard way) about how to turn all those pins and repins and boards of the Pinterest universe into actual money.

But sometimes, you just gotta SEE it.

So, in this final chapter, I will share with you some companies I think are doing a GREAT job on Pinterest, and in particular, what area of Pinterest I think they are killing it in.

Don't be intimidated if some of them are big brands and huge companies. There are plenty of big companies who suck at Pinterest, if they have any Pinterest presence at all.

Just collect ideas you can use for your own Pinterest marketing efforts, and before you know it, you might be one of the big guys yourself.

PINTERST ALL-STAR NO.1: CHOBANI GREEK YOGURT

The company that made Greek yogurt a national food phenomenon knows what it's doing with Pinterest.

Not only do they have boards that extoll the many benefits of Greek yogurt — it's healthy for you ("Fit With It" board), it's great baked ("Baked With Chobani"), it's awesome frozen ("Chilly Chobani") —

but they also do a fantastic job of recognizing their fans ("Chobani Champions") and creating little nuggets of inspiration that have nothing to do with yogurt ("Nothing But Good" and "Go Real").

All-Star Resource: http://pinterest.com/chobani

Pinterest All-Star No.2: Etsy

Etsy, that handcraft marketplace that rejuvenated more craft rooms in America than the glue gun, was practically made for Pinterest and its visual revolution.

Of course, Etsy has plenty of themed boards that show off their awesome wares — ("Etsy Jewelry," "Cool Spaces", "DIY Projects") — but they also utilize the guest contributor feature quite well, with their series of "Guest Pinner" boards.

Also, the "Etsy Kids" and "Etsy Weddings" boards show this company ain't just about buying cool, handmade stuff made in a rural Pennsylvania farmhouse.

It's about being creative, and teaching the next generation that not everything should be made in a factory overseas.

All-Star Resource:http://pinterest.com/etsy

Pinterest All-Star No.3: Gap

The company who can't seem to decide on a logo they want, actually has a pretty good Pinterest strategy in place.

They don't have a ton of boards, but the ones they do have do a lot more than just show off the latest back-to-school styles.

Gap does a great job of getting their followers to post pictures of themselves wearing Gap clothing ("Styld.by You") and they've also created a clever board, called "GAPgrams," where users put their Gap outfits together in anthropomorphic poses…and then share them on Instagram. (Sounds weird, but it totally works.)

Note: Notice how many of their product photos have a white background…not a coincidence.

All-Star Resource: http://pinterest.com/gap

Pinterest All-Star No.4: Whole Foods Market

They call it food porn for a reason. But the Whole Foods Pinterest page offers a lot more than pretty pictures of soy burgers and seaweed grass smoothies.

It also offers fitness and nutrition tips for kids ("Kids: MOVE That Body," "A LunchBox That's Tops"), creative holiday boards ("Creative Christmas Projects"; "Spring Gatherings"), information on the company itself ("#WhyAustin") and the most popular of all, a board that allows followers to express their thanks for the role food plays in their life ("#foodthanks").

I'm not sure what I think about them putting their logo on NEARLY every pin, but overall it's a good brand to emulate.

All-Star Resource: http://www.pinterest.com/wholefoods/

A Final Note

If the Internet is still in its infancy. Then Pinterest is in its first trimester.

It's still not clear how the whole business model will shake out for Pinterest.

- Will external websites get pissed off Pinterest is monopolizing their traffic? (Flickr sure is mad. Wonder who's next?)
- Will Pinterest charge users?
- Will they push paid placement like Facebook, Twitter and Instagram have?

What we know, due to its overwhelmingly quick rise up the social media charts, is that Pinterest has hit a NERVE.

And that **nerve** is all about photos and videos that inspire and motivate people.

So, as you dip your toe into the Pinterest marketing waters, remember though the tactics of this super-trendy social network may change...

The strategy is here to stay.

- Keep it visual.
- Keep it simple.
- Keep it positive.

I have real doubts that people will actively read long-form text on a screen in the future. (And as an English major, that mortally offends me.)

But the more you can present the story of your company in a simple, compelling image...

...the more your business will be poised to not just **survive** these crazy, chaotic economic times.

But thrive. (And what could be more inspiring and motivating than that.)

Here's hoping YOU thrive and kick some serious ass in your Pinterest efforts.

Vol.5
of the Small Business
Marketing
COLLECTION
INSTAGRAM
MARKETING
in 2019
MADE
(STUPIDLY) EASY
Michael Clarke

Instagram Marketing in 2019 Made (Stupidly) Easy

Vol.5 of the Small Business Marketing Made (Stupidly) Easy Collection

PROLOGUE:
Yeah, But How Do You Make Money With Instagram?

Unless you've been living under a Kardashian-free rock, you'll no doubt have heard Instagram is the NEW (gotta-use) marketing platform to reach ANYBODY under the age of 40.

The numbers are staggering, Instagram has nearly one billion monthly users. With year-over-year growth rates of nearly 200%. (Take that, Twitter.)

And there's a REASON Facebook paid 750 million dollars to acquire Instagram. They KNOW Facebook may be the perfect platform for Mom to connect with her book club. Or Dad to talk smack with his fellow Fantasy Football nerds. Or Grandma Jo to share some weird cat meme picture she found. ("Look, honey...the cat is playing a keyboard guitar!")

But the young, 18-35 demographic eyeballs — who have tons of discretionary income — are ALL on Instagram.

Big question for us marketers is how we get noticed in a sea of mirror selfies and shaky 15-second nightclub videos. (#DontThesePeopleHaveAJob)

Well, getting noticed, introducing these folks to our brand — and eventually getting them to give us their hard-earned (or sometimes hardly earned) Millennial cash is what this book is all about.

But before we jump into the trenches of Instagram marketing, before we dig into creating content and building a tribe of rabid Instagram followers, let me tell you the #1 way NOT to market to folks on Instagram.

And that is...

Sell.

Much ink has been spilled trying to "figure out" the consuming habits and core values of the "Millennial."

But one thing that's abundantly clear from all the research is folks aged 18-40 DON'T trust institutions or anything that smells "corporate."

It's as if they see life like some "Hunger Games" scenario where reality is a struggle over scarce resources, such as a full-time job or a free burrito at Chipotle. (While the corrupt adults who run companies sit back and watch.)

And if you intend to barge into Instagram with a formal, corporate "Go here and buy this thing" attitude then let me save you the time. It won't work.

Try Google AdWords. Or a Goodyear Blimp.

But if you're willing to show a hipper, more irreverent side of your business...

If you're willing to spend time "liking" and "commenting" on your tribe's posts...(nothing these folks love more than approval)

If you're able to connect your product or service with an aspirational lifestyle that makes Millennials look smart, beautiful and morally superior to the world (and that includes OTHER Millennials)...

...then you'll crush it on Instagram.

Still not convinced?

Don't worry if you can't quite see HOW it's all going to come together. I'm not gonna ask you to delve into complex HTML or spend hours a day "liking" and "commenting" on Instagram accounts.

I won't even ask you to take any selfie shots of your six-pack abs. (Or in my case twelve-pack abs.)

But I will encourage you to put your impulse to "sell" and "convert" on the back burner as you:

- Step #1 - Post stuff on Instagram that doesn't suck (which gets you followers and fans)

- Step #2 - Which leads to followers and fans clicking on the link in your Instagram bio that sends them to your lead-capture page
- Step #3 - You make a crap load of money and invite me to your party in Aruba when Facebook acquires your company

The Instagram crowd has a very refined radar for detecting B.S. marketing messages. But if you can get past the radar — in this book I'll show you how to do that — then not only will you find a ton of leads (and future customers) on Instagram.

But you'll find a motivated (and highly connected) army of young people who'll share your message…for FREE!

And that makes enduring a nightclub video or two worth it.

So, if you're ready to grab your crossbow…let the "Instagram Hunger Games" begin!

Introduction:

Newbie's Guide to Instagram FAQ

"Thorough preparation makes its own luck."

-Joe Poyer

If you're an Instagram expert already — if you spend 11 hours each day finding the "perfect" sepia filter for your Instagram posts — then move on to Chapter 1. (You already KNOW everything I'm gonna cover here.)

But for those who have no clue how this popular, if strange, network works — or why people under 40 spend so much damn time on it...

...here are 5 Instagram FAQs to help guide you through the Instagram marketing process (and make you appear way smarter and hipper than you actually are.)

Instagram FAQ #1: What the Hell is Instagram? (And Why Is It So Damn Popular?)

Instagram is a photo-sharing social network that allows users to post photos to their profile — then tweak those photos with old-timey picture filters — which lets them share those pictures with their friends. (And with over 400 million monthly Instagram users, there's a lot of friends out there.)

As for WHY is it so popular, there are THREE key reasons:

1) **The lo-fi photo filters are cool.** These are the optional filters users can employ to give even the most ordinary photos drama and intensity. (Not to mention make everybody look like a way better photographer than they actually are.)

2) **Instagram makes it easy to SHARE photos & videos with friends on the phone.** Unlike the mobile Twitter and Facebook app — which can take that extra 13 seconds to share a pic or video — Instagram is dead-easy to use from a user perspective.
3) **People use photos as their default "status update" increasingly.** This, my friends, is the WHOLE reason Facebook purchased Instagram. (It wasn't the filter technology.) They looked into their crystal ball and realized things are only gonna get more visual — and more attention-span challenged — and people typing more than a sentence or two on their phone is going the way of the Dinosaur.

Instagram FAQ #2: Can I Use Instagram on My Laptop?

Uh…sorta. (But they don't make it easy.)

To get started though, you MUST download the Android or iPhone app to your mobile device to be deigned worthy...I mean, be able to register for an Instagram account.

This is done to cut down on the amount of spammy accounts. Or maybe it's just a way to keep businesses away from their prized users. (At least those who won't pay the Instagram advertising toll.)

What you CAN do on your desktop computer is update your information in your all-important bio. (We'll go over this in some detail in the first chapter.)

But for interacting and actually using your Instagram profile, I recommend you do most on your mobile weapon of choice. (If just to ensure what you're putting out there doesn't look like total crap.)

Instagram FAQ #3: Any Weird Instagram Terms I Need to Know About?

Thankfully, Instagram is generally free of the social-media jargon that plagues most social platforms. But here are essential Instagram terms you gotta know:

- **Post** - This is the finished Instagram product after you upload your photo, tweak its appearance and add your caption. This is the jet fuel that makes Instagram go.
- **Filter** - This is the photo filter — what the "kids" call the "old-timey look"— that made Instagram so popular, so fast. (We'll go over filters more later, just know this is the "secret sauce" to Instagram's initial success.)
- **Hashtag** - Like it sounds, this is the word that follows a pound sign (#) which organizes and categorizes Instagram posts. (We'll go over these in more detail later.) They are very important — even more important than hashtags in Twitter.
- **Feed** - The generic term for that unending stream of Instagram goodness produced by the accounts -- and hashtags -- that you follow. (This used to display chronologically -- whatever is newest gets displayed first -- but Instagram is tweaking with alternatives.)

Instagram FAQ #4: Sounds Great...How Do I Make Money With Instagram?

Woah there, Turbo! I love your enthusiasm but ya gotta learn to walk before you run over to the cash register and count your money.

Don't worry: we're gonna go over the nitty-gritty of building your Instagram following and creating killer Instagram content that inspires folks to give you hard currency.

But to satisfy your terminally impatient mind, making money with Instagram is not unlike other social networks, such as Facebook, Twitter or Pinterest:

- Share a bunch of cool photos (Yours included)
- Build up a rabid fan base
- Occasionally share a photo that links to some special offer
- Let your rabid fan base buy your crap
- Rinse and repeat

INSTAGRAM FAQ #5: CAN INSTAGRAM REALLY HELP MY BUSINESS?

Unless you're selling "New Coke" or "Blockbuster Video" franchises…yes, it can help.

That said, there's no question Instagram (like Pinterest) caters to products or services that are more aspirational in nature.

Less "I need a personal injury lawyer, so I think I'll go find one on Instagram" and more "Oooh, check out those cool steampunk artisanal socks. Think I'll buy one."

But I've got clients in non-aspirational fields such as mortuary services and life insurance who've used Instagram successfully.

Because what Instagram does really well — besides tell us which rappers are fighting over a girl — is give REAL personality to a business.

And considering Instagram is so damn EASY to use — for both users and devious marketers like ourselves — with just 2-3 minutes a day you can find a new, untapped audience that's just waiting to buy your stuff.

Especially considering how few of your competitors are already on Instagram.

And figuring out how to connect with that untapped audience is what we'll cover in the first chapter.

INTRODUCTION Key Takeaways:

- **Instagram is a photo-sharing social network.** Kind of like a souped-up, photo-heavy version of Twitter. (Difference being Instagram actually makes money.)
- **Instagram is popular because it's easy to use, it's got cool photo filters, and it's become the "new" status update.** For many, under 40, it has become the default camera (and social media) app on their phone or tablet.
- **It's all about the mobile experience.** Sure, you can update your bio on your desktop computer, but most of your Instagram duties — including the creation of your account — will be done on your mobile device.
- **There's not much jargon you gotta learn.** (Thank God.) Just the "post," the "filters," the "hashtags" and the "feed."
- **You make money with Instagram by inspiring (or entertaining) people.** And then either let people find your products or services through your bio or subtly throw in a special offer here and there to an excited fan base. (Or both.)
- **Instagram is great at giving a personality to your business.** (Even a faceless, corporate drone army.) And with just a few minutes a day you could see some awesome results.

Chapter 1:

The Art of the Perfect Instagram Marketing Funnel

"

Perfection is not attainable, but if we chase perfection we can catch excellence."

-Vince Lombardi

I know you're just itching to get your Instagram account set up — and browse for that photo filter that will make you look even more amazing and attractive than you are.

But before we do that, we've got a few things to set up. (Namely create ways to turn what we do on Instagram into actual money.)

Having all this in place, before you post your Jack Russell Terrier pics and selfies from your shop, will ensure you don't miss out on possible leads being added to your funnel.

And will help you make progress, even when you don't feel you're making any.

So, here are my 5 Keys to a Kick-Ass Instagram Marketing Funnel:

Instagram Marketing Funnel Key #1: Create a Freebie Thing-a-Majiggy to Give Away

Here's the bitter truth: overt selling on Instagram doesn't work. (I've tried.)

The Instagram crowd is too cynical (and marketing-savvy) to be coerced into heading to your sales page and buy whatever crap you're hawking just because you ask them to.

However, if you give them something for FREE, and it's something they want, you'll not only find your opt-in conversion rates skyrocket — but you'll make a lot more money (both in the short- and long-term.)

Now what you give away will depend on your business. But here are a couple of things that have worked really well for me:

- Coupon (or discounts)
- Video series
- Special Report
- Cheat Sheet
- Insider Guide
- Resource List

The general rule is, if I'm selling actual merch I'll go with a coupon or discount (either on a specific product or on the entire inventory). If I'm selling education/information, then I'll go with some kind of short, quick-hit insider guide.

INSTAGRAM MARKETING FUNNEL KEY #2: HAVE A WAY TO COLLECT EMAIL ADDRESSES

You didn't think you were gonna just give that stuff away for FREE for no reason. No, you'll be exchanging that coupon or cheat sheet guide for the most valuable thing a consumer can give you… their email. (Far more valuable than a "Facebook like" or "Instagram follow" any day.)

Now, there are a ton of companies who handle the collection and maintenance of your email marketing efforts. (I use ConvertKit but other ones include iContact and MailChimp.)

Just make sure you've got something, or you'll be leaving money on the Instagram table.

Instagram Marketing Funnel Key #3: Create a Web Page That Collects Email Addresses (in a Non-Sucky Way)

Ya gotta have somewhere to send those people to get their email address, don't ya? And that's where a dedicated email capture page comes in. (Called a "landing page" in the weird, over-hyped Internet marketing business.)

And this is an AREA where most marketers screw up because they send their prospects to a page on their blog that has way too much CRAP on it.

It'll have their website navigation, sidebars, blog excerpts, social media icons, pictures from their 11th-grade yearbook, etc.

This is the BIGGEST mistake you can make when collecting email subscribers. (And one that'll absolutely SINK your opt-in rates.)

Your email capture page should only have:

- A picture
- A headline (letting people know who the freebie is for)
- A paragraph (telling people what the freebie entails)
- A place for people to type in their name and email

And that's it!

I use a tool called LeadPages — PunkRockMarketing.com/Lead — which provides me out-of-the-box templates that make my pages look awesome. (Without me having to know any code or contain a scintilla of graphic design talent.)

But you could also use a tool like Instapage. (I've heard great things about them, and they tend to be cheaper than LeadPages.)

The nice part about these is they're all mobile-responsive, so they'll look great across any device.

What I wouldn't do is try to design the page yourself — or outsource it to somebody else. (The things you and I don't know about web design would fill a library. So let's not work on an area that somebody else has already mastered.)

Instagram Marketing Funnel Key #4: Have Something to Sell on Your Email Subscriber Thank You Page

Here's another BIG mistake marketers make. They go to the trouble of signing somebody up to their email list and then neglect to offer them something to BUY right on the "Thank You" page.

Your "Thank You" page is your most valuable piece of web real estate. After a lead signs up for your list they are at their MOST motivated to buy something from you.

So, why not let them?

Now, I wouldn't offer them your big-ticket $12,000 suite of consulting services. Make it small. (Something under $20.)

But if you set things up right, roughly 25% of the folks who subscribe to your list will buy your first offer. (Which can let you spend more money on advertising than your competition…yeah!)

Note: Both tools I mentioned earlier, LeadPages and Instapage, let you create snazzy "Thank You" pages that look awesome, and totally convert.

Instagram Marketing Funnel #5: Install Retargeting Code On Your Website

Now, if what I said — "retargeting code" — sounds like something from a bad sci-fi novel, that's okay. Don't worry about the "tech" side. (You can always have somebody far more left-brained and fearful of sunlight than you to handle it.)

This is how "retargeting" works:

- **You place an invisible piece of retargeting code on your ENTIRE website** (This includes your email capture page and your thank you page) — This is easier than it sounds, usually done with a plugin
- **You create a "retargeting" ad —** can be video or text — that reminds people how awesome your freebie is (and how they'd be an idiot not to sign up RIGHT NOW)
- **You create "retargeting" ad campaigns**, on Google and Facebook, that target folks who "visited" one of your pages but did NOT reach your "Thank You" page
- **You swim around in your newfound cash** (like Scrooge McDuck)

Now, again it's off-topic to go into too much detail about "retargeting" in this book on Instagram. But let me tell you, if you haven't tried it, it is AWESOME.

And at little cost, it will help turn casual window-shoppers into possible long-term customers.

Chapter 1 Key Takeaways:

- **Create a freebie that doesn't suck.** (Coupons and discounts work great for physical products. Cheat sheets and insider guides work great for info products.)
- **Have a way to collect email addresses.** If you don't already have an auto-responder, such as ConvertKit or MailChimp, invest in one. It'll be worth it.
- **Build an email lead-capture page that doesn't suck.** All ya want is a headline, brief paragraph describing the freebie, a picture of your freebie, and a box for visitors to sign up for your list. Lead-Pages and Instapage are great web page template tools for creating these.
- **Offer something to sell on your "Thank You for signing up" page.** (Just don't make it a big-ticket item, something under $20 would work.) This is when people are most motivated to buy something from ya…so don't stand in the way.
- **Install Facebook and Google "retargeting" code on your entire website** — and that includes opt-in and thank you pages. If you don't know how to do this, just hire somebody to do it. (Setting up "retargeting" campaigns based on Instagram visitors is like "found" money.

Chapter 2:

Six Steps to a Profitable Instagram Profile

"There's nothing worse than a sharp image of a fuzzy object."

-Ansel Adams

Okay, now you've got a rough understanding of Instagram, let's jump right in with creating you a supremely awesome Instagram profile that not only boosts your exposure — but also lets you collect leads (while you sleep.)

Now, as I mentioned in the last chapter, Instagram is primarily a mobile platform. And much of the Instagram profile creation I'm about to go over will be done on your mobile device of choice.

But the LAST step, the most important step, we're gonna do on your good, old Dinosaur-ish computer. (Remember those?)

So, let's jump right in with my 6 Steps to a Profitable Instagram Profile:

Instagram Profile That Doesn't Suck Step #1: Download the App

I know you need another app on your phone or tablet like you need another hole in the head. (Or another Kardashian spin-off.) But this is the price of doing Instagram business.

And it's easy, just head to your app store and grab the FREE Instagram app. When you open the app, you'll be asked whether you want to SIGN in with Facebook or your email address.

If you plan to have only ONE primary Instagram account, if you've only got one business you're running, then go with the Facebook option. If you're Mark Cuban, helping run 12 different businesses, then go with your email address.

But the choice is entirely yours. Because once you do that, you'll be ready for...

Instagram Profile That Doesn't Suck Step #2: Choose a Non-Sucky Profile Photo

Now, this isn't something you have to do right at this moment. (And you can always go back and change it.) But your profile photo is probably the MOST important factor in your ability to get noticed on Instagram. (That and your ability to get Bruno Mars to mention you in a post.)

Here's what you gotta know about Instagram profile photos:

- **The ideal size for a profile photo is 500x500 pixels.** Anything smaller and you'll look more pixelated than a Minecraft game.
- **Your profile photo will be resized to a square ratio**. So, if you don't want to look like you've been decapitated, size your bio photo to 500x500 before uploading.
- **If the account is gonna represent a corporate brand, go for a simple logo (without words.)** Forget that picture of your team on the front steps, or that logo with the text at 4-point font. (It'll look crappy on a phone.) Just stick with a simple, eye-catching logo.
- **If the account is gonna represent YOU as a brand, go for a high-quality photo that shows you off.** Avoid head-to-toe shots, unless you're a fitness instructor and you wanna show off your six-pack abs. Otherwise go for a shoulder-up shot that shows off that winning smile of yours. (Or in my case, slightly exasperated grin.)
- **Go easy with filters on your bio photo.** We're gonna go over filters in more detail later but try to avoid going heavy with the filters on your bio photo. (They can make your pic look too dark.)

You can also grab a photo from Facebook or snap a quick selfie right there in the app. Just ask yourself: "would I buy something from somebody who spent less than 10 seconds on their Instagram profile pic?"

Instagram Profile That Doesn't Suck Step #3: Find Some Friends (If You Have Some)

Right after you create your profile you'll be taken to a screen called "Find Friends." (If only that screen were available when I was in high school.)

You DON'T have to choose this option at the moment you create your profile. You can always go back later and select the "Find Friends" feature from your profile.

But there are three powerful options Instagram offers here to find friends:

1. Find friends from your Facebook account (Did we mention Facebook owns Instagram?)
2. Find friends from your phone contact list
3. Find friends from your email address

Unless you're Edward Snowden — or you want none of your inner circle knowing what you do for a living — I recommend you take advantage of this powerful tool.

It'll make getting some serious traction with your posts much easier down the road.

Instagram Profile That Doesn't Suck Step #4: Choose a Username That Doesn't Suck

So, before I give you my tips on creating a username, let me be clear right at the start.

In the Instagram world, "username" and "personal name" are different. (Confused? Yeah, I was too, the first time.)

The username is your Instagram handle — Example: "@facebookceo" — while the personal name is just what it sounds like, your name — Example: "Mark Zuckerberg."

The personal name field is simple, use your name. (Or whatever alias you're using to evade the cops.) And you can change this information as many times as you want.

But it's your username that will drive much of the "branding juice" of your Instagram account. And it can be rather challenging to find the right username, especially if somebody has already taken one related to your given name or your business. (Welcome to the "Wild West" of social media.)

If you're having a tough time finding that perfect username then here are a couple of pointers:

- **Use periods (".") and underscores ("_") between words to help you find a unique username.** This won't always work — with my name "Michael Clarke" I only happen to be competing with 4 million other people — but it can be beneficial in the right situation.
- **Add a "The" or "The Real" prefix to your name or business.** This is a trick I got from a LinkedIn seminar. (The seminar was horrible except for that one tip.) If Joe Schmidt is taken, maybe it's time you embrace your inner superhero and become "TheJoeSchmidt" or "TheRealJoeSchmidt."
- **If your company name is taken add a ".com" to the end of it**. Or ".org" or whatever the extension of your domain is. Not only can it let you hold on to your branding identity, but it also (not-so-subtly) encourages folks to check out your website.

Instagram Profile That Doesn't Suck Step #5: Create That All-Important Bio

Of the five steps in this chapter, creating your bio is by far the most important. That's because your bio is not only where you get to throw in some keywords related to your business or field, but it's also where you get to place that all-important call-to-action. (And where you get to add a juicy link back to your website.)

Now, as I alluded to before, it is POSSIBLE to update your bio through your mobile device, but I don't recommend it. That's because adding text to your bio, through your mobile device, will CLUMP all the text together.

No matter how many times you hit the return key, Instagram doesn't seem to recognize line breaks when it comes to your bio.

So, what's an enterprising marketer to do? Simply update your bio — on your desktop computer — using this simple process:

1. **Download a FREE copy of my Instagram bio text template.** You can find it at PunkRockMarketing.com/InstagramBio. This is a simple text document to ensure your line breaks and formatting is just how you want it.
2. **Use the template to fill in the relevant info for your bio.** I recommend line #1 of your bio be used to describe your role in the business ("Author. Entrepreneur. International Man of Mystery") and lines #2-#4 be used to craft a CTA (call-to-action) that gets people to act ("To grab a FREE copy of my special report: "7 Ways to Download a Special Report") head over to:")
3. **Head over to https://instagram.com/accounts/edit/#** and log in to Instagram.
4. **Paste in text from your Instagram bio template EXACTLY**, adding no additional characters or line breaks.
5. **In the website field, insert the relevant web page** you're asking people to visit (This will automatically show up as the final line in your bio.)
6. **Click "Save" and you're good to go.**

Now that's the HOW of setting up your Instagram bio. But that doesn't tell us the WHAT, what the heck should we be pitching in our Instagram bio. (What's the best way for us to use that space in an effective and profitable way?)

Well, this will depend on your particular business model. But here are a couple thoughts to keep in mind:

- **Resist the urge to hawk multiple things in the same bio.** If you want people to "like" you on Facebook, do that. If you want people to try your "Columbia House 12 CDs for a penny" offer, do that. Don't do both. (The confused mind always says no.)
- **Links to sales page and offers — unless it's an irresistible offer — tend to NOT work.** Now this might not be a deal-breaker for you. Perhaps your sales page offer is so inviting, and your conversion rates so high, that all ya need is eyeballs. But mostly anything over $10, direct sales links don't convert that awesomely.
- **Free giveaways or super-cheap offers work REALLY well.** If you've got ANY way to spin your product or service into something free(ish) then go for that in your Instagram bio. (Will pay off huge down the line.)
- **If you have nothing to give away**, you could always just ask people to "follow your account" or "like your pictures" or follow you on any number of other social media channels. (Snapchat and Pinterest work really well — others not so much.)
- **Don't just encourage people to "Check out your website" or "subscribe to your newsletter."** Nobody cares about you. They want to know what's in it for them. So give them a reason to check out your stuff, beyond the fact you finally figured out how to FTP a WordPress website.
- **Use active verbs to tell people what you want them to do.** Don't be shy. (Nobody on Instagram is.) Tell people exactly, what you want them to do. "Download your FREE report; Click to grab your complimentary offer; Buy every single product I sell... Now!"

Instagram Profile That Doesn't Suck Step #6: Link Up Your Instagram Account With Your Other Social Media Channels

You don't have to do this now; you can do it later. But at some point, you'll want to sync up your Instagram account with your social media accounts — including Facebook, Twitter, Tumblr and Flickr.

This will make the sharing of your posts to your various social media properties way easier. (And you'll boost your engagement and reach of your posts without having to do a damn thing.)

Just REMEMBER not to go all "Andrew Dice Clay" with your Instagram posts. (Your grandmother might see it on Facebook and you won't get that $5 check for Christmas.)

CHAPTER 2 Key Takeaways:

- **Ya gotta create your Instagram account on a mobile device.** Price of doing business, don't stress it.
- **To create a profile photo that doesn't suck remember to resize your image to 500x500 pixels.** (Otherwise it'll look Pixelated.) Also, keep it simple with non-text logos and head shots.
- **Use the "Find Friends" feature to locate people** in your email contact list or Facebook friend list who you can add to your Instagram tribe.
- **Creating a username that doesn't suck is harder than it sounds.** (Many names are already taken.) IF you're stumped, use periods/underscores, domain extensions or a simple "The" or "TheReal" prefix to get around this.
- **For your bio make sure to a) update it on your computer** (not mobile device) b) Use my FREE Instagram Bio text document to keep formatting correct (PunkRockMarketing.com/Instagram-Bio) c) Just pitch ONE THING in your bio.
- **Sync your Instagram account with your other social media accounts**, such as your Twitter, Facebook, Tumblr and Flickr accounts.

Chapter 3:

Spying on the Competition for Fun and Profit

"A horse never runs so fast as when it has other horses to outpace it."

-Ovid

Okay, so we've got your Instagram profile set up and your bio looking spiffy and chock-full of marketing potential.

But before you shoot pics and uploading your Instagram posts of awesomeness, there's ONE important task to complete. And that is to…

…blatantly SPY on your competition! (But in an ethical way.)

Not only will it give you ideas on the kinds of Instagram content you SHOULD — and should NOT — create, but it will also give you some much-needed intel on the best way to get your content discovered. (Which #hashtags should accompany your content.)

So, here are my 3 keys to spying…err…researching what your industry is currently doing on Instagram:

(Note: I know you're tempted to skip this part. But resist that inner teenager inside ya who wants to just go play video games. This will make you money down the road.)

Instagram Spying Key #1: Learn the Ways of the Enemy

One of the quickest ways to learn the Instagram mores of your target audience is to figure out how competitors are ALREADY communicating with your target audience on Instagram.

This includes paying attention to things like:

- How often do they post on Instagram? (Every day? Twice a week? Once every Presidential election?)
- What kind of CTA (call-to-action) do they have in their Instagram bio? (If any)
- What kinds of #hashtags do they include with their posts? (Are their #hashtags unique to their brand? Or are they "popular" #hashtags intended to throw a much-wider Instagram net?)
- What kinds of Instagram content do they share? (Product shots, behind-the-scenes stuff, blatant offers and coupons, how-to content, stuff created by their fans, etc.)
- And what things would you like to STEAL from their campaigns? (And what would you never, under any circumstances STEAL?)

Now to make this process easier, I've created an Instagram Marketing Research excel sheet, which you can grab TOTALLY FREE by heading over to PunkRockMarketing.com/Instagram-Research.

All you gotta do is:

- Head over to Instagram
- Type in keywords related to your business (or if you already know a competitor is on Instagram, put them in)
- Find at least 5 competitors (who have a minimum of 1000 followers)
- Scan their bios and photo feed (and fill out your Instagram Research sheet)

Now you DON'T want to copy every single thing these brands do. (Many have no frickin' clue what they're doing with Instagram.)

In the Instagram Marketing Research sheet I give you some examples I did with those high fructose syrup giants - Coke, Pepsi, and Dr. Pepper.

Even with these huge multi-billion-dollar companies I still don't love everything they do. (I love Coke's use of user-generated content and their clear CTA in their bio. But their photos feel too "artsy" and "couture" for me.)

And Pepsi may evoke a nice family-friendly, holiday BBQ feel that ties in with their demographic. But that their bio has no CTA is mind-boggling.)

But doing this exercise — should only take you 20 minutes — will give you a virtual B.A. in Instagram Studies. (Without the need to take out a single student loan.)

INSTAGRAM SPYING KEY #2: FIND YOUR FUTURE PARTNERS

So, once ya got your list of competitors, it's time to up your game and get your full-on Master's Degree in Instagram Studies. And you do that by making a mongo list of Instagram influencers.

Now, these are not competitors. These are brands and/or personalities who are related to your business.

For instance if I was a golf club manufacturer, then influencers would include:

- Golf pros
- Golf instructors
- Golf courses
- Golf magazines
- Golf bloggers

...folks who have an audience that is interested in what I offer. (But are not in direct competition.)

And don't forget about "Instagram enthusiasts" who simply LOVE (or pretend to love) everything about a topic related to your business.

These folks can have HUGE follower counts — some over a million — and will even "sell" a sponsored shout-out to their audience.

For now just dig through Instagram by:

- Type a keyword related to your business in the Instagram search bar
- Find 5-10 influencers with at least 1000 followers (Keep searching until you find a decent mix of magazines, websites, bloggers, enthusiasts, manufacturers, etc.)
- Scan their profiles, and input their info in your Instagram Research sheet, under the "Influencers" tab (Grab their email or social contact info, if provided)

Instagram Spying Key #3: Make a List of All-Powerful Hashtags

Once you've done some early reconnaissance on the competition and influencers who might help you down the line...

...it's time to make your master list of hashtags you'll be using for each of your Instagram posts.

Huh? Hashtags? Do I really have to do this?

Uh...yeah.

See, in the Instagram universe #hashtags are valuable currency. (Even more valuable than they are on other social platforms such as Pinterest or Twitter.)

Because there is just NO more reliable way to get your Instagram posts discovered than to have a ton of #hashtags.

And here's the interesting part about Instagram #hashtags:

- Studies show the MORE hashtags you have, the MORE your posts get engaged with
- Instagram allows you up to 30 hashtags per post. (I recommend keeping the number around 15-20, but still that's a lot of hashtag real estate we can be using.)
- Hashtags are best — just like your stock portfolio — when they're diverse. (Meaning you should have a mix of mega-popular hashtags, semi-popular hashtags, and less-popular hashtags.

The good news is hardly anybody goes to this much trouble when including hashtags in their posts. (Which lets you and I take advantage of their ignorance and get our posts to the front of the Instagram line.)

So, here's what ya do:

- Open up that Instagram Research Worksheet (head over to the third tab, entitled "Hashtags")
- Head to Instagram and type keywords in the search bar related to your business.
- Your goal is to find FIVE hashtags with at least 1000 results, FIVE hashtags with under 1000 results, and FIVE hashtags with under 100 results (This doesn't have to be exact but get as close as you can.)
- Include your own branded hashtags in the sheet — this will probably be related to your company name or hashtag slogans you've used in the past

Now this Master List of Kick-Ass Hashtags will evolve as you get more familiar with Instagram. (You may find new ones or take some off the list.)

But try your best to get a nice, diverse mix of hashtags that can leverage super-popular hashtags and slightly less-popular hashtags.

If you're able to complete your Instagram Research worksheet, and I know you are, then you will be ahead of 92.6% of all the other marketers out there. You'll have a Ph.D. in Instagram Marketing Readiness.

And then the next step will be creating some killer Instagram content, which is what we'll cover in the next chapter.

CHAPTER 2 Key Takeaways:

- **The best way to learn the ins and outs of Instagram is to study the competition.** (Warts and all.) Find out when and how often they post, along with ideas on content (and what they promote.)
- **Another key resource are influencers, profiles that have an audience who'd be interested in your products, but not in direct competition with you.** These can be things like blogs, magazines, websites, manufacturers and deranged enthusiasts.
- **Hashtags are super-important in Instagram.** So collect a batch of hashtags you can use for your future posts. (Try your best to find a mix of popular, semi-popular, and somewhat niche hashtags to help your discoverability.)

Chapter 4:

Seven Ways to Create Killer Instagram Content

"Creativity is knowing how to hide your sources."

-C.E.M. Joad

Okay, we're here! We're finally gonna create some visually delicious, lead-generatin' Instagram content!

But before I share with you my 7 Secrets to Creating Killer Instagram Content — and I use these secrets over and over — I need to lay out my...

[BORING BUT IMPORTANT LEGAL DISCLAIMER]

I know the Internet can feel like the "Wild West" sometimes. But Instagram has made it a priority to crack down on people posting photos they don't hold the rights to.

And though Instagram tends to be a bit conservative, as social media companies go, it's their sandbox. (So we need to play by their rules.)

That means:

- Don't grab a photo off the Internet and post it to Instagram, without the permission of the rights holder. (Usually they'll give it to you, if you ask.)
- If you get permission to use the photo, be sure to credit them in the caption.
- Don't assume adding a "filter" to an existing photo makes it "yours." It doesn't.
- When in doubt, grab a photo from one of the many royalty-free photo collections out there. (Such as MorgueFile, Wikipedia, or Pixabay.)

- The EASIEST way around this conundrum is to simply take your own photos.

Got it? Don't post photos unless ya got permission.

And if you want to use a photo that you didn't take, grab it from one of the royalty-free sites.

Okay, enough of the boring legal stuff. Let's jump right in with…

KILLER INSTAGRAM CONTENT METHOD #1: SHOW OFF YOUR PRODUCTS & SERVICES (IN CONTEXT)

This is probably the MOST effective Instagram marketing strategy there is, showing off your product or service in all its glory. But most companies who do this, execute it so clumsily they hardly get any marketing bang from it. (Which is a shame.)

Here's how to strut your company stuff (effectively):

- **Go for pictures of humans using/interacting with your products NOT staged product shots.** Try to put a person in the shot when featuring your products. It boosts engagement and leads to higher conversions.
- **Your team IS a part of your products and services.** So, why not show off that hard-working (or moderately hard-working) staff of yours? Studies have shown that the more people know about a company's employees, the more likely they are to buy…so why not use it to your advantage?
- **Before-and-after shots work great.** If your business revolves around some kind of transformation — whether physical fitness or interior decorating — add great "before-and-after" photos to underscore the power of your product or service. (In Chapter 7, I'll go over tools that can help you create these types of pictures.)
- **Photos from live events and product launches work really well.** You and I both know how boring business events can be, but our audience doesn't have to know that. Have somebody take a bunch of pics of your event and throw them up on Ins-

tagram. (This boosts your presence as an authority and gives you Instagram content you can use for weeks.)

- **Humor goes a long way with your product/service photos.** There is so much blatant self-promotion on Instagram, it's refreshing to see a business who brings wit and self-deprecation to their product pics. So, don't take yourself, or your business, too seriously. And have fun (while you promote.)

Killer Instagram Content Method #2: Promote Your Events or Limited-Time Offers

This is what MOST companies love to share on Instagram: endless posts about whatever promo crap they're hawking. And these types of posts CAN be profitable (if you do them right.)

Here's what I've learned about doing a few hundred of these:

- **Don't assume people will get the message of your offer from your caption.** You GOTTA put a text overlay on the image that spells out exactly what the offer is.
- **Don't put TOO MUCH text over the image.** Keep it simple. Use active verbs that indicate clear benefits. And let your sales page do the talking.
- **Include time-limits or discounted prices in your image.** Make it urgent that people CLICK NOW, not later, to check out your stuff. (Scarcity and discounts work really well.)
- **Pictures of people enjoying your event or product work best for overall promotion.** Far better than boring, generic product photos.
- **Short videos are a great way to boost interest in your event or product launch.** Hardly anybody does these. Which is fine with me — lets you and kick serious marketing ass. The key with these is to sell your "excitement" — not the product. (Let your sales page do the heavy lifting.)
- **Tease events and product launches in the days leading up with some Instagram posts**. I have no idea why people would be in-

terested in watching us "prepare" for a launch or event — but they do. (Trust me.) So build anticipation with pre-launch videos and images that let people know WHEN it's coming.

- **Tell people EXACTLY what they need to do to get your offer.** "Click here to..." or "To grab your FREE offer..." Don't be vague. Tell people what you WANT them to do. (And they'll usually do it.)

Killer Instagram Content Method #3: Inspirational (Feel-Good) Crap

These types of posts are created by putting inspirational quotes in a text overlay over a photo of a sunrise. Or a mountain. Or a redwood forest. (Man, they love redwood forests.)

And I, personally, find these vapid and annoying. But I am in the vast, cynical minority.

But here are a few tips to keep in mind:

- **To create these quote posts use a tool, such as Canva or PicMonkey.** These are FREE tools that let you easily cobble together a textured background image (with your devastating quote of choice.)
- **If you can, pick a quote from a speaker most of your audience has heard of.** That insight from that 19th-century physicist may be profound, but its impact will be lessened if nobody has heard of 'em.
- **Pick a short, clever quote.** Don't go with a super-long paragraph on a topic. Keep it short and simple.
- **Find quotes at sites like Brainy Quotes or GoodReads.** These are good, FREE places to find quotes to use with your feel-good crap.
- **Pick a quote that has resonance with your audience.** If you're selling fitness equipment, go with something about "goal-setting" or "determination." If you're selling financial services, go with something about "wisdom" and "experience." Choose the right bait for the right fish.

- **When in doubt, go with something about "overcoming adversity."** That's something we can all relate to. (No matter what kind of crap we're looking to buy.)

Killer Instagram Content Method #4: Random, Personal Stuff About Your Day-to-Day

This is another category I could do without. (But I'm a cranky malcontent who spends time in his bunker waiting for the zombie apocalypse.)

People love getting to know more about people. And that includes:

- What movies you're watching
- Books you're reading
- Struggles you've overcome
- Goals you've accomplished
- Anything to do with kids and/or pets (This stuff is Instagram crack)
- Those ever-annoying "selfies" of wherever you are throughout the day

I know. Sounds like 5th ring of hell stuff. But people love commenting and liking this crap.

And, when you think about it, one of the most powerful motivators in the world is the "need" to be valuable. To contribute something to the tribe. (And for a lot of folks, this makes them feel like they're contributing something, even if they're just sitting on their be-hind.)

Killer Instagram Content Method #5: Sharing Your How-to Expertise

Your business may not use content marketing much. (You know that annoying method where you give away your best stuff — so they're tempted to buy some of your crappier stuff for money.)

But there's nothing people LOVE more than learning secrets, tips, strategies, and shortcuts that'll help them feel smarter than other people…I mean…lead better and more impactful lives.

Couple things to keep in mind when promoting content with an Instagram post:

- **Videos and photo galleries do well** when promoted on Instagram. 5200-word essays? Not so much.
- **Pair a benefit-focused text overlay with an eye-catching image** to promote your content. And by "benefit," we mean a "benefit" to the user…not you. (Just sayin'.)
- **Use a benefit-focused headline that doesn't sound like homework**. I know the headline of your blog post may be "124 Ways to Improve Your Life." But keep it simple. Use phrases like "Discover the #1 Secret…"; "Learn my #1 Strategy…" Keep it simple and non-threatening.
- **Try to have the image you use in your Instagram post be the SAME** as the one featured on the webpage you're promoting. This is an overlooked technique, but you wanna make the transition from Instagram to website as quickly as possible. (And using the same creative will help that.)
- **Make it clear what KIND of content you're promoting (especially if you're promoting a PHOTO or VIDEO.)** For some, and by some I mean most, people just don't want to click on something that sounds like work. But photos and video don't sound like work, they sound like goofing off.

Killer Instagram Content Method #6: Ask for User-Generated Content

This might be the MOST under-utilized type of Instagram content there is. Which is a shame because it's not only content you DON'T have to create — but it also boosts the engagement of your audience.

And user-generated content like this can come in many forms:

- Users submitting photos of them using your product
- Users submitting photos of them striking a unique or interesting pose (This works really well — no idea why)
- Users giving feedback on a question you pose
- Users creating a video response to one of your posts
- Users/customers giving video testimonials

And that LAST ONE is worth its weight in gold. (And worth more than 100 sales pages combined.)

Now, this strategy won't be effective until you've amassed somewhat of a following on Instagram. (And in Chapter 6, we'll go over methods for building your Instagram zombie army.)

But all you gotta do is just upload an eye-catching photo — with a text overlay "asking' people to upload their own photo and adding a branded hashtag of your choosing — and you've got your every own content marketing army. (Without having to break a sweat.)

Killer Instagram Content Method #7: Good, Old Video

So, we've touched on video in the first six Instagram content methods. But I want to encourage you to give video a try. (And the Instagram app makes it so damn easy. Just hit the record button and then the pause button and you've shot a scene.)

Now the maximum time allowed for Instagram videos is 60 seconds. (So, no Presidential convention speeches allowed.) But I've seen clever things done with videos on Instagram:

- Answer a single question
- Offer a single tip
- Show off a singular fitness trick (or dance move)
- Give a daily update on what's going on in somebody's lives
- Give customers a chance to express their opinion, show off their creativity or offer a testimonial

If you're a cantankerous English major like me — who reads 1200-page 19th-century novels for fun! — then this 60-second limit to videos will seem like a sign of the impending fall of civilization.

But to many of your would-be customers, it is the perfect length for them to get a taste of what you (or your business) is all about. And the companies that are able to manage this short (but powerful) method of communication are poised to make a crap load of money. (Pretty good for 60 seconds of your time.)

CHAPTER 2 Key Takeaways:

- **One of the best ways to use Instagram is to show your products or services in context.** (And by "in context" we mean actual, breathing humans using your stuff, not just stock-photo models.)
- **Promoting live-events and special offers is another great way to use Instagram.** Just be sure the KEY information is in a text overlay on the image. (Don't expect the caption to do all the work.)
- **Inspirational (touchy-feely) quote posts work well on Instagram.** (Even though I hate 'em.) Just use a tool like Canva or PicMonkey, and throw a short, clever quote from a speaker "some" people have heard of.
- **Random, personal (but not-too-personal) snapshots of your day are another great way to engage with your audience.** (Doesn't necessarily have an immediate ROI, but can build some serious goodwill later on down the line.)
- **Promoting your how-to content — especially videos — on Instagram can seriously boost your marketing.** Just be sure to indicate the benefit of the content (and whether it's a video) in the text overlay on the image.
- **User-generated content can be some of the most powerful and easiest type of content to create.** Just ask your followers to respond to questions, show off their style, film themselves using your products…just be sure to wait until you got a decent following first.
- **Posting videos straight to Instagram is an under-utilized — yet staggeringly effective — form of marketing.** Yeah, you only get 60 seconds, but it works really well for testimonials, behind-the-scenes tidbits, and quick mini-tips.

Chapter 5:

The Perfect Instagram Post Checklist

"It takes real planning to organize this kind of chaos."

-Mel Odom

All the prep work is done. We're (finally) going to upload your delicious Instagram content for the world to see! (And hopefully inspire them to buy some of our crap.)

In the next chapter we'll delve into the creation of your Instagram fan base and go over how to attract those smartphone-addicted masses to follow — and engage — with your Instagram activity.

But BEFORE THAT I encourage you to upload at least 10-15 posts FIRST. And for Instagram posting, feel free to follow my Perfect Instagram Post Checklist.

This is the 7-step checklist I use each time I post my Instagram goodness, and it'll ensure you maximize the potential of your posts — and wring every ounce of marketing juice out of your Instagram marketing efforts.

So, without further Instagram adieu, let's jump right in with:

Instagram Post Checklist Item #1: Pick a Goal That Doesn't Suck

Now, you need not spend hours on this. (Please don't.) But it's a good idea to have SOME idea what the hell you're trying to accomplish with a particular marketing activity, before actually doing it.

And with Instagram posts the goals will usually be from the following list:

- Boost exposure for a product or service (Product/service shots, behind-the-scenes, videos)
- Increase engagement with your Instagram account (Questions, Feel-good quotes, contests, user-generated content)
- Gather sign-ups for your email list (How-to content, free offers)
- Drive sales (promoted events, product launches, behind-the-scenes videos, user-generated content)
- Ramp up exposure for your other social media properties (videos, behind-the-scenes, feel-good quotes, user-generated content)
- Pad your Instagram follower account (Almost any type of post)

The key thing to remember is that an Instagram post CAN have multiple goals. (You can sell stuff AND pad your Instagram follower count.)

But I like to have ONE primary goal and 1-2 tertiary goals. And, for my business, my THREE most successful goals are:

1. Gather sign-ups for my email list
2. Increase engagement
3. Boost exposure

Direct selling from my Instagram account doesn't always pay off for me. (I prefer to do that through my email marketing.) But your funnel might support linking to a sales page.

And I don't focus too much on increasing my Instagram follower count with a specific post. (That happens anyway.)

But you'll want to tweak and test to see what works for your business. Just get in the habit of choosing ONE primary goal — and 1-2 tertiary goals. (Don't I just sound like an English major with my throwin' around "tertiary?")

Instagram Post Checklist Item #2: Pick a Posting Time That Doesn't Suck

Okay, now we're getting to some juicy ninja-hack stuff. WHEN should we be posting our Instagram stuff?

To be fair, Instagram is such a NEW platform — and the user base will change as it gets adopted by people who are over 30 and don't have lip piercings — but for now the best data suggests that optimal Instagram posting times of the week are (in descending order):

1. Wednesday
2. Thursday
3. Tuesday

With "Mondays" being the absolute WORST day of the week. (I think that's because most Instagram users are hungover...uh...I mean, focusing on their work.)

But if you can only do 1-2x a week — be sure to post somewhere in that Tuesday-Thursday range.

Now, when it comes to time of day, there are essentially THREE sweet spots:

- 5:00 p.m. (EST)
- 10:00 p.m. (EST)
- 1:00-2:00 a.m. (EST)

This will depend on your particular audience, and their nocturnal habits. But try these out first, and then do your own testing. Again, if you're only gonna post a couple times a week, you could do worse than follow these general industry benchmarks. (And in Chapter 7, I'll show you some super-simple apps you can use to schedule all your Instagram goodness.)

Instagram Post Checklist Item #3: Upload That Photo and Make It All Pretty-Like

The HOW to upload your photo is very simple. (So simple a Kardashian could handle it.) You:

- Open Instagram on your phone or tablet
- Click on the big blue camera button (or click on the "+" button on the bottom)
- Find the photo on your device using "library"
- ...and upload

But it's those all-important Instagram filters I want to walk you through. Because they can be confusing, and unless you've got some serious photography skills you'll spend THREE hours trying to find the right filter. (Or you'll end up with Instagram posts that make you look like a zombie.)

So, here are a few things I've learned about Instagram filters (and again I'm no photo-filter expert!)

- **Don't just stick with the "Normal" filter.** It's boring and nobody will love you. (Okay, maybe that's strong. But go crazy...it's Instagram!)
- **When in doubt, go for the "Earlybird" filter.** It's the most forgiving — makes you look more "bronzed" and "golden" than usual — and it's the most popular filter out there for a reason. It makes every shot look dramatic and interesting.
- **If you want your picture to look dramatic** and have dark edges around the corner — like an old-time photograph --go for "X-Pro II."
- **If you don't want a "dark" photo and you want to boost the "lightness" of your pics** — and I'm thinking mostly here of product launches, event promotions, and links to content — then go with "Valencia." (It's a dramatic filter, without the "undead" look.)

- **Go with "Hefe" if your picture has lots of color and you need sharpness and vibrancy.** And not "bright" in a hipster band photo sort of way.
- **If you're going for that artistic, discolored (post-apocalyptic wasteland) look,** where the color is washed out, then "Brannan" is your filter of choice.
- **And finally if you wanna go "light" with the filters** and use the Instagram bells-and-whistles, then "Nashville" is a great add to your Instagram toolbox.

But again, don't take hours and hours poring over all the filters. Just try a few out and see if you like the results. (And when you're posting something that requires immediate action, go easy on the hipster, starving-artist filters.)

Note: If you don't see any of the filters I mentioned above, click on "manage" to specify which filters you see in your dashboard.

Instagram Post Checklist Item #4: Create a Killer Caption

Aside from the photo you take, this is the MOST important part of the Instagram posting process. That's because your caption has to do so many things:

- Tell people what the picture is about
- Ask people to comment and/or share your post
- Add a call to action (if relevant)
- Add those all-important hashtags (15-20 if ya got them)

I know this seems daunting. And the first couple of these you do may appear awkward and ineffective. But stick with the process I'm about to show you and you'll master creating captions in no time. (And you can always go back and edit your captions later if you screw up.)

So, here's what I do:

1. **Open your Facebook app on your phone or tablet.** Huh? Facebook? Yeah, we're gonna type our status update there, so it recognizes any line breaks we add. Otherwise our caption will look more scrunched than a rush-hour NYC subway. I know this seems like a pain — and you don't have to do it if you don't want to — but once you get used to it you'll see it pay dividends.
2. **Start off by telling folks about the back story of the picture.** (Don't start off promoting.) Nobody cares about YOUR marketing. But do they care about your story — the WHY you took the picture? Where you were WHY you took it. And WHAT you were thinking when you took it. ("Here's my view from the hotel lobby of the Waldorf Astoria in NYC at the Evil James Bond Villain Convention!")
3. **Hit "return" and add a line break.**
4. **(Optional) Add your CTA (call-to-action).** This will either be a) Click on this link to get more info or buy something or b) Comment, like and share this post. (Or both.) Either way make it friendly but CLEAR what you want them to do. ("If you'd like to find out how to be a James Bond villain get my FREE "How to Be a James Bond Villain" report by clicking on the link in my profile."; "What would your James Bond villain name be? Let us know in the comments!"
5. **Hit "return" and add a line break.**
6. **Add them Hashtags.** You should already have a nice list of hashtags assembled. (I recommend having them in a text document in a cloud storage app like Dropbox, so you can easily copy and paste them.)
7. **Copy and paste the text from the Facebook app to your Instagram caption**. And you've completed your first caption!

Note: Instagram does NOT allow you to embed links right in your caption. (No bueno.) But in Chapter 7, I'll show you a super-sneaky ninja way to get links right in the caption.

Instagram Post Checklist Item #5: Tag Other Instagram Users

This won't be entirely relevant when you're first starting out and have no followers to speak of. But tagging other Instagram users, who might be interested in what you're posting, is a cool way to get INSTANT engagement. (And build your follower base in no time.)

Again, not required, but it's nice if you like to engage and talk with other human beings.

Instagram Post Checklist Item #6: Tag Your Geographic Location

You wouldn't think this was important. God knows I don't care WHERE somebody is posting from.

But having a geo-verified Instagram post has proven to boost both engagement and conversion rates. Maybe it's like a subtle form of account verification.

Whatever it is, unless you're in the Witness Protection program and want nobody to know where you are, tag your geographic location.

Instagram Post Checklist Item #6: Promote Your Post on Your Other Social Media Sites

As we went over in Chapter 2, you can link up your Instagram account with your Twitter, Tumblr, Flickr and Facebook accounts. (There are also a bunch of other accounts I've never heard of.)

Now you DON'T have to share your Instagram posts on these other platforms. (And you can pick which ones you want to use for promotion at the time of posting.)

But unless you go off your meds and are knee-deep in a Charlie Sheen-esque rant…why not? Give your posts as much exposure as you can.

PUNK ROCK MARKETING
AMPLIFY YOUR MESSAGE

CHAPTER 5 Key Takeaways:

- **You can have more than one goal for your Instagram posts.** But keep it limited to one or two primary goals. My favorite goals are boosting exposure for a product, increasing engagement on my account, and gathering sign-ups.
- **Tuesday-Thursdays (5:00 p.m. and 10:00 p.m. EST) are the best times of the week to post on Instagram.** Avoid Mondays if you can.
- **Add "some" kind of filter to your Instagram posts.** (Normal filters are boring.) There are many to choose from, but if in doubt go for "Earlybird."
- **The ideal Instagram caption tells people what the pictures are about, asks folks to comment, provides a call-to-action and has 15-20 relevant hashtags.** (Don't forget to create your post captions away from your smartphone, if possible.)
- **Tagging other Instagram users with your posts is a great way to boost engagement** and show super-cheap social proof.
- **Don't forget to promote your Instagram posts on your other social media sites.** That includes Twitter, Tumblr, Flickr and Facebook.

Chapter 6:

How to Create a Rabid Tribe of Zombie Instagram Followers

"A friend is someone who knows all about you and still loves you."

-Elbert Hubbard

Congratulations! If you've read this far that means you're in the upper 75% of all breathing humans on the planet. (Most of whom never read more than half of ANY book…EVER!)

Hopefully, you've dipped your toe into the Instagram waters. (And picked up a few followers along the way, by simply being an awesome person.)

But in this chapter we're gonna put that Instagram tribe-buildin' muscle of yours on steroids. (And we're gonna do that with my seven favorite strategies for acquiring an Instagram zombie army…I mean…passionate Instagram following:

Instagram Tribe Buildin' Tip #1: Post More Than You Think You Should

I know this is gonna sound obvious — which it is — but the MORE ya post on Instagram, the more you get noticed. (And add to that zombie army.)

Instagram is more like Twitter and Facebook, than it is Pinterest. Though posts can be found through #hashtag searches, recent content ALWAYS gets noticed and consumed far more than older stuff. (And with the attention span of most Instagram users hovering somewhere near that of a housefly, it's no surprise that consistent content is the key to getting discovered.)

In the last chapter I went over general guidelines about optimal times of the week to post (Tuesdays and Thursday evenings) but once you get the hang of this…

…as long as you're saying something interesting, post as much as you damn well want. (Nobody'll throw you in Instagram jail — and you might just get a ton more sales.)

Instagram Tribe Buildin' Tip #2: Put a "Follow Me On Instagram" Button on Your Website

The actual creation of the button is super simple. Just head over to ShareThis.com, put in your account name, specify your text ("Follow Me/Us on Instagram" works) and it'll spit out a gorgeous piece of code you can put on your website. (Best of all, ShareThis lets you create buttons for all the major social platforms. Nice!)

Though you can certainly put the "Follow Me on Instagram" code wherever you want, I would absolutely recommend you put it in places such as:

- Your website sidebar
- The footer of each of your blog posts
- Any "About Me" Pages on your website

But you shouldn't just stop with your website. You could also put it in…

- Your Tumblr posts
- Your Twitter bio
- Your email signature
- Your message board profiles
- Anywhere else you can think of!

Now, your audience may not be super Instagram-savvy…yet. But don't worry, in a year your efforts as an Instagram marketing pioneer will pay off.

INSTAGRAM TRIBE BUILDIN' TIP #3: LIKE, FOLLOW AND COMMENT YOUR WAY TO STARDOM

This is probably the MOST EFFECTIVE way to build your fan base. But it's not an overnight strategy, and requires spending short, consistent bursts of time interacting with fellow users on Instagram. (I know, not exactly a "night at the movies.")

But here's how it works:

- Find a batch of Instagram users you want to interact with. Either use a relevant hashtag (such as #socialmedia) or just head to the followers of an influencer your target audience would be likely to follow. (You should have a list of influencers in your Instagram Research Worksheet we went over in Chapter 3.)
- Scanning the list of users, follow SIX accounts who fall into the demographic and interest patterns of your ideal audience. (Tip: Make sure they've got at least 500 followers themselves, and at least a line or two in their bio. Otherwise they probably spend little time on Instagram.)
- For THREE of the SIX followers you just followed, check out their posts and "like" at least THREE, per user. (To "like" a post just click on the "heart" icon in the lower left.)
- For the OTHER THREE followers you just followed, check out their posts and "comment" on at least ONE of their posts. (Be sure it's not a generic "nice post" comment. But something unique and authentic...and something a robot piece of software couldn't do.)
- Do this 2-3x a day, during the hours of 5:00p.m. — 10:00p.m. EST.

And before you freak out I'm asking you to give up your late-night viewings of "Castle" — just remember each of these "following sessions" should take only 2-3 minutes a piece. (Four minutes if you've already had that second glass of wine.)

And trust me, those four-minute flurries of following, commenting and liking, not only will help you avoid the Instagram spam police and build up your follower counts exponentially...

...but you'll also create some serious Instagram goodwill you can convert later on for some hard currency.

Instagram Tribe Buildin' Tip #4: @Mention and Spotlight Your Existing Followers

Once you've got a fairly decent collection of followers, and if you follow Tip #3 you'll have that before you know it, then you'll want to use three of my favorite strategies for boosting engagement with your existing followers:

1. @Mention followers in your Instagram posts (You do this by adding their @username in a post caption)
2. Share a follower's image in your own feed (You can do this by taking a screen shot with your phone and then cropping and uploading to your own feed. Be sure to ask permission FIRST!)
3. Share a follower's post on one of your other social media channels (Facebook, Pinterest and Twitter are ideal for this. Be sure to ask permission FIRST!)

And why would we want to embark on this bit of altruistic spelunking? Because this follower will pay it forward, by sharing your post with your inner circle. (Which will get you a new swath of followers and possible customers.)

Trust me: This is effective. But ya gotta schedule it, just like them following sessions. (Otherwise you'll never get around to it.)

Instagram Tribe Buildin' Tip #5: @Mention Celebs and Influencers

This is like the previous tip, only this time the person you are "mentioning" has the last name of Kardashian. (Or is a big influencer within your industry.)

And just like in the previous step, all you have to do is add the @username of the person you're trying to reach in your post caption.

Now you don't want to be a spammy jerk. Don't just add people for the sake of getting access to their followers. (It's not cool, and it frankly doesn't work.)

But if you have a genuine response to something a fellow Instagram user has said or created — let's say you've been moved by a book somebody wrote, or you think the influencer or celeb might be interested in your post…

…then knock yourself out. (Just don't lose sleep waiting for Katy Perry to get back to you.)

Instagram Tribe Buildin' Tip #6: Add a QR Code for In-Store Users

So, I have to be honest: I know next to nothing about how QR codes work. But apparently there is this witchcraft that lets you generate magical code…

…which you put in your place of business. (And which allows customers to scan with their phones and instantly lets them become a follower of your Instagram tribe.)

Like I said, I'm a real QR expert.

But, having worked with enough clients who have physical stores, I can tell you the Instagram QR strategy works (especially if your clientele is under 40)…

…as long as you give them an incentive to actually follow you. Just being added ain't enough. (Ya gotta do better than that.)

So, here's what I recommend:

- Create your QR code — Through whatever wizard means you do that)
- Create a compelling incentive — Follow us on Instagram to get 10% off your order or Follow us to be entered into a contest to go on a date with Natalie Portman (if only)
- Print out the QR code (or conjure it) and put it next to your register — Your clientele will see it

Wait? Contest? What's this about a contest? How do I do an Instagram contest?

So, glad you asked…

Instagram Tribe Buildin' Tip #7: Run a Frickin' Instagram Contest

This is more of an advanced tribe-buildin' tip, and one I wouldn't jump into until you've got at least 1000 followers. (Otherwise you won't see serious gains.)

But once you've got those 1K followers, I highly recommend you try it. (I schedule at least one contest every three months and always see a huge boost in LEADS and SALES.)

So, how do you run an Instagram contest? Here's the four-step process I follow each time:

1. Choose a non-sucky prize. Gift cards work great. (Especially if you're a brick-and-mortar shop or an e-commerce site) If you're a service business, then some kind of consultation or value service is a great prize.
2. Announce the rules of the contest in an Instagram post. It'll be some action that requires followers to a) Upload a photo of them expressing themselves or using your product and b) Using a predesignated contest hashtag
3. Keep an eye on the hashtag. It's important you choose a unique hashtag. #SummerFun might sound like a great way to describe your contest, but it'll be a nightmare figuring out who actually entered the contest. (I generally go with something like #CompanyNameSpringContest…or something like that.)
4. Announce the winner. You can do this either through a specific Instagram post or direct message to the winner yourself. (Or both.)

Like I said, su-per simple.

Once you get the hang of running a contest or two, you can try out different variations, such as:

- Have people comment, like or share to enter a contest
- Have people VOTE on an item of yours (with the winning item going on sale at deep discount)
- Have people tag their friends (Example: "Tag a friend who is into the 'smoky eye' look…") — This type of contest is so popular it's got a dedicated hashtag — #TagAFriend
- Any other fun and visually interesting (though legal) activity you can dream up to have your followers do

There's no limit to the weird and wonderful ways you can use a contest to build your tribe (and put money in your pocket.)

Just don't have them watch one of those awful "Twilight" movies. (No prize is worth that.)

CHAPTER 6 Key Takeaways:

- **It's simple, the more you post the more followers you get.** Recent content will always be king.
- **Gather new Instagram followers by simply asking for them on your website.** Generate "follow me on Instagram" code and place it in key areas such as your site's "About Me" page, sidebar and the footer of blog posts. (But don't forget about other places such as email signatures and Twitter bios.)
- **The most effective form of tribe-buildin' is to like, follow and comment on Instagram users.** Schedule 2-3x minute-long sessions where you like, comment and follow folks who represent the demographics of your ideal customer.
- **Boost your follower count by spotlighting your followers and fans.** Just mention their @username in a post and you'll not only get their engagement on a post — but most likely they'll share it with their own tribe.
- **You can also ping celebs and influencers with the same @username method.** The key is not to be too spammy — or too stalker-ish because Taylor Swift didn't get right back to ya.
- **Though the author knows nothing about the witchcraft that is QR codes, he knows it works.** Just make sure you give people an incentive to follow you on Instagram.
- **Instagram contests work super frickin' well.** Choose a unique hashtag and a prize that doesn't suck. (Gift cards and one-on-one coaching sessions work best.)

Chapter 7:

Five Ninja-Hack Tools & Apps That Will Make You Money

"The best investment is in the tools of one's trade."

-Benjamin Franklin

We've come to my FAVORITE part of this book! (And it should be your favorite too.)

That's because I'm about to share with you my favorite ninja-hack apps and tools that'll not only save you a crap load of time...

...but also make you a crap load of money.

Now, some of these apps/tools are more on the advanced side. (For example, I don't recommend you jump right out and run an Instagram contest with Wishpond your first week out.)

But if you add these slowly, over the course of the next few weeks, you'll be shocked how quickly your Instagram efforts will start to pay off.

Quick word of warning: many of these apps have the lasting power of an NBC sitcom. (Not much.)

For instance, one of my FAVORITE tools ever — Iconosquare — was FREE for years. (Until they started charging $200/month. Yikes!)

So, do your due diligence before signing up for any of these apps/tools recommended below.

Okay, let's jump into the deep end of the Instagram app pool:

Instagram Ninja-Hack Tool #1: HootSuite (Instagram Post Scheduling Tool)

Posting on Instagram with your smartphone or tablet of choice has three major drawbacks:

- It's tough to type out lengthy captions without making a typo (or inducing carpal tunnel in your hands)
- Copying and pasting 15-20 relevant hashtags into a post is a nightmare
- Posting consistently during optimal Instagram times can be as difficult as 12th-grade pre-calculus

But worry not, Instagrammers, we have our champion! And that is the social media management tool, HootSuite.

HootSuite is a web/mobile app that lets you manage nearly ALL of your social media activity — I use it to churn out all my LinkedIn, Facebook, Instagram and Twitter activity — in one simple, convenient location.

Best of all, it's FREE. (Though they have paid options, if you want more user accounts and broader analytics.)

Now HootSuite isn't PERFECT. (You can schedule posts for anytime — but in order to "publish" you have to "approve" a mobile notification for the post RIGHT before your scheduled publish time.)

And it doesn't work well when you repost other people's stuff (more on that next.)

But for a FREE tool that lets you do MOST of your Instagram activity right on your computer, it's a DAMN good addition to your overall Instagram marketing plan.

Instagram Ninja-Hack Tool #2: Repost for Instagram

HootSuite works great for posting original Instagram content you create. But what about reposting other people's stuff? (Which is one of the most effective ways to get your profile noticed…notice other people first!)

That's where the Repost for Instagram app comes in.

Forget spending HOURS each week finding content you can repost and share with your followers. With this app you can scour Instagram, using keywords, to find users who might make for ideal prospects. (Lets you schedule a week's worth of Instagram content in just a few minutes.)

Here's how it works:

- Download the Repost for Instagram app
- Fire up the Instagram app
- Use keywords to find users who have interesting content AND who you'd like expose to your brand
- Click on one of their posts and then click on the three dots in the upper right
- Select "copy link"
- Open up your "Repost" app (the app will automatically recognize the post you copied a link for)
- Then when you WANT to…open the Repost app and publish the repost

Now it doesn't give you the ability to schedule posts. But it lets you create a reservoir of content, in just minutes, that you can then go back and publish when you need to fill your quota. (I recommend 5pm and 10pm EST Tuesday -Thursday, at the least.)

This may not pay huge dividends right away. But if you stick with it, you'll slowly build a legion of Instagram followers.

And then you'll be ready for…

Instagram Ninja-Hack Tool #3: Follow Liker

The FollowLiker app is so powerful I almost don't want to tell you about it.

It's that good.

But if you want to build your follower numbers up to 2-3k, in a matter of weeks, you must:

- Follow a ton of people in your target audience
- Like posts by your target audience
- Unfollow folks who didn't follow you back
- Keep doing it for hours and hours each week until your finger bleed

And if that sounds fun, and if enjoy getting your teeth drilled, then don't let me stand in your way. But if you'd like to skip all the manual work, and let automation take over, then Follow Liker is a great way to go.

Here's how it works:

- **Purchase FollowLiker.** Yep. Sorry. It's not FREE. But at $75 it's worth it.
- **Find a computer you use little.** That old laptop you spilled coffee on will work.
- **Set parameters to the software.** (More on that soon.) And let it do it's thing in the background.
- **Watch as your follower count climbs**.

Before you freak out that a tool that does things like mass following, liking and unfollowing will get you exiled to the Instagram prison colony, just know with the conservative settings below you'll ensure you don't risk censure from the Insta-Police.

When setting up your FollowLiker account you'll want to:

- **Skip one day off a week.** Using this tool 24/7 is a great way to get your account banned.
- **Operate only during the day.** Or at night. But not both.
- **Impose daily limits.** I like to limit the tool to only 100-150 follows per day, only 100 unfollows per day, and only 200 likes of individual photos per day. Stick with those and stay well within bounds.
- **Insert a 60-second delay between actions.** You don't want the tool just going non-stop. You want it to appear organic. And adding a one-minute delay will do that.

Instagram Ninja-Hack Tool #4: A Second Instagram Account (For Super-Sneaky Hyperlinks)

This is my FAVORITE ninja-hack on the entire list. Mostly because it's really effective and NOBODY else uses it. (Except for me and my crazy clients.)

But here's the basic concept:

- Instagram DOESN'T allow LINKS in the captions of your Instagram posts - The only external link you can have is right below your bio
- Instagram DOES allow you to link to other Instagram accounts - by simply adding @username in the caption of the post
- So, what we do is create a SECOND Instagram account (such as @mybusinessfreebie) and add that to our caption
- And when users click over to that 2nd Instagram account they see our promotional goodness (and we get around the NO LINK Instagram caption rule)

I know this may sound like a lot of work. All you're doing is creating a dedicated SECOND Instagram account and then creating 3-4 Instagram posts (with great images and strong text call-outs) that promote that all-important special offer or freebie giveaway you're hawking.

Because here's the funny thing: you'd think research would show that these extra "hoops" you're making people run through would be bad for conversions. (Actually the opposite is true.)

The more you keep asking people for "small" commitments, but still keep them in their "native" Instagram environment, the more likely they'll take a positive action you want when they finally reach your landing page.

Now, again your offer needs to be good. It needs to be a great discount or freebie giveaway...or amazing offer that nobody can resist. (Don't just hawk expensive crap nobody wants.)

But the cool thing is you can create as many of these PROMO Instagram accounts as you want. (Maybe one for each of your products and services.)

So, give this technique a try. (Just promise not to share it with everybody you know. We gotta hold on to our competitive advantages as long as we can.)

Instagram Ninja-Hack Tool #5: WishPond (Instagram Contest App)

So, as we went over in the last chapter, Instagram contests are a fantastic way to build your Instagram following. (And even turn those followers into warm leads.)

But some logical, tech-y contest stuff can be a pain to deal with. That's why I recommend a contest tool, such as WishPond.

Basically what WishPond does is offer you:

- **Templates for creating mobile-responsive contest landing pages** (that you can then publish on your website, Facebook page or Twitter stream super EASILY)
- **And then they handle the collection of all the leads.** (My favorite type of contest is the Instagram hashtag contest — and the awesome thing is WishPond will collect all the photos…so you don't have to sift through them.)
- **Most importantly: WishPond takes care of all the contest terms of service and regulations.** (This can be a pain and they make sure you totally comply with Instagram's rules of the contest road.)

Now, WishPond has a ton of different payment options, depending on how many leads you acquire (and how many internal users you need.) But they have a 14-day trial I highly recommend you check out. (Even if just to try out your FIRST contest.)

CHAPTER 7 KEY TAKEAWAYS:

- **HootSuite is a fantastic FREE tool that lets you create and schedule your Instagram posts ahead of time.** You will have to "approve" each scheduled post on your mobile device, but this FREE tool will save you a crap load of time.
- **The Repost for Instagram app is a marvelous way to gather content** to fill your Instagram coffers in just a couple minutes a week.
- **FollowLiker is a great tool for automating the liking and following of folks in your target audience.** Be sure to use the limits outlined above to avoid a crackdown from the Instagram police.
- **A second Instagram account is the ideal super-ninja way to get around the "can't link in Instagram posts" rule.** Just create a dedicated second account, for a particular offer or product, and then fill that account with posts that direct users to your location of choice.
- **WishPond is the perfect Instagram contest tool.** They let you create mobile-friendly contest landing pages and handle all the lead collection and hashtag monitoring for you. (Big time-saver!)

EPILOGUE:
"Toto, I Don't Think We're in Kansas Anymore"

I wish I could tell you Instagram was just a blip on the marketing radar screen.

That its practitioners' obsession with hashtags and selfies and sepia-toned pictures of...God knows what...is just a slight deviation from an otherwise straight trajectory toward a more nuanced and refined society.

But you and I both know that just ain't the case.

Things are only gonna get more vain, more narcissistic, and more superficial — future academics will call it the "Kardashian factor" — and Instagram is the ultimate reflection of a generation absolutely consumed with presenting themselves in the most hip and attractive way. (So they can be validated with a flurry of likes, comments and follows.)

But having plumbed these Instagram depths for the last year I can tell you that underneath the shallow Instagram posts and the inappropriate and stupefyingly inane comments is something far darker and more profound...

...a need to be seen. (And heard. And understood.)

And if you're able to offer your message (and your products) not in some antiquated 50s sales-y way...

...but as an opportunity for young people to get noticed in a world that's as distracted as a four-year-old on Red Bull...

...then you'll not just sell more stuff. (Which is always nice.) But you'll create an army of loyal (and socially connected) users who can spread your company's message faster and far more cheaply than you ever could. (Even with 30 seconds during the Super Bowl.)

So, look past all the pouty-lip selfies and the six-pack ab mirror pictures and just ask yourself…how can my product or service make my tribe look smarter/hipper/more attractive/morally superior than their friends?

If you're able to do that, then your business will have more momentum than a four-year-old on Red Bull.

LinkedIn® Marketing in 2019 Made (Stupidly) Easy

Vol.6 of the Small Business Marketing COLLECTION

Michael Clarke

LinkedIn Marketing in 2019 Made (Stupidly) Easy

Vol.6 of the "Small Business Marketing Made (Stupidly) Easy" Collection

PROLOGUE:
Why LinkedIn Might Be the Most Amazing Marketing Tool (You're Not Using)

I shouldn't be writing this book.

I should probably keep my LinkedIn marketing insights to myself.

I should probably tell you to REFUND this book and get your money back because:

- LinkedIn won't work for your type of business (Especially if you don't play in the B2B (business-to-business) space)
- LinkedIn ad costs are ultra-expensive (Minimum of $2/click)
- LinkedIn sends out more spammy email notifications than ProFlowers (and I didn't think that was possible)

So, there's nothing for you to see here. LinkedIn marketing won't do much for your business and I'm sorry to have wasted your time.

Except…

…LinkedIn might possibly be my favorite method for lead-generation for a few, kick-ass marketing reasons:

- **People who visit LinkedIn are "ready" to do business.** This is not a social networking site filled with cat meme pictures and videos of a Trump presidential rally. This is a social platform about making connections — and furthering one's career.
- **The average household income for LinkedIn users is 109K per year.** MUCH larger than any other social network.
- **LinkedIn is a perfect place to contact, not just future custom-**

ers, but future partners. Even if the only people who buy your products are sixteen-year-old shut-ins who play "World of Warcraft" all day, LinkedIn is perfect for connecting with strategic partners who can help move the needle on your business.

- **LinkedIn Groups (I predict) will become the new email list.** Creating, owning and running a LinkedIn Group will soon be more profitable than conventional email lists 10x as big.
- **LinkedIn is mega-respected by the Googlebots.** Meaning a tricked-out LinkedIn Company profile is not only good for your branding, it's vital for your SEO.
- **LinkedIn provides me and my clients the biggest ROI in terms of marketing time, and money spent.** The more ads we buy and LinkedIn emails we write, the more money we make. It's that simple.

And in this humble tome you're holding (or listening to) I will walk you through each of these methods every step of the way. (And show you my favorite, no-brainer lead generation technique…no matter what you're trying to sell.)

But you're probably not interested in any of that. You're probably just fine marketing things the way you are currently. And if so, awesome. I wish you much luck. (And I'll look for you on "Shark Tank.")

But if you'd like to learn how to use LinkedIn Marketing in some powerful (if slightly sneaky) ways, then I encourage you to keep reading.

All I ask is you take the solemn oath of the "League of Inner Circle LinkedIn Marketing Ninjas…"

And that is by holding up your right hand (or left, we're not picky) and solemnly declare:

"I hereby promise to use my newfound LinkedIn Marketing skills for good and not for evil. (And by evil we mean selling more of those "Big Mouth Billy Bass" singing wall hangings.)"

So, if you're ready to proceed, in a non-Billy Bass world, let's begin by creating you the most kick-ass, awesome LinkedIn Profile that ever existed.

Chapter 1:

5 Steps to a Kick-Ass LinkedIn Marketing Funnel

"Perfection is achieved not when there is nothing more to add, but when there is nothing left to take away."

-Antoine De Saint-Exupery

Before we jump into the nitty-gritty of LinkedIn marketing — and cover the ins and outs of LinkedIn groups and that oddly named "LinkedIn Pulse" — there are a few things we gotta have in place to make sure your LinkedIn efforts actually make you money...

...and not just "pad" your LinkedIn follower count.

Many of these steps you might already have checked off your marketing to-do list. But if it's been awhile since you looked at these pillars of your business, I encourage you to give each of these a software upgrade.

Leads generated on LinkedIn can be some of the most valuable contacts you make in your business. (But having your marketing funnel set up beforehand will save you not only time — but a crap load of money.)

So here are my 5 Steps to Developing a Kick-Ass LinkedIn Marketing Funnel:

Kick-Ass LinkedIn Marketing Funnel Step #1: Create A Bite-Sized Freebie Thing-a-Ma-Jiggy (That's Easy to Consume)

I know we'd all LOVE to post links to our sales page on LinkedIn and sit on a beach in Aruba sipping $18 drinks with umbrellas in them as we count our profits.

But that's not quite how marketing on LinkedIn works. Instead, the process works something like this:

1. Turn strangers into connections
2. Turn connections into email subscribers/partners/media contacts
3. Turn subscribers into customers
4. Leverage customers/partners/media contacts to promote our business on LinkedIn
5. Rinse and repeat

Now we're gonna cover each of these in more detail as we go, but for now know if I could give you just one LinkedIn ninja-marketing hack it would be this...

...offer folks an INCENTIVE to be added to your network of connections.

I know you feel your dazzling wit — and immense job experience — is an instant draw to any would-be LinkedIn connection...

...but people NEED more convincing. (Especially since they fear a torrent of spammy LinkedIn emails if they accept your invitation.)

However, if you offer something SMALL and FREE to would-be LinkedIn connections, then you'll separate yourself from the rest of the LinkedIn marketing pack.

Now this FREE THING doesn't have to be BIG or comprehensive. Just a bite-sized (but juicy) tip that helps your ideal customer with one of their biggest, annoying obstacles. (And which lays the groundwork for them to opt-in to your email list.)

Which is why you'll need…

Kick-Ass LinkedIn Marketing Funnel Step #2: Create a Slightly More Expansive Freebie Thing-a-majiggy (That Converts)

Now this FREEBIE is more comprehensive than the freebie in Step #1. (As it should be, you are asking for more of a commitment here — such as an email address or phone number or both.)

And the FREEBIE can take the form of things like:

- Case studies
- Insider guides
- Cheat Sheets
- Webinars
- Seminar
- Special reports
- Resource guide

What works best is if this FREEBIE builds on the topic presented in your earlier freebie.

For instance, with one of my clients who works in the network security space, his "mini-freebie" is: "My #1 secret to safeguarding your business from DNS attacks from abroad (and it takes 5 minutes to set up.)"

This one is a great (bite-sized) tip that crushes it for gathering connections from CTO (Chief Technical Officers) with companies of all sizes.

And then his "larger freebie" is a (recorded) webinar in which he walks prospects through the "5 Biggest Mistakes CTOs Make When Choosing a Network Security Solution."

But both are connected to each other. (And "feel" to the consumer like one extended conversation.)

Now NOT every single new connection you get will opt in for your BIGGER freebie. But we usually get a 50-60% opt-in rate for new connections.

And considering our "connection rate" is most likely to be up 50%, because of our mini-freebie, this is found money.

Kick-Ass LinkedIn Marketing Funnel Step #3: Set Up a Way to Collect Email Addresses

You most likely already have this in place. So I won't belabor the point.

But you'll need two things in place to make your "larger freebie" translate into future profits. And that is:

- **A Landing Page** (Where prospects provide their email and/or phone number)
- **An email autoresponder** (That collects the contact info and then delivers the FREEBIE)

I use LeadPages (for my landing page duties) and ConvertKit (for my email stuff). Both are affordable and make my business appear way more professional and organized than it is.

But you can use any number of companies who offer that service. Just make sure your landing page is as simple as can be and that means:

- A picture of your freebie
- A place to collect contact info
- Headline copy that lets people know what they're gonna get

Kick-Ass LinkedIn Marketing Funnel Step #4: 2-3 Follow Up Emails (That Tell Stories)

This is where most folks' LinkedIn marketing efforts fall short. (Well, that, and their constant need to fill their profile with "certifications" nobody has ever heard of.)

When somebody FIRST opts in to your email list they are both at their most skeptical — "Who is this guy and why does he want to keep emailing me?" — and they're most likely to buy something from you.

They do after all have a problem/concern they need help with. And they want it solved…YESTERDAY!

The key is to write an email follow-up sequence for new opt-ins (I like to send 2-3 over that first week) that tells stories (and subtly sells.)

Forget overt sales pitches and "Grab your 50% off coupon" missives. They don't work anymore.

Instead tell "stories" about you — or your customers — and how they overcame their challenges. (And don't sell until email #3.)

If you're unsure how to do this, just follow this oldie-but-goodie formula:

- **Email #1** - Problem (Touch on the biggest problem your leads are facing, hint at solution)
- **Email #2** - Agitate (Make the problem emotional, urgent)
- **Email #3** - Solve (Offer 'em the solution — which is your product)

At the risk of being a shill, I wrote an entire book on the subject — "Email Marketing Made (Stupidly) Easy" — so check it out if you need a more thorough walk-through.

But if you need the "Cliffs Notes" version, write three emails — following that problem/agitate/solve — and you'll stand out from the rest of the LinkedIn marketing pack.

Kick-Ass LinkedIn Marketing Funnel Step #5: Take a Tour of Your Marketing Funnel

So, this is a tip I got from a super-expensive, otherwise-worthless Mastermind seminar — trust me I'd rather have the Home Theater system I could have bought with the 10K — in which one member mentioned every three months he "plays" prospect and goes through every aspect of his marketing funnel, as if he were a customer.

And whether you follow the stringent 3-month directive, I recommend before you plunge headlong into the deep end of the LinkedIn marketing pool, you go through your own marketing funnel. (Or have a critical friend or family member do it for you.)

- Does the sales copy adequately speak to the needs of your new leads/subscribers?
- Are you missing any opportunities for upsells — or down sells — or affiliate income that could boost your bottom line?
- Is there a disconnect, at any point, between the message you're trying to send out (and the market you're hoping will receive it)?

Doing this alone will boost your conversion rates, each step of the way, at least 15%. (Which will put enough money in the bank for you to buy those home theater speakers you've had your eye on.)

PUNK ROCK MARKETING
AMPLIFY YOUR MESSAGE

CHAPTER 1 KEY TAKEAWAYS:

- **Having your LinkedIn marketing funnel set up beforehand will save you time** (and make you more money.) The author wishes he had done this. God, how he wishes he had done this.
- **Once someone has become a "connection," you'll want to move them over to a subscriber.** And for that you'll want a more comprehensive, detailed freebie. (Special reports, resource guides, and cheat sheets work great for this.)
- **Most likely you'll already have this, but you'll need a landing page that collects email addresses** (I use LeadPages) and an email autoresponder to send out automated email messages and deliver your freebie. (I use ConvertKit.) But you can use whatever you like.
- **One of the most neglected parts of a LinkedIn marketing plan is the follow-up emails.** I recommend three emails (spaced out over a couple of days) that follow the tried-and-true formula of Problem/Agitate/Solution. (And then in the third email you link up the solution to YOUR product.)
- **The final STEP to a kick-ass LinkedIn marketing funnel is a quick (though highly effective) tour of your marketing funnel** — from start to finish. You could either do it yourself, or have somebody else do it, but checking every element for any weird messaging or unclear benefits will make you money down the line. (Oh, I wish I had done that earlier.)

Chapter 2:

How to Create a LinkedIn Profile That Doesn't Suck

"Nothing succeeds like the appearance of success."

-Christopher Lasch

Even the most novice of LinkedIn users knows it's a platform which is a) business-focused and b) is all about the power of an individual's profile.

That's because a LinkedIn profile isn't just a collection of vital statistics. It's a:

- Virtual resume
- Lead-generation tool
- High-profile Google search result
- Company billboard
- Future employee recruiter
- Fantastic place to showcase any piece of content that you or your team creates

Unfortunately, having a LinkedIn profile that's incomplete, or complete with the WRONG self-serving info — or a profile as boring as a Downton Abbey marathon — will not hurt your chances to gain new business. (But act as a 24-hour repellent for any future LinkedIn marketing activity.)

So, here's my 7-Step LinkedIn Profile Awesomeness Checklist:

(Note: I'm gonna assume you already have a LinkedIn profile created. If not, head over to LinkedIn.com/start/join and create one. It's dead-easy, and they make it simple to find new contacts through your email address.)

LinkedIn Profile Awesomeness Step #1: Create a Marketing-Friendly Public Profile URL

Your LinkedIn public profile URL is the web address where people can find all your LinkedIn goodness. (Example: Linkedin.com/li/PublicProfileURL.)

But what most people don't know is they can change this Public Profile URL anytime they want, up to five times every 180 days.

Not like Facebook, which requires you enlist your firstborn into indentured servitude to change your Fan Page username.

Now you don't want to change your URL as often as Taylor Swift changes boyfriends.

But if you don't quite have your LinkedIn marketing presence built out just yet, or you find your public profile URL as boring as a C-SPAN congressional vote, then think about including one of the following in your public profile URL:

- **The name of your business** (LinkedIn.com/BillsHouseofPotpourri)
- **Your name accompanied by occupation** (LinkedIn.com/MattJonesDenverRealtor)
- **Keyword-based URL** (LinkedIn.com/BestPortlandPizza)

You want to balance common-sense discoverability — what would look good on a business card? — with search-engine keyword considerations. (Your LinkedIn public profile URL will by and large determine your profile's Google popularity.)

LinkedIn Profile Awesomeness Step #2: Upload a LinkedIn Photo That Doesn't Suck

I'm sure you already know this, but you need a good, professional photo to make an impression on LinkedIn. (And dim, shaky, out-of-focus smart phone selfies won't cut it.)

Now I'm not a pro photographer (by any stretch) but I can tell you:

- **Outdoor photos — and well-lit interiors — are the best way to go.** No quick pics taken in the hallway of your neon-lit office hallway.
- **Mornings and early evenings are the best times to take outdoor photos.** The light is best then.
- **Always try to keep the light behind the camera, facing the subject.** Light pointing directly into the camera will make you look like a zombie.
- **Find a talented (and under-employed) photographer on Craigslist to help you out.** Especially if nobody on your team can help you out. They're cheap, and most of the time you'll get great results.

LinkedIn Profile Awesomeness Step #3: Upload a LinkedIn Background Photo of Your Team (or Customers) That Doesn't Suck

Again, I am NOT in the graphic-design caste, so I can't give you a ton of "creative" suggestions for your LinkedIn background photo.

But here's what I've learned so far:

- **The ideal size for these background photos is 1400 x 425 pixels.** And they mean it! Anything not in that ratio will look awful.
- **Pictures of people, including you, work best.** Super-large logos and bit call-to-actions come as spammy and annoying.
- **You — or your customers — working directly with your products or services work best.** Give people a snapshot of the inner-workings of your business. (Worth 1000 words of sales copy.)
- **If you don't have a product, just set up a "faux" speaking event.** Fill a conference room with employees, or random strangers, and take a picture of you "working." (It'll be way better than a logo.)

LinkedIn Profile Awesomeness Step #4:Use Your "Name" Field Like a Total Marketing Ninja

This might be my most favorite (though sneaky) trick in this whole profile bunch. And that is use your "name" field to maximum marketing exposure by including both your "name" and "occupation."

So it would look something like this: "Tom Brady - New England Patriots QB - Professional Uggs Model."

Why would we want to do this? Don't we specify our occupation in the "Professional Headline" section?

A couple of important reasons we want to do things this way:

- **Your "name" field is one of the biggest SEO on-page factors for your LinkedIn Profile**. Why not get in any occupational or business keywords in there to help you get found in the LinkedIn Search bar?
- **It helps your profile stand out**. Hardly anybody does this.
- **We're gonna use the "professional headline" section** to an even more devious marketing end.

Speaking of devious marketing…

LinkedIn Profile Awesomeness Step #5: Ask a Question in Your Professional Headline

I can tell you, without exaggeration, this one technique alone has helped me and my clients boost our LinkedIn marketing lead acquisition by 200%.

And the strategy is simple: instead of using the "professional headline" field to tout your particular occupational expertise — which nobody cares about — instead use this space to ask a compelling, emotional question that speaks to possible leads. Such as:

- "Need Help With Your Network Security?"

- "Looking for a Denver CPA Who'll Save You Money?"
- "Need a Dallas Financial Planner Focused on Results?"

Notice how each of these (subtly) insert a valuable keyword in their LinkedIn profile — in a prominent spot — and ask a hot-button emotional question that a prospect already has in their head.

Trust me: If you do nothing else in this book, give this "professional headline" as a lead-generation question a try.

LinkedIn Profile Awesomeness Step #6: Create a LinkedIn Summary of Unstoppable Power

Mountains of advice have been written about how to craft the "perfect" LinkedIn profile. The only problem with much of this well-meaning advice, is that it ignores one simple fact: nobody (not even perspective employers) cares as much about your "expertise" and "experience" as you do.

So, instead I recommend you do the following with your LinkedIn profile summary:

- **Use all 2,000 characters if you can.** Don't worry, NOBODY will read the whole thing. You just want to take advantage of the plethora of keyword opportunities a long summary gives you.
- **Write your opening paragraph as if it you were writing sales copy**. Instead of dithering on about yourself in some super-boring, official way ("Big Brother, Inc. offers a full-service suite of software solutions to help businesses with their integrated HR solutions…") get right to what people care about, solving THEIR problems. (Your freebie.) "Feel like your employees spend most of their time goofing off? (While they're supposed to be doing work for you?) Get a FREE Trial to our "Big Brother" software which tracks every single thought your employees have…"
- **Share the emotional (and passionate) mission of your business.** Not just a catalog of everything clever you've ever done.

Tell us WHY you're so committed to getting results for your clients and customers. (And what results you can create.) Get YOU out of the picture. (Nobody cares!)

- **Tell non-boring stories.** It's okay to put personality in your summary. (Please do!) Tell 'em about things you've learned — follow that old "Problem, Action, Result" formula every job counselor told ya about. Just be human and passionate about your business. (Chances are, total strangers will be too.)
- **Break up them paragraphs**. For the love of all that is good and true, PLEASE break up those paragraphs to a maximum of two or three sentences. And throw in a couple super-short sentences. (Helps the pacing of your summary.)
- **Break up your entire summary with subheads.** This is just a simple ALL CAPS heading to break up different aspects of your summary. (Use strange characters such as asterisks and brackets if you like.) This helps the readability of your summary. (Also helps get in some keywords.)
- **Use a primary keyword (at least twice) in your summary, and 2-3 related keywords.** You probably already know this, but it's important to get relevant keywords in your summary. But don't just settle for that ONE keyword to rule them all, go for related keywords so you can grab people no matter how they're searching.
- **Add visual content that supports the message of your business.** Great things to include would be YouTube videos, SlideShare presentations, photos of you and your team, case studies, reports...anything you can think of that would break up all that laborious text and give attention span-challenged folks a chance to check out your stuff...visually. (All you gotta do is add the link and LinkedIn will dynamically pull the info.)
- **Put in your contact info.** This is one many marketers neglect to do with their summary. But contacting people through LinkedIn email can be a pain — so if you want to hear from prospective clients and customers, throw in your contact info (such as phone number and email) to make it easy for them to reach you.

- **If you're a local business, be sure to throw in your zip code and city info.** You'd be shocked how having a zip code in your summary can help your Google results when people search for businesses in their area.

LinkedIn Profile Awesomeness Step #7: Fill Out the "Rest" of Your Profile Goodies

I don't want to hurt your feelings, but most people will never get "past" your summary. (Especially if they aren't considering you for a position.) And this includes areas like "skills and endorsements" and "projects" and "experience."

That doesn't mean these areas AREN'T important. You want to get your LinkedIn profile to 100% completion, otherwise you end up looking like a total tool.

But the most important element of all these random LinkedIn profile categories is....keywords! You want them in areas like your:

- **Work Experience** - Put all those key industry buzzwords in your current and previous occupations.
- **Skills & Endorsements** - Ask your friends and colleagues to help you out with this (Give before you get).
- **Projects** - Don't have any projects? Make one up that might appeal to your future customer. (If somebody asks you about it, might be time to create it.)
- **Honors & Awards** - Tread carefully with these. Nobody really cares about these. (Unless they prove how YOU can help them!)

And whatever you do, don't wait till you have the "rest" of your profile set up before you dive headlong into the LinkedIn marketing end of things.

This is definitely something you can work on as you go. Spend the majority of your energy on your name, professional headline, and summary. That's where a majority of your marketing gains will come from.

Because when you've got that ready, it'll be time to create that most rare and hardly seen item in the universe: a LinkedIn Company page that boosts the bottom line.

PUNK ROCK MARKETING
AMPLIFY YOUR MESSAGE

CHAPTER 2 Key Takeaways:

- **Don't feel constrained by your current LinkedIn public profile URL — you can change it!** Five times, every 180 days. (Get industry and occupational keywords in there, if you can.)
- **Don't skimp on your LinkedIn profile photo.** Make it look professional, well-lit and not something you had a colleague shoot in an interrogation room.
- **Use the background photo spot to highlight your team or customers.** (Or both.) Showing humans interacting with your product or service is IDEAL.
- **Your name field is valuable real estate** — so don't waste it by putting your moniker in there. Instead, put your occupational title in there.
- **The most ninja LinkedIn tip I can give ya** is to use your professional headline not as a brag zone for your job title — but as a place to ask a compelling question your customer is dying to know the answer to.
- **Use the first paragraph of your summary not as a place to tout your expertise**, but as if it's a de facto sales letter. (Which it is.)
- **Be sure to fill your summary (and the rest of your profile fields) with plenty of industry and occupational keywords.** (It's how people will find you.)
- **Add subheadings, unusual characters, contact info and lots of paragraph breaks to your summary.** (Make it easy for your prospects to find you and reach out.)
- **Add any visual content, such as video, SlideShares, or pictures — to your summary.** (These can turn even the most boring LinkedIn profile into a kick-ass machine of marketing awesomeness.)

Chapter 3:

How to Create a LinkedIn Company Page of Total Awesomeness

"The way to get started is to quit talking and begin doing."

-Walt Disney

I have to be honest, this is a part of my own LinkedIn profile I just didn't get for years — and neglected.

Reason was I didn't check out other company pages — so why the hell should I work on mine. (What an idiot!)

That's because having a fully stocked LinkedIn company page gives you the following opportunities:

- Access to additional LinkedIn marketing goodies (that you can't get otherwise)
- A chance to put a spotlight on your best employees — and favorite customers
- A place for you to feature all your testimonials and customer feedback
- A place to persuade future partners (and cynical media members) to help take your business to the next level.

And considering your LinkedIn Company page will be the second or third search-engine result when people type in your "company name" it's worth spending time on this powerful — but often overlooked — element of LinkedIn marketing.

So, here are my 7 Keys to Building a Kick-Ass LinkedIn Company Page:

LinkedIn Company Page Key #1: Create Your Page (and Fill It With Goodness)

Creating your actual LinkedIn company page is so simple even a Kardashian could do it. (All ya gotta do is log in, head to the "companies" tab and click on the "create a company page button.")

But here are key guidelines when creating your LinkedIn company page:

- **Don't waste the "overview" and "description" part of your company page.** This is super-vital real estate. So make sure you got something that, yes, includes keywords, but is also all about SOLVING problems. (Not just making your company sound important.) Tip: The more personal and fun this part sounds — the more people will respond to it.
- **Resize that logo image before uploading.** The ideal upload size is 300 x 300 pixels. Be sure to resize this first, before uploading. Otherwise LinkedIn will make it look Minecraft-pixelated.
- **Your background image should be sized 1584 x 396.** And you could use this spot to feature: your company tag line (sorta boring, but can be effective), behind-the-scenes pics of your business, or shots of customers using your product or service. (Probably the best way to go.)

But don't spend too much time on this initial set up. Because you want to get to…

LinkedIn Company Page Key #2: Fill Thy Company Page With SEO-Friendly Showcase Pages

If you're not familiar with LinkedIn showcase pages, it ain't your fault — they're a relatively new feature. But showcase pages are a brilliant way to squeeze keyword-awesomeness into your Company page, at the same time you get to feature various segments and/or products within your business. (Pretty much as close to a LinkedIn win-win as you can get.)

Here's what I've learned so far implementing this new(ish) LinkedIn promotional tool:

- **Creating them is su-per simple.** You head over to your company page, click on the "edit" drop-down and choose the "create a showcase page" option.
- **The username and description of your LinkedIn is supremo SEO important.** Be sure it's titled something that packs a serious search-engine punch for your business.
- **The header image for your Showcase page differs from your Company page.** I know. Confusing, right? Still you'll want to make sure your header image for your showcase page is at least 976 x 360 pixels. (And be creative with these — they can be powerful, when done right.)
- **With a FREE LinkedIn account you're limited to just 10 showcase pages.** (At least for the time being.) So, don't waste it on elements of your business that are low-priority.
- **What should you create showcase pages about?** Well…almost anything: products, services, company initiatives…any of the major pillars that make your entire business run like the well-oiled machine it is.
- **When you're done creating these showcase pages link to them from your website, and your many social media accounts.** These are wonderful little silos of company information that shouldn't be locked up inside the LinkedIn confines for good.

LinkedIn Company Page Key #3: Build a Company Update Schedule

Company updates are LinkedIn's version of the Facebook status update — without all the cat meme pictures. And your Company page needs them, or else your page will look as desolate as a Sears store during "Black Friday."

LinkedIn's own advice regarding company updates is good — "We recommend company updates stay authentic, relevant, and brief" — and the key with these updates is to mix with the helpful with the (subtly) promotional.

Here's what I suggest you do:

- **Plan to post 1-2 company updates per week to your company page**. I'll go over ideal posting times later in this book, but I think Tuesday and Thursday mornings are an ideal starting point.
- **Organize your company updates according to the following ratio:** 50% Helpful, How-to Stuff; 25% Genuine News About Your Company; 25% Subtle Promotional Stuff (If you post 2x a week, this would break out to four how-to updates, two news updates and two subtle promo updates.)
- **If you're promoting something, give it an "educational" spin.** Instead of saying "We launched our brand-new product. Go buy it!"…lead with, "Here's ONE thing I learned from the launch of our new product." (Win-win on both sides.)
- **Links to external content (you didn't create) is okay, in moderation**. Don't go overboard just sharing cool stuff you came across. That's what LinkedIn groups are for, this space is about your company. So mix it up with stuff you've learned and come across yourself.
- **Motivational quotes are always good if you have NO IDEA what else to share.** I think they're insipid, but everyone else likes them.
- **Company updates are perfect for getting feedback or giving stuff away.** Just make it sound collaborative, not so sales-y.

But how do I get people to actually "follow" my page so they can see these company updates? Good question…because that leads us to…

LinkedIn Company Page Key #4: Place a "Follow Me on LinkedIn" Button on Your Website (or Wherever Else You Can Think Of)

To get people to actually "follow" your company page, and receive notifications whenever you make an update, you need to create some kind of handy-dandy button that makes it easy for people to add themselves to your LinkedIn company tribe.

Luckily, LinkedIn makes this process super-super easy. All you gotta do is:

- Head over to Developer.LinkedIn.com/Plugins/Follow-Company
- Put in the company page you want to create the button for (I'm assuming you don't want to help promote somebody else's page)
- Spit out code
- Place that code wherever you think it might help you (Including the footer of your blog posts, website sidebars, guest blog posts, email signatures…even in LinkedIn pulse blog posts)

Your company page follower updates may not skyrocket overnight — but give it a couple weeks and you'll see results before you know it.

LinkedIn Company Page Key #5: Invite Employees (and Happy Customers) to Follow Your Page

If you REALLY wanna boost your Company page follower count, there are four key areas where you can find would-be tribe members:

- Current employees (Gently "suggest" they follow your company page)
- Happy clients and customers (Skip the unhappy and deranged)
- Partners (Anybody you work with)

- Members of your existing LinkedIn network who you think might be interested

You don't want to just spam everybody you know — or whatever innocent victims were nice enough to accept your connection invite. Just reach out to people who have a strategic link to your business.

LinkedIn Company Page Key #6: Fill Thy Company Page With Employee Wonderment (and Customer Testimonials)

Company page recommendations are exceptionally valuable, especially for finding new clients and customers on LinkedIn. But like asking somebody to watch your three chihuahuas for two weeks while you head to Hawaii, it can be a big imposition.

So, be sure to reach out to folks who genuinely have something nice to say about your business. (Or can fake it with a proper amount of begging.) And don't forget, especially with clients and customers, to ask if there's anything YOU can do for them on LinkedIn.

LinkedIn Company Page Key #7: (Optional) Buy a Little Exposure for Your Company Page

You don't have to spend a single penny on promotion to see gains from your company page. (Especially when you implement some strategies we will go over in this book.)

But there are three advanced LinkedIn company page promo strategies I would feel remiss not sharing with you:

1. **Promoted Company Updates** - We're gonna cover LinkedIn ads in a lot more detail in Chapter 7. But for now just know that if you've got an exceptionally juicy company update you're excited about — I'm thinking freebie giveaways and promotions disguised as how-to education — then creating a couple "promoted" company updates to your ideal customer demographic

wouldn't be a bad idea. (Just tread carefully with these, LinkedIn ads can be very expensive if you're not sure what you're doing.)

2. **Fiverr SEO Backlinks** - If you're not familiar with the freelance marketplace, Fiverr, let me introduce you to your new best friend. For just $5-$10 you can buy a couple of cheap "SEO" gigs that will build backlinks to whatever URL you choose. And your LinkedIn company and showcase pages are perfect for this SEO boosting on the cheap. (I like to "SEO" gigs that include "social bookmarks" and "link pyramids.") Just make sure you include those all-important SEO keywords when creating the gig.
3. **Press Releases** - I know what I said about most people NOT caring about your latest business update. But press releases serve two functions: promote your brand and build SEO link juice to your company page. So, if there's a notable company update or showcase page you'd like to highlight, think about heading over to Fiverr and have some talented (and underpaid) English major write you up a press release.

CHAPTER 3 Key Takeaways:

- **One of the biggest keys to outfitting your LinkedIn company page** is to ensure your description and overview are filled with keyword-filled, non-sucky copy that makes your business not sound as boring as an insurance seminar.
- **There are two key photos to upload to your LinkedIn company page.** They are the logo image — which should be resized to 100x60 — and the background image — which should be resized to 646x220. Be sure the background image shows off humans (whether customers or team members) interacting with your product or service.
- **"Showcase pages" are not only a great way to feature your many product offerings** — and categorize your business sectors in ways that customers can easily find — but it's also a fantastic way to get some much-needed keywords in your LinkedIn presence.
- **To ensure your LinkedIn company page is primed for maximum non-suckiness create a "company update" schedule** that you or somebody on your team can handle. (1-2x a week, somewhere between Tuesday-Thursday is perfect.)
- **Follow a "company update" ratio of: 50% helpful stuff, 25% news about your company, and 25% subtle promo stuff.** (Make your promos subtle by indicating what you "learned" — not just what you're selling.)
- **Sometimes the best exposure you can get is that which you pay for.** You can create "promoted company updates" — using the LinkedIn ad platform. Or you can use the freelance marketplace Fiverr, to promote your company page (and showcase pages) with backlinks and press releases.

Chapter 4:

7 Keys to Getting 1000s of New Connections in 30 Seconds

"Everyone should build their network before they need it."

-Dave Delaney

Connections are the rocket fuel that powers the LinkedIn universe. They're really frickin' important — and it's important you create a strategy that helps you constantly build on your network of targeted connections.

And why are they so important? Well…

- You can't contact anybody who is not a 1st-degree connection to you (More on that in a second)
- Any time you make a LinkedIn update, your 1st connection folks get notified
- It's the TOLL BOOTH for reaching out to new leads and future clients on LinkedIn

Okay, great. I need some LinkedIn connections. How do I do that?

Well, before we jump in with the whole LinkedIn connection world tour, let me take a moment to make sure we are all on the same "connection" page.

How the Whole LinkedIn Connection Thang Works

Remember that whole "Six Degrees of Kevin Bacon" game where you'd try to link any movie — or any Hollywood star — within six degrees of the famed star of "Footloose."

Well, LinkedIn works (sorta) the same way.

There are three degrees of connection in the LinkedIn world:

- **1st-Degree Connection** - This is where you or another person have accepted an invitation to connect on LinkedIn. You can contact these people by emailing through LinkedIn. (People in the same groups as you are, are considered 1st-degree connections.)
- **2nd-Degree Connection** - These are people who are connected to YOUR 1st-degree connections.
- **3rd-Degree Connection** - These are people who are connected to YOUR 2nd-degree connections.

It isn't exactly rocket science, but your job is to build out your 1st-degree list of connections as quickly as possible — which then puts you in a position to send out "connect" invitations to your 2nd-degrees.

Don't worry if this seems confusing — or downright pointless. There are LOTS of different ways to reach your future customers, clients and partners in the LinkedIn world. (And we're gonna go over a bunch of 'em in the chapter.)

So, let's jump right in with my 7 Keys to Getting a Crapload of LinkedIn Connections:

LinkedIn Connection Key #1: Have Something to Offer

Wait...what? Aren't I supposed to just send out spammy LinkedIn connection requests?

Well, yes, you could do that. (And most everybody else does.)

Or you could have something special you give away to new connections and find your connection request success rates jump by 50-60%.

Now this "something" you're offering doesn't have to be extensive, or the complete 100-page guide to "anything."

It could be your #1 ninja-hack strategy secret thing-a-majiggy that you think your ideal customer on LinkedIn would take advantage of. Or it could simply be a LinkedIn connection-only coupon or discount. (Or if you're selling more high-ticket items, it could be a free consultation.)

What's key is that ONCE you have your free thing nailed down, you want to go back in and add a reference to the FREEBIE in the first line of the "summary" of your LinkedIn profile.

Example:

"If you'd like to discover my #1 Secret Insider Tip for Keeping LinkedIn From Sending You 1200 Emails a Day…then connect with me on LinkedIn and I'll send it over to ya."

Why do things this way?

Because when somebody gets your "connection request" the first thing they will do is check out your profile.

And if your "summary" text is all about what YOU can do for THEM — instead of a laundry list of your accomplishments — they are much more likely to connect with you. (And start what might hopefully be a profitable — and beautiful — friendship.)

LinkedIn Connection Key #2: Make Sure Thy Profile is Complete

This should go without saying. But so should the dangers of "backyard wrestling." (And yet people still do it.)

• Before you send out your 100s of "Hey! Let's connect on LinkedIn" emails, take a moment to fill out all your key profile elements. That includes:

- Profile picture
- Background picture
- Name (Which includes your name and title)
- Professional headline (Which includes your hot-button question your prospective customers need help with)

- Summary (Which includes a reference to your freebie for LinkedIn connections and plenty of keyword awesomeness.)

This doesn't have to be perfect. But you want to get it looking like you give a crap what people think on LinkedIn.

LinkedIn Connection Key #3: Reach Out to Your Inner Circle

I'm not gonna spend much time on this — because chances are you've already done this.

But in case you didn't do this when you created your account — send "connect requests" to folks you already know. (And by "already know" — I mean people who would instantly recognize your name if it showed up in their email.)

Don't worry if they don't get back to you right away. (LinkedIn sends out so much damn spam, it can take a while for people to get back to you.)

But at the least you want to reach out to:

- Email contacts (This is usually done automatically for you upon account creation)
- Employees (past and current)
- Customers (past and current)
- Die-hard social media fans (they call these evangelists, I think)

So what do you say when you approach the folks? Well, whatever you do, try NOT to use the generic "I'd like to add you to my professional network." (Sounds as robotic as a Presidential debate.)

Instead add in your own personality. (And show the person you're sending the request to that you took an extra 12 seconds to write something just for them.)

For example, if I'm reaching out to somebody I've worked with in the past, but who may not recall just who the hell I am, I'll do something like:

"Hi there,

"I don't know if you remember me, but (Insert reason for connection: "We did some contracting work for you a few years back"; "We got stuck in an elevator last week for 27 straight hours") and I wanted to add you to my professional network .

"If you prefer not to connect for any reason please click "Ignore" instead of "I don't know this person." Thanks so much!"

The keys to this request are 1) I tell them HOW we're connected (not force them to figure it out) and 2) I ask them to select "Ignore" instead of "Don't Know."

This is because LinkedIn keeps track of the number of people who claim they DON'T know you. And if you send too many requests to people you DON'T know, LinkedIn will cap the number of requests you get to send out. (No bueno.)

Now, for folks who will recognize your name right away, get more conversational and intimate with your request.

"Hey Kim Kardashian,

How have you been? Sounds like you've had a busy couple years. What with being married to Kanye West — good luck with that — and being one of the most famous people in the world despite having not a single ounce of talent."

Let's connect on LinkedIn. (Just don't send me a copy of your book.)

Talk soon

LinkedIn Connection Key #4: Become a Thriving (Productive) Member of 5 LinkedIn Groups

In the next chapter I'm going to cover the somewhat-strange — but very effective — strategy of creating (and running) your own LinkedIn group. (Easier than you think; more profitable too.)

But for now, here's what you GOTTA know about LinkedIn Groups:

- **LinkedIn Groups are STILL one of the best ways to find new connections.** No matter how many ways people try to screw it up.
- **Ya gotta be an active member to get much benefit.** That means liking, commenting and sharing way MORE than promoting.
- **It's better to focus all your energies on 4-5 groups, than split your efforts on 15-20 groups.** This one took me forever to figure out, but, trust me, the real benefits come from focused group activity — not a shotgun approach to promotion.)
- **If you can only check in a couple times a week, make sure it's Tuesday through Thursday.** These are when most people are on LinkedIn.
- **Don't overly promote.** For every blatant promotional update you share — and some groups may not even allow this — try to have 3-4 status updates that offer advice or help others out.
- **Learn the lay of the land before posting a ton.** Each LinkedIn group has its own schedules and tendencies. Join 4-5 groups and just observe for a couple weeks before making any demands.
- **To find groups where your ideal customers are hanging out, put in keywords related to your industry in the "Groups" search engine.** Don't worry if you must wait for approval. It's often worth it.
- **Spend time "commenting" and "liking" other people's stuff each week.** And by "commenting" I mean more than just "Thx!"

LinkedIn Connection Key #5: Collect Your "Magic 100"

The "Magic 100" is more than just a vague term I made up because I wasn't creative enough to come up with something more exciting.

It's a targeted list of LinkedIn users you'd LOVE to add to your network. This could include future:

- Customers and/or clients
- Partners

- Vendors
- Journalists
- Bloggers
- Podcast producer
- Industry governing bodies
- Anybody who could move the needle on your business
- To create your "Magic 100" all ya gotta do is:
- Open a text document in your text editor of choice (I use "Notepad")
- Make a list of occupations that are relevant to your ideal customer. These includes terms such as "owner," "reporter," "founder," "Head of the Jedi Council."
- Make a list of industry-specific keywords. Such as "restaurant," "plumbing," "dental," "light saber technician."
- Head over to the LinkedIn search bar and put in different combinations that incorporate one occupation and one industry keyword (all in quotes) — with the word "AND" (all in caps) between them. Examples: "pizza" AND "owner"; "partner" AND "law firm"; "Sith Lord" AND "Galactic Empire."
- Scan these search results — bookmark them as well — and add anybody who you want to reach out to in your handy-dandy Excel sheet (or some other word processor that doesn't feature a paper clip as its mascot.)

Now you don't have to limit yourself to just 100. You could do 1,000. Or 12 billion. (Although that may take a while.)

But it's good to have a tangible goal to build up your army of future LinkedIn connections. Which we'll need when we work with…

LinkedIn Connection Key #6: Create a Weekly "Connection Request" Schedule

Once you've got your profile looking sharp, and you've joined some groups — and have your list of "Magic 100," it's time to begin the methodical (though often profitable) process of reaching out to (somewhat) strangers and asking them to join your network.

Now, how much "connection requesting" you're willing to do will depend on your schedule. And how many college-age interns you've got in your own "Galactic Empire" but my own connection request schedule looks something like this:

- **Monday 8am** — 3 connection requests to fellow members of Group #1; 3 connection requests to "Magic 100 bloggers"
- **Tuesday 8am** — 3 connection requests to fellow members of Group #2; 3 connection requests to "Magic 100 future clients/ customers"
- **Wednesday 8am** — 3 connection requests to fellow members of Group #3; 3 connection requests to "Magic 100 journalists"
- **Thursday 8am** — 3 connection requests to fellow members of Group #4; 3 connection requests to "Magic 100 future clients/ customers"
- **Friday 8am** — 3 connection requests to fellow members of Group #5; 3 connection requests to "Magic 100 future partners"

Now you could do more than this. (And I usually do.) Or you could organize WHO you target differently.

You may have no interest in partners — and instead may want to focus 100% of your energies on future customers and clients.

But try to come up with some minimum weekly amount of requests that hit all the MAJOR pillars of your overall LinkedIn promotion marketing plan.

And when you send out your connection request, I recommend you use the following template:

"Hi There,

My name is Michael Clarke. I'm the founder of Punk Rock Marketing (Insert reason you found them: "I noticed an update you shared in a group we belong to"; "I found you in a LinkedIn search I was doing) and I'd like to add you to my professional network.

If you prefer not to connect for any reason, please click "Ignore" instead of "I don't know this person." Thanks so much!

P.S. Please don't report this as spam."

Again, you want to tell them

- Who you are
- How you found them
- That you'd prefer they click on "Ignore" over "I don't know this person."

And that's it!

Trust me: If you keep sending these out, week-by-week, and use the customized (non-generic) templates we've gone over — besides checking in with your LinkedIn groups a couple times ago — you'll see such a response rate you'll wonder what ELSE can I do to broaden my LinkedIn network. (Which is what we'll tackle in the next chapter.)

CHAPTER 4 Key Takeaways:

- **The LinkedIn network is organized by degrees of connection.** (1st-degree connections are those who've accepted your invite to connect; 2nd-degree connections are those connected to your 1st-degrees; 3rd-degree connections are those connected to your 2nd-degrees.)
- **The #1 key to getting more connections is to have something to offer new connections.** Doesn't have to be big — just a small thing you think connections would like.
- **Make sure your profile is complete before you go searching for new connections.** (This includes all the typical stuff — summary, job experience — but also those pesky background pictures that everybody forgets about.)
- **Reaching out to people you KNOW is the easiest way to build your network.** This includes employees, customers, social media fans, and email contacts. (Just be sure to make that LinkedIn invite personal. No robotic queries!)
- **One of the fastest ways to build your LinkedIn network** is to become a kick-ass member of five LinkedIn groups. (Don't join 50. Stick with five and go from there.)
- **Creating a "Magic 100" list of folks you'd like to connect with is a great way to build your network** — and your profit margin. This includes future clients, partners and vendors — besides bloggers, journalists and industry experts who can spread your message at light-speed.
- **The best way to ensure consistent building of your network is to schedule your sending of weekly connection requests**. I like to do three fellow group members and three off the Magic 100 — each Monday-Friday. But whatever you choose, go with a schedule you can keep to. (You'll see great results if you do.)

Chapter 5:

Blatant Profiteer's Guide to Creating (and Running) LinkedIn Groups

"The single greatest 'people skill' is a highly-developed and authentic interest in the other person."

-Bob Burg

Huh? Create and run a LinkedIn group?

I'm sure you need ONE MORE THING to manage in your business like you need a tax audit.

But "owning" your own LinkedIn group offers you a ton of super-ninja marketing benefits:

- **Your number of connections will go through the roof** — There is just no better way to connect with new people than a LinkedIn group)
- **You'll become an authority in your industry** — Even if you don't have the certification — or standing — to be an authority
- **You'll drive traffic to your website** — Or wherever you send folks
- **It's a helluva lot easier to get media attention** when you run a LinkedIn group
- **You get to send out a weekly message to EVERY single person in the group** — Huge game-changer!

And it's that last one where I think the real gains of a LinkedIn group can be found. I have a feeling LinkedIn groups are gonna be the "new" email newsletter. (Or at least how email newsletters used to be back in the Mesozoic era of 1997.)

If you could send out a weekly email to 2500-5000 leads — that you didn't have to pay for — would you do it? (Hell yeah!)

Well, LinkedIn groups can offer that to ya. But you gotta set things up right. (And spend time each week cultivating that LinkedIn group.)

But if you can get past the initial growing pains, running a successful LinkedIn group might be the most lucrative promotional vehicle you can have.

But enough of the talk, let's jump right in with my 5 Pillars of a Profitable LinkedIn Group:

Profitable LinkedIn Group Pillar #1: Brainstorm Ways to Serve Your Industry (NOT Just Ways to Sell 'Em Stuff)

Oh, I know you want to sell 'em stuff. (And you will, trust me.) But your initial objective with your LinkedIn group should be more altruistic.

All ya gotta do is reverse-engineer the process. Ask yourself: "Why do I join groups in the first place?" Generally it comes down to you committing to:

- Make new connections
- Figure out how to make your business more profitable
- Promote something

So, whether you organize your group by occupation ("Long Island Plumbing Network") or by industry ("Direct Response Advertiser Collective") or some other demographic ("League of Extraordinary San Diego Marketers") try to come up with a compelling reason WHY the group should exist. (And find a name that attracts your ideal customer.)

Profitable LinkedIn Group Pillar #2: Create Your Group for Maximum Awesomeness

Creating the group is simple. (Just select "Groups" from the navigation, and then click on "My Groups." You'll then see a prompt for "Create a group.")

But there are a few things to keep in mind as you fill out the group's information to completion:

- **Keywords are gold** - You'll want to include them in your Group Name, Summary and Description. And these aren't necessarily Google-friendly keywords — though that can certainly be helpful — but these should be LinkedIn keywords (such as occupation and industry) that people are likely to use to find your group. (Not sure what keywords to use? Just find out what other groups are using to get ideas.)
- **Your summary should be both description and an invitation to join** - The summary is the "short description" of what your Group is all about. And that's important. But you also want to tell people what they need to do to join the group. The question is do you want to have to "approve" everybody who wants to join the group. (I recommend you do.) If that's the way you want to go, then just put in some text that says something like "Join group to apply for membership." (This lets them know they have to hit "join" — but that membership isn't guaranteed.)
- **The description is your long (ish) detailing of what you'll cover in the group** - Don't worry not everybody is gonna read this entire thing. You just want to put enough description — and enough keywords — to give people an idea of what they can expect from joining the group.
- **Be sure to upload a logo image that's no bigger than 100 x 60 pixels** - I know, that's tiny. But these are rules as delivered upon

high, so to make sure your image doesn't get horribly manipulated, give the LinkedIn police exactly what they want.

- **Under website, choose a URL that promotes opt-ins** — Don't send people to your homepage. (Unless your homepage is stocked and ready to convert.) Instead, put in a link to a page that can offer your freebie — and collect a lead at the same time.

Profitable LinkedIn Group Pillar #3: Set Some Ground Rules

This is where the real challenge in managing a group comes — making sure other people don't ruin it with their spammy or abusive comments.

Now, most people will be perfectly polite citizens in your LinkedIn group domain, but there are always a few loons who see it as their LinkedIn-given right to do whatever the hell they want.

Luckily, LinkedIn allows you to set "group rules" for your little patch of LinkedIn real estate. This is where you lay down what you will — and will not — allow in your group.

I've actually created a template for you to use; you can grab your totally FREE LinkedIn Group rules template over at: PunkRockMarketing.com/GroupRules.

But no matter how you style your particular "group rules" make sure you have at the least the following:

- Make sure people post in English. Unless your Group caters to a non-English-speaking audience. This isn't xenophobia, this is to combat spam.
- Always insist on respectful comments. Otherwise this can get out of hand.
- Insist on relevance. A post on Digital Marketing has no place in a Group dedicated to D&D players. Encourage people to keep things focused.
- Be clear that promotions and job postings belong in the "promotions" and "jobs" tabs. This will probably be the #1 bane of your

LinkedIn group existence. (And a little leeway can be allowed.) But you want to avoid your group being over-run by shameless promoters. (Like yourself.)

- Encourage people to share their insights, knowledge and opinions. Tell 'em you want them to share what's going on — just to do it in a respectful, non-spammy way.

PROFITABLE LINKEDIN GROUP PILLAR #4: CREATE A WEEKLY POSTING SCHEDULE

So the real "job" of running a LinkedIn Group — aside from keeping the spam robots from hijacking the enterprise — is to come up with some kind of regular posting schedule that will keep the Group from dying on the vine.

Now how often you post — and what you post — will depend on your particular industry. (And how much time you have to devote to the Group.)

But here are a few guidelines that have worked for me regarding the what, when and how of posting to LinkedIn Groups:

- **1-2x a week is ideal.** With once a week being an absolute minimum.
- **Tuesday - Thursday is your sweet spot in terms of LinkedIn Group activity**. So if you will only post a couple times a week try to have it be in that time range.
- **The best time of day to share is 7am-8am…maybe.** This will depend highly on who you're trying to reach. If your ideal customer segment is corporate — and they're likely to be in front of their desks all day — then mornings are great. But if your ideal audience is on service calls all day, then post in that 5pm-6pm range.
- **Don't just share links.** Mix up the kinds of stuff you share: quotes, insights, discussion topics, blog posts, videos, slideshares, infographics.

- **Keep your ratio of posts to 80% industry-related helpful stuff, and 20% promotional stuff.** This is a good rule for any kind of social media platform but do your best not to violate this rule.

So, for example, here is a monthly posting schedule for one of my LinkedIn Groups:

- **Week One:** Tues morning (Blog Post Link); Thurs morning (Question of the week)
- **Week Two:** Tues morning (Infographic/Visual Content Link); Thurs morning (Question of the week)
- **Week Three:** Tues morning (Video Link); Thurs morning (Question of the week)
- **Week Four:** Tues morning (News Item Link); Thurs morning (Question of the week)

Now your particular posting schedule may look different. But you'll notice I mix up the TYPES of stuff I shared in my LinkedIn group — not all boring 5000-word essays.

I also tend to post my "Questions of the week" on Thursdays. (This is because people's brain-cell capacity for consuming content tends to go down as the week goes on — but their ability to share their opinion never wavers.)

However you slice it, if you stick with a rough schedule like this one, you'll ensure your LinkedIn Group stays as vibrant — and helpful — as possible.

Profitable LinkedIn Group Pillar #5: Create a Weekly Maintenance Schedule

And by "maintenance" I simply mean checking on your LinkedIn group. Making comments. Removing any offensive posts. Keeping the spam to a minimum.

Again this doesn't — and shouldn't — take hours of your time up each week. But in my experience, unless this is scheduled, it'll never happen.

So, here's what my weekly maintenance schedule looks like:

- Tuesday Evening (5 mins)
- Thursday Evening (5 mins)
- Saturday Morning (5 mins)

You'll notice I do my posting in the mornings, but I do my maintenance in the evenings. This lets me a) respond to any comments or questions I got from my earlier posts and b) manage any weird stuff that comes up.

Also, though I know Saturdays aren't big LinkedIn consumption times, it's good to take just a few minutes on the weekend to make sure things are looking good. (And free of zombie spammers.)

Profitable LinkedIn Group Pillar #6: Come Up With a Weekly Email Schedule

So this is where LinkedIn Groups get exciting. (And really profitable.) And that is by sending out "LinkedIn group announcements" you control — and that get delivered right into your group member's inbox.

Now you're limited to ONE announcement per week. (But really sending more than one of these per week will get really annoying, really fast.)

And what should you promote in these announcements? Well, you could promote all kinds of things:

- Content you created
- A survey you hope folks take
- A freebie offer (probably the most effective thing you can promote in these announcements)
- A special, limited-time offer (just for members of the group)
- An affiliate product (you've actually used and that you highly recommend)
- Anything you think could help members of your group (and perhaps also your bank account)

I don't recommend you promote stuff people have to pay for EVERY single week. (You'll get a ton of churn in your LinkedIn group.) But I think promoting something people can buy, 1-2x month, is fine.

And what should you put in these announcements? Well, I think, at the very least, you need:

- A quick note about why you're writing them (and why it's IMPORTANT they read on)
- A call-to-action (with hyperlink) of what they should do next
- A brief breakdown of the benefits if they click on the link and act
- A "What do you think about this topic? Leave a comment below!" piece at the end

Here's an example to show you what this might look like in real-life:

"Hey Small Biz Ninjas,

We all know analytics are vitally important to running a successful business. (It's just that they're so dang confusing — if not monumentally boring.)

That's why I've put together a super-quick cheat sheet called "The 5 Metrics EVERY Business Must Track (and How to Set 'Em Up)" which you can grab TOTALLY FREE!

Just head over to: PunkRockMarketing.com/AnlayticsAreBoring

In it you'll get a down-and-dirty guide to learning:

- *How to track where your web traffic is coming from (Even social media!)*
- *How to set up analytics goals that ACTUALLY affect your business*
- *And how to set up actual profit projections — not just guesses — for your business*

Did I mention it's free?

By the way, I'd love to know WHICH metrics you think are most important for your business? Share in the comments below!

Michael Clarke"

The reason we want to add the whole "What do ya think" angle is that when you schedule the announcement, you will be able to turn it into a "featured discussion." (Which you wanna do! You want your promo stuff to become somewhat "viral," if it can.)

And as for WHEN to send these announcements? That will depend entirely upon your particular corner of the business universe. But generally I like to send these out early Saturday mornings. (Less competition on the weekends.)

But do some testing. See what works for you. And be sure to use this most valuable aspect of LinkedIn Group management.

Profitable LinkedIn Group Pillar #7: Build an Army of Group Members

Many of the strategies we've gone over earlier, in building our network of connections and gathering company page followers, can also be applied to building up one kick-ass LinkedIn group.

But just in case aliens wiped the hard drive of your brain…err… you may not have memorized every word I put to paper, here are a couple of no-brainer people to reach out to build your LinkedIn Group member count:

- Members of your existing network (who might benefit from the group)
- Fellow members of other LinkedIn groups you belong to
- Clients/customers
- Vendors
- Partners
- Influencers/Media
- Employees/Colleagues
- Anyone on your "Magic 100" — the list of folks you'd like to be connected with
- Experts in your industry
- Subscribers to your email list

- And to promote your LinkedIn group to the big-bad Internet universe, you could do a few no-brainer things: (Most of which can be outsourced to a freelancer on Fiverr)
- Publish a press release about the group
- Share featured group posts on Facebook, Twitter, and Google+
- Buy SEO backlinks to the URL of your LinkedIn Group
- Put links to your LinkedIn Group page on your website, blog, business card, etc.

The cool thing is if you do just a few of the promotional things I've mentioned — and you see steady growth in the popularity of your group — LinkedIn will definitely meet you half-way.

And before you know it LinkedIn will feature you in their prized search-engine results, and you'll see so much free traffic (and additional group members) that you'll have more connections, subscribers and customers than you'll know what to do with.

And that, my friends, is a "group" all of us would love to spend time in.

CHAPTER 5 KEY TAKEAWAYS:

- **Creating and running your own LinkedIn Groups are a fantastic way to find new clients and customers on LinkedIn.** (And the author thinks they will eventually become the "new" email list of the future.)
- **When creating a LinkedIn Group, brainstorm ways of creating a resource for others.** (Not just an excuse to promote your crap.)
- **Fill out the vital details of your LinkedIn Group** — and that includes the summary, title and description — with plenty of keyword goodness.
- **You gotta set ground rules for your Group before you get the ball rolling.** To get my sample template of LinkedIn Group rules head over to: PunkRockMarketing.com/GroupRules
- **To keep your Group vibrant — and full of lead-generating activity — create a weekly posting schedule.** (1-2x a week is ideal, with a mix of how-to-stuff, discussion topics, and promo stuff.)
- **To keep your Group from being overrun** with hijacked discussions and spammy users, set aside time for LinkedIn Group Maintenance. (Just 5 mins, 3 days a week should do)
- **You can send ONE email a week** to members of your LinkedIn Group. (Be sure to take advantage.) Share insights, content, resource guides, and at least 1x a month something you're selling.
- **To build up your army of LinkedIn Group members** reach out to employees, colleagues, vendors, customers and clients. (Ask what you can do for them.)

Chapter 6:

How to Use LinkedIn Pulse for Complete (and Total) World Domination

"Adapt what is useful, reject what is useless, and use what is specifically your own."

-Bruce Lee

It's possible this entire chapter will be irrelevant to your business.

You may NOT have any use for content marketing — the practice by which you create a piece of content in the hopes this content will bring your business exposure (and hopefully additional leads.)

And you may have even less interest in taking the time to CREATE a piece of content that lives on the LinkedIn servers.

But having worked with clients in businesses whose target audience you wouldn't think would be receptive to content marketing — such as the craft beer industry and the carpet-cleaning mafia — I can just say...you'd be surprised how powerful content marketing is.

Because there may be no more powerful force in this universe than the need to NOT feel dumb — and feel SMARTER than everybody else.

And you sharing your expertise — in whatever field — is a fast-track way to win the hearts, minds (and wallets) of your ideal customer.

And as for your content "living" on somebody else's real estate...I hate to break it to ya...but I think the days of people visiting individual websites to consume content are gonna go the way of Lindsay Lohan's career.

So, before you poo-poo using content marketing — and specifically the LinkedIn Pulse platform — keep an open mind and give this method a chance. You might just be shocked how powerful (and profitable) it really can be.

Okay, so let's jump right in with my LinkedIn Pulse Marketing FAQ:

LinkedIn Pulse Marketing FAQ #1: Just What the Hell is "LinkedIn Pulse?"

LinkedIn Pulse — yeah, I hate the name too — is LinkedIn's dedicated content platform in which users can publish content using a variety of mediums — text, video, images, SlideShares, cave paintings, etc.

LinkedIn Pulse was originally an invite-only platform. Meaning you had to wait for an invite from Richard Branson — hey, Richard, I'm still waiting for a ride on the jet — to use it. But now it's available to all LinkedIn users.

LinkedIn Pulse Marketing FAQ #2: How Is Pulse Different From Regular Content Marketing?

Simple...the content LIVES on LinkedIn. (Meaning you can't control its placement and you can't retarget to consumers of that content later on.)

But the advantages outweigh the disadvantages:

- Your post will rank MUCH higher in the search engines
- Your post will be accessible in the LinkedIn search engine
- Your post will have the chance to be discovered by a much-larger audience (especially media)
- Your post (if it gets momentum behind it) will be put in "LinkedIn Spotlight" (which can get you thousands of readers in no time)

Just so you know, I struggled with the whole "publish on my site or publish on LinkedIn" debate?

And I would say, if you think a good portion of your target audience is already on LinkedIn AND you're trying to establish your expertise with your marketing — not just a faster, cheaper, better mousetrap — then I would encourage you strongly to focus a good portion of your energies on creating content for LinkedIn Pulse.

LinkedIn Pulse Marketing FAQ #3: What Should I Write My Pulse Articles About?

Well, first off, you don't have to necessarily "write" anything. There are plenty of other modalities — such as video, image or SlideShare — that you can use to create "Pulse" content.

But I love you're asking the question FIRST — not after you've already created the content.

Many clients I work with, who've tried "Pulse" with virtually no success, have encountered problems because they didn't brainstorm strategically their content before creating.

So, here's a quick step-by-step guide to creating killer "Pulse" content:

1. **Search "Pulse" for topic ideas.** Why do all the heavy-lifting yourself? Just search the "pulse" platform — type in your industry — and see what other topics people have covered. (Tip: If you still can't find anything, check the Table of Contents of books in your industry on Amazon. Those are a treasure trove of ideas.)
2. **Determine your target audience (and what end results you'd like them to have)**. I know you might think you have ONE audience — but I'm sure within that one audience you have different segments. So, decide WHO exactly this content is for — and what end result/insight you'd like them to come away with.
3. **Group your "Pulse" post into logical sub-headings.** This will likely be the "three steps" or "five keys" or " seven big takeaways" related to your topic. (You'll notice I do this shamelessly throughout this book. That's cos it works.)

4. **Come up with a schnazzy title that would get noticed on a smartphone.** Pretend like you're a 22-year-old intern/journalist working for one of those "clickbait" farms like BuzzFeed. What kind of compelling title could you come up with? ("5 Things Every Contractor Needs to Know About the New Tax Laws"; "How to Not Royally Suck at Your First Radio Interview.") Make it sound fun — even if the topic is dry.
5. **Write the damn thing.** Don't feel like just because it's LinkedIn you gotta make your content sound all official and business-y. Write in a conversational tone like you talk. Your content — and your marketing message — will be received much better if you can.

LinkedIn Pulse Marketing FAQ #4: How Do I Publish on LinkedIn Pulse?

The actual mechanics of your posting on "Pulse" are super easy. All you do is:

- Click on "Interests" (top navigation)
- Select "Pulse"
- Select "Publish a Post"
- And type (or paste) in your textual LinkedIn goodness

But let me give you a couple rules-of-the-road to ensure your post gets the maximum amount of awesomeness possible.

- **Put a call-to-action in your footer and a LINK to your website in the body of your post.** Your footer call-to-action can be your usual standard "If you'd like more information, head over to… blah…blah…blah." But the real SEO benefit will be in putting a keyword (linked to your website) in the body of your post.
- **Insert at least 2-3 images in your post.** The longer your post, the more images you should have. (Optimal amount seems to be seven, but that seems like a lot more work than I'm willing to do.)

- **Add any relevant video, SlideShares and infographics to your post.** Doesn't have to be stuff you created. (I love throwing YouTube videos in my posts — if only to break up the monotony.) Just try to use "rich media" to boost your "likes" and "shares."
- **Add plenty of headings (h2 button) to separate content.** This not only makes your content easier to read — but also provides extra SEO juice to your headings. (So, if you can get a keyword in there…do it!)
- **Add lots of relevant tags when publishing.** This will help the discoverability of your post.
- **Publishing on "Pulse" is a cumulative effect.** Don't freak out if you don't see results instantly. It is a long-term, though effective, strategy.

LinkedIn Pulse Marketing FAQ #5: How Do I Promote My Pulse Article?

The short answer is: any damn well way you can. But a couple of my favorite go-to ways to promote "Pulse" posts include sharing with:

- LinkedIn groups you belong to (or manage)
- Followers of your company page
- Any notable LinkedIn connections (including media)
- Twitter followers
- Facebook fans
- Email subscribers
- Google+ plus-ers

In addition, if you wanted to get super-ninja about your "Pulse" promotion, you could:

- Publish a press release
- Post an excerpt on your blog
- Buy backlinks to the post (with Fiverr)

- Take out a few Facebook (or LinkedIn) ads
- Share it on Quora (as an answer to an existing question)
- Share it in any message boards or forums you belong to

There's virtually no limit on the many ways you can promote your "Pulse" posts. (And once ya get a buzz going, LinkedIn will take over from there.)

LinkedIn Pulse Marketing FAQ #6: How Often Should I Publish on "Pulse"?

There's no hard-and-fast rule to this. (Unfortunately.) The more you publish, the more chances you give your future clients and customers to find you.

But you do lean more toward quality than quantity. (No point in churning out three mediocre posts a week, when one really good post would prove more beneficial.)

In my experience, publishing ONE quality "Pulse" post a week is usually all you need to accomplish your goals. (Besides you don't want to over-saturate your network with constant "look at me!" content promotion.)

What I would recommend you do, however, is to write about 3-4 of these before you start publishing. (This will give you a month of regular "Pulse" content, which will give you time to test and tweak different promotion methods to see what works best.)

And there's no question LinkedIn rewards content producers who are consistent. And if you show — right out of the gate — that you aren't a total slacker, you'll have a much higher likelihood of getting a future "Pulse" post featured by the LinkedIn gods.

Which just might get you that much closer to a weekend invite from Mr. Branson.

PUNK ROCK MARKETING
AMPLIFY YOUR MESSAGE

CHAPTER 6 Key Takeaways:

- **"LinkedIn Pulse" is a powerful — if oddly named - content marketing platform** in which you create content that lives on the LinkedIn servers.
- **Yes, it's scary to create content for real estate you don't control**, but the author is skeptical about how viable company websites will be in the future.
- **The best way to figure out what to create content "about" is to research** what's already been covered on "Pulse." (OR check out Amazon book "Table of Contents" for suggestions.)
- **When you publish your content to "Pulse" don't forget** to add any relevant videos, SlideShares, or photos. (Breaks up all that text.)
- **Promote your "Pulse" articles to whoever you think might be benefited.** This includes: fellow LinkedIn group members, social media fans, notable LinkedIn connections, Lady Gaga, etc.
- **Publishing 1-2x a week is ideal.** (More than that and you risk over-saturating your audience.)

Chapter 7:

Your Super-Quick Guide to LinkedIn Ads That Don't Suck

"Creative without strategy is called 'art.' Creative with strategy is called 'advertising.'"

-Jeff I. Richards

Before we jump into the strange (though often profitable) world of LinkedIn ads, I have to be upfront with you.

Though I love LinkedIn ads, and recommend them for all my B2B clients using LinkedIn, the platform is so new I am by no means the ultimate LinkedIn ads expert.

But having organized a few hundred of these campaigns, for both myself and my clients, I'm pretty jazzed about the potential that LinkedIn ads gives us as marketers.

That's because:

- LinkedIn ads are still the best — and most reliable — source of social media lead-generation around. (Way better than Twitter or Facebook — the key is to make sure it's at a price you can live with.)
- No other ad platform offers the occupational, educational and company targeting that LinkedIn ads do.
- LinkedIn ads offer the fantastic ability for users to choose the option of having you "follow up" with them personally.

Now as with any advertising platform, the key is to make sure the cost of lead acquisition fits comfortably within the goals of your funnel. (No amount of fuzzy math will make up for the fact that LinkedIn ads are on the expensive side.)

But if you know WHO you want to reach — and you've got a message you're fairly certain will resonate — then LinkedIn ads offer you a unique opportunity in the digital marketing world: cut through the bullshit and communicate directly with the decision-makers of companies all over the world.

So, with that "caveat emptor" out of the way, let's jump right in with my 5 Keys to LinkedIn Advertising Awesomeness:

LinkedIn Advertising Key #1: Figure Out HOW MUCH You're Willing to Spend

There are two (somewhat) daunting facts about LinkedIn advertising:

- The minimum CPC bid is $2.00. (And that doesn't guarantee placement, that's just the minimum.)
- The minimum daily budget is $10/day or $300/month.

And though this may induce zombie apocalypse level anxiety in even the most confident marketer as long as you know what you're willing to spend — both on a daily scale and total campaign level — then you'll be less likely to encounter "sticker shock" when the ads run.

In my experience this all comes down to what a single lead is worth to you. (And what your current lead-acquisition costs are.)

Generally I recommend marketers budget at least a minimum of $100 in their total ad spend with their initial LinkedIn ad campaign. This will give you enough information to find out if:

1. Your offer resonates with folks when they click on your ad
2. Your ad grabs the attention of the LinkedIn universe.

Once you've got a winner — or at least something that is converting at a rate you are comfortable with — it's just a matter of scaling it up.

But stick with the minimum $10/day daily budget at first. (No need to burn through your budget until you've got a handle on how your ad is performing.)

LinkedIn Advertising Key #2: Decide on What Type of Ad to Run

There are two kinds of ads you can run on the LinkedIn ad platform — although if you eventually become a LinkedIn partner you get a bunch of other advertising options. (But if your business is at that level, chances are you're not reading this book right now.)

The two most common types of LinkedIn ads are:

- **Sponsored content** - Where you boost an existing status update made by your profile, group or company page. Best results from this one, especially with content.
- **Dynamic Ads** - Where you deliver personalized ads in the sidebar that send people to your website. Good, if they convert. Expensive if they don't.
- **Text Ads** - Like they sound, short text ads with a small picture. You only pay for clicks you get, so can be a good strategy. But won't send a ton of traffic your way.
- **Sponsored InMail** - I have not had good success with these. So, I can't recommend them. Maybe you'll do better than I did. In which case email me and let me know.

In my experience, unless you're selling REALLY big-ticket items and need just a few leads to make the numbers work, the "sponsored updates" don't always pay off in the long run.

This will depend on your particular funnel. But these kinds of "content-type" ads can get expensive, fast.

Instead, I recommend — especially if this is your first time out with LinkedIn ads — you start off with display ads. (Which entice users to click on your ad to be taken to a web page of your choosing.)

Now as for whether to go with video or text, the data I've collected seems to suggest that text ads convert better. I know this is counter to the whole "everything is going mobile and visual" mantra that surrounds marketing.

But from what I've found, LinkedIn is something people STILL do at work, in a professional setting. (And putting on headphones so they can listen to you yammer on for three minutes isn't always the best way to entice prospects.)

But you'll want to do your own testing to see what works for you. And if you've already got a well-converting video, that's crushing it on other ad platforms, such as Facebook, then definitely explore putting this video up on LinkedIn.

LinkedIn Advertising Key #3: Nail Down WHAT You Want to Promote

I know this'll sound wishy-washy, but again this will depend on YOUR business. But my recommendation is to always send "cold" advertising traffic to an email opt-in page.

That's because:

- Opt-in pages convert better than sales page with "cold" traffic
- Sending "cold" traffic to opt-in pages lets you retarget those folks — even if they don't opt-in — on platforms like Google or Facebook

Now what this opt-in page looks like will depend on what you're asking people to sign up for.

If it's a simple PDF case study or cheat sheet resource guide, then just having a picture of the freebie — along with a widget where they can put in their name and email — will suffice.

If you're asking people to give you a serious investment in time — such as a webinar — then I'd think about perhaps having a quick video introducing yourself — and the webinar you're giving away.

Bonus Tip: Create a dedicated landing page that mentions "LinkedIn" somewhere — such as "Hey Fellow LinkedIn User! Feel free to grab my FREE Case Study!"

I know it seems trivial, but this small customized tweak can lower a prospect's resistance to your marketing message just enough to boost the conversion rate of your page by 10-15%.

LinkedIn Advertising Key #4: Determine WHO You Want to Target

This is where LinkedIn ads derive much of their marketing power. (And the reason I so wholeheartedly recommend them for folks trying to reach specific occupations or businesses.)

Because with LinkedIn ads you can use the following criteria to target would-be leads:

- Job title
- Job function (sometimes even better than title)
- Industry
- Geography
- Company name
- Seniority
- Age
- Gender
- LinkedIn Group
- School
- Skill

There's virtually no limit to all the awesome — if super "Big Brother-y" — ways you can target LinkedIn users.

For instance, I've helped clients target "Male senior accountants over the age of 40 who went to Texas A&M University AND belong to the International Accounting LinkedIn Group…"

Or: "Oral surgeons over 50, who founded their own practice, have been in the industry over 25 years AND belong to the Oral and Maxillofacial LinkedIn Group." (Take that, Facebook!)

Now getting to this level of demographic sophistication will require you to know WHO the hell your ideal customer actually is.

For instance, one of my clients sold network security software. (At a high price.) And one would THINK that we wanted to target the "Head of IT" for "Fortune 500" companies.

Turns out, that was NOT our customer. In a corporate structure it's the CTO (Chief Technical Officer) who makes all the software decisions — not the "Head of IT." (Much to the chagrin of IT folks.)

Also, getting Fortune 500 companies to commit to software purchases is just slightly harder than understanding the federal tax code. (Most of these big companies are like "aircraft carriers" and getting them to commit to any decision is like herding cats.)

Instead, we needed to target CTOs of mid-sized companies. (But to discover that we needed to talk to get out of the ivory tower and talk to the sales guys and girls in the trenches.)

So, before you spend time — and hundreds of dollars in ad spend — take time conversing with your team (even if your team is just you and your Jack Russell Terrier) and figure out exactly who you want your ad to reach.

LinkedIn Advertising Key #5: Write Your Copy (Gather Your Creative)

So, the actual creative of your LinkedIn ad is very similar to the Google AdWords platform.

You must gather:

- A headline (That tells people who the ad is for)
- Some ad copy (Telling people what yer offering and what they need to do)
- Destination URL
- An image

Again, I am not the world's biggest LinkedIn expert. But here are a few things I've noticed having run a couple hundred of these types of ads:

- **Ask a question in your headline if you can.** The brain just responds differently to questions than it does commands. (Ask yourself which you would be more likely to click on "Reach New

Customers" or "Wanna Reach New Customers?") And that "question mark" character also helps your headline stand out in a sea of other LinkedIn noise.

- **But...that doesn't mean your headline can be long.** You've only got 25 characters to play with, so make 'em count.
- **Get. To. The. Point.** (With your ad copy.) You don't have a lot of room here, so just start off with a verb telling people what you want them to do. ("Grab my FREE dental marketing cheat sheet & boost your business today!")
- **Put a female face in your image.** I know this might be a bit controversial. And objectifying. And not the most enlightened view of humanity. But all my testing has shown, putting a female face will boost click rates.
- **Resize your image to 50x50 pixels before uploading.** And make sure you can see what's going on in the image before publishing.
- **Add targeting to your destination URL.** Whether it's Google Analytics — or some other tracking — you definitely want to have some kind of tracking in place, so you can see how well — or not well — your ads are doing.

LinkedIn Advertising Key #6: Create That Ad (and Set Your Budget)

We've gone over most of this already, but all you do is:

- Head over to LinkedIn.com/Advertising and create a business account
- Upload your assets
- Set your daily budget (Remember start slow with $10/day and then raise from there)
- Set your CPC bid — I like to usually go $1-$2 over the minimum suggested bid (Don't worry — you won't be paying that)
- Create three different versions of your ad — Try different tweaks (such as different headlines, pictures, or ad copy)

- Allow people to have you "follow up" with them personally, as opposed to "clicking." (It's called lead collection, and it's awesome.)
- Let 'em rip (and by "rip" I mean go out there and make ya some money)

LinkedIn Advertising Key #7: Monitor (and Tweak)

I know this isn't exactly the sexiest part of marketing — constantly futzing with ads to make sure they're performing.

But it is where the REAL money is made.

That's because minor tweaks — or sometimes major tweaks — to your ad creative and targeting can make a huge difference down the line in terms of lead cost.

So, how do you know if your ad is successful? Well, here are a couple of guidelines to keep in mind:

- **Give your ad at least three days** before freaking out…I mean… adjusting the ad.
- **A click-thru-rate of .025% or higher for a LinkedIn ad is a winner.** So, if you've got a particular ad variation that's reached that…you have your "control." (If not, keep trying out new variations.)
- **Once you've got a winner, create variations of the "control."** Not create "new" variations out of thin air. (Otherwise you won't know what works, and what doesn't.)
- **If your CTR is good** — but your opt-in rate or conversion rate is poor…your issue is that your offer isn't clear on your landing page. (Don't forget it's all about: Benefits! Benefits! Benefits!)
- **Break your ads into different campaigns, by company, occupation, title, etc**. When you can get this to work — you'll have hit upon the "hidden gold" of LinkedIn ads.
- **Create "retargeting ads"** — using Facebook and/or Google — to follow those folks who don't opt-in. (Lets you get more profit out of the same amount of LinkedIn ad spend.)

And that's really what LinkedIn ads are all about. Wringing out more profit from every drop of LinkedIn ad spend. (Because when you can do that, the only question will be how I make even more money — by doing even less work.)

And that's what we will cover in the next chapter.

Punk Rock Marketing
Amplify Your Message

CHAPTER 7 Key Takeaways:

- *LinkedIn ads can be a fantastic way* to reach the most targeted professional audience anywhere. (Just be aware of the high CPCs.)
- *Be prepared to spend at least $100* in a LinkedIn Ad campaign. With a minimum daily bid of $10/day, this will give you plenty of time to test and tweak to find a winning ad.
- *There are TWO types of ads: display ads (text or video) or sponsored updates*. In my experience, display ads provide a bigger ROI.
- *Promote STUFF that puts folks into your funnel, first.* This usually means some kind of email opt-in or lead-collection. (Links to sales pages don't convert very well.)
- *The MAGIC of LinkedIn ads comes from its targeting.* You can target based on things like Job Title, Job Function, Industry, Geography, Company Name, Age, Gender or LinkedIn Group.
- When writing ad copy try to put questions in your headlines — and keep your ad description focused on benefits.
- REAL ad success comes from finding a "control" — an ad that is currently working — and then tweaking that ad to make small, incremental improvements. (Doesn't sound earth shattering, but it will make a huge difference.)

Chapter 8:

Tools & Apps You Just Absolutely Gotta Have

"The best investment is in the tools of one's trade."

-Benjamin Franklin

Awesome! You have made it to my FAVORITE part of this tome.

Namely all the cool tools and apps that help you get a helluva lot done — and look like a total productivity wizard — even while you sit in your hammock setting your rotation for your Fantasy baseball team.

Now before we jump into my most indispensable LinkedIn marketing tools, I need to tackle one rather thorny and controversial topic...and that is third-party LinkedIn apps. (Or the obliteration of third-party apps.)

There was a magical time — back in the Paleozoic era of 2013 — when LinkedIn would let third-party companies, such as Amazon and WordPress, create applications that let you "decorate" your profile with things such as your:

- Amazon reading list
- Calendar
- Evernote

And you can STILL do a ton of cool ninja-app stuff with your LinkedIn profile. You gotta be sneakier about it. (Don't worry I'm gonna show you how.)

But I tell you this because MUCH of the information out there about LinkedIn apps is outdated and just plain wrong. (And I don't want you to waste your time looking for features that aren't there anymore.)

So, now I've got the official "safety cop" lecture out of the way, let's jump right in with my 4 Super-Killer, Must-Have LinkedIn Marketing Apps:

Must-Have LinkedIn App #1: IFTTT (If This, Then That)

If you're not familiar with IFTTT — and why would you be with such a weird name like that — prepare to have your mind blown.

IFTTT is a super-powerful app that lets you set up "rules" across any number of your digital footprints in the world. (And I mean ANY.)

For instance, you could set up rules that:

- You get an email each time a Silver-Age comic book is posted on Craigslist (or eBay)
- Your phone sends a text message to your kids when your near school to pick them up
- Your refrigerator sends you an email when it's time to change the water filter (No joke)
- You receive an email when someone you follow on SoundCloud or Spotify uploads a new song (Or you can even receive a summary of all the songs you've liked that week)
- Your Fitbit exercise sessions — are automatically saved to a Google spreadsheet (In my case, this would be a short spreadsheet)

Now this all depends on your fridge or automobile having this technology in place. (Don't think my '83 Honda Civic could handle it.)

But these "recipes" — as they call them in the IFTTT parlance — can be super-powerful ways to stay productive, even while you sleep. (And this is especially true with our many social media properties.)

For instance we could set up "recipes" that:

- "If" we publish a new blog post — or YouTube video — "then" it's shared on our LinkedIn Profile
- "If" a link is posted on our Facebook page, "then" a copy is posted on LinkedIn
- "If" there's a popular article on the New York Times in my area of expertise, "then" it's shared with my LinkedIn followers
- "If" you broadcast on Periscope, "then" it's posted as an update on LinkedIn
- "If" it's Christmas (or someone's birthday), "then" that person receives a template message from us on LinkedIn

Now as you can see there literally thousands of ways to skin this LinkedIn cat. (And, trust me, you can spend hours looking through the many variations. I have.)

But, as a general rule, I would avoid having content you update many times throughout the day — such as Twitter or Instagram or a Foursquare check-in — automatically re-purposed on LinkedIn. (Fatigue will set in for your followers.)

But, for any pillar content — such as a blog post, video, or Facebook page update — I would definitely create some killer IFTTT recipes to help promote it. (Not to mention you might find that rare "Silver Surfer" comic book from the 70s you've been looking for.)

Must-Have LinkedIn App #2: Evernote (With IFTTT)

Evernote is another one of those life-changing apps I don't know how I survived without for so long. Although for years I thought the same thing about Netflix. ("You telling me I can watch episodes of "Columbo" AND "Rockford Files" ANYTIME I want!")

In case you're not familiar with this awesome tool — with the strange green elephant logo — Evernote is a FREE app — though you will need to pay $2.99/month for this feature I'm about to show you — that lets you store, gather and track almost everything you need in your life. (Articles, receipts, your boarding pass, that manifesto about the Arsenal football club you've been working on for 10 years.)

And what makes Evernote so powerful is that it syncs all this "content" across all your devices — both mobile and desktop. (And keeps all the formatting native to whatever you put in there.)

But the reason I LOVE Evernote so much — from a LinkedIn perspective — is its power to "scan" business cards on the spot and pull the contact info and send an instant LinkedIn connect invite. ("F&*in brilliant!")

This strategy gets even cooler when you pair it with IFTTT and set up a "recipe" that: "If I scan a business card with Evernote, then LinkedIn automatically sends that person an email of my choosing."

I can't emphasize enough how frickin' cool this is. How many times have you been at some conference and collected a crap load of business cards and then typed them into LinkedIn hoping they'll add you? (And then big whoop! So they add you! What next?)

Whereas, with this strategy, you can scan their card and if they "connect" with you, you'll have a customized email ready in place to capitalize on that new connect by:

- Providing them more information about your products and services
- Offering them a freebie
- Inviting them to check out testimonials about your product

Most people are so impressed with this little trick — especially if I show it to them in person — they assume I've got every other part of my business and life as sorted out. (How little they know!")

Now to set up this devilish piece of marketing Mojo you have to go through a couple of hoops. Luckily, I've created a little step-by-step process on my blog. You can access it over at PunkRockMarketing.com/EvernoteBizCard.

Must-Have LinkedIn App #3: HootSuite

So, HootSuite (the social media dashboard tool) isn't as earth-shattering as the first two. But it provides a valuable service: it lets you manage all your LinkedIn groups — and profile activity — in one tab. (Meaning you don't have to navigate around the LinkedIn universe to all the various groups — but instead can do everything from your smartphone or tablet.)

The tool is FREE — though they have paid options. (Haven't needed that yet.) And all you do is:

- Sign up for an account
- Download the app (If you like)
- Sync your HootSuite with your LinkedIn profile
- Create "streams" (these are Hootsuite's' versions of tabs) for each of your primary LinkedIn groups

And you don't have to JUST use HootSuite for LinkedIn. I use it primarily for my Twitter activities. (I don't recommend you use it for your Facebook page management. Facebook, in my experience, penalizes accounts that do their Fan Page publishing with a third-party app.)

But with the weekly LinkedIn Group interactions I recommend, primarily between Tuesday-Thursday, HootSuite is an absolute time-saver and stress-reducer. Not bad for something that costs you NOTHING.

Must-Have LinkedIn App #4: Social Lead Machine (Chrome App)

I've left this tool for last, because, frankly, it is the most expensive ($40/month) and, if put into the wrong hands, can get your LinkedIn account banned quick.

But…if you've tried everything in this book, and you've got your LinkedIn profile and marketing funnel dialed in right where you want it, then I recommend you give this super-powerful tool a try.

Okay, so why's this tool so powerful?

The reason is simple: one of the easiest ways to get "noticed" by folks on LinkedIn — who are not already in your existing network — is to "view" their profile. (We're all vain and want to know who the heck checked out our profile.)

But this process can be laborious. (I mean, there's all those episodes of "Treehouse Masters" to get through.)

Unless you've got a piece of software such as Social Lead Machine. The process works something like this:

- You get your profile maximized for awesomeness (They've got some tutorials to help you with this)
- You determine who your ideal buyer or client is (You should already have a good idea if you've gone over the strategies outlined in this book)
- You search, using keywords, for LinkedIn users whose profile you'd like to visit.
- Let the software do its thing

I know what you're saying: sounds unbelievably spammy. You're right. It risks going into the dark arts of the LinkedIn Hogwarts School. (And there are many other products out there that cross the line.)

But having used a few of these products from the underbelly of the LinkedIn marketing world, I can tell you the guys over at Social Lead Machine go to great lengths to ensure the tool isn't used for nefarious means.

And in my experience, the BEST way to ensure that this strategy is effective (and ethical) is to ensure everything in your profile is inviting and relevant to folks you're viewing. (Not just something that sniffs of a sales-y fishing expedition.)

And I probably wouldn't recommend you try this powerful (though expensive) tool right out the LinkedIn marketing gate. But once you've got your funnel dialed in — and your profile primed for optimal lead-generation — this is a tool that can, within just a few weeks, provide a huge BOOST to your business. (Not to mention your ability to catch up on "Treehouse Masters.")

PUNK ROCK MARKETING AMPLIFY YOUR MESSAGE

CHAPTER 8 Key Takeaways:

- **The author loves tools and apps because he's intrinsically lazy** — and likes to appear more productive and organized than he is.
- **The author has a slightly-uncomfortable man-crush on IFTTT (If Then, This That***).* This app lets you create "recipes" or "rules" which will automate tasks. (Such as posting any new WordPress blog post or YouTube video or Periscope broadcast on your LinkedIn profile.)
- **Another great app — especially when used with IFTTT — is Evernote.** With these two tools you can "photo scan" somebody's business card, connect with them on LinkedIn, and send them an email touting your latest product or service — in less than five seconds.
- **HootSuite is a great way to manage all your social media activity — not just LinkedIn stuff.** The author uses it to monitor all his LinkedIn Groups, Twitter accounts, and Instagram activity.
- **Social Lead Machine ain't cheap, but it's one of the most powerful tools for automating your lead-generation** duties on LinkedIn. When you've got everything dialed in, give their 15-day FREE trial a chance.

Epilogue:
Okay, What Next?

What next, indeed?

It's hard to know what the social media landscape — and that includes LinkedIn — is gonna require of us marketers over the next few years.

Is Facebook gonna take over the universe — and implant a microchip in our brain — to become the #1 search engine/media company/local business guide in the world…like most people think?

Maybe.

Will the Internet become a mish-mash of Pinterest pins and Tumblr .gifs and 60-second Instagram selfie videos? With anything longer than 250 words, or more substantive than a BuzzFeed article, left by the wayside. ("Five Reasons You Need to Read This Article (and #3 Will Shock You!)"

Maybe.

But I have a feeling no matter how visual and "click-bait-y" social media gets…

…there will always be a place for career-minded people who get up before 11 a.m. and would rather spend their weekends working on a marketing plan — than build a PVC pipe castle at "Burning Man."

And as LinkedIn rolls out more services and apps, the LinkedIn profile will be the default resume/portfolio/personal website. (Even more important than a company website.)

So the relationships you build on LinkedIn won't just help pad your earnings — which it will — but will put your company (and your career) in a prime strategic location for the future.

Where you won't be shocked by anything that comes your way. (Including "Reason #3 You Need to Read This Article."

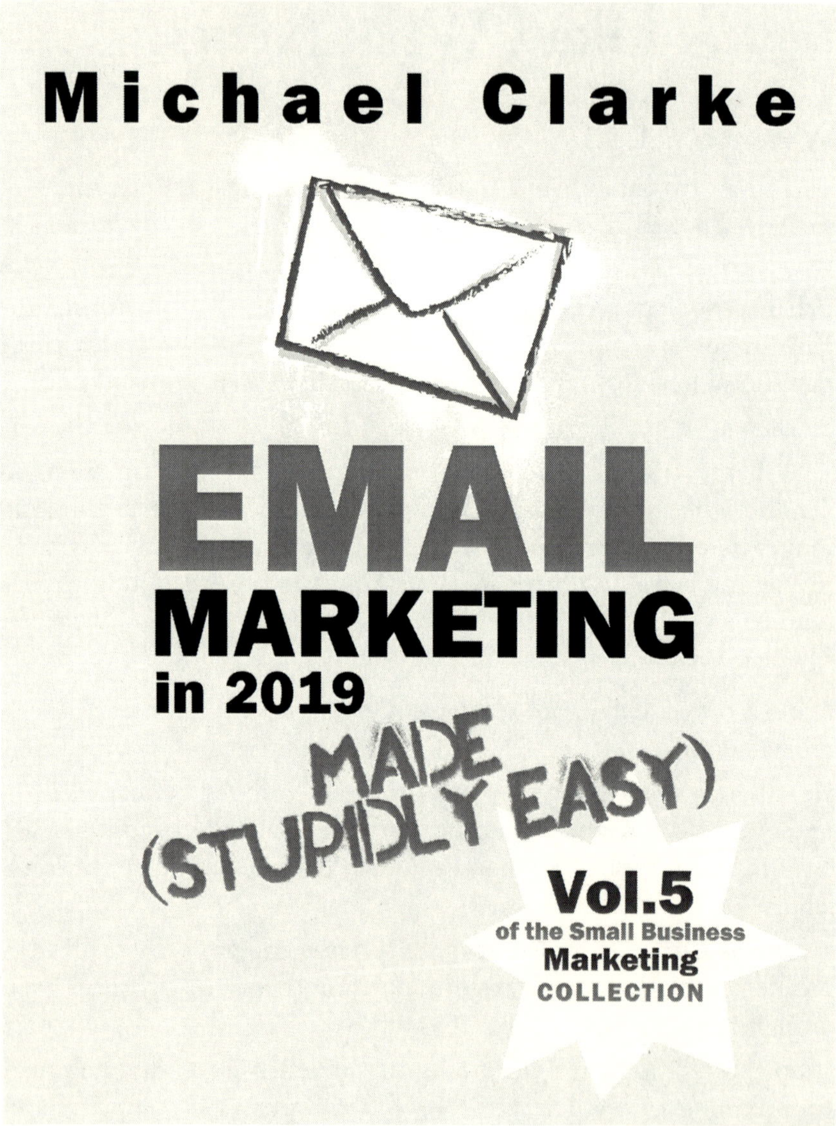
Michael Clarke
EMAIL
MARKETING
in 2019
MADE
(STUPIDLY EASY)
Vol.5
of the Small Business
Marketing
COLLECTION

Email Marketing in 2019 Made (Stupidly) Easy

Vol.7 of the "Small Business Marketing Made (Stupidly) Easy" Collection

PROLOGUE: Email Marketing is Dead, Long Live Email Marketing

Why are you reading this book?

I mean it.

Didn't ya get the memo?

...that email is old-fashioned?

Behind the times.

Something your grandmother uses to send you the latest chain-letter message she came across. ("Look out, dear. The government is keeping your emails in a vault in Cleveland.")

That it's nearly impossible to make email marketing work when:

- Email open rates are down.
- Email click-through-rates are WAY down.
- Email conversions are abysmal.
- Email providers, like Google, keep changing the rules and making things terminally impossible.

And that in a world of tweets and likes and pins and status updates that email is the 21st-century version of the rotary phone. (Quaint, but impractical and obsolete.)

'Cept...

Have you noticed when all those nifty social-networking tools want to let you know about all those tweets and likes and pins and status updates they're dying to share with you...

...they send you EMAILS.

Still.

So, while it's true email marketing doesn't work for most people. (Or works so poorly that it's hardly worth the effort.)

It isn't because the medium is dead. (It's that most marketers have no idea what the hell they're doing.)

But if you KNOW what you're doing, if you tell stories and talk to people like humans…

…instead of chirping on and on like some drone in a robot-marketing army…

Then not only can you make email marketing a cheap, cost-effective part of your marketing arsenal, but you will dramatically stand out from the rest of the morons in your business niche.

And by following the tips in this book, your customers will look forward to your emails. (I know! Crazy, right?)

When that happens, you'll be scooping in so much new business and raking in so much extra moolah…

…that you might even have the funds to make that investment the Finance Minister of Nigeria emailed you about.

All right…let's get this (email) party started!

Chapter 1:

3 Things You Absolutely, Positively Gotta Have

"Give me six hours to chop down a tree and I will spend the first four sharpening the axe."

-Abraham Lincoln

We will get to the nuts-and-bolts of email marketing: "What do I write, when do I send it, and how do I get people to buy my crap?"

Promise.

But before we do that, we need to make sure you're ready to do serious email marketing battle. (And not, to quote one of my favorites movies of all times, bringing a "knife to a gunfight.")

So, here are my Top THREE Email Marketing Tools you gotta, gotta, gotta have before you can crush the competition with your email marketing awesomeness.

Must-Have Tool No.1: Autoresponder Service (Paid)

An auto-responder service, such as Aweber or MailChimp or InfusionSoft — there are many — does a ton of cool things you absolutely NEED to kill it with email marketing:

1. **Handles ALL your mass email sends** (so your regular email account doesn't get banned by sending out hundreds of emails at the same time.)

2. **Drastically IMPROVES your open rates and delivery rates.** (They work hard to remove blacklists that anal email service providers just love to use.)
3. **Lets you write your welcome emails** and follow-up emails months, if not years, in advance. (THIS. IS. HUGE.)
4. **Lets you AUTOMATICALLY add people** to your email list if they buy something from you.
5. **Provides a ton of email templates** that let you send out CUSTOMIZED and super-interesting newsletters and emails.
6. **Provides you some nifty little CODE** you can put on your website or blog, so you don't have to handle the email addresses yourself.
7. **THE BIGGIE** - Lets you visualize and map out your entire marketing funnel.

Some auto-responder services, such as 1 Shopping Cart, even let you have e-commerce checkout system baked into your account.

If you had asked me, just a year ago, what my personal weapon of choice was, I would have told you Aweber. (With a cost of $20 a month for up to 1k subscribers, great deliverability and a 30-day trial it's a great way to dip your toe in the auto-responder waters.)

But then I switched over to Aweber competitor, ConvertKit, and I was blown away by all the cool features. Friendlier interface, funnel workflow dashboards and tags — which let you segment users by behavior — such as sending a follow-up email to everybody who clicked on a link in your email.

Already, within a year I'm seeing a huge impact on my bottom line with the switch to this robust, but very affordable, tool.

But don't let the tech scare you off. Better to choose something imperfect now rather than wait for the perfect solution four months from now.

Must-Have Tool No.2: A Landing Page That Doesn't Suck (Free or Paid)

And by doesn't suck, I mean a landing page, with an email opt-in form that converts pretty well. (And by pretty well, I mean somewhere in the 20-35% range.)

Most marketers have landing pages that suck because they:

- **Put too much CRAP on their page.** Your Landing Page should do one thing. Ask for an email address. (Not SELL your entire line of Justin Bieber memorabilia.)
- **Their landing page is UG-LY.** (Looks like it came out of an AOL members' page from the mid-90s.)
- **They have their email opt-in BELOW the fold**. (People gotta scroll down to see it and getting people to "scroll down" for ANYTHING is a chore.)
- **They DON'T tell people** what they'll get by opting-in.
- **They focus on features, NOT benefits.** (People don't buy the All-Wheel Steering. They buy the FEELING of driving like James Bond.)
- **Their headline is BORING and sucky**.

Now, the last three points touch on the rather involved craft of copywriting. (I don't have room to go into the complete ins and outs of copywriting here, but there are a ton of good books on the subject. My favorite is "The Copywriter's Handbook," by Robert Bly.)

As for how your landing page LOOKS, my favorite weapon — no matter whether your site is on WordPress or not — is a tool called Lead Pages. (I've secured a FREE 14-day trial over at PunkRock-Marketing.com/Lead)

This thing comes LOADED with a bunch of templates to outfit your squeeze pages, sales pages and membership pages.

In addition, it's dead easy to use. (And they handle all the split testing for you. No need to fuss with code.)

Trust me, this tool will make you look more talented and smarter than you actually are.

If you're on a serious budget then try having a designer code something up for you at Fiverr or Upwork. Both sites have plenty of talented, but underworked, web professionals who can hook you up.

Just make sure:

- **The page is responsive**. (Meaning it works on a mobile device.)
- **The page has one simple Call-to-Action**, not 25 things the user can do.
- **The page has an image (or video) and an opt-in box**. (And not much else.)

MUST-HAVE TOOL NO.3: A COOL, FREE THING YOU'RE GIVING AWAY

As marketers, we may believe asking folks to hand over their email address is NO BIG DEAL.

But our (future) customers don't see it that way.

Most people KNOW giving their email address to somebody may lead to:

- A clogged email inbox
- Annoying, spammy emails they don't want in the first place
- Tough decisions (Such as: "Do I buy this thing from this person I've never heard of?")

So, if you will ask people for an email address, make sure you give them something COOL.

Like a FREE eBook, video, report, CD, Cheat Sheet, Insider's Guide or a NEW CAR!

Something!

Not only does it act as a flavorful carrot to entice people to give you their email digits...

...but, let's say, you do a halfway-decent job of delivering quality content with your FREE THING...

...they'll be BLOWN AWAY.

- **They'll think you're an awesome trustworthy human person.** (Instead of a shady marketer.)
- **They might actually want to read your emails**. (Which makes marketing your emails that much easier.)
- **They might (someday) be way more likely to BUY** something from you.

So, what kind of freebie (or "lead magnet" as the hipsters call it) should you give away?

I think that entirely depends on what your strengths are. If you like writing, then I'd do an eBook or report. If you like video, then a screen-capture vid or talking-head video would be good.

If you're more graphical, then maybe an infographic or PowerPoint presentation would be right up your alley. (Infogram is my favorite place to create infographics for FREE.)

The HOW is not as important as the WHAT, which should be some form of a:

- Cheat sheet
- Insider guide
- Mini-Course
- Tip, or series of tips
- A solution to a problem

People are lazy. And the more you can provide easy solutions to hard things, the more you will be able to convince total strangers to give you their email address. (And their money.)

CHAPTER 1 Key Takeaways:

- **Sign up for an Auto-responder service** such as ConvertKit to handle all your email deliver-ability needs.
- **Make sure your landing page does one thing: collects email addresses**. (Use a tool like Lead Pages to make it look super pretty, and mobile-friendly.)
- **Give something FREE away**, so people will opt-in to your email list, instead of just offering a crappy newsletter that nobody wants.
- **Boost your headline and copywriting game** by picking up a book such as "The Copywriter's Handbook."
- **Create a nifty, cool FREE thing** to give away to your email subscribers, such as a cheat sheet, insider's guide, training video, or mini-course.

Chapter 2:

How to Get Tons of Subscribers...FAST!

"Only those who risk going too far can possibly find out how far one can go."

-T.S. Eliot

Okay, so ya got your email-marketing tools set up!

Hopefully by this point you've:

- Signed up for an auto-responder service.
- Placed code (courtesy of your autoresponder company) on your website that will let people "opt-in" to your email list.
- Created some enticing FREEBIE that people actually want... and will happily give over their email address to get access to.

So, once you've got those things crossed off your list, it's now time to go out there and get some good old subscribers to your email list.

So, here are my FIVE Super-Ninja Email Subscriber Methods:

Email Subscriber Method No.1: Video...and Lots of It

Not only is video cool and makes you look like a total expert - even if you aren't - but it also converts. (In some of my markets, my YouTube videos convert at nearly a 60% rate. That's huge!)

The keys are:

1. **Make sure your videos solve problems and don't sell (overtly).** People don't like straight-up marketing messages and YouTube

will probably crack down on your overly promo videos at some point. Just teach what you know can help other people.

2. **Choose video titles that incorporate SEO-friendly keywords**. Opt for "How to Clean a Jacuzzi," NOT "Joe's Pool Supply Tips".
3. **Have a clear Call-to-Action that mentions your FREEBIE in the Video.** This means you need to tell people what to do when the video ends. Like, "Head over to my website NOW and get this free thing!" (Not just ramble on about your "branding.")
4. **Promote first!** Have the first thing in your video description be a LINK to your FREEBIE. Most people won't hit the "more" button and see the rest of your description. (And you'll miss out on a chance to create a new lead.)
5. **Ask viewers to do things.** Such as: Facebook Like, Retweet and give a Thumbs Up to your videos. (Having all this social activity swirling around your videos make them much more visible.)

Email Subscriber Method No.2: Tweet a Link to Your FREEBIE

This one's a no-brainer. And yet, so many marketers neglect it. (I guess they've got more important stuff to do on Twitter. Like, find out what Kim Kardashian is wearing.)

At least once a week tweet out a link to your FREE lead magnet. Just be sure to tweet out other non-promotional stuff the rest of the week, so you don't come off like some kind of Twitter spammer.

Here are a couple ways to get the most out of these freebie tweets:

- **Mention the word FREE…in all CAPS.** There's a reason it's the most powerful word in the English language.
- **Mention a specific benefit of your FREEBIE, not just the FREEBIE itself.** Go with — "FREE guide shows how not to get ripped off when you buy a new car" instead of "Download this 67-page guide today."

- **Ask people to RT (Retweet).** Folks on social media are lemmings and will do what you tell them to do. So tell 'em to share your promo tweet.

Email Subscriber Method No.3: Facebook Ads

I have had huge success using Facebook ads in building up my email list.

Facebook page status updates…eh…not so much!

I find Facebook Page status updates are great conversation starters, good for getting people to talk about something. (Usually themselves.) Not so awesome for getting people to plunk over their email info.

But Facebook ads can be a great to generate a ton of (relatively) cheap email sign-ups. As long as you start slow and gradually boost your budget when you see things working. (Slow and steady not only wins the race - but it keeps you from going bankrupt.)

Now I know there are TONS of Facebook ad gurus out there who'll be happy to teach you EVERY single thing you need to know about Facebook ads. (For the low, low price of $2000.)

But let me JUST give you the process that has worked for me OVER and OVER:

1. **Take that same video you uploaded to YouTube and upload it to your Facebook page as a "video status update."**(Don't just share the YouTube video - directly upload the video to Facebook. And don't show a sales-y video…yet!
2. **Boost the post to your existing fan base for a just 5 or 10 bucks for a couple days**. (This is to help your video get approved faster, not to reach the masses.)
3. **After the "boost post" promotion ends, create a video ad.** When you create your ad target the "fans" of 5-10 Facebook pages that are similar or in competition with your business. (You want to aim for a target audience that is at least 400K large.)
4. **Set up a daily budget of $10 and run the campaign for 7 days.**

This will let you get .02 cent video views. Super cheap! (And let you create a "custom audience" of folks who watched your videos. These will be "warm" prospects!)

5. **After that campaign is over, set up ANOTHER video campaign.** This time you target that "custom audience" with a video encouraging them to sign up for your email list. (Something like "Hey, you watched our video now come sign up for our freebie thing-a-majiggy.")
6. **Run that campaign for as long as it is profitable to do so.** (Or until you become so powerful you end up becoming a Facebook shareholder.)

Did that sound totally confusing? It's okay. Basically what you're doing is serving ads to a content-only video. (With the expressed intention of creating a "custom audience" of people who raise their hands ever so slightly.)

Then serving that "custom audience" with ANOTHER video encouraging them to sign up for your email list.

I know TWO videos and TWO campaigns sounds like a lot of work. But it's not. And it is the best and most effective way I've found to consistently make Facebook ads work for me.

If you've tried Facebook ads in the past, with little success, give this strategy a try. You'll be shocked by how awesome it is.

Email Subscriber Method No.4: PPC Traffic

In case you aren't familiar with the term, PPC stands for Pay-Per-Click marketing. And it refers to those ANNOYING ads you see on search engines, like Google or Bing, that are positioned right above the results you ACTUALLY care about.

And, yes, it's true. People do click on these.

The way you buy that ad inventory is by bidding on certain *keywords* such as "quit smoking" or "used baseball mitt" through ad platforms such as Google AdWords or the Yahoo/Bing Ad Network.

PPC traffic can be good. And very profitable. (These are people looking to solve problems.)

It can also make you broke, fast, if you're not careful.

But if you have a product that solves a specific problem - and isn't in the super-competitive areas of financial services and weight loss - then you might just be able to make it work for you.

I am by no means a PPC expert; there are way more qualified left-brained folks out there who know far more than me. But here's what I've learned, the hard way, with running PPC campaigns:

- **Stick with "long" (3-5 word) -phrases when setting up your keywords.** Skip "weight loss" and go for "how to fit in a prom dress." Cheaper and more profitable. (And frankly way more specific.)
- **Go with phrases that seem to have a commercial intent.** (Meaning people will spend money.) "Free ringtones" ain't such a big winner. But "Lady Gaga ringtones" might be more up your alley.
- **Make sure your website landing page has a good amount of content on there.** This'll keep your PPC costs low. Now, you don't have to write a book, but maybe throw in 200 informative words about that specific keyword, to keep the Google police off your back.
- **He who tests, wins.** There is no magic overnight solution for PPC ads. You gotta check your performance every day to make sure things are looking good. But if you can do that…and keep tweaking to improve your results…then it can be some of most reliable and profitable traffic you'll find anywhere.

Email Subscriber Method No.5: Finding Leads Anywhere You Can

Whenever I'm building a new email list, I like to create opt-in opportunities anywhere I can.

So here are a couple of my favorite — both online and offline — ways to find new email subscribers:

- **Put a notice on the store counter.** If ya got a brick-and-mortar business, this is a must.
- **Every single "About Me" field in every social media profile I can think of.** This includes my YouTube channel, my Pinterest pin board, my Facebook profile, and my Twitter bio. Wherever you can, throw in a link to a website landing page.
- **Message board and forum signatures.** You don't want to spam folks, but if you answer questions in a relevant online forum, and then have a link in your forum signature to your FREEBIE, people will check it out.
- **Press releases.** This one can be a surprisingly consistent form of steady traffic.
- **An opt-in box on your "checkout page."** This can actually help convert more buyers.

CHAPTER 2 KEY TAKEAWAYS:

- **Create YouTube videos**, with keyword-friendly titles, to send traffic back to your landing page.
- **Tweet out a link to your FREE THING** a couple times a week on Twitter.
- **Use Facebook ads** to get super-cheap email subscribers. Use the TWO video strategy to hack the whole process. (And pay way less than your competition does.)
- **Dip your toe into the PPC world**. But be sure to stick to long-tail keywords that keep out the freebie seekers.
- **Put a link to your landing page everywhere** — both online and offline — that you can think of.

Chapter 3:

My Ultimate Email Marketing Formula

"Make a customer, not a sale."

-Katherine Barchetti

Most business folks — even those with high-priced degrees from impressive academic institutions — usually drop the ball with email marketing.

And that's because they do one of THREE things:

1. **They sell way too early** in the email marketing process.
2. **They send out episodic emails** that have no connection to each other.
3. **They email their subscribers WAY TOO MUCH**. (Or not ENOUGH.)

This is known as the *"Till They Buy or Die"* philosophy. The system goes something like this:

1. Add tons of people to your email list.
2. Send them an email every couple days selling your latest "thing."
3. Keep sending them emails until they unsubscribe or buy something.

And, sure, if you've got a big enough email list, and an unlimited budget, this can totally work.

But it can be REALLY EXPENSIVE.

And if you constantly harass your readers with emails pitching crap they don't want, then you'll have an extremely high rate of churn.

And you won't be able to take advantage of long-term (1 year+) email relationships with your customers. Any successful marketer will tell you, long-term customers are where the REAL MONEY is.

So, how do we avoid those mistakes?

How do we make the most of your lead-acquisition budget and build dedicated, consistent customers who give us money repeatedly?

How do we develop long-term customers who feel connected to us and respond consistently to our email marketing?

We stop marketing so damn much.

The Punk Rock Email Marketing Formula

I can't take all the credit for this approach. (Even though I really want to.)

One of the absolute masters of email marketing is Andre Chaperon.

But here's the bare-bones formula in a nutshell.

We start off by giving each new email subscriber an initial sequence of emails that slowly tell a story and build our credibility by positioning ourselves as somebody who doesn't just want to sell crap, but actually cares whether they succeed or fail.

And then we transition them slowly into a more spaced-out, weekly email schedule.

A good calendar would look something like below. I'll share my formula with more detail in the following chapter (it looks a little different, but the same principle… gotta find what works for you!)

Phase 1: The Initial "Get to Know Ya" Sequence

Day 1- Day 5: An email every other day (I send emails on Day 1, 3 and 5) that gives your subscribers a tip, solution, or story that relates to their problem/need. (We don't SELL ANYTHING directly during this time. But we provide Resource Links at the bottom of our emails where people can always buy stuff if they want.)

Day 6: We offer something to buy. (But in a cool, not super-obvious way.)

Day 7- Day 21: An email EVERY THREE DAYS (or less often, depending on the market) that gives people more tips, more solutions, more stories.

Day 22: We offer them ANOTHER something to buy. (Could be our product or somebody else's.)

Phase 2: Infinity and Beyond

Day 23-End of Time: We send them a weekly or bi-weekly email, which goes out to our entire list talking about some tip or story that can help them with their lives.

Phase 3: The Sales Sequence

Occasionally, no more than once a month, we will have something to sell. (Something different than what we've already offered them.)

To do this we will send them THREE EMAILS over THREE DAYS. The first TWO emails setting the stage for the THIRD email where we actually offer them something to buy.

Why This System Works

Okay, so before you freak out and say: "I can't do this! That's way too much work. I'll never be able to pull this off."

A few things:

1. **Yeah, it's a little work.** That's why nobody else does it.
2. **The initial sequence gets rid of freebie seekers by the sheer volume of email.** (And if that's what they are, you don't want them on your list anyway.)
3. **Don't think of it as TEN TIPS or TEN STORIES.** Instead, think of it as one extended story with five episodes. (In the next chapter, I'll talk more about how to pull this off.)

4. **You don't have to do it ALL at once.** You can write, and rewrite, and tweak as you go. (Slowly building up your catalog of emails.)
5. **The emails don't have to be long.** Maybe 200-500 words apiece.
6. **The 21 days is deliberate.** It takes 21 days for somebody to develop a habit. Here, YOU are the new habit.)
7. **You will give your readers tons of opportunities to BUY STUFF.** (It just won't feel like you're hounding them 24-7.
8. **I repeat…nobody else does this.** To your new leads they will be astounded that somebody took the time and care to help them out this much, without "selling" so much. (And the concept of "obligation" is hard-wired in the human brain. At some point, a very large amount of people will BUY something.)

…and that "something" might as well be your product or service.

CHAPTER 3 Key Takeaways:

- **Don't sell, tell stories.** Most email marketers make the huge mistake of SELLING from the get-go, and by sending out emails that have no connection or sequence.
- **Start off with an initial sequence for the first 21 days** that emphasizes content-only emails and infrequent sales offers.
- **After 21 days, we recommend shifting to a weekly-email format.**
- **Products and services can be promoted through three-day sales sequences** that don't sell a thing until the third email.
- **This works because: nobody else does it** and it conditions your subscribers to look forward to your emails while building up the feeling of obligation in your subscribers.

Chapter 4:

Your Initial Email Sequence (Or How Not to Be a Stalker)

"The beautiful part of writing is you don't have to get it right the first time, unlike, say, brain surgery."

-Robert Cormier

There's nothing like a "new" romance.

The sun shines brighter. The birds sing louder. And the world feels like it's all unicorns and rainbows...

I remember once meeting this beautiful, slightly crazy, punk-rock girl who worked at my local neighborhood used-record store.

After chatting for a while, I realized we had SO MUCH in common. ("Wait, you mean you love late 70's British punk and have a slightly irrational fear of clowns? Me too!")

Things were great, until halfway through our SECOND DATE, when she asked if I wanted to move in, as her current roommate was moving out.

We didn't have a third date.

"You Had Me at Hello"

That's what happens when you ask somebody to give you money the first or second time they get an email from you. You cause all kinds of "Danger: Will Robinson!" signs to go up, and ruining a possibly good (and profitable) relationship.

That FIRST WEEK of your email "relationship" with your subscribers is CRUCIAL. Sets the tone for the entire life of your (email) conversation.

It cements in their mind whether you're in their corner, and truly want them to succeed, or you're just like every other huckster out there.

Because for most your subscribers, they have NO IDEA who the hell you are.

It's one thing for Amazon, Tony Robbins or Oprah Winfrey to pitch something in the first week of "gettin' to know ya" emails. They have a frickin' 300-acre vault of goodwill to lean on.

You and I, unfortunately, do not walk on fire or give away cars to our studio audience. We're marketers, and we've got to do WAY more romancing and courting than Overstock.com.

And that involves selling LESS of our crap and telling MORE really cool stories. (Ironically, if you tell good stories, you end up selling way more stuff.)

So, here is a closer look at how I approach each of my email marketing campaigns…

…and how I've used this same system to sell products and services in markets as diverse as self-publishing, golf and even the restaurant business.

Day 1 - Day 7: The First Story (One Email Every Other Day)

This is where you explore the PAIN your subscribers have, and how it relates to the FREE LEAD MAGNET you created. Then, at the end of the story, you give them a chance to buy something cool from you.

I usually structure things like this:

Email 1: (Day 1) The "Please Allow Me to Introduce Myself" Episode

- **Thank them (and welcome them) to your tribe** - "Hey there, welcome to my "inner circle" newsletter! Thanks so much for me giving me the chance to help you save more money this year."

- **Give them the LINK to their freebie** - "To grab your special report '10 Things Every Denver Entrepreneur Should Know About Taxes' head over to SavvyCPA.com/freebie"
- **Give them (self-deprecating, personal) background on YOU** - "I've been a successful CPA in the Denver area for 30 years - and I'm also the owner of the world's most neurotic Jack Russell Terrier."
- **Tell them what they can expect from you** - "Over the next couple of days I'm gonna send you some of my best/favorite tips for learning how to keep more of your income from good, old Uncle Sam."
- **Ask them to answer a question in the P.S.** - "Before I let you go, I've got a question for ya. Whatd'ya think is the biggest mistake entrepreneurs make with their tax return? I'll dig into the gory details in the next email…but if ya think you know the answer hit "REPLY" and let me know what you think."

Note: You may wonder why we go to the trouble of making them feel like they're part of a tribe or ask them to hit "reply" to a P.S. question.

Our job for this email is to get them to open the next one. To "look forward" to our emails. Later on we can sell them stuff but for now we are "training them" to trust our emails.

And by getting them to "reply" to our emails we virtually guarantee that our emails get out of the spam folder…and into their valuable inbox.

Email 2: (Day 3) "I'm Mad As Hell and Won't Take It Anymore" Episode

- **Offer a blistering emotional rant about an area of your field of business - usually aimed at your (cheaper) competitors** - "Ya know what really galls me? Those tax prep "chop shops" that send out the 18-year-old kid spinning "tax prep" signs dressed as the Statue of Liberty. Not only do those tax prep "professionals" usually miss opportunities for you to save thousands of dollars, but they offer upsells up the wazoo!"

- **Apologize (sorta) for going off** - "I'm sorry about the rant. It's just that rip-off artists pretending to run tax prep services really make me mad. This is a noble and honorable profession, in which most of us care deeply about helping our clients get the biggest refund. (And most of us don't have to dress up like a theme park mascot."
- **In the P.S. tell 'em you'll answer the question from Email 1 in the NEXT email** - "Sorry! I forgot to answer the question from Email #1. (I ran out of room!) I promise, in the next email I'll get to it."

Note: I know a going on an email rant about a sector of your business may not seem like good email marketing, but it is. You are drawing a line in the sand. You are saying clearly what you are NOT. (Far more powerful than saying what you ARE for.)

If people don't unsubscribe after this email, then you know your message resonates with them. And they are more likely to stick with you in the long-term.

Email 3: (Day 5) The "Everybody Hurts" Episode

- **Answer the question you posed in the first email** - "So…what's the biggest mistake families make with their tax returns? It's using business deductions that raise serious red flags for the IRS."
- **Elaborate on WHY the answer is so DAMN important - namely the pain and pitfalls your subscriber will feel if they don't act right away to fix whatever this issue is** - "Things like deducting a home office, phones, meals - if not done correctly - can not only open you up to audits down the line but possibly incur some serious penalties from the big, bad IRS."
- **Hint at a way to turn a crisis into a huge opportunity - and promise to answer it in the next email** "Here's the cool thing: if you get this whole home office thing RIGHT. Not only will you save more money on your taxes, avoid the evil dragon IRS, but you can also write-off a myriad of fun stuff. Like vacations and entertainment. And in the next email I'm gonna show you a way to do it in a super, seamless way."

- **Add a "Recommended Resource" link below the text of your email** that sends people to your flagship product that solves the problem hinted at in the email

Email 4: (Day 7): The "Here's Something to Sell" Episode

- **Start off by telling a personal story, either about you or customer who encountered a problem** - "I got this friend Jim. And he was a successful entrepreneur. But after his youngest daughter got sick with a mysterious illness - don't get me started on insurance companies - Jim needed to find a way to keep more of his money."
- **Finish up the story by linking up the happy ending to your product** - "And so after trying out my Tax Deductor software - which analyzes your email inbox for untapped deduction opportunities - we saved an extra $1400 which Jim could use a helluva lot more than the IRS."
- **Tell people the product is NOT for everyone** - "Now Tax Deductor is not for everybody. If you think your money is better served in the coffers of the IRS then go ahead…knock yourself out. But if you'd like a simple, done-for-you way to find untapped deduction opportunities then I encourage you to look at Tax Deductor."
- **Include a link where they can learn more, if interested (Sell the click, not the product)** - "If you'd like to learn MORE about Tax Deductor head over to SavvyCPA.com/Deduct"
- **Add a "Recommended Resource" link below the text of your email** that sends people to your flagship product that solves the problem hinted at in the email
- Now, before you run off and write your FOUR EMAILS remember:
- **Keep these emails short, but not too short**. More on this later. A good page to a page and a half (double spaced) in MS Word is a good barometer.

- **Write them from the point-of-view of a PERSON**. I had success writing a campaign from the POV of my mom. (Boy was that strange.) Emotions sell way more than logical, boring arguments.
- **Don't forget to put in mistakes you've made, or other people have made, and how your readers can avoid them**. People LOVE reading about these.
- **And the MOST IMPORTANT RULE OF ALL: Be sure to tease the end of each email**, talking about the next one. (More on this in Chapter 6.)
- **Don't worry about what days of the week to send these emails**. Just send them in sequence and trust people will be interested in your stuff. But I recommend sending in the morning, about 3:00 a.m.-6:00 a.m. local time for the subscriber. (All the major autoresponder services let you do this.)

Day 8 - Day 27: Story Cycle #2

So, people have gone through your first story.

Just because they didn't buy doesn't mean they don't want to hear from you. (Don't worry, they'll unsubscribe if they don't want to hear from you.)

Perhaps the thing you were offering just didn't appeal to them. Now, it's time for story cycle two.

It's similar to cycle one, but with some slight tweaks. You're going to email them every three days, or perhaps even less than that. (It's good to give them a break right after you hit them with that first week.)

Again, this will lead to another product or service pitch at the end…

But here's what I like to do:

Email Day 10:

Write a quick email on the state of your industry. What you see as the future trends of your area of business. (This will brand you as the expert.)

EMAIL DAY 14:

This time write about what those future trends/changes in your industry mean for your reader. (We're going from the global to the more personal.)

EMAIL DAY 17:

Offer a Quick Tip addressing some of the challenges/obstacles your subscriber/customer faces going forward with these changes.

EMAIL DAY 20:

Tell a story of somebody who experienced a pain point similar to your subscriber. (Hint at a solution at end of email.)

EMAIL DAY 24:

Finish up the "story" and link to a video or article "describing" the solution. (This should link to a sales video or sales letter.) But DON'T tell them you're selling anything - let the video or article do the selling!

EMAIL DAY 27:

Answer the 2-3 most common objections prospects have about the product. (And link back to your video or article. Don't sell!)

Here are a couple of tips for Story Cycle Two:

- **Make sure the product/service you are pitching in this story cycle is MORE EXPENSIVE** than the first product/service. This is your marketing funnel and now you start ascending them up the chain.
- **Use the cliffhanger tease** at the end of each email. Again.
- **Again, don't worry about which days of the week to send these**. No matter what day of the week, I like to send them between 3:00 a.m.-6:00 a.m. local time for the subscriber.

Though my conversion rates are generally lower for Story Cycle Two than they are for Story Cycle One, my profit margins are usually higher. (Because of the higher price point.)

But the cool thing is, once you write these 12 emails — I like to bust them out over a week — they're done. You don't have to really touch them, unless you see that some of them aren't working. (More on that in Chapter 9.)

Then you can turn your attention to where the real big money is… that is the weekly emails. (Which we'll cover next.)

PUNK ROCK MARKETING AMPLIFY YOUR MESSAGE

CHAPTER 4 KEY TAKEAWAYS:

- **Email marketing is like a new relationship**. So chill out and don't be such a stalker at first.
- **Write your emails from one person's point of view**. Could be you, a former customer or Harry Potter.
- **Focus on expressing pain and objections** in Story Cycle One. (Wait until Email #4 before you overtly ask for a sale.)
- **Focus on setting yourself up as an expert, and voice in your industry**, in Story Cycle Two.
- **Offer a higher-priced item in Story Cycle Two.** Conversion rates are lower, but profit margins are higher.
- **Don't forget to express urgency**. They need your product or service NOW.

Chapter 5:

Zen and the Art of the Weekly Email

"We read to know we are not alone."

-William Nicholson

All right, we've come to the piece of email marketing that most people are familiar with.

And that's the weekly email blast which is sent to all, or a good portion, of your subscribers.

This can be in the form of a Newsletter, a Quick Tip, a Weekly Essay, an inbox magazine, or just your bitter, angry ramblings about a society gone awry. (I prefer the latter.)

The actual form of media isn't as important as the frequency. (Which is weekly.)

Does have it to be weekly? I mean, weekly is so much work and I've got things to do and there are all those episodes of "Rockford Files" on Netflix to catch up on…

'Fraid so.

I have found that anything less than weekly, actually hurts response rates and leads to a much higher rate of unsubscribes. People will literally forget they signed up for your newsletter minutes after opting-in to your list. Let alone THREE WEEKS later.

To get the consistent results you want, you'll need to keep putting yourself out there. And emailing every month, or every couple of weeks just won't help you reach your goals. (Trust me, people's inboxes are crowded and busy. It's much better to send TOO MUCH than not SEND ENOUGH.)

So, before you dig in your heels and create your weekly email editorial calendar, here are guidelines to keep you on track with your weekly email marketing efforts:

What Should I Put in My Weekly Email?

Well, this will be entirely up to you and the business you're in. I like the newsletter/magazine format for many markets I'm in, which includes:

- **A main message** or quick tip.
- **A spotlight on one of your email subscriber**s (people love these).
- **A motivational quote** (people love these even more).
- **A link to recommended resources:** Perhaps a weekly coupon or offer, or a link to your own products and services, or products you're an affiliate of.
- **Social Media Icons** at the bottom so people can stay "in touch" with you. Creepy, but effective.

Yeah, But Do I Have to Put All That Stuff in My Weekly Email?

No. You don't.

I have an email list which caters to CPAs. Motivational quotes don't really do much for them.

They want the actionable tip and then want to get on with their lives. (Which usually involves billing their clients hundreds of dollars an hour.)

But then I've also got an email list focusing on songwriters. That crowd loves quotes and anecdotes and recognition. Mostly because songwriters make slightly less than poets.

And if I were running a brick-and-mortar business, then I may want to just put in a weekly "Offer of the Week." (More on subject lines later.)

What Should My Weekly Email Look Like? (How Pretty Does It Need to Be?)

I'm the world's worst graphic/web designer person. So I wouldn't want to give you stray advice on these matters.

But all of the auto-responder services I mentioned in Chapter 1 (Aweber, ConvertKit (my favorite), Mail Chimp) have a ton of easy-to-use templates to make your weekly email look as awesome or boring as you like.

Here are a few things I've learned, the hard way, about making your weekly emails all pretty:

- **Make your font big.** (At least 14px) Shows up better on mobile devices.
- **Don't go crazy with images.** Most are blocked by email providers, anyway.
- **If you have an awesome HTML-designed newsletter, be DAMN SURE you have a text-only version as well.** (Most auto-responders have this by default.)
- **Check your email on various devices and email clients.** The same email can look drastically different depending on which overpriced smartphone you're using.

When Do I Send It?

Ah, yes. Send times.

There might be no bigger cause for debate in email marketing circles — yes, those circles exist; and they are dorky — then when to send your weekly email blasts.

Some folks will tell you to avoid weekends. Because most people have their primary email tied to work hours.

Other people will tell you Sunday mornings are great because most people "catch up" on their emails then. (How sad is it we spend Sundays getting through our email backlog?)

I can only tell you what I've found in MY experience. (Test to figure out which send time is right for you.)

Here are my not-so-hard and fast rules about send times:

- **Avoid Mondays.** Most emails are sent this day. Engagement is high. But you are likely to get lost in the email shuffle.
- **Avoid Fridays.** People start to get email fatigue about Friday. (Which is not a good for email marketers.)
- **Avoid Saturdays.** Unless you've got a limited-time offer or something to sell. Then Saturdays can be good.
- **Tuesdays-Thursdays are great.** My personal favorite is Thursday, as people are generally "thinking" about the weekend already, which makes it easy to tap into their "escapist" emotions.
- **Sundays are good, but it depends on your market.** Open rates are generally down on Sundays. But CTR's (Click-Through-Rates are higher.) There's a lot less competition on Sundays, but you can sometimes get people skipping your email, or reading it days later. (Which can be okay, depending on your market.)

But I Don't Know What to Write About!

A lot of email marketing gurus will tell you to come up with a list of the 20 most common questions/obstacles your customers have and just go down one-by-one and write an email about it.

And that works…okay.

But I use something a little more nuanced. Here's what I suggest you do:

- **Come up with a list of problems/obstacles your email readers may be having/experiencing.** Say your email list caters to contractors, it could be the rising cost of supplies, difficulty of finding good workers, truck maintenance issues, etc.
- **Come up with a tip/solution/insight you have connected to that issue.** Keep it focused and short.
- **Tell a story about a person…**either yourself, somebody on the team or one of your customers who encountered that same problem.

- **Give a happy ending/solution.**
- Notice the difference between these two:

VERSION 1:

"Finding reliable construction workers to add to your team can be a challenge.

"Despite a thorough screening process it's difficult to find quality employees that match your company's needs.

"Here's a resource which may benefit your small business…"

VERSION 2:

"I got the call last Thursday at the job site.

"My tile guy wasn't gonna make it. He was sick. Or hungover. (Who knows?)

"Either way I was behind schedule, the client was mad and I was in danger of another horrible Angie's List review.

"But then I came across something that saved the day…"

See how different those read?

It's the same TIP, but a completely different emotional experience.)

And that's what you want with the weekly emails, emotional experiences.

I'M CONFUSED. HOW DOES THE WEEKLY EMAIL WORK WITH THE INITIAL SEQUENCE?

Here's what happens, the moment somebody signs up for your list they get your initial sequence of emails. (We went over this in Chapter 4.)

While that's playing out they will also get your weekly or biweekly email blast.

Yes, there will be overlap. Yes, some people will be knee-deep in your initial sequence, while they may get a few weekly emails.

That's okay. If it's too much for them, they'll un-subscribe. (Trust me.)

When the initial sequence plays out, then the weekly email blast will be the ongoing touch-point of our email marketing relationship.

Why Don't You Start With the Weekly Email Blast? Why Waste Time With the Initial Sequence?

Because the MOMENT somebody signs up for your email list they are at their most vulnerable.

They have a problem that needs solving. (Otherwise they wouldn't have found you.)

And while MOST of the world will try to sell them crap, you will — through the initial sequence — be taking them from confusion to solution.

Even if they don't buy from you in that sequence, they'll see you as somebody they can TRUST. Somebody who's in it for more than just the quick buck.

And when you have something to sell, and the offer is something they are interested in, they will pounce on it. (Which is what we'll cover in the next chapter.)

PUNK ROCK MARKETING
AMPLIFY YOUR MESSAGE

CHAPTER 5 KEY TAKEAWAYS:

- **You can put as little or as much** in your weekly emails as you like.
- **Common elements include:** a weekly tip, spotlight on a reader, recommended resources, social sharing icons, book reviews and recommended resources.
- **Tuesdays-Thursdays are good days to send your weekly email,** but Sundays can be good too, depending on the market.
- **Write about solving people's problems**, but from a personal POV. (Not just dry, boring lectures.)
- **It's okay** if weekly emails and initial sequences overlap.

Chapter 6:

3 Steps to Huge Email Marketing Profits

"Your customer doesn't care how much you know until they know how much you care."

-Damon Richards

Finally, you're saying. We're gonna get to what I REALLY care about. Making moolah!

Hold on there, Turbo!

At this point, you should already have made a ton of sales, through the links at the bottom of all your emails and from the direct pitches at the end of your initial sequence.

But, let's get one thing clear: The EMAIL, as a medium, is an exceptionally crappy way to make your sales pitch.

People SCAN emails, they don't really READ them with the attention and focus that's needed for a financial decision.

But...

...emails ARE superb for developing relationships. (Which is what we've done through the initial sequence and the weekly email.)

And, once you have a product or service to sell folks, emails are a GREAT WAY to send people to a sales page on your website.

And before I show you an absolutely devastating way to make a ton of sales through emails, let's talk a bit about your sales page. (And make sure it's where it needs to be to set you up for success.)

A Super-Quick Guerrilla Guide to Sales Pages

What should be on that sales page of yours?

Well, it's beyond this book to cover every bit of sales-page techniques, but let me give you some quick down-and-dirty tips when using email to send your subscribers to a sales page.

- **The headline is the most important part of the sales page.** Keep it short. And make sure it's clear WHO this page is for. (And, as a result, who the page is NOT for.)
- **Make sure headline is part of the conversation already going on in your customer's head.** Example: "Is your 401K in the crapper?" is better than "Training Course reveals things you should know about your 401K."
- **Write 10 headlines.** Then write 10 more. Pick the best one.
- **If you can, do video.** Converts much better than those super-long sales pages and has a much better engagement rate.
- **Follow the good-old formula of "Problem, Agitate, Solve."** Example:
- **Problem:** "As a business owner you know employee theft is an issue…"
- **Agitate:** "But you may not know for every dollar you earn, 45 cents is walking out the door…"
- **Solve:** "Here's my patented system for catching employee thieves. It's called a pit bull."
- **Get as many testimonials as you can.** Video testimonials work even better.
- **As you write your copy, and/or record your video, think about the word: URGENCY.** They need this NOW. Not later, NOW!

The Sales Trinity of Awesomeness

So, again, I didn't invent this here technique.

It's a hybrid between a technique used by Internet marketer Frank Kern and the great work done by the aforementioned Andre Chaperon.

But the trinity goes something like this:

- **Email 1:** Feel Their Pain
- **Email 2:** Help Them Understand Their Pain
- **Email 3:** Offer a Pain Solution

Let's go over these in some depth.

EMAIL NO. 1: FEEL THEIR PAIN

As the old sales adage says, you are not selling the hammer. You are selling the hole in the wall.

Every product or service is relieving some kind of pain. That pain could be as simple as:

- Wanting a new pool
- Wanting a better-tasting pizza
- Looking desperately for adequate day-care
- The inability to keep roses alive in the front yard
- The primary goal of this first email is to…
- Establish what the pain point is.
- Discuss your own connection to the pain point. ("Believe me, I know how stubborn those damn gophers are!")
- Hint that there is a possible solution to this pain.

Note: Do not sell in this email. Do not pitch. You are letting them know you understand.

And the tone here should be emotional, empathetic, understanding. NOT abstract or official!)

EMAIL NO.2: HELP THEM UNDERSTAND THEIR PAIN

This is where you get to flaunt your expert status a bit.

This is where you give them insight into the BIGGER PICTURE of where their pain point fits in with the grand scheme of things.

In the day-care example, you've already, in Email No.1, talked about the pain of not being able to find quality day-care. (The hectic schedule, the lack of certainty, the anxiety over who to trust.)

Now, you can dig deeper into the problem of adequate day-care. Such as:

- No unified certification system
- Tough to find honest feedback on providers
- Too expensive
- No reliable database of names
- No monitoring system

You've appealed to their emotion around the pain. Now you've given them insight and education about the problem. (And made them feel smart, no small thing.)

Now, it's time to move to the solution…

Email No.3: Offer a Solution

This is where you give them the way out of this pain.

This is the day-care membership site, the premier pizza club, the state-of-the-art fiberglass pool, the Golfinator 5000…etc.

Just remember to focus on the benefits and paint successful word pictures in which they can "see" what it's like to have the product or service.

People don't care about the titanium alloy of the Golfinator 5000 Club. They care about "seeing" their cocky friends look impressed as their golf ball ZOOMS hundreds of yards down the fairway.

Note: Let the video, or sales letter, do the selling. All you want in the email is to tell people to "check out the solution."

How to Sell Stuff and Not Piss People Off

Now you could just send these three emails to your ENTIRE list.

And that would be (sorta) okay.

If you're offering a low-ticket item you know everybody might be interested in (such as a 2-for-1 entree deal, then that would be fine.)

But remember, the whole problem with Groupon was they sucked at tailoring their offers effectively. (Don't know how many emails I got from them offering me deals on facials and chemical peels.)

My personal recommendation would be to create a NEW email list in your auto-responder, focused exclusively on this product offer, and then invite your larger list to opt in to the new list.

This is called List Segmentation. It sounds like a lot of work. (It isn't, and it's super effective.)

Here's how I do it:

- Write my three emails in the Sales Trinity of Awesomeness.
- Create a new email list based on the product or service I'm selling, and load up the three-email sequence in that list.
- Grab the "opt-in code" for that NEW list and create a page on my website where I can send people to sign up for that NEW list.
- Email my ENTIRE LIST asking if they're interested and send them to that webpage to opt in.
- Sit back and count my money.

Say, I run a golf store. And I've got 1500 people on my list.

And let's say I've got this ultra-awesome golf club that just came in — The Golfinator 5000 — which promises to add forty feet to your drives, and with a picture of a Cobra in flames on the side, promises to make you look like a supreme stud on the greens.

Well, everybody on my list MAY NOT want a golf club with a cobra on fire. (I know. Crazy, right?)

So, what I would do is: send out an email that said something like:

SUBJ: Ready to Start Being Awesome?

Hey There Golf Dudes and Dudettes,

Well, we've had an interesting week here.

I might have come across the biggest technological advance in golf I've seen in the last 20 years.

Now, it may not be for everybody. (It's pretty bold, and could add some serious juice to your drives.)

But again, it's not for everybody.

*So, if you'd like to hear more about it head over here (*Link to Website page with sign-up code for your new email list.*)*

What's the point of this?

Well, you avoid alienating your main email list with offers they have no interest in.

And so when you promote something else on your email list, whether it's a computer-graphics class or a 24-foot yacht, you'll know you'll be speaking to people who are interested, and motivated by your offers and have the potential to boost your profits enormously.

PUNK ROCK MARKETING
AMPLIFY YOUR MESSAGE

CHAPTER 6 Key Takeaways:

- **We use a three-step email sequence called the Sales Trinity of Awesomeness** to sell our products and services.
- **The first email should establish you feel your reader's pain**, the second email should help your reader understand their pain, and the third email should give them a solution. (Your product or service.)
- **To avoid email list fatigue, look into list segmentation**, in which you create a separate list for that product or service.

Chapter 7:

How to Make Sure Your Emails Get Opened

"It is not enough to conquer, one must learn to seduce."

-Voltaire

Most businesses suck at email marketing.

Want to know how I know?

Though it can fluctuate by market, the average industry standard open rate for email marketing is 10.8%.

You read that right. Nearly 90% of all folks out there don't open the email they get in their inbox.

Now, hopefully you've learned over the course of our email marketing journey together that some techniques can help you stand out from the pack.

But if people never open your email, as they are inclined to do, then all the great initial sequences and sales funnels won't do a bit of good.

So, here are my Top FOUR TIPS to help you get out of the Inbox Slush pile, and into the rarified air of your subscriber's undivided attention.

Tip No.1: Ask Your Subscribers to Add Your Email to the Safe Sender List

This doesn't seem like a big deal, but it is.

Most email clients are as anal as a tax auditor and are looking for any excuse to banish your precious email message to the Siberia of the spam folder. (Especially if you have any "dodgy" words in your subject line or message body.)

The fix is simple: just ask your subscribers to "whitelist" you, or add you to the "safe sender" list.

I usually do this in my "welcome" email — the one they get right after they sign up for my email list. And I tell them, straight up, why it's important they do this:

"Hey There. Just a quick reminder Please add my email address to safe sender list. (I want to make sure you get all the cool bonus tips I got for you coming down the pike."

Even better, you could ask them to "reply" to your email to ensure they got it. (This will ensure all your emails get delivered in their inbox.)

Tip No.2: Write a Kick-Ass Subject Line

Poor open rates can always be traced back to a subject line that either confused, intimidated, or simply bored the reader.

Here are a few down-and-dirty tips for subject lines:

- **Avoid spammy words such as FREE in your subject line.** Readers don't like 'em and the email filters will throw you in the spam folder. A fate far worse than death. (Here's a list of spam words to avoid, from the folks over at HubSpot. PunkRockMarketing.com/SpamWords)
- **Leave your dictionary at home.** Use conversational words and a conversational tone. (Example: "How Big Bird Ruined My Business" NOT "An Examination of the Many Layered Effects Public Television Has on Consumer Spending.")
- **Keep it short. I mean it.** Shoot for under 50 characters. (Most email providers, much like the orchestra at the Academy Awards, will end up cutting you off anyway.)
- **Make your subject lines personal if you can.** (Example: "Oops! Biggest Mistake I Ever Made in Business" NOT "The Mistakes Business Owners Must Avoid.)

- **Use specific numbers, not rounded numbers.** This one seems weird. But it totally works. (Example: "How One Pool Cleaner Saved $1,467" NOT "How One Pool Cleaner Saved Over $1,000")
- **Make the subject line either TOTALLY WEIRD or TOTALLY focused on a BENEFIT.** Both work, but mediocre stuff in the middle doesn't work so hot. (Example: "I Brought Home a Penguin Today…" AND "The #1 Reason Your Facebook Marketing Sucks" are both subject lines I've used with success.)

TIP NO.3: MAKE YOUR "FROM" NAME PERSONAL

All auto-responders will allow you to customize the FROM email address that subscribers see when they scan your emails.

And unless you're Pepsi or Target or Home Depot — a HUGE brand with INSTANT name recognition — I would advise you to use your name, followed by your company. (Either spelled out or abbreviated.)

So I might do something like:

"FROM: Michael Clarke (Punk Rock Marketing)"

Or…

"FROM: Michael Clarke (PRM)"

If I used the abbreviation, I would want to let my subscribers know early on what the "PRM" meant. (If I wasn't super clear, somebody might think a political action committee was emailing. Which ain't what I'm going for.)

The point is to get through people's natural distrust of organizations.

Most people scan their inboxes quickly. And they figure emails from "companies" usually involve coupons or offers that they can "get to later."

But emails from PEOPLE are different. They may be time-sensitive. There might be important information in there.

There might be something I need to act on right now. So, make the change and watch your open rates skyrocket.

Tip No.4: Go Easy on the Images

A lot of people check their emails at work, and email clients such as Microsoft Outlook provide the subscriber a snapshot of your email, without them actually having to open the email.

And if your email has got a ton of images, or one large image, then chances are that image will be blocked, until the subscribers click on the "Display images below."

I know. So what's the big deal?

Well, aside from the fact that people are inherently lazy and any single thing that makes it HARDER for them to see your email I'm wholeheartedly against…

…some email clients, such as Outlook, will automatically send emails with photos into the spam folder. (If your subscriber didn't already set up a filter to block image emails.)

Either way, it's an awful lot of risk for the sake of a pretty image.

So, keep the images to a minimum and small. (Maybe just your logo.) And get to the meat of your email content.

Your open rates, and a grateful (email) nation, will thank you.

PUNK ROCK MARKETING
AMPLIFY YOUR MESSAGE

CHAPTER 7 Key Takeaways:

- **In your welcome email, have new subscribers add you to their "safe senders" list.** (Or even better, have them shoot you a quick reply.)
- **Keep your subject lines: short**, interesting, personal, non-spammy, specific and conversational.
- **Put your name in the From Address.** (Don't just put your company name.)
- **Leave your big images for your website.** Hurts open rates.

Chapter 8:

How to Make Sure Your Emails Get Read

"To understand the man, you must first walk a mile in his moccasin."

-North American Indian Proverb

I had a gig once as an A&R guy — you know those people who gets paid virtually nothing by a record label to go see a lot of crappy bands, hoping to find the next Nirvana.

I remember on my first day on the job, probing my boss for some veteran words of wisdom.

Me: "What's the biggest thing I should look for in a band?"

Him: "Brevity and heartbreak."

I thought he was kidding. He wasn't.

Turns out you can tell a hell of a lot by a band by the length of a band's repertoire.

That's because everybody's songs are TOO long.

Their intros are too long, their choruses are too long.

And that artful, clever, self-conscious banter in between songs is the longest thing of all.

And the songs would usually have the dumbest, most cliché lyrics; lyrics that even a Celine Dion fan would think was sappy...

But every once in a while, I would see a band that got it.

A band who realized songs that got the point quickly, and kept people entertained, and expressed some devastating heartbreak or emotional minefield, was a better way to sell a trunk load of CD's, T-shirts and bumper stickers than any twenty-minute incoherent speech by the lead singer.

"Hit Me Baby, One More Time"

I contend emails should be written exactly the same way.

To the point. Personal. And not boring.

Now, I don't believe all your emails have to be a certain length. (Some of my emails get long.)

But I make sure they are NOT boring. If they are, what's the point of sending them?

I try to get some of my personal mojo in there.

So, here are my Top FIVE Tips for writing compelling emails that get people engaged, interested and willing to listen to what you have to say:

Tip No.1: Bring the Emotion…Fast!

Please don't write:

"In this email I will cover the three challenges most small businesses face…"

But instead…

"Okay, I'll just say it. This economy sucks ass."

Now, you don't have to borrow my liberal use of the English language, but you need to go for the jugular.

Get to the HEART AND SOUL of the issue. Fast. It's the only way to break through the inbox clutter.

Tip No.2: Tell a Story Through Your Main Character's Eyes

When I say "main character," I don't mean you have to write your emails through Hannibal Lecter's perspective. (Although, wouldn't that be cool…)

No, just that people relate to people, and that it's much easier for people to get emotionally invested when you're placing your email message in the covers of a "character."

- This can be the subscriber. (In fact, most times it will be.)
- This can be a former/present customer.
- This can be you.
- This can be your business.
- This can be Donald Trump's hair piece.

If it's a sales-y email, don't just say:

"We have 200 units of the Golfinator 5000 in overstock. Grab yours today."

Make it personal!

"I'm a moron. I ordered too many Golfinators. (They are currently taking up residence in my employee break room.) Help give my employees a place to eat their Lean Cuisine and grab an awesome club today."

If it's a quick tip, don't just say:

"One issue homeowners have is understanding how fiberglass pools differ from other kinds of pools."

Instead…

"Fiberglass gets a bad rap. (Had a customer once tell me he'd rather root for the Dallas Cowboys than put in a fiberglass pool.)

'Well, get your Tony Romo jersey ready,' I told him, because here are a few reasons fiberglass pools are so awesome…"

Tip No.3: Cover Just One (Main) Thing

Ever forget to put something on your to-do list?

And then when you did the task, you put it on your to-do list just so you could cross it off. (I know you have, so don't even pretend.)

That's because us human-types are always looking for small, little areas of our life where we can feel like we're getting stuff done.

And there's nothing more satisfying than cruising through our inbox and getting through the sludge of email that's backed up.

But when a subscriber opens your email and sees 12 links, 14 paragraphs, three tips and tons of calls-to-action…

…then most subscribers will prefer to just delete your email — i.e.: cross it off their list — then actually go through the effort of reading your email. (Even if the info is really helpful and good.)

So, just keep your email to one simple concept or idea. (Have three tips for the new homebuyer? Stretch it out over three emails. Have three products you're offering? Send three different emails talking about each one.)

Tip No.4: Break Up Your Paragraphs.

As you can tell how I've organized this book, I like to keep my paragraphs short.

Now, you might find this mortally offensive and against every rule of grammar…

…but, here's the thing, reading words on a screen is hard. (And nobody, except my mother, prints out emails to read.)

I like to keep my paragraphs to about two sentences max. (And I like to throw in plenty of one-sentence, or even one-word, paragraphs.)

Tip No.5: Use a Cliffhanger at the End

We touched on this earlier in Chapter 4 where we covered your initial sequence. But let me show you how it's done.

Basically you want to end every email with a tease for the next email.

There are many ways to do this:

The Upfront Technique

"And you think that's cool? Wait till you see the next email where I show you how to make a 27" HDTV out of chicken wire and old cellphone parts!"

The "Sorry, I Ran Out of Room" Technique

"Sorry. This email is getting a little long. I'll have to give you my #1 Way to Avoid Federal Taxes tomorrow. But I promise to deliver tomorrow. Scout's honor."

The Soap Opera Ending" Technique

"And which famous film director said he would find me and break my kneecaps? Well, you'll have to tune in tomorrow to find out."

The "Gotta Get Permission Before I Can Tell You" Technique

"And which famous actress is using our skin product to look ten years younger? Well, I can't reveal that. Yet."

"I'll try to do that tomorrow. But I'll give you a hint. (It rhymes with "Peg Dyan.")

CHAPTER 8 Key Takeaways:

- **Go for an emotional hot button** quickly in your email.
- **Each email should have a main character**. Could be you, could be a customer, could be the President of the United States.
- **Each email should cover one topic**. Break up large topics into much smaller topics.
- **Keep your paragraphs short**. Embrace fragments.
- **End each email with a cliffhanger** that teases what will be covered in the next email.

Chapter 9:

5 Secrets to Total World Email Domination

"If people do not believe math is simple, it's because they don't realize how complicated life is."

-John von Neumann

Quick confession: I hate spreadsheets. And Math.

And anything that smells like it came out of a high-school statistics class.

But at some point, even a right-brained English major like me, realizes to be an entrepreneur and avoid having to get some soul-sucking cubicle job…

…my email campaigns have to make a profit.

And the real question isn't about HOW MUCH MONEY you're making.

It's how much money am I willing to spend to acquire new subscribers? (And how can I do it for cheaper than my competition?)

And while there are certainly many ways to lower your Google Pay-Per-Click costs or reduce your Facebook advertising expenses, the REAL way to slash your lead-gen costs is to make your email marketing as kick-ass as possible.

And to do that, you gotta tweak, you gotta test. You gotta dig into the numbers. (As much as my Shakespeare-lovin' heart disapproves.)

So, what TWEAKS should you make? What should you pay attention to?

Where can you trim the fat, and boost the performance of your email marketing efforts?

Well, here are my FIVE Email Tweaks to Help You Dominate the World and make a lot more profit, without spending more money:

Email Tweak No.1: Remove Your Unsubscribers Every Month

Just because somebody unsubscribed from your email marketing campaign does not mean the auto-responder service has removed them from your list. Most likely they will keep the email address in your database. Which means you continue to pay for that lead.

Get in the habit, every month, of removing every person who unsubscribes from your email list and save yourself money.

Email Tweak No.2: Create New Subject Lines to Boost Open Rates

Often you'll find, by digging into the reports of your auto-responder, that there's an email or two in your sequence that goes over, as my father used to say, like a "lead fart."

When there's a huge drop in open rates, inevitably it's the subject line.

So, write out a couple of options and try the best ones that don't seem quite as sucky and plug 'em in. (Keep tweaking until you get the open rate back to where you want it.)

Email Tweak No.3: Sharpen Calls-to-Actions to Boost Click-Thru Rates

This will depend on what you're asking people to click over to.

I'm usually sending people to a sales page that I'm linking to in the bottom of the email. You may ask people to go to a blog post or a video or a press release.

The key here is to find out which outbound links are working in an email, and which aren't. The only way to do this, with any certainty, is to use analytics. (I know, I hate that word too.)

Google Analytics is my weapon of choice. (It's free and fairly easy to use.) And works perfect when you drop in that extra piece of code on the end of a link.

This is absolutely vital when you provide multiple links to the same destination.

Once you get your data, you'll want to look at:

- **Changing the location of the outbound link** by moving it further down the email, or closer to the top.
- **Changing the Call-to-Action verbiage** "Click here," "Check Out this Link" or "Download Now." They all say very different things.
- **Changing how the link looks**. Is it "http://yoursite.com/offer" or "http://yoursite.com/?9sf3" or "http://bit.ly/424" or "Click Here Hyperlink"? I prefer pretty URLs, like the first one, but this will require some testing on your part.
- **Changing how the link is presented.** Is it in bold? Is it in italics? Does it have arrows like this — "==>http://yoursite.com<==" — try different variations to see what grabs your email readership.

Email Tweak No.4: Split-Test Your Squeeze Page

All the traffic in the world won't help if nobody is opting into your list. You should, comfortably, sit at about a 25-35% opt-in rate.

If not, refer to Chapter 2 for ideas on how to tweak your landing page. (And if you are above 35%, keep tweaking anyway. You're onto something great.)

But one other VITAL way to boost your conversion is to split-test two different versions of your squeeze page. (This allows you to show TWO DIFFERENT VERSIONS of the same page randomly to web traffic.)

I like to test things such as:

- Video vs. Text
- Headline #1 vs. Headline #2
- Orange "Get Access button" vs. Yellow "Get Access" button. (You think I'm kidding. I'm not. It matters.)
- Bullet points vs. No bullet points
- More copy vs. Less copy

Again, Google Analytics offers a FREE way to do this with its content experiments service.

You'll have to install Google Analytics on your website — it's a bit too involved to go into here — but once you do, you just create two different pages on your site and let good old GA do the rest.

Email Tweak No.5: Track Your Sales

This will depend on what you are, in fact, selling.

If you're selling a simple product online then this will be pretty straightforward and you can track, using Google Analytics, how many people are clicking on a link in your email and eventually reach the "Thank You" page they see when they purchase something.

But if you're a brick-and-mortar business — say, you're a sandwich shop — then you'll need to do something a little more nuanced.

I suggest promoting a coupon, that's only available for your email subscribers, in which they have to either mention some EMAIL CODE WORD or print out the email and bring it to your business.

At the end of each month, you can track your sales percentage against the amount of new leads you get from your email campaign and see how you're doing.

Hopefully, if you follow the techniques we've gone over in this book, you'll have a healthy 10-15% conversion rate.

But many marketers make a great living off of a 1-2% conversion rate. (So don't beat yourself up too much if it's low at first.)

PUNK ROCK MARKETING
AMPLIFY YOUR MESSAGE

CHAPTER 9 Key Takeaways:

- **Tweaking your email campaigns is an easy way to make more money**, without increasing your ad spend.
- **Rewrite any under-performing subject lines to boost open rates.** Open rates ALMOST always have to do with subject lines that aren't connecting with readers.
- **Remove any unsubscribers from your auto-responder database each month.** You're paying for them, anyway.
- **Use Google Analytics to track your click-thru rates** and split-test your squeeze pages.
- **Track your sales either through Google Analytics**, or with a simple coupon code.

Bonus Chapter:

Let's All Thank Google for Ruining Everything

It pains me to write this extra, bonus director's-cut chapter of Email Marketing That Doesn't Suck. (Mostly because I had other really important things to do. Like binge-watch "Breaking Bad" for the twelfth time.)

But there's an elephant in the email marketing room…and it's called Google. See, Google has this nasty habit of changing everything. (And I mean everything.)

And I didn't feel it was fair to leave you without a tip or two on how to handle this Gmail tab wasteland we find ourselves in.

Fortunately, the harder Google makes it for marketers, the easier it will be to stand out from the rest of the pack.

Here Be Monsters (and a Crappy Open Rate)

So, in case you have no idea what I'm talking about, Gmail completely changed how it filters emails for its users a couple years ago.

The old interface used to dump all the email for a subscriber into one single vertical location. (And required its users to filter and organize and figure out how to avoid email overwhelm.)

But then the Google brain trust came up with an idea to divide all email into three tabs: Primary, Social and Promotions. (By the time you're reading this there might even be a new categorization system even more nefarious.)

As a Gmail user, I love it. As a marketer, and somebody who has to make a living in a capitalist society, I HATE IT.

Because:

- Gmail will (most likely) deem our broadcast emails as "promotion," even if they aren't. (Unless we take action.)
- People are lazy and probably won't look at the promotions tab very much. (I know I don't.)
- Sales will suffer. (Which is bad, bad, bad.)

"I Got a Remedy"

So what do we do? Bribe Google? Quit our job? Start an alpaca farm in Pennsylvania?

No.

We take some simple, but super-effective actions that not only can help us survive as marketers in a post-Gmail tab world…

…but actually help us stand out from our competition even further.

So, here are my Top THREE Ninja Tips for Gmail Tab Survivalness

Gmail Tab Tip No.1: Ask Your Subscribers to Make You a Primary

There are a lot of email marketing gurus who advocate teaching your subscribers to manually "turn off" the Gmail tab organization.

I think that is way overkill. (And frankly a bit unethical. I mean, if they want the tabs, why should you ask them to do something like that?)

But instead, you could film a very quick screencast video showing people that by "dragging" your email from the "promotion" tab to the "primary" tab they'll be sure not to miss out on all the great content you'll be sending them.

Add a link to this tutorial video in the welcome message you send to your new subscribers. They'll thank you for the cool way to organize their email and you'll make sure your delivery rates stay high.

And do this in your FIRST email you send out. (Don't wait till your stuff gets piled up in the email slush pile.)

Gmail Tab Tip No.2: Ask Your Subscribers to "Reply" to You

This one totally works. (And also helps you look like a really helpful, cool person.)

Ask your new subscribers in your first email to "reply" to your message. Tell them you want to make sure they got access to the free goodie you're giving away and you want to hear from them if they have any questions about your area of expertise.

Not everybody will reply to you. But A LOT of people will. Once they do, you will automatically be filtered as a primary contact in their inbox.

Best of all: the questions you get from subscribers can give you some great ideas for future content. (Bo-nus!)

Gmail Tab Tip No.3: Do More Social Stuff

If the first two don't seem to help with the whole Gmail tab thing, then ramp up your social media efforts. (Because I have a feeling that the social tab in Gmail will be visited far more than the Promotions tab.)

So, when people sign up for your email list, make sure your Thank You Page has links where they can "Follow you on Facebook" and "Follow Us on Twitter" or "Subscribe to Us on YouTube."

Doing this will help ensure your messages, whether informative or of a marketing nature, get delivered, read and eventually taken action on.

"...And Now for Something Completely Different"

I actually think the Gmail interference is a good thing for us. (In the long run.)

Because:

- Our competition won't have a clue what to do. (And will abandon email.)
- If we tell good "stories" with our email marketing, and we truly send out stuff that helps people, then we have a superb chance at being THE EXPERT in our space.

And when we do that, we have a superb shot at selling way more stuff. (Which is never a bad thing.)

PUNK ROCK MARKETING
AMPLIFY YOUR MESSAGE

BONUS Key Takeaways:

- **Don't freak out over the whole Gmail Tab thing**. (It's big, but not earth-shattering.)
- **Record a quick video** showing your new subscribers how to add your promotional emails to the Gmail primary tab.
- **Ask new subscribers to "reply"** to your messages to ensure you get looped into the primary list of emails.
- **Push your new subscribers to follow you** on your many social media platforms so you don't miss an opportunity reach your tribe.

EPILOGUE:
This is Just the Beginning

Hopefully, I've made the case to you that email Hopefully, I've made the case to you that email marketing is more than just weekly newsletter updates.

It's a profound marketing tool that lets business owners cut through all the noise and social media bull-crap that surrounds modern life, and allows you to speak to your subscribers/customers in a personal and meaningful way.

Now, I seem to have misplaced my crystal ball at this moment, so I can't tell you exactly what emails are going to look like in the future. (Will we be able to send video emails? Facebook chats? Twitter feeds? Instagram Mail? Embedded emails in a brain micro-chip?)

But the core asset of email marketing will never change. Having a list of people you can talk to, over and over again.

I don't know a single marketer or a business person who makes a living EXCLUSIVELY from social media mediums such as Facebook or Twitter. (Unless of course they are selling guides to making a living EXCLUSIVELY from mediums such as Facebook or Twitter.)

I do know plenty of entrepreneurs, myself included, who routinely make serious money from just sending out "emails."

But, if you stick with this email "thing," you'll do far more than make a lot more money for your business.

You'll hear from thankful subscribers who feel like you wrote that email message "just for them."

You'll get handwritten thank you notes and home-baked cookies sent to your house as appreciation for what you do.

You'll find people asking your opinion about a myriad of subjects, because they see you as an "expert" in your field.

And no matter what marketing tool or social media platform comes along in the future, solving people's problems and understanding their pain will never go out of style.

SEARCH
ENGINE
OPTIMIZATION
in 2019
MADE (STUPIDLY)
EASY
Vol.6
of the Small Business
Marketing
COLLECTION
Michael Clarke

Search Engine Optimization in 2019 Made (Stupidly) Easy

Vol.8 of the Small Business Marketing Made (Stupidly) Easy Collection

PROLOGUE:
What the Hell is SEO? (and Why You Should Care?)

It used to be so easy.

Way back when grunge music was all the rage and Mariah Carey still sang high notes that made her sound like a porpoise.

The only thing you needed to dominate the search-engine rankings with your web property was to:

1. Create a website.
2. Submit your website to a couple of ultra-shady directories.
3. Tell Yahoo what keywords you wanted to rank for.

And things were great. (Unless you didn't do any of that stuff. Then you were screwed.)

But then a tech start-up in Mountain View, with a ridiculous name, came on the scene. And Google did more than just provide "relevant" results, or a (boring) clean interface.

It brought law to a lawless land.

"There's a New Sheriff in Town"

See, back then the Internet was like the Wild West.

If you ran an "adult" site but wanted to be seen in the search engines as a "dating" site…

…all you had to do was set up a couple of word list campaigns, optimize your meta keywords, do some spam submissions, and you were all good. (Unless you were the unsuspecting user searching for eHarmony.)

ANY website could say they were anything they wanted.

The only way to know if a search engine result was valuable or worthwhile was to follow that result down the rabbit hole and see where it took you.

Most times, it was to a not-so-nice place.

But Google figured out that what the early World Wide Web needed more than anything else wasn't faster load times, prettier graphics or more links crammed into a single web page.

It needed a Wyatt Earp to come in and tell the good guys from the bad guys.

"What We Have Here is a Failure to Communicate"

Trouble was, how do you tell a reputable website from a disreputable one? (You know, without screening each website by hand.)

The (somewhat) elegant solution Google came up with was to create an algorithm — whose secret sauce is guarded religiously to this day — that determines which sites have "authority" (the good guys) and which do not — the not-so-good guys).

And although there are tons of factors that go into this algorithm, the basic equation is built around three factors:

1. **What YOU say your website is about** (content, keywords, domain name, alt tags, meta keywords, h1 tags, title tags, etc.)
2. **What OTHER PEOPLE say your website is about** (backlinks, directories, social mentions, social sharing, etc.)
3. **What visitors' behavior says about your website** (Bounce rate, 404 errors, time spent on site, social bookmarking, etc.)

And this whole system WOULD work just fine.

If the bad guys didn't keep dressing up like the good guys.

It Ain't Easy Being Green (or a 14 Billion-Dollar Company)

So, why should we care about Google's problems?

Well, because Google is that bratty kid who keeps threatening to "take their ball and go home" if people don't play right.

And in this case, they OWN the ball. The playground. The parking lot across the street. The entire TOWN.

There may come a day when somebody ELSE rules the Search Engine universe. (Facebook is trying its damndest. And Amazon might have the best shot of them all, with its massive media empire disguising itself as a place to buy socks.)

But let nobody fool you: Search Engine Marketing is all about getting the Google Housekeeping Seal of Approval.

And although social media is certainly the brand-new shiny thing every marketer is in love with, organic search-engine traffic still kicks major ass because:

- It's free.
- People are conditioned to TRUST Google search results.
- People searching on Google are looking for a solution to their problem NOW.

So, as we go through the various "ninja" SEO tactics in this book, and I've got quite a few in store for you, just remember Google tweaks its algorithm as often as Taylor Swift changes boyfriends. (Which is to say, a lot.)

But the core concern for Google remains the same, they don't want people to CHEAT.

They don't want people to over-optimize their sites and cut to the front of the line.

While you may be tempted to try some slightly shady Google Sniper software, or give in to the promises of some overpaid SEO "expert" who positively, absolutely guarantees you a Google page one placement RIGHT THIS INSTANT...

...follow the techniques and tips in this book.

Give the strategies outlined here some time to percolate and do their magic.

You may not get to the front of the line immediately.

But before too long, you'll be stepping over the competition. (And making a ton of money in the process.)

Chapter 1:

Everything You Know About SEO is Kinda, Sorta, Mostly Wrong

"Know the rules well, so you can break them effectively."

-Dalai Lama XIV

Okay, maybe not everything you know is wrong. But a lot.

And it's not your fault. I mean, you're busy.

Having a life. Running a business. NOT spending time in dorky SEO message boards. (Like me.)

That's because, due to Google's desire to keep the recipe to their secret sauce...you know...secret, there's a lot of speculation/fortune-telling that goes on with Search Engine Marketing. (And that even more horrible word, Search Engine Optimization.)

- Do keywords still matter?
- How much does a keyword in your domain help you?
- What's the deal with backlinks? (And how do you get good ones?)
- Can some SEO hack who called me up during business hours REALLY guarantee me to be on the first page of Google?

So, before we dig into the nitty-gritty of Search Engine Optimization, I'd like to answer some common SEO questions business owners like you have, to give you the latest findings on this ever-evolving, and somewhat complex, area of marketing:

Search Engine FAQ No. 1: Do Keywords Still Work?

Even the most web-challenged business owner knows a little something about "keywords."

Keywords are the semantic phrases that "real" people use to search for stuff. (And that Google uses to determine what a page is about.)

And it used to be that to "rank" a page for a certain term, such as "hair loss remedies," all you had to do was write an article on your website that looked something like this:

Hair loss remedies are very desirable for people who are losing their hair. Hair loss remedies come in many shapes and sizes. Propecia is one of the many successful hair loss remedies out there. It works. That's what hair loss remedies do.

And on and on and on. Obnoxious keyword stuffing at its finest.

This technique used to work. No longer. (Thank God.)

In fact, for most ultra-competitive keyword phrases, the "main keyword" shows up about .1% of the time in the web content.

What's important now is the main phrase COUPLED WITH related phrases that are connected to the main keyword phrase. I'll show you how to do this in Chapter 4 so it doesn't look like it was done by a robot.

SEO Verdict: Don't keyword stuff. Doesn't work, and the content reads like it was written by someone who just came out of a coma.

Search Engine FAQ No. 2: Do Exact-Name Domains Still Work?

An exact domain is when you include a keyword phrase in the address of your website with something ludicrous like:

- *MartinD28Guitar.com*
- *RazorElectricGoKart.com*
- *Chapter7BankruptcyAttorney.com*

Ridiculous, right? I mean, who would do something so idiotic as create a site with that URL? (Me, it turns out. As I owned all of those.)

But those days are long gone. Google no longer gives (much) weight at all to exact-match domains.

And the advantages of a cool-sounding, branded domain, such as GoKartNinja.com or BankruptcySolutions.com, far outweigh whatever small benefit an exact-domain match might possibly give you.

Far more important are how you title individual pages or posts within a website.

So, for example, if we wanted to rank for the term "Denver Bankruptcy Attorney," then a good way to optimize that page would be: "CowboyJoe.com/Denver-Bankruptcy-Attorney."

SEO Verdict: Don't use an exact-name domain. Use your business name or some other branded name to make your site much more appealing to humans. (And, as a result, search engines.)

Search Engine FAQ No. 3: SEO is All About Backlinks, Right?

Backlinks, in case you're not up on your SEO terminology — and why should you be? — are the links that outside, external sites place on their domains that link back to your site.

And, Google weighs these very carefully in determining who are the good guys and bad guys. (They act as "votes" in separating the crap from the awesome.)

Trouble is, for years backlinking was nothing more than an arms race to mediocrity.

Whoever could get the most backlinks, and it didn't really matter where you got them from, ultimately won.

But one day, not too long ago, the sleeping Google Giant woke up and finally realized that a home's value isn't just in the drywall and thatched roof. It's the neighborhood as well.

So, hanging out in some dodgy web neighborhoods, and getting some very skeevy backlinks not only doesn't help, but it also hurts.

The key, instead, is to go for high-quality neighborhoods. I'll show you how in Chapter 5.

SEO Verdict: Go for a few reputable backlinks. And leave the sketchy backlink neighborhoods to the spammers.

SEARCH ENGINE FAQ NO. 4: CAN ANYBODY GUARANTEE PAGE ONE PLACEMENT ON GOOGLE?

Well, they CAN guarantee all they want. But can they deliver?

Maybe.

For a little while.

But ask yourself, if the tactic is that easy, why isn't he/she doing it for their own site? (And why do you need them at all?)

There's no question that getting on the first page of a search-engine listing is VITAL. (Especially in the top 3-4 results of a page.)

But who gets on the FIRST PAGE of a SERP (Search Engine Results Page) can fluctuate wildly. (I've seen my own sites randomly move up and down over the course of a day.)

In Chapter 7, I'll share with you some cool tricks for getting your company right there on good old Page One. But just be aware, it's a position of constant flux. (And not something to worry about terribly.)

SEO Verdict: Fire that $2,500/month SEO consultant you've got on the payroll and build your SEO efforts the right way.

CHAPTER 1 Key Takeaways:

- **Keywords are still important.** (Especially in the title.) But keyword stuffing is not.
- **Exact-name domains are spammy.** Stay away. Unless you have a compelling business reason to use them.
- **A couple quality backlinks are way, way better than a bunch of trashy backlinks** from CrappyArticleDirectory.com
- **Watch out for wild claims by SEOs**, guaranteeing page one placement. (They might also have a magical elixir to sell you.)

Chapter 2:

Why Your Website Sucks at SEO (and What You Can Do About It!)

"Everything that looks too perfect is too perfect to be perfect."

-Dejan Stojanovic

In the next chapter we will talk about the actual content on your website. (You know, the stuff that gets people to do things like "buy stuff.")

But right now let's talk about the GUTS of your website. The ENGINE underneath the hood.

Or what overpriced web consultants call "site architecture." (Yeah, I think it's pretentious too.)

But often it's the way a website is organized that some of the quickest SEO fixes for a marketer can be found. (And some of the biggest gains.)

So, here are 6 Website SEO Hacks you can apply to your website (pain-free) to give you a serious SEO boost:

Website SEO Hack No.1: Make Sure Your Site is Responsive

And by responsive we mean friendly to the mobile devices out there. Because I hate to break it to you but the days of people reading your website on a desktop or laptop are going the way of the 8-track cassette.

If your site is NOT mobile-friendly and responsive to different screen sizes, you are throwing money out of your pocket.

How to make your particular website responsive will depend on what platform your site lives on. I use WordPress and MOST website themes are responsive out-of-the-box. Same thing if your site lives on a template service such as Wix or SquareSpace.

But if your site is a custom build, made by your crazy uncle five years ago, then you might need to have a developer look your site over.

Either way, with the encroaching popularity of mobile, it's a worthwhile investment.

Website SEO Hack No. 2: Tell Google (and the World) Who You Are

This one took me a while to figure out. Google doesn't exactly come right out and tell you precisely what you need to do to make your website uber-compliant.

But one of the most important things you need to do on your website is to make clear:

1. Who you are: (The "About" page.)
2. What your site does: ("The Terms of Service" page.)
3. What you will never, ever do: ("The Privacy Policy" page.)
4. How people can get a hold of you: ("The Contact Us" page.)

Now, there are lots of plugins and boilerplate templates floating around the Internet that you can use to automatically churn these out.

Don't. Use. Them.

Google wants to see original content here. They want to see your website is an authority, something closer to a magazine than some scammy website.

So here are a couple of tips:

- **Put lots of info on the "About" Page.** Including info about everybody on your team, and all the people who write for your website. (Names and pictures are great.)
- **Terms of Service.** This is where you tell people what your site is about. If it's e-commerce, then you need to go into shipping procedures. If you're an affiliate, you need to be VERY CLEAR that you make money off the products you endorse. Don't be coy, be clear. Google doesn't like coy.
- **Make your privacy policy original.** Write it in your own voice. You can use other sites as a template, but don't copy. (Google hates boilerplate Privacy Policies.)
- **Include phone numbers, email addresses, names, and everything else you can think of on your "Contact Us" page.** Think of this like a masthead at a newspaper. Let people know how they can reach you.
- **Put links to all these pages in the footer of your site.** Don't make them hidden or in grayed-out text. Make them super clear.
- This may all seem silly. It's not. It's super-important and Google pays attention to it.

Website SEO Hack No. 3: Drink the Blog Kool-Aid

The word "blog" usually conjures up images of self-centered twenty-year-olds sharing every thought they have in their brain as they prepare dishes from a Julia Child cookbook.

But to Google a blog is a form of website content organization. And it's a content organization Google loves.

That's because the organization of a blog screams: This Sucker Gets Updated Frequently! (Which makes it easier for search engines to crawl and index your website.)

And the WordPress platform, in my not-so-humble opinion, is the best solution for this. (Head over to WordPress.com to check it out.)

It's free, there are a ton of plugins that go with it, and Google has a stalker-ish obsession for WordPress.

So, think about moving your static HTML website over to a blog format.

If you have ZERO technical skills, head over to contractor websites such as Upwork and find a developer to do it for you on the QUICK and CHEAP.

Website SEO Hack No. 4: May All Your URLs Be Pretty

And by "pretty" I mean something that humans can understand. And doesn't look like a robot set it up.

For example, let's say I want to create a blog post entitled "Is SEO Really Dead?"

That post's URL (the web address users see when they visit your site) could be displayed any number of these ways:

- PunkRockMarketing.com/page=5
- PunkRockMarketing.com/2019/4/sample
- PunkRockMarketing.com/PageId=874
- PunkRockMarketing.com/is-seo-really-dead

I'll let you guess which is better from an SEO and user standpoint. (Hint: It ain't the ones with numbers.)

The way to accomplish this is to set up a site permalink structure, the way your links automatically generate, so the data pulled isn't tied to a number but instead to the title of a particular page or post.

Confused, yet? Don't worry. It's easy.

- If you have your site set up in WordPress all you do is:
- Go to "settings" and click on permalinks
- Paste this bit of code into the custom structure field: "/%category%/%postname%/" (Do not include quotation marks)
- Save Changes

- When you create a new page or post, make sure you include the keyword in the title, and then remove all words, except for the keyword phrase, from the URL

If you have your website living on a different platform than WordPress, or you have your own DIY website installation, you may need to have a web-developer type do some tweaking. (Trust me, it'll be worth it.)

All you do is tell your developer to set up a permalink structure that includes:

- Domain.com/Category/PostName (for blog posts)
- Domain.com/Page Name (For pages)

That's it.

And this is where many small business owners STOP. But they miss out on one key aspect of page URL structure.

When they have content optimized for a particular keyword phrase, to have a URL that contains THAT keyword…and NOTHING else.

For instance, let's say I want to create a new blog post entitled "Google SEO Tips So Simple a Caveman Could Do It." And the keyword phrase I want to optimize this post for is "Google SEO Tips." (Horribly competitive, but let's give it a whirl.)

The way most people have their site set up is that the URL of that post would be:

PunkRockMarketing.com/SEO/Google-SEO-Tips-So-Simple-A-Caveman-Could-Do-It

And they mistakenly believe because the URL CONTAINS the keyword phrase that this is ideal search engine optimization.

But this gives Google mixed messages. It tells Google your page is ABOUT the following:

- Google SEO tips

- Cavemen
- Simplicity

Too much thinking for the Google algorithm to handle.

Instead, you want to set up your links of keyword optimized content to look something like:

PunkRockMarketing.com/SEO/Google-SEO-Tips

In the next chapter we'll go over why you want to have SOME content that is keyword-focused and SOME content that is NOT.

But for now just remember this:

- **Step One:** Set up a permalink structure that organizes content by websitename.com/Category/PostName or websitename.com/PageName.
- **Step Two:** If it's a page not intended to be optimized for a keyword phrase, you're done. Hit Publish.
- **Step Three:** If the page is intended to be optimized for a keyword phrase, remove all words that are NOT the keyword phrase and then hit publish.

Website SEO Hack No. 5: Jump on the Category Train

So in the above example (PunkRockMarketing.com/SEO/Google-SEO-Tips) you'll notice I have the phrase "SEO" before the post name of my blog post.

This is a category and search engines love categories. (Makes their job easier.)

Suppose you're a bankruptcy attorney with a website that has 10 or so how-to articles on the various forms of bankruptcy. (Some on Chapter 7, a couple on Chapter 13, maybe a couple on Chapter 11…)

And this may make total, intuitive sense to you, but it can confuse search engines as they try to determine what your website is actually ABOUT. (Search engines are as clueless as a Kardashian sometimes.)

The solution?

Create "focused" categories that organize the content on your website. This will not only boost your rankings in the search engine, but also make for a better user experience.

With Mr. Attorney here, I might come up with categories such as:

- Chapter 7 Bankruptcy
- Chapter 11 Bankruptcy
- Medical Bankruptcy
- Avoiding Bankruptcy
- Bankruptcy and Divorce
- Bankruptcy and Probate

...and so on.

Then my permalinks would look something like:

- LawyerBob.com/Medical-Bankruptcy/How-to-Survive-a-Hospital-Judgment
- LawyerBob.com/Chapter-7-Bankruptcy/Chapter-7-Avoid

This not only streamlines your website for optimal awesomeness, as far as Google is concerned, but can also help give you an editorial framework for future articles.

Website SEO Hack No. 6: Create a Circle of Life

Don't worry. I will not ask you to sing an Elton John song. Unless you want to. (Stick with the early stuff.)

I WILL, however, advise you to have every page on your website connect (through article text or dedicated links in the sidebar or footer) to another page on your website.

The advantages are numerous:

- **It keeps users on your site longer** and increases the chance of a successful conversion.

- **It boosts the average "Time Spent"** on your site, which directly affects your search-engine rankings. (We'll go over this in Chapter 7.)
- **It provides a more satisfying user experience** for your visitors.
- **It tells Google which pages of your website are the REAL BIGGIE** authority pages on your site. (Google loves it when you make their job easier.) One way to do this is to have internal linking, where words and/or phrases in your content are linked to other pages on your site.

How do we implement this?

If you're using WordPress there are a ton of plugins, such as *WP Internal Links*, that do this automatically.

You choose a certain phrase and the destination you want that internal link to go to, and the plugin will automatically create an internal link to that page everywhere on your site that word appears.

For example, every mention of the phrase "how to find cheap flights" would link to TravelNinja.com/cheap-flights/how-to-find-cheap-flights while every mention of "last minute flights to Baltimore" would link to TravelNinja.com/last-minute-flights/last-minute-flights-to-Baltimore

There will be times, however — and we'll go over them in the next chapter — when you write content that doesn't focus on a keyword phrase. Such as content that is more opinion- or news-driven rather than how-to and instructional. ("How the New Travel Restrictions Will Affect Flight Prices")

Don't stress it. Just do the best you can by linking to another page that might provide good information for a user.

Don't worry if a couple of your pages don't have internal links. This isn't the tax code. You won't be audited if you don't follow things to the letter of the law. You just want to put best practices in place that serve you and your business.

CHAPTER 2 Key Takeaways:

- **Pages that tell Google who you are and what you're about are important, not just vanity.** This includes your "About" page and "Contact Us" page. They legitimize your business.
- **If you haven't already, think about moving your website over to a blog framework.** It's not just a way to express your inner tortured artist, but a way to organize your content that Google prefers.
- **Set up your permalinks so they automatically become friendly URLS** when you create new content.
- **When creating content focused on a keyword, remove all words that are not part of the keyword** phrase from the URL.
- **Create categories for your website** based on the most logical subjects of your site's content.
- **Try to have each page of website content link** to another page on your website.

Chapter 3:

5 Secrets to Kick-Ass SEO Content

"If I waited till I felt like writing,
I'd never write at all."

-Anne Tyler

I hate the word content.

Not sure why, got no rational explanation for it.

It's probably all those years I spent in conference rooms — how come nobody can ever get the air conditioner to work in those? — where some advertising rep would talk on and on about the need for high-quality CONTENT...

...and how we needed to have a c**ontent strategy** to *leverage our current content offerings* and how important it was to create a **content platform** that utilizes user-generated *interactivity.*

Ugh.

Talk like that makes content sound like government regulation, instead of, you know, words that connect with human beings.

And for years that approach worked.

Creating web content that search engines LIKED, and would be rewarded with high placement, was like following a cake recipe.

"First, we need a half a cup of long-tail keywords. Then a quarter cup of bolded H2 tags, and then top it off with four tablespoons of backlinks..."

Companies like eHow and Ezine Articles specialized in this sweatshop method, becoming factories for 300-word optimized balls of content shite.

But then Google woke up from its article-directory coma and unleashed its cute, furry animals of SEO doom in the form of the Panda and Penguin updates.

When Penguins and Pandas Attack

Today, content that boosts the SEO rankings of your website doesn't follow so much a crude SEO checklist that any knucklehead with a Warrior Forum log-in can execute…

…but rather a skill that requires actual thought, time, and the tiniest sense you know what the hell you are talking about.

So, here are my FIVE Tips for creating SEO-Friendly Content for your site:

SEO Content Tip No.1: Create Diverse Content

What do I mean by "diverse?" I mean, content that comes in different shapes and sizes. Publishing nothing but 2000-word blog posts might be noble — and tendonitis-inducing — but it's not what Google wants.

Google wants your content to be a mix of:

- Long-form written content (Over 1,000 words)
- Short-form written content (400-700 words)
- Video
- Audio
- Picture Gallery
- PowerPoint presentation
- Q&A

This isn't just good from a user experience, to help grab people in different ways, but Google sees this as a sign your site is reliable and newsworthy.

Even if it's not.

And you don't have to do every single type of content out there. Just mix it up. One week do a video, the next week do a blog post, the week after that do a podcast.

And while you're creating this mix of content you want to have:

- 75% of your content be keyword-focused
- 25% of your content NOT be keyword-focused

Why the hell would we want to do something like this?

Well, in the old days we wanted to have every single piece of content optimized for a keyword phrase. But this is now as suspicious as writing off your purchase of Starburst© candy as a tax deduction.

You want to have a mix of optimized content and non-optimized content to make your site seem natural and organic.

I know this is contrary to what all the books, blog posts, and gurus tell you. But in the long run, if you adopt this strategy, it will not only make you look good to the Googlebots but also make you more money.

SEO Content Tip No.2: Create Regular Content

How frequent should you create/publish content on your site?

Well, it will depend on the goals of your site. And how much time, energy and staff you have to devote to this endeavor. But my recommendation is to pick a schedule you can live with and STICK to it.

If you can create one piece of content a week, then pick a day of the week — Tuesdays-Thursday are good — and publish at the same time, on the same day, each week.

If you can create two pieces of content per month, then pick a day — 2nd and 4th Wednesdays — and publish at the same time, on the same day, each week.

Google favors sites that have a regular posting schedule. Makes them look more professionally and journalist-y.

They do not favor the "cram for the exam the night before" approach. If you get inspired over the weekend, and write four blog posts, don't think you should publish them all at once because you think Google will reward you. Far better to space those out and schedule them over the course of your regular publishing schedule.

SEO Content Tip No. 3: Create Content for a Native Speaker

It sounds simple, but you'd be absolutely shocked how many business owners are still trucking in lousy outsourced content from overseas to fill their website.

Problem is: Google is getting great at detecting content whose syntax is (slightly) off.

Note: *Syntax is just a fancy word for how words are arranged. Bad syntax is one of the first tip-offs that content is written by somebody for whom English is not a first language.*

Not only are you wasting money with your newfound international content pipeline, but it's got a great shot of actually getting your site banished from the most-favored SEO nation status.

So, if you're not a great writer yourself, find somebody on your team who likes to write. (Or look for an unemployed college graduate in your hometown. God knows there's a ton lying around.)

SEO Content Tip No. 4: Create Content That Solves People's Problems

I work with business owners all the time who get stuck about what content to publish on their site.

And I ask them the same question: "What do you KNOW that could save somebody pain, time or money?"

People LOVE insider tips. Cheat sheets. Quick guides.

Anything that will save them the trouble of having to go and learn the damn thing, your website should talk about.

Some of my favorite content subjects include:

- **Q&As** ("Car Buying Q&A")
- **Biggest Mistakes People Make** ("5 Biggest Mistakes Brides Make on Their Wedding Day and How to Avoid Them")
- **Secrets to Achieving a Result** ("3 Secrets to Clear Skin Through Diet)

- **Steps to Solve a Problem** ("The 6 Steps to a $2,000 Tax Refund")
- **The State of the Industry** ("A State of the Union of the Cruise Ship Industry")
- **Upcoming Trends People Need to Know About** ("5 Trends Every Homeschool Parent Needs to Know About")
- **How One Unrelated Area of Life Can Teach You About Another** ("What Lindsay Lohan Can Teach You About Brand Reputation")

SEO Content Tip No. 5: Create Content With Keywords You Can Rank For

I left keywords for last, because the first five tips are way more important than which keyword you use.

Keywords won't help your blog post get shared on Facebook 329 times. Writing cool, non-sucky content will.

But there is still a function and a place for keywords. They are, after all, connected to the phrases that people use to find the information they want.

The two big mistakes small biz owners make regarding content keywords are:

- They target keywords WAY OUT of their league
- They target keywords that aren't relevant
- When targeting keywords, here is what I recommend:
- **Fire up whatever SEO keyword tool you like.** There are tons of paid options — WordTracker, SEM Rush, Moz — but I still like to use the Google Keyword Planner. It's not always accurate, but it reflects what Google thinks. (And what Google thinks is important.)
- **Type in keywords related to your business.** Put 'em all down. Anything related to your business. (Don't forget competitor brand names.)

- **Filter your results.** I like to search for keywords that get LESS than 1k searches a month and have LOW competition. This isn't an exact science. But by doing this I ensure I don't go after impossible phrases like "marketing tips" or "mindfulness" that have super-high competition. But I do target keywords that SOMEBODY is looking for.
- **Remove irrelevant phrases.** This could, depending on your business, mean removing anything with the word "free" or "cheap" or "open source." Or maybe there's just a phrase that has no relevancy for potential buyers. Even if a phrase has decent search numbers, and low competition, does not make it a good fit for your site. Remember the end goal: find people who might buy stuff from you.

PUNK ROCK MARKETING
AMPLIFY YOUR MESSAGE

CHAPTER 3 Key Takeaways:

- **Create diverse content for your website.** Publish a mix of text (both long and short), video, audio, photo galleries — whatever you feel spreads your message the best.
- **Have 75% of your content be keyword-focused** and 25% be whatever you want.
- **Stick to a regular content schedule.** Whether 1x a week or 1x a month, keep it regular and consistent.
- **Publish web content that was written by a native speaker.** And not some spam robot.
- **Solving people's problems** will always help your SEO efforts.
- **Create keyword-focused content that actually have a shot to rank for.** Good rule of thumb: target keyword phrases that get less than 1k searches a month and have LOW competition.

Chapter 4:

Your Ultimate SEO Content Publishing Checklist

"I am free no matter what rules surround me.."

-Robert A. Heinlein

Creating killer content that addresses people's questions, solves their problems and, is centered on a potentially lucrative keyword, is just the first step to SEO content awesomeness.

Once you've got that content created, in whatever form, it's time to optimize it and get it ready for prime-time. (So, it can get discovered and make you a bazillion dollars.)

And though I'd like to tell you the following items are guaranteed to work, until Google opens their vault and shows us exactly how they rank content, we must just use experience and insight to guide our way.

Just remember no matter what tactics change in the SEO content game, one strategy will always be the same:

Search engines want to deliver relevant and non-sucky content to users. (Follow that and you can't go wrong.)

With that said, and until the day Google spills the beans, here is a checklist I heartily recommend you use to get your content as optimized as humanly possible before publishing.

Note: If you're publishing a piece of content not optimized the keyword, skip the first four items.

Checklist Item #1: Find Somebody Else to Do Most of the Items on This List

You might resist me on this one. You might think it's better for you to have your finger on every SEO pulse of your website and business.

But once you've done this checklist a few times, you'll quickly realize: "I would love to have somebody else do this crap."

So, as we go through the items think about somebody on your team — or inner circle — who these tasks might be a good fit for.

Or if you don't know anybody, visit a site like Upwork.com and find somebody you can add to the fold.

Checklist Item #2: Come Up With a Secondary Keyword

Huh? You mean I've got to have a secondary keyword *too*? Man, this is a lot of work.

It's not that big a deal…

All you do it look over your list of approved keywords — those that are relevant, have decent search volume and have low competition — and then find another related keyword.

For example, if I'm optimizing a piece of content for the phrase "mystery writing tips," then scanning my list I might find the phrase "thriller story ideas."

Sounds like a good pair to me.

Then, just take the two phrases and paste them into a text-only document, such as Notepad or TextEdit.

After that, you're ready for…

Checklist Item #3: Fix Your Meta Data

Meta is defined as: information "about" something. In the Web world, metadata is the information on a web page that tells the search engines, and humans, what a web page is actually ABOUT.

And it's important.

In the old days, metadata was easy to abuse. Spammy web publishers would cram the "meta keywords" field full of words they wanted to rank for, even if the page had NOTHING to do with those terms.

And though Google has tightened its policy toward metadata — meta keywords don't figure into Google's search algorithm anymore — it's still a vital part of your web page structure.

There are four areas you need to focus on in relation to metadata for each page you create:

1. Title Tags
2. Meta Description
3. Meta Keywords
4. Meta tags

Let's take these one at a time:

Title Tags: This is the phrase, or title, a visitor sees at the top of their browser when they visit your website. Some content management systems will pull it directly from the title of a page or a blog post. But most content systems will allow you to customize this.

You want to have your main keyword phrase appear as early as possible in the title tag.

Example: "Mystery Writing Tips From the Pros" is better than "The Unique and Wonderful and Strange and Bizarre History of Mystery Writing Tips."

Meta Description: This is the short, text description that you see below the actual hyperlink, when you do a web search.

And this one is important, because humans actually see it, and it has a huge bearing on whether people will click on the result.

What you want to do in the meta description field is to get BOTH your primary keyword and your secondary keyword in there.

Example: "Want to know what mystery writing tips you can learn from your fave author? Here are tips to aid your thriller story ideas."

Meta Keywords: But wait a minute! I thought you said meta keywords weren't even used in Google's algorithm.

Yes. That's true.

But if you ever end up doing any kind of PPC (Pay-per-click) campaign with Google AdWords or Facebook or LinkedIn, then meta keywords can make a slight difference in how much you pay for your advertising. (And unless you like wasting money, optimize it now to gain benefits later on.)

The process is simple: just add your primary and secondary keywords to the meta keywords field.

Meta Tags: Okay, now I've totally confused you. "Title tags" and "Meta tags?" Who can keep this SEO stuff straight?

Don't worry. Here's which meta tags you need:

- One for your primary keyword ("Mystery writing tips")
- One for your secondary keyword ("Thriller story ideas")
- One for the category of the page or post ("Mystery writers")
- Any other relevant tags that tie into your website ("Fiction writers; Horror fiction; Self published authors")

Checklist Item #4: Add Keywords to Your Content

This is another area where many small biz owners trying to outfit their site with SEO goodness misstep. And that is cram their content with obvious keywords.

Example:

"Mystery writing tips are good to have when writing mysteries. Mystery writing tips come in many sizes. Which mystery writing tips are good? Read this article on mystery writing tips to find out."

Unless you're on 150mg of Thorazine, this won't resonate.

A better strategy is to make sure your keyword is included in the following:

- Primary keyword in the first paragraph and **BOLDED**
- Secondary keyword in the first three paragraphs and *ITALICIZED*

- Primary keyword used as a HEADING
- Primary keyword used in last paragraph and *ITALICIZED* (I usually do this in the form of an invitation for people to comment or respond)

Geez. Seems onerous.

Not really.

This is what it would look like in practical terms:

Which **mystery writing tips** can you learn from your favorite author? Are there any nuggets of wisdom we can glean from the pros to boost our ability to come up with compelling *thriller story ideas*?

Here are strategies every mystery writer can add to their toolbox to improve their craft and reduce their learning curve.

5 Mystery Writing Tips You Can Use Right Away (this is a heading - you indicate this by highlighting and choosing the <h2> option in your Web Editor

Pro #1: Stephen King

Stephen King always starts off each horror story by playing a Metallica CD to help get him in the mood. Which CDs help evoke a mood for you?

........blah, blah, blah....

So, those are some of our favorite *mystery writing tips* from the pros. Do you have one or two mystery writing nuggets that you've picked up along the way? Let us know in the comments below.

What the heck does this accomplish?

By using a mix of italics, bold, and headings you are telling Google — in different ways — what this one page is about. And by adding a secondary keyword — and italicizing it — you are putting the keyword in context with other keywords.

Google loves context.

You've also asked people for their input. Which can boost engagement and send even more social signals to Google that this is important content.

But even if nobody leaves a comment, you have done Google a favor by making it explicitly clear what this content is about. (And Google will often return the favor by sending traffic your way.)

Okay, but what do you if you do if you're publishing a video or a podcast or SlideDeck with little text?

It's okay. Breathe. Everything is going to be okay.

In that case, skip the heading. And write 3-4 sentences that describe the content you're publishing, and which includes the primary keyword (bolded and italicized) and the secondary keyword (italicized)

This is not a pass-or-fail exam. You're just trying to make your content as optimized as possible. If doing so compromises the user experience, don't do it. Just do your best and rejoice because most people won't do this.

Checklist Item #5: Optimize Your Images

I will assume you use images in your website content. If not, I encourage you to leave the 19th-Century and join us here where people love visual stuff and have no attention span.

That said, there are a few things you can do to make your images are as SEO-friendly as possible:

- **Add a filter to your images (for stock photos only)** - If you're uploading a photo that you or somebody on your team took, then don't worry about this one. But if you are using a photo from a stock photo platform, then I recommend you throw that photo into some kind of editing tool (Canva is a great FREE tool) and change the saturation or some other visual element of the image. Doesn't have to be extreme; just a subtle filter and your photo will be seen as original by Google, instead of some cookie-cutter image you got from a stock image factory.
- **Compress your images** - Google penalizes pages and sites that have slow load times. And nothing loads slower than HUGE images. So, before you upload your image to your site, go to a

place like CompressJpeg.com (it's FREE!) and compress your image to a smaller size. You'll hardly recognize the difference. But Google will and that's what's important.

- **Rename your images** - This is simple. If you're publishing a keyword piece, name the image file with the keyword, hyphens separating the words ("mystery-writing-tips"). If you're writing a non-keyword piece, then just use the title of your page, ("how-do-mystery-writers-make-money")
- **Add primary keyword to your image alt tag** - Alt tags are image attribute tags that describe what an image is about. (Used with screen readers for the blind to aid accessibility.) Not only is it a good thing to do, ethically, but it's another opportunity to tell Google what a page is about.

CHAPTER 4 KEY TAKEAWAYS:

- **Find somebody else** to do the items on this list. (Eventually.)
- **Come up with a secondary keyword.** This establishes the context of your content.
- **Optimize the metadata of your content.** This includes title tag (primary keyword), meta description (primary and secondary keywords), tags (primary and secondary keywords), and meta keywords (Primary and secondary keywords)
- **Add keywords to your content.** Aim for primary keyword (Bolded) in the first paragraph, secondary keyword (italicized) in the first three paragraphs, primary keyword as <h2> heading, and primary keyword (italicized) in last paragraph.
- **Optimize your images.** This means compressing them to a smaller size, adding a filter (to ensure originality) and adding a primary keyword in the ALT tag.

Chapter 5:

How to Get Backlinks That Don't Suck

"It is better to be alone than in bad company."

-George Washington

Ah, yes. Backlinks. The hard-earned currency that makes the SEO world go round.

Contrary to popular opinion, backlinks — which are nothing more than external websites linking back to your website — are still a super-vital part of search engine optimization.

It's just that Google has systematically closed down a lot of the counterfeit backlink shops...

...making it much harder to get good quality backlinks. (And, as a result, making them much more valuable.)

"We Don't Need No Stinkin' Backlinks!"

There was a time, not too long ago, when you could buy some automated software, named something ridiculous like Google Annihilator or Article Spinner Samurai Mojo, to help you rack up thousands of "targeted" backlinks to your site in just 24 hours.

Say, you wanted your site to rank for the phrase "Pool Cleaner Phoenix."

Well, the old way to do business would be to hire some poor outsourcer, who knows nothing about pool cleaners (or Phoenix), to write a crappy 300-word article for you...

...which you, or your SEO team, would then put into your new software to "spin" 1,200 times — don't get me started on "article spinning" — which would then be "published" on a bunch of other crappy websites that only search engines ever visit…

…in the hope that the anchor text — the exact hyperlinked phrase that points back to your website — would help boost your website in the rankings.

And, it became a huge backlinks arms race, where dueling SEO strategists tried to find the latest article marketing ballistic missile to crush the competition.

But Google did two things to turn this equation upside-down:

1. They reduced the value of anchor text keywords.
2. They penalized websites for having too many backlinks from crappy Internet neighborhoods.

"You'll Never Find a More Wretched Hive of Scum and Villainy"

For many marketers, these two changes alone destroyed years of SEO effort and created a chaotic environment of search-engine confusion.

So, what do we do now?

How do we create valuable backlinks without, you know, begging and pleading every website we know to link back to us?

Fear not!

Here are FIVE Ways to Build Backlinks that are awesome, effective and will (probably) last FOREVER:

Ethical Backlink Method No. 1: Guest Blogging

This is probably my favorite form of backlinking right now.

Here's how it works:

1. You approach a blog owner who's in a similar field as yours.
2. Ask them if they'd like free content. (They will say yes. Trust me.)

3. Write killer content.
4. Specify where on your website you'd like to be linked back to, along with a brief call-to-action about the cool, awesome free thing you are giving away. (Or special offer you've got going.)

Not only is this a totally fair and equitable way to build a backlink, but it can put your brand in front of an entirely new (and qualified) audience.

Sure, it may seem like work. (Because, you know, writing is like… hard.)

But if you have absolutely no idea what to write about, just do a Q&A in your knowledge wheelhouse. (People will appreciate those more than anything else you'll do.)

So, how do I find guest-blogging opportunities?

I use good old Google and do the following searches: (replace [keyword] with your particular area of expertise)

- "Write for us" [keyword]
- "Become a contributor" [keyword]
- "Submit guest post" [keyword]
- "Bloggers wanted" [keyword]
- "Becoming a contributor" [keyword]

You can either bookmark these searches or set them up as Google Alerts so you can get the latest results emailed to you. Don't get much easier than that.

Ethical Backlink Method No. 2: Blog Commenting

There's a lot of misinformation about blog commenting. Many people will preach that you have to be the FIRST person to comment on a blog post to get any backlink love. (Not so.)

Or you have to write a dissertation-length comment to get any traction from it. (Not so.)

But it helps if you know what you're doing, and not be a total spambot.

So, here is my step-by-step process for blog commenting:

1. Choose 4-6 high-traffic blogs in your general industry. (Not competitors.)
2. Sign up for the RSS feeds of those blogs. (These are the orange icons, with the three lines next to them, you'll usually find on the blog home page.)
3. Check your RSS Feed Reader, such as Feedly, to find out when new blog posts are published.
4. When a new blog post is published, head over to the post location and make a decent/interesting comment that is moderately long, couple sentences, replies to the first commenter, if that isn't you, mentions the blogger by name (super important!) and something BESIDES "Nice post" or "Good point," and include a link to your website.
5. Use a pinging service, such as PingOMatic or Pingler, to "ping" the URL of your comment. (All you have to do is enter the URL and click "ping.")

Doing just 2-3 of these a week will boost the backlink awesomeness of your website.

Ethical Backlink Method No. 3: Forums/Message Board Commenting

Message boards can be tricky. They can be a great way to find new customers and promote your business to a whole new audience.

They can also be an incredible time suck, and a great way to induce an anxiety attack as you deal with bitter, angry forum trolls.

So, here's how to tread carefully and get the most out of forum backlinks:

1. Choose 2-3 message boards where your customers might hang out. Any more than that and you'll totally get overwhelmed. (BoardReader.com is a great resource for this.)

2. Create a profile that includes a link back to your site and a call to action that promises something FREE and COOL in your profile signature. (Example: "For a FREE Carpet Cleaning Business Guide head over to…")
3. Comply with forum rules. Some profile signatures will allow HTML, and some won't. You must read their terms of service to find out what you can and can't do.
4. Commit to making three contributions in each board a week. (Reply, question, or new thread.)
5. For the first three weeks, just reply to other people's threads. Don't promote. Don't appear as a know-it-all.
6. After a couple of weeks of feeling out the vibe, throw in an occasional "Hey, if you want to check out my cool free thing here…"
7. Be helpful, be cool, be funny. (If you're funny.)

Most people are irrational and/or too sales-y in forums. By being different you'll stand out big time! (And you'll get a ton of traffic from the forum.)

Ethical Backlink Method No. 4: Article Marketing

Most people will tell you the whole article marketing thing doesn't work anymore.

Most people would be wrong.

It's true that the whole article marketing thing, where you publish articles in directories for the sole reason of a backlink to your site, got thoroughly abused by the spammer faction.

But with Google's clampdown, it has filtered out a bunch of the knuckleheads and left room for "normal" marketers like us.

So, here's where I make article marketing worth the considerable time and effort it takes:

- **Choose 1-2 article directories to focus on and don't worry about the rest.** I like EzineArticles and HubPages. But by the time I finish typing this sentence there may be another one popping up.
- **Publish unique articles on each article directory site.** Not just "spun" article junk. (These are great opportunities for interns to show their worth.)
- **Don't fuss with anchor text.** Anchor text is where you link a keyword to a page optimized for that keyword, such as "frisbee golf supplies" being linked to a page about "frisbee golf supplies." It's not that valuable and it's an easy way to get caught in the spam ring. Instead, just link back with your web address. Example: For more information on cool ways to waste time check out FrisbeeGolf101.com.
- **Try to include two different versions of your keyword in the title of your article.** Example: Hummingbird Feeders - Everything You Need to Buy a Hummingbird Feeder. Title tags are still a huge part of optimization for these directories.
- **Use keywords, but don't over-do it.** The knuckleheads do this.

You are not a knucklehead. (Or at least not anymore.)

ETHICAL BACKLINK METHOD NO. 5: USER PROFILES

In the next chapter, we will dig deep into the morass of social media backlinking. (It's a strange little world.)

But for now, just know this: Every SINGLE social network or forum or user group or...whatever...you sign up for, make sure there is a link in your profile back to your website.

Not only is it a cheap, easy way to get a bit of traffic. But it's also a cheap, easy to get down-and-dirty SEO juice.

And for many tools like Twitter, GooglePlus and Pinterest, it's possible that your one profile link will be included in numerous lists, directories, and compilations that will bring in backlinks long after you're done creating them.

CHAPTER 5 Key Takeaways:

- **Offer to do guest blogging** for notable websites in your niche.
- **Set up RSS feed alerts to help you leave comments in related blogs.** (Don't forget to mention the author's name and respond to the first commenter.)
- **Choose 2-3 forums to frequent** and become an active member. (Along with an infrequent promoter.)
- **Dip your toe into article marketing**. Choose one or two directories to focus on and always post unique content.
- **Make sure every social media profile** you create has a link back to your website.

Chapter 6:

What Social Media Can – And Can't – Do For Your SEO

"The best way to engage honestly with the marketplace is to never use the words 'engage,' 'honestly,' or marketplace."

-Jeffrey Zeldman

Google didn't want to do it.

They didn't want to use likes, shares, retweets, pins, etc. — what are called "social signals" in the biz — as part of their search algorithm.

And for years, they resisted any method that might reward Facebook, their biggest and most hated rival.

(If you think the two companies aren't at odds, look where Facebook is poaching most of its talent from. It's Google.)

But then Google was forced into a corner.

Once they got rid of that whole spammy backlink culture, they had to find some alternate ways to determine who's an expert author and who is just some schlocky content spam artist.

And the answer was staring them right in the social-sharing face.

Fact and Fiction About Social Media SEO

So, there's what we know, there's what we think we know, and then there's what Google tells us about SEO.

Google is very cagey about which social signals actually help your website's SEO rankings. They don't want to create the same spammy culture they had with backlinks by giving away the secret social signal recipe.

But according to SearchMetrics, there are five different social media factors that absolutely (no doubt) affect a web page's SEO. They are:

1. The # of people who like your Facebook Page
2. The # of likes for a specific post that contains a link to your site
3. The # of Facebook shares of that post
4. The # of Twitter followers you have
5. The # of retweets of a post that contains a link to your site

Does this mean Facebook and Twitter are the ONLY social media networks that affect SEO?

Heck no, techno! (As my twelve-year-old cousin would say.)

What this REALLY means is, after years of denying it, Google is finally admitting that all of this social stuff really makes a difference.

(And will only continue to become more and more important as Google refines this some more.)

So, keeping in mind this is still an evolving method, here's my FIVE-Step Process for Using Social Media to crush your competition with SEO:

Social SEO Step No. 1: Sign Up for (Almost) All the Major Social Networks

What are the major ones? Well, my very unofficial action list would be:

- **GooglePlus:** I know you never use Google Plus. Nobody does. (And they're doing away with their personal profiles, so there's that.) But Google still allows company profiles. And they reward GooglePlus-endorsed content with SEO juice.

- **Twitter Account:** This is probably the easiest social network to use for SEO. A must-have.
- **Create a Facebook Fan Page:** No-brainer here. You SHOULD have a Facebook Marketing plan. If not, do it NOW!
- **LinkedIn Company Page:** This is overlooked by many marketers.
- Much to their peril.
- **Create a YouTube Channel:** Google owns YouTube. 'Nuff said.
- **Pinterest:** Google loves Pinterest. It's like the girl in a love triangle, where Facebook and Google fight over the affections of Pinterest all the time. This is a gut feeling, but I think Google really wants to use Pinterest as a jumping-off point for creating a visual search of the web. (Could be wrong, but I don't think so.)
- **Instagram:** Instagram is like Pinterest, but with more ab selfies and LESS pictures of shoes.
- **Whichever other ones you enjoy:** If you like, you can also do StumbleUpon and Tumblr or whatever other ones you're interested in. But if you hate social media, as much as I do, then just stick with the ones you like.

Social SEO Step No. 2: Optimize Your Profiles With Keywords

We talked about adding links back to your site in all the profiles you create.

But it's also important to get all those awesome keywords in social network profile spots, such as:

- A keyword as the name of your YouTube channel.
- Right after your website link in your Facebook Fan Page "ABOUT" section.
- Your Twitter Bio section.
- Your LinkedIn Company "ABOUT" section.
- Your Pinterest company info, and in all of your Pinboard captions.
- Your Instagram profile description.

SOCIAL SEO STEP NO. 3: BUILD A TRIBE

So, there's no question that retweets and Facebook likes and shares, and all that other social-media goodness, makes a difference in your content's SEO.

But before you promote your content, it's a good idea to build up the audience that you'd like to eventually add into your marketing funnel.

Now, I don't expect you to be a social media rock star in all the different networks, but if time is short, then I would spend most of my time working on these three that can have a real impact on your business:

- Your # of Twitter Followers
- Your # of Facebook Fans
- Your # of YouTube Channel Subscribers

Of all three, my favorite is the YouTube channel subscribers. This is because each time you upload a new video, your subscribers get an automated email update. (I'll take that over any old Tumblr ping any day.)

SOCIAL STEP NO. 4: PROMOTE YOUR CONTENT AND ASK FOR SHARES

Okay, finally! We're going to share our stuff. Here's how I do it:

Day 1: Tweet my content. This gets it indexed in the search engines pretty fast. I also ask for a retweet to hopefully get it shared quickly.

Day 2: Post my content on my Facebook page and put a question at the end to get people commenting and talking about it. I also ask for a Facebook Like.

Day 3: Add the content to my Google Plus profile.

Day 4: If it's a text article, I usually read it aloud and record it as a video and upload it to YouTube (with link back to the original blog post.) I also ask for a like or channel subscription at the end of the video.

Day 5: Upload image of post on Pinterest, with link back to the original blog post. (Set it up so it automatically does the same on Instagram.)

Day 6: Post link to blog post in status update of LinkedIn profile and my Company page. (And post link in any relevant LinkedIn groups I belong to who might find it interesting.)

Quick Note: If the content you're sharing is a video, and video is mucho awesome for sharing, then be sure to upload your video separately to your Facebook page.

Facebook heavily favors its own videos over the ones its rival has on YouTube. (Funny, huh?) So play to their vanity, and you'll be rewarded with better placement in the good old Facebook feed. (Which will lead to increasingly more sharing.)

PUNK ROCK MARKETING
AMPLIFY YOUR MESSAGE

CHAPTER 6 Key Takeaways:

- **Concentrate on the big social networks:** LinkedIn, Twitter, GooglePlus, Facebook, YouTube and Pinterest
- **Don't forget to add keywords i**n all your social media profiles.
- **Link your blog content to your GooglePlus account** to get a thumbnail in the search results, and an extra SEO boost from Google.
- **Build a following by focusing** on Facebook fans, Twitter followers and YouTube subscribers.
- **Promote your blog/website content by following this simple 6-day promotional system:** Tweet, Facebook share, Add to GooglePlus, Turn text article into YouTube video, Upload image of post to Pinterest, Post link on LinkedIn company page and LinkedIn groups.

Chapter 7:

Standing on the Shoulders of (Billion-Dollar) Giants

"Authority without wisdom is like an axe without an edge, fitter to bruise than polish."

-Anne Bradstreet

And now for something completely different...

We've talked a lot about creating search-engine friendly content that humans will actually read and respond to.

We've also talked about how to acquire quality backlinks that aren't spammy and will stand the test of (SEO) time.

But in this chapter, we're going to think **outside the box**.

We will build little islands of SEO awesomeness, and "borrow" credibility from the biggest media platforms in the world, that will not only help your SEO effort and lead-generation campaigns...

...but put your business in a vastly better position for years to come.

The Website is Dead, Long Live the Website

It's hard to predict what the web will look like in the future.

Will we still be blogging?

Or tweeting?

Or setting up WordPress sites with pretty backgrounds? (Hard to say.)

But I'm damn sure we'll still be:

- Buying books (Amazon)
- Listening to music (iTunes)

- Watching videos (YouTube)
- Sharing photos (Pinterest)
- Connecting with friends (Facebook)

...and probably doing all of it on our phone, or the microchip inside our brain, as we ignore the humans sitting next to us.

The cool part for us as marketers is: As hard as it is to get our own site ranked for the choice keywords that move the needle in our business...

...it's SUPREMELY SIMPLE to get one of big-platform entities ranked for that very same keyword. (As long as we know what we're doing.)

So, here are my Top FOUR Ways to Use the Big Media Platforms for our own nefarious SEO means:

SEO Platform Step No. 1: Create an SEO-Friendly Facebook Fan Page (or Two)

Google hates Facebook. But they also respect them. (They kinda have to.)

And one sure sign of respect is how Facebook Fan Pages, not profiles, can show up supremely high in search-engine results.

Now, it's important to clarify that status updates are not (currently) indexed by Google, so stuffing keywords in your next status update won't do any good.

But having a keyword-friendly name of your page can do absolute wonders. (Along with keywords in the "ABOUT" section, mission statement, and page description.)

So, what do you do if you already have a Facebook fan page that is named after your company or brand?

Well, create another Facebook page. (There's no limit to the number of pages you can have.)

One technique is to break your business into different areas of focus and have a Facebook page for each of those areas.

Say, you were a dentist in the Seattle area. Well, maybe you have a general practice, but then you also have a sub-specialty just for kids.

Then create one Facebook page that is "Seattle Dentist 101," but then another that is "Seattle Dentist for Kids." (Or whatever that keyword may be.)

Don't worry if it sounds like a lot of work. You don't have to do all of your primary social activity here.

Just update it a couple times a week and have clear calls-to-action for how people can get more information about you.

SEO Platform Step No. 2: Get in the News

As much as Google HATES Facebook, they love press releases. (Which is weird, as most press releases I come across totally suck.)

I suppose Google sees them as somewhat reputable, or perhaps they (mistakenly) believe that spammers won't go to the trouble of creating press releases about things that are lame and totally useless.

Either way, sending out a keyword-focused press release can be an absolutely awesome way to boost the SEO of your website and get a ton of extra traffic. (I continue to get traffic from press releases I sent out years ago.)

What do you send out a press release on? Well, almost anything you want.

New products, new services, new company announcements… some people I know even do it for each new blog post. (I wouldn't go that far.)

If you've got a big budget, then you can go for something like PR Web. A release there will cost you about $200-$250.

But I prefer WebWire because they're good, they're cheap, and press releases there work.

Don't forget to include keywords in the title, body, and footer of your press release.

As always, write a press release from the third person:

"Michael Clarke, founder of Punk Rock Marketing, continues to show why he is the most dynamic human being that ever walked the earth..."

...NOT:

"We here at Punk Rock Marketing think Michael Clarke is wicked cool. Here's stuff we sell to prove it."

SEO Platform Step No. 3: Boring Slideshows for Fun and Profit

Okay, I gotta admit it: I hate slideshows and PowerPoint presentations. It does absolutely nothing for me.

But I am in the **minority**.

Lots of people ENJOY looking at recycled slide decks on the web, in a variety of subjects. (Maybe it gives them the takeaways of a meeting without, you know, actually attending the meeting.)

The number one player in this area on the web is SlideShare, a site that allows you to upload your PowerPoint presentations, word docs, Keynote projects, and Adobe PDF portfolios.

Not only does uploading your deck to SlideShare allow you to reach a new, unique audience — it's great for B2B stuff — but Google thinks SlideShare is just the most amazing thing around right now.

And as a result, ranks their pages very highly. (The fact they are owned by LinkedIn probably doesn't hurt either.)

I have to admit this is a rather new form of media for me, so I don't have a ton of experience with it. (For instance, I know you can insert YouTube videos in your decks. But haven't done too much of it personally.)

But I know it can get you some major SEO results fast. (And additional traffic, if you make your call-to-action cool and non-sucky.)

SEO Platform Step No. 4: Embrace Your Inner Writer

Now this may not be for everybody. Not everybody has a "book" in them.

But...if you have some expertise you'd like to share, then I highly recommend you write and self-publish a book on Amazon with a strong keyword in your title. (You are reading one now, as we speak.)

A "book" doesn't have to be 70K words. (Like most traditional publishers demand.) This book is approximately 15K words and took me four weeks to write.

But the cool thing is, you can literally "own" a very competitive keyword, not just on Amazon but on Google, with a good book that helps solve people's problems.

Don't forget to include a link to your website to offer people more stuff, more info.

Also, once you've published your book, you can create a "Listmania!" list, based around that keyword, with your book included amongst other books in your field.

Doing this, will give you two great CHANCES to show up on page one of Google, without a single thing added to your website.

CHAPTER 7 Key Takeaways:

- **Create Facebook Fan pages with keyword-based names**. Don't forget to also include keywords in the "About" and "Description" sections.
- **Send out a press release for any new announcement** or product you want a little SEO love for.
- **Take your boring PowerPoints and throw them into SlideShare** for a super quick SEO boost.
- **Write a short (ish) book**, with a keyword-based title, and self-publish it on Amazon, if you can.

Chapter 8:

It's About User Experience, Stupid!

"Truth builds trust."

- Marilyn Suttle

Google is many things.

Ambitious. Persistent. Stubborn. Pious. Bipolar.

Ruthless when it comes to exploiting user's personal data.

But its entire business model is based on:

1. Giving away cool, free tools that users become really addicted to (Gmail, Google Docs, Google search, etc.)
2. Using the data those free tools provide to serve users "relevant" ads and "helpful" search results.
3. Charge advertisers a boatload for serving those ads and search results.

It's that "relevant" and "helpful" that Google has built its entire empire on. Once users stop "trusting" Google to give them what they want…Google is toast.

When an advertiser sends a user to a crappy sales page, or some SEO guru tweaks the search results to send some user to a misleading squeeze page…

…it's Google that looks bad. (And Google doesn't like to look bad.)

Google is so desperate to make that user experience supremely awesome that they have spent TONS OF MONEY developing FREE TOOLS that website owners like you and I can use FOR

FREE to make our sites informative, interesting…and capable of keeping people on our page. (Which helps boost our sales.)

Conversely, when you don't KEEP people on your site, and they quickly move on to a different site — what in the web world is called "bounce rate" — then Google has failed.

And they will bring the SEO hammer down on ya.

The shame is that Google has a ton of FREE TOOLS marketers can use to help them avoid this hammer. (And create a website that keeps users on the site longer.)

So here are the Top FIVE Free Google Tools you can use to improve your website's conversion rate, increase your site's SEO rankings, and totally rule the world:

Google Tool No. 1: Google Webmaster Tools

Webmaster Tools is like the auto mechanic for your website. They may not turn your Toyota Corolla into a Maserati, but they will have your compact sedan running the best it possibly can. (You can find it by heading over to http://google.com/webmasters/tools.)

Most website owners totally drop the ball here.

Installing Webmaster Tools requires a bit of website know-how. If you're not the webmaster of your site, then have him/her to set it up for you.

But once you've got it running you can use Webmaster Tools to:

- **Find out where your website traffic originates from.** And give you insight in creating content that addresses that region.
- **Discover which of your links are broken.** This DIRECTLY affects your search-engine rankings. Boring, but important.
- **Learn if you've accidentally blocked any of your content from the search engines.** It happens. It's your job to catch it.
- **Specify your important site links.** These are the sub-pages that show up in your search engine results, below the main page result. Very, very helpful to build out your authority.

- **Find out which of your pages are missing title tags, or non-existent meta descriptions, or have duplicate metadata!** This alone makes it worth it.

...and it sort of goes without saying. Google respects sites that have webmaster tools installed.

Google Tool No. 2: Google Analytics

This one is the Self-Help Life Coach for your website; the tool that will help take your site from mediocre and under-performing, to total website rock star. (You can find Google Analytics at http://google.com/analytics.)

While there are lots of cool things you can find out about your site, such as where in Russia most of your traffic comes from, the real "money" is found in analyzing the user experience of your website.

Setting up Google Analytics is a bit easier than Webmaster Tools. (There are even some WordPress plug-ins that do a lot of this for ya!)

But you still have to add code to your website. (Again, non-techies could use their webmaster or hire somebody over at Fiverr for a couple of bucks to do it for them.)

Once you get it up and running, here are some super-useful things you can do with Google Analytics:

- **Find out how well your squeeze page(s) convert.** (Anything below 20-25% should be tweaked.)
- **Create "goals" which determine the form of web traffic that converts best.**
- **Implement "content experiments" which allow you to split-test squeeze pages.** (This is the old Google Website Optimizer.)
- **Discover the average time spent on your site.** (Time spent, many believe, is a big part of the Google search ranking algorithm.)

Of the above features, the MOST IMPORTANT is the TIME SPENT. Or what percentage of visitors are "bouncing"— or leaving your site within 10 seconds.

A bounce rate of 50-60% is pretty decent. Anything higher than that and you'll want to tweak your website content until it comes back down to earth.

Things you can do to counter a high "bounce rate" include:

- Adding a "recent articles" widget on the right or left side of your website's navigation.
- Adding social proof components such as Facebook Like boxes and other social media junk to your pages.
- Inserting a picture of you or your team to add credibility and authority to your site.
- Making sure the content on your page fits what people are looking for.

And the last one, making sure your content fits your visitor's needs, is accomplished with the following three Google tools.

GOOGLE TOOL NO. 3: GOOGLE TRENDS

Google Trends is your resident hipster teenager. This lets you know what's hot, what's cool, and what people are looking for on the Internet at this very moment. (Embrace your inner hipster over at http://google.com/trends)

You can also project what will be hot and cool in the future. By viewing the history of a search term over a long period, you can find out WHEN and WHERE the sweet spot for your particular keyword phrase is.

A phrase such as "social media marketing" is generally white-hot in January and February. Not so much in November and December.

There's another sneaky, awesome way to use Google Trends…

For instance, I can tell you when it comes to the phrase "social media marketing," the county of Bletchley in England is number two, right behind London.

Would this kind of info be helpful for something like Facebook advertising campaigns? (You frickin' bet!)

If I created a landing page that said something like: "Welcome Blethchley Social Media Pros!"…would that be more relevant than most other webpages? (Hell yeah!)

Google Tool No. 4: Google Keyword Planner

Chances are, you're probably already familiar with this tool. (It's the best FREE keyword research option out there and we talked about it in an earlier chapter. The URL is on the complicated side, so to find it just Google the phrase "Google keyword planner.")

But there's a whole lot more you can do than just find out how many times a month a particular phrase has been searched.

Here are a couple of ways I use this tool every single day:

- **Find long tail keywords that most people miss.** Most marketers don't worry about keywords below 1,000 searches a month. Big mistake. There's money in them keyword hills, and here's where you find 'em.
- **Find which keywords you SHOULD optimize your site for.** Just throw in your website URL, and you'll find what Google thinks your site is about. (Good way to find out if you're sending out the SEO signals you truly mean to.)
- **Find good websites to advertise on.** With the Placement Tool you can put in a search term and Google will spit out a bunch of websites that are good spots to advertise on for that phrase. (Then you can contact the sites directly and get a much cheaper ad placement than Google would ever get you.)
- **Research the competition for a particular keyword.** Just because a term has high competition, doesn't mean you can't rank for it. (Just means it might take longer.)
- **Find new keywords and subjects you'd never think about exploring.** This is may be the biggest advantage. By putting in a

bunch of keywords in the keyword tool, you'll automatically get a bunch of ad group ideas that may or may not have been on your radar.

It's possible to get a little lost in the Keyword Tool. Just stay focused and have fun. (Or at least as much fun as keyword research can be.)

GOOGLE TOOL NO. 5: GOOGLE ALERTS

To keep the strained metaphor going, good-old Google Alerts is like the small-town sheriff of your website. It keeps an eye on everything, so you don't have to.

There's so much you can do with Google Alerts. (http://google.com/alerts.) Besides find out how many times your name is mentioned on the Internet.

I use Google Alerts for the following jobs:

- **Keeping track of all new external links to my site.** Simply put in "link: mydomain.com" in the alert field to set it up.
- **Finding out every time my blog or website is mentioned**, by creating an alert for my company.
- **Ensuring nobody steals my content.** This happens. Trust me. An easy way to find out if this is happening is to put a fairly large paragraph in the alert field and see what pops up.
- **Get all the latest info, news and tips in your industry.** By creating a couple of area-specific alerts you can appear way more knowledgeable and connected than you actually are. (Just create an alert for 2-3 keywords of your industry, and you're golden.)

PUNK ROCK MARKETING
AMPLIFY YOUR MESSAGE

CHAPTER 8 Key Takeaways:

- **Webmaster Tools can help you find broken links** in your site and tell you which of your pages need title tags and better meta-data.
- **Google Analytics is an awesome/free tool** to help you track the conversion rates of your squeeze pages and find out where your website traffic is coming from. (And how best to increase that number.)
- **Search Google Trends to find "hot" topics** you can incorporate into your content and discover the best time of year for specific areas of content to focus on.
- **Use the Google Keyword Planner Tool to find long-tail key-words you can rank for**, discover advertisers you should approach with your PPC campaigns, and find out what Google thinks your site is about.
- **Employ Google Alerts to track how often your website/company is mentioned** and easily collect any third-party content in your industry you can share and/or write about.

EPILOGUE:
What I Learned as a Black-Hat Underground SEO

I know more about prom dresses and lower-back Celtic Tattoos than any red-blooded man you'll ever meet.

That's because my first "real" job, after my band broke up and my girlfriend kicked me out of her studio apartment, was writing hundreds of horrible SEO web content articles…

…and that includes 100 articles about tribal tattoos, and a mere 72 articles about illuminating topics such as "Discount Prom Dresses," "Gothic Prom Dresses," and that ever-controversial subject, "Modern Prom Dresses."

And it was my job to not only create those collections of textual crap but promote them.

In the most skeevy, shady ways.

I would create numerous fake blogs, with fake profiles and fake concerns and fake links to these horrible articles. ("Hey guys, I just found this great article on *Discount Prom Dresses* that I found very helpful, and so will you.")

And then I would create additional fake profiles which would comment on these initial fake posts.

And then I would put all of this into some strange software, whose name I can't remember, that would suddenly create thousands of backlinks to these blogs and comments in a matter of minutes.

The whole thing would have been utterly ridiculous if it didn't work so well.

Really well.

Anyway…

Most of those shady techniques don't work anymore. I'm sure there are other, even shadier, techniques that have taken their place.

But there's one memory that sticks out in my mind from that time. (Besides the fact that I wrote about prom dresses for eight hours at a time.)

Every Thursday we'd have a company strategy session; this was a chance for the team to map out which niches we'd be focusing on.

At this meeting, writers, like me, would throw out different ideas for markets the company could dive into. (Examples: "Car insurance," "Autism tips," "Living Trust attorney")

And our boss would look at the results of the competition for that keyword on that first page of Google. And depending on what he saw, he would say, "Yeah, sounds good," or "Hell, no, are you insane?"

So, one time I asked him: What makes you decide whether to go into a market?

Is it the size of the company you'd have to go up against?

Or how long your competitor's domains have been around?

He said, "No. Got nothing to do with any of that."

He told me he could compete with almost anything a competitor could throw at him:

- The number of backlinks
- The age of the domain
- The number of pages on the website

The ONE THING he hated to go up against was: Websites run by owners that actually "give a damn."

Everything else he could outmaneuver and outrank.

But when somebody was writing about something they were really passionate about, and they really, truly wanted to help people out, they produced a lot of content. Good content.

And content like that gets retweeted, liked, forwarded, commented on, shared in forums, printed out and put on the refrigerator.

And the whole **job** of SEO starts to become less and less important. And you start "ranking" for stuff, almost by accident.

So, as you dip your toe, or maybe your entire body, in the deep end of the SEO pool, and get slightly frustrated that things aren't happening overnight….

…realize there will always be some latest tool, some new gimmick that you might be tempted to throw in your toolbox.

But, if you're really passionate about your business, and write like a normal human being, then you'll have an advantage no piece of SEO software, or your competition, can compete against.

Authority.

"Regrets, I've Had a Few..."

By the time I finish typing this sentence...

...There will be a BRAND-NEW social network that you and I absolutely HAVE to drop everything we're doing and sign up for.

It'll be called "Social Zoom" or "FriendyBot" or "BluMeanie." And everyone you know — and don't know — will tell you the only way to market your wares in the 21st century is by spending 17 hours a day "posting" or "sharing" or "zweeping" on these must-have social platforms.

Or even worse, the strategies and techniques and methodologies I've outlined in this humble tome will become horribly — and painfully — outdated by the time I hit "publish."

Facebook will suddenly decide, without warning, that all Fan Page owners MUST not only "pay" for their content to be seen, but they must also get a "I (Heart) Mark Zuckerberg" neck tattoo to boost the visibility of their status updates.

Twitter, in the future, may feel 140 characters is far too verbose for its users, and require that all tweets contain no more than 20 characters, and be written in one-word sentences. ("Here. Coupon. Buy. RT.")

And posting a 12-second video on YouTube may force you to take a blood oath of allegiance to the Cult of Google. ("I hereby swear, to never turn ON my Gmail privacy settings...")

But...

...whether the tools and platforms outlined in this book change — and they will change, trust me — the big-picture strategies we've gone over will NOT change.

In my never-humble opinion, we've reached a point of no return.

Boring, old, business-as-usual marketing — "Here's my thing! Buy it now!" — just doesn't work anymore. (If it ever did.)

Consumers don't want anything that has the "whiff" of marketing. More than deals, offers, sales and coupons, they want…a story.

They want the buying experience to be, just that, an experience.

They want to be able to tell their friends about that cool, handcraft jewelry maker they found on Facebook and bought a necklace from.

They want to blab about that artisan pizza joint — run by those whacky hippies from Vermont — who send out those funny email newsletters.

They want to recount the time they won a video contest on Pinterest, which got them the 60-minute coaching call that changed their life.

And the more we can keep things visual, fun, interactive — and give our customers plenty of opportunities to be recognized and feel "wicked smaht" — then no matter what social media platform comes down the pike…

…we'll be in a position to crush anything our competition — and those pesky big-box retailers — can throw at us.

Here's hoping this book has given you a strategy or two to begin your quest for world (marketing) domination.

Talk soon,

Michael Clarke
PunkRockMarketing.com
Michael@punkrockmarketing.com

Made in United States
North Haven, CT
04 November 2026

21760240R00307